Founding the
American Presidency

Founding the American Presidency

edited by
Richard J. Ellis

ROWMAN & LITTLEFIELD PUBLISHERS, INC.
Lanham • Boulder • New York • Oxford

ROWMAN & LITTLEFIELD PUBLISHERS, INC.

Published in the United States of America
by Rowman & Littlefield Publishers, Inc.
4720 Boston Way, Lanham, Maryland 20706

12 Hid's Copse Road
Cumnor Hill, Oxford OX2 9JJ, England

British Library Cataloguing in Publication Information Available

Library of Congress Cataloging-in-Publication Data

Ellis, Richard (Richard J.)
    Founding the American presidency / Richard J. Ellis.
        p.   cm.
    Includes bibliographical references.
    ISBN 0-8476-9498-4 (cloth : alk. paper).—ISBN 0-8476-9499-2
(pbk. : alk. paper)
        1. Presidents—United States—History Sources.   2. Executive
    power—United States—History Sources.   I. Title.
    JK511.E46   1999
    352.23'0973—dc21   99-19012
                                                                  CIP

Printed in the United States of America

♾™ The paper used in this publication meets the minimum requirements of
American National Standard for Information Sciences—Permanence of Paper for
Printed Library Materials, ANSI Z39.48–1992.

For my students

Contents

APPENDIXES

Preface

This book was born out of frustration—frustration at not being able to do justice to the founding period in teaching my course on the American presidency. Even the best collections of readings on the presidency generally limit students' direct exposure to the framers to little more than a few of Alexander Hamilton's *Federalist* essays (typically nos. 69–70). As powerful as these classic essays are, they cannot begin to capture the richness of the founding debate over executive power. Of course, the essays can be supplemented with reliable secondary accounts of the creation of the presidency (e.g., Cronin 1989; McDonald 1994; Milkis and Nelson 1994, chaps. 1–2; Pious 1996, chap. 2), but even the best summaries of the founders' debates, speeches, and essays cannot take the place of reading the documents themselves. Moreover, in my experience, even the best secondary accounts can inadvertently promote a passive mode of learning because students often lack alternative sources of information that would enable them to argue back. Having students read primary documents allows them to become more engaged, to argue with each other and with the teacher, to think about the Constitution for themselves. The secondary account, in my experience, tends to be absorbed, memorized, and then forgotten at the completion of the exam. Having to wrestle with the primary sources helps give students a more lasting appreciation for the richness of the founders' debate and the importance of their institutional creation.

Or so I believed. But what was such a teacher to do? As I cast around, I found no such collections. I could, of course, assign Max Farrand's multivolume *Records of the Federal Convention* (1937), but that hardly seemed satisfactory, since less than a quarter of those 1,300 pages of debate relate to the presidency. Moreover, simply assigning some part of the convention debates still left out entirely the ensuing ratification process, in which the debates are often fundamentally unlike the debate that took place at the Constitutional Convention. Hundreds of relevant essays and speeches are scattered throughout the multivolume collections of Elliot (1888), Storing (1981), and Jensen,

Kaminski, and Saladino (1976–), but few teachers have the time or knowledge to make judicious selections from these many intimidating volumes.

The challenge, as I saw it, was to craft a collection that went beyond Hamilton's greatest hits without getting lost in the thicket of the founding debates, to offer up a generous helping from the founders that students would still find digestible. I have created this book in the faith that there are other teachers out there who share my belief that it is invaluable for students to grapple seriously with the political thought and political compromises that were responsible for the invention of the institution of the presidency. The book is designed for those who would like to spend more than just a single class session or lecture on the founding of the American presidency.

Reading this diverse collection of documents may, I hope, prompt teachers and students to ask what is lost when we rely only on a few essays by Hamilton for our understanding of the nature of the presidency. At the Constitutional Convention his views on executive power went well beyond what others were willing to accept. His June 18 speech, in which he proposed a president for life, was praised for its erudition but, as William Samuel Johnson noted, "supported by none" (Farrand 1937, 1:363). Moreover, Hamilton missed virtually all of the debates that related to the presidency, including the crucial period in which the convention hammered out the all-important compromise regarding the electoral college. It has always puzzled me that teachers of the presidency know so much about Hamilton, who was at best a bit player at the Constitutional Convention, and so little about James Wilson, who was arguably the most influential framer with regard to Article 2. The opportunity to read speeches by largely forgotten figures like Wilson will, I hope, promote a more nuanced appreciation of the founders' thought on the meaning of executive power.

If selecting Hamilton to exemplify all Federalist thought on the presidency is problematic, the difficulty of choosing a representative voice on the Anti-Federalist side is even more pronounced. In their excellent collection of readings on the presidency, Pfiffner and Davidson (1997) select "Cato" as representative of the Anti-Federalist position, but in truth there was no single Anti-Federalist position on the presidency. The most influential Anti-Federalist pamphleteer, the "Federal Farmer," for instance, spoke appreciatively of much that the framers had done in Article 2. Some Anti-Federalists, like many of those at the Pennsylvania ratifying convention, were worried less that the president was too strong, as Cato feared, than that his weakness would make him a tool of the Senate. Although the Anti-Federalists lost, and some of their complaints may strike the reader as antiquated and overwrought, many of their concerns and fears about presidential power still resonate today.

One of the things I hope this book helps students to grasp is that many aspects of the presidency that we take for granted were once intensely debated *choices.* Moreover, many of these choices were only made at the last minute. If the convention had ended its work at the end of August rather than the middle of September, we would have had a president elected by the legislature for a seven-year, nonrenewable term, without the power to appoint judges or ambassadors or to make treaties. How different would American politics have looked with this radically different framing of the presidency? Among my aims is to prompt readers to think counterfactually about how American politics and political development might have been different had the founders framed the presidency differently.

This book focuses on those parts of the presidency that were discussed most at the federal convention and the ratifying conventions. Since some important constitutional provisions relating to the presidency received little or no attention at the convention, not all the significant clauses of Article 2 are examined here. For instance, the reader will find no examination in these pages of section 1, clause 5, which stipulates the qualifications for being president: at least thirty-five years of age, a natural-born citizen, and a resident for fourteen years. The convention adopted these qualifications late in the convention without any explanation, though they did extensively debate the issue of qualifications for legislators (see Nelson 1989). Another important provision of Article 2 that received little or no attention at the convention or in the debate over ratification is the requirement in section 3, clause 1, that the president "shall from time to time give to the Congress Information on the State of the Union, and recommend to their Consideration such Measures as he shall judge necessary and expedient." My omission of these clauses is in no sense a judgment on their importance, but rather an admission that the primary documents used in this book are not well suited to understanding these particular clauses.

Most of the book is organized thematically, with separate chapters on the appointment power, the veto power, the selection process, the impeachment process, and so on. Although the convention structured its business so that debate was usually focused on one specific provision at a time, debate over a particular clause sometimes spilled over into connected issues. For instance, whether the Senate or the president should appoint judges or make treaties had consequences for the deliberations over whether the judiciary or the Senate should try impeachments. And, to take another example, how much power could be safely vested in the president depended in part on how the president was to be selected. For the most part, however, the debates lend themselves quite readily to the sort of conceptual compartmentalization employed in this book. The postconvention debates, however, were less constrained by the need to discuss the Constitution clause by clause. Opponents of the Constitution, in particular, often felt that a clause-by-clause critique played into the hands of those who favored adoption of the Constitution. Their objection was often less to a particular clause than to the entire package of powers that had been vested in the president. The final chapter thus focuses on those postconvention critiques and defenses that did not aim at any one particular power or clause but analyzed the presidency considered as a whole. In these writings we confront the macro-question that Americans continue to debate: Is the presidency too strong or too weak, or is it just right?

Because this is a book designed for students, I have made changes in the texts wherever I felt that it would make comprehension easier. For instance, in the invaluable notes James Madison took at the federal convention he frequently misspelled delegates' names: Ellsworth was rendered as Elseworth, Pinckney as Pinkney, Paterson as Patterson, Gorham as Ghorum, and so on. In an attempt to avoid spreading confusion, I have corrected the spelling of delegates' names. To take another example, where Madison abbreviated words, as he often did in his effort to record what was said, I have written out the entire word. I have also changed punctuation, capitalization, or spelling where I thought doing so would make the document easier to follow. Occasionally, too, I have added or omitted a word when I felt it would help the reader.

I could not omit, however, the people who have helped me write this book. Without the support of the Earhart Foundation I would not have commenced work on this project, and without the support of Jim Ceaser, Erwin Hargrove, Sid Milkis, and Mike Nelson, Earhart would probably not have aided me. Mike Nelson was also invaluable as a reader for Rowman & Littlefield, as was Andrew Busch. I was also helped by the good counsel of Gaspare Saladino and Fred Woodward, and the generous assistance of Michael Stevens of the State Historical Society of Wisconsin. Emily Middaugh and Karen Bond performed with grace and patience the thankless task of typing each of the primary texts. Special thanks are owed to Jennifer Knerr for her early faith in the project and her sound advice throughout. I am also grateful to production editor Scott Horst and copy editor Chrisona Schmidt for their able assistance. My task was made easier by the work of other scholars who have collected primary documents from the founding period. Particularly useful to me were Philip B. Kurland and Ralph Lerner's magisterial five-volume collection, *The Founders' Constitution,* the heroic multivolume *Documentary History of the Ratification of the Constitution,* edited by Merrill Jensen, John Kaminski, and Gaspare Saladino, Herbert Storing's seven-volume *The Complete Anti-Federalist,* and Morten Borden's useful *The Antifederalist Papers.*

My greatest debt, though, is to my students, who have taught me most of what I know about teaching. It is for them that I have written this book.

Richard J. Ellis

Notes on Reading the Text

This text has several different parts. Each chapter has an introduction by the author to the topic at hand. Within each chapter are one or several documents. Each document is numbered; there are 52 documents total within the text. Each document has its own introduction by the author, and the source of the document is found at the bottom of the page on which it begins in an unnumbered note. The document itself is set in a slightly different typeface from the rest of the text, so in addition to being numbered, the documents are easy to find and distinguish from the author's introductory and interpretive text. At the end of each chapter is a set of Questions for Discussion. These are designed to put the reader in the place of participants in the events described in the documents. We hope these elements, together with the helpful notes, appendixes, and references included, will guide readers through the book.

Introduction: Prelude to the Presidency

> Every gentlemen who has turned his thoughts to the subject of politics, and has considered the most eligible mode of republican government, agrees that the greatest difficulty arises from the executive—as to the time of his election, mode of his election, quantum of power, &c.
>
> Edmund Randolph

The American presidency was a deliberate creation, an invention. In this respect the presidency is unlike the office of the British prime minister, which evolved gradually during the eighteenth century without ever being codified. No one can definitively say who was the first prime minister, but every schoolboy and schoolgirl knows that George Washington was the first president. Prior to 1787 there was no American presidency; indeed, there was no national chief executive of any sort. There was an office with the title of president under the old national confederation, but it bore no relationship to the presidency established by Article 2 of the U.S. Constitution. Between 1775 and 1787 the president was elected annually by the Continental Congress from among its members and served as little more than the presiding officer of that body; it was an office "more honorable than powerful" (Jillson and Wilson 1990, 94).

Rebelling against the British monarchy meant not only declaring war on the mother country but avoiding any institution that even vaguely resembled kingship. In the state constitutions drafted in 1776 and 1777 the American revolutionaries systematically emasculated the power of the governors. And at the national level, the Articles of Confederation—endorsed by the Continental Congress in 1777 though not ratified by the last state until 1781—made no provision for an independent executive branch of government, let alone a chief magistrate. Such powers as the national government had (which did not include the power to tax the states or to enforce its laws) were vested entirely in the Continental Congress. At first Congress attempted to carry out admin-

1

istrative and executive functions largely through ad hoc or standing (that is, permanent) committees made up of its own members, but dissatisfaction with this arrangement led Congress in 1781 to set up several executive departments—foreign affairs, finance, war, and marine—and to place at the head of each a single person with control over and responsibility for subordinates. Neither the executive head nor the subordinates were members of Congress, thus achieving a separation of administrative and legislative personnel that had been lacking in the confederation's early days.

The establishment of executive departments improved the confederation's administration, but the executive branch remained an appendage of the legislature. The department heads were appointed by Congress and served at its pleasure. Moreover, Congress could issue specific directives to a department head whenever it saw fit; throughout the confederation period Congress continued "to settle matters of minute detail on its floor" (Thach 1923, 62). The power and even the shape of the executive was dependent upon the disposition and makeup of Congress. The creation of executive departments with a single head in 1781 owed much to the turnover in congressional membership that occurred that year; when Robert Morris resigned in 1784 as head of the finance department, a new Congress, with the war now over, abolished Morris's position and replaced it with a three-person board (McDonald 1994, 144). Lacking constitutional authority, the executive branch could do little to resist legislative will or caprice.

The concentration of all federal power in a single legislative body was oddly out of step with the colonists' professed attachment to the separation of powers. Four of the state constitutions drafted in 1776 and 1777—Georgia, Maryland, North Carolina, and Virginia—had explicitly provided (in the words of the Virginia constitution) that "the legislative, executive, and judiciary department, shall be separate and distinct, so that neither exercises the powers properly belonging to the other" (Thorpe 1909, 7:3817). Uniting all powers in the hands of any body of men, many colonists believed (following Montesquieu),[1] was the very definition of tyranny. "No man, or body of men, ought to be intrusted with the united powers of Government," the town of Boston instructed its legislative representatives in 1776. "It is essential to Liberty that the legislative, judicial and executive Powers of Government be, as nearly as possible, independent of and separate from each other." The Continental Congress itself praised the "immortal Montesquieu" and lectured the people of Quebec in 1774 that history had demonstrated "the truth of this simple position, that to live by the will of one man, or set of men, is the pro

---

1. "When the legislative and executive powers are united in the same person, or in the same body of magistracy," wrote Montesquieu, "there can be then no liberty." Nor can there be liberty "if the power of judging be not separated from the legislative and executive powers" (1977, 202 [bk. 11, chap. 6]).

duction of misery to all men. [The device] of the several powers being separated, and distributed into different hands, for checks upon one another [was] the only effective mode ever invented by the wit of men, to promote their freedom and prosperity." At both the federal and state level, then, there was, as historian Gordon Wood has emphasized, a marked "discrepancy between the affirmations of the need to separate the several governmental departments and the actual political practice" (1969, 150–53).

How did revolutionary Americans resolve this conflict between their words and deeds, between the ideal of separation of powers and the reality of legislative supremacy? At the federal level, the conflict could be resolved by pointing to the weakness of the federal government. Denied the powers to tax or coerce the states, the confederation was so weak that few worried about its becoming tyrannical, even if all its powers were vested in a single legislative body. More important, when Americans invoked the separation of powers, they were, as Wood points out, "primarily thinking of insulating the judiciary and particularly the legislature from executive manipulation." The main threat to liberty, in the eyes of the colonists, came from the executive's capacity to corrupt members of the legislature by "appointing them to executive or judicial posts, or by offering them opportunities for profits through the dispensing of government contracts and public money, thereby buying their support for the government." Massachusetts governor Francis Bernard, for instance, had used his patronage powers in 1766 to dismiss colonels in the militia who had opposed him in the legislature. Looking across the Atlantic, colonists saw further evidence of executive influence corrupting the people's representatives: "Royal Ministerial, and Parliamentary managers," lamented a Pennsylvania writer, "cajole, tempt and bribe the people, to commit suicide on their own liberties" (Wood 1969, 157). Separation of powers in 1776 was thus invoked primarily as a means of constraining what was perceived to be the most dangerous part of government: the executive.

After 1776, experience at both state and federal levels began to modify Americans' single-minded dread of executive power. Executive power was still to be feared but so too, many Americans were learning, was unchecked legislative power. In *Notes on the State of Virginia,* Thomas Jefferson, having just completed two frustrating years (1779–1781) as Virginia's governor, observed that in Virginia, "all the powers of government, legislative, executive, and judiciary, result to the legislative body." Though the constitution paid lip service to the separation of powers, in fact "the judiciary and executive members were left dependant on the legislative, for their subsistence in office, and some of them for their continuance in it. If therefore the legislature assumes executive and judiciary powers, no opposition is likely to be made; nor, if made, can it be effectual." Members of the legislature, Jefferson lamented, have "in many instances, decided rights which should have been left to judiciary controversy: and the direction of the executive, during the whole time of their session, is becoming habitual and familiar." Experience had taught that "173 despots would surely be as oppressive as one" (1954, 120).[2]

At the federal level, the absence of separation of powers taught a different lesson. Here its absence was criticized not for creating a tyrannical government but for fostering a feeble government. Writing to a friend toward the end of the summer of 1787, while the delegates at the federal convention in Philadelphia were seeking to complete their labors, Jefferson expressed his conviction that it was essential "to separate ... the Executive and Legislative powers." "The want of it," he continued, "has been the source of more evil than we have experienced from any other cause." The problem, in Jefferson's view, was that by becoming absorbed in "executive details" Congress's attention had been diverted from "great to small objects," which makes it appear "as if we had no federal head" (Thach 1923, 71). Alexander Hamilton, writing at the outset of the decade, identified the lack of a separate and independent executive branch as one of the major defects of the confederation. Congress, he complained, "have kept the power too much in their own hands and have meddled too much with details of every sort. Congress is, properly, a deliberative corps, and it forgets itself when it attempts to play the executive. It is impossible such a body, numerous as it is, and constantly fluctuating, can ever act with sufficient decision or with system" (Thach 1923, 64). For Jefferson no less than for Hamilton, then, separation of powers was a means to strengthen and not just restrain central power.

Those who wished to revise the federal constitution found the doctrine of separation of powers a powerful rhetorical tool. It was difficult to deny that the Articles of Confederation blatantly violated the ideal of separation of powers, and only a few Americans were willing to defend the status quo by repudiating the ideal. Even those who distrusted Hamilton's vision of a powerful central government could not dispute Hamilton's contention that "confounding legislative and executive powers in a single body," as the Articles of Confederation had done, was "contrary to the most approved and well founded maxims of free government which require that the legislative executive and judicial authorities should be deposited in distinct and separate hands" (Casper 1997, 16–17). As the Constitutional Convention began, there was general agreement among the delegates that a separate executive branch was necessary (McDonald 1985, 240). Even the New Jersey (or Paterson) Plan, which attempted to preserve the basic structure of the Articles of Confederation, including a unicameral legislature, was defended by its proponents on

---

2. James Madison agreed with his fellow Virginian. In notes he prepared in 1784 for a speech advocating revision of the Virginia constitution, Madison invoked the authority of Montesquieu, arguing that the "Union of powers" in Virginia's government was the essence of tyranny (Hutchinson et al. 1962–, 8:78).

the grounds that "a distinct executive & Judiciary also were equally provided by this plan" (Farrand 1937, 1:251).

Though the delegates agreed that the new constitution should establish a distinct executive branch, they had very different ideas about what that branch should look like. The delegates faced a host of contentious questions. Should the executive, for instance, be plural or single? If single, should the executive have to seek the advice and consent of an executive council, as most state constitutions required the governor to do? Should the executive be selected by the legislature, as was true in all but two states, or should the delegates follow the lead of New York and Massachusetts and make the executive directly elected by the people? How long should the executive's term of office be, and should the executive be eligible for reelection? What powers should the executive be given? Should the executive have the power to veto legislation, a power that no governor possessed? Should the executive be given the power to make appointments, grant pardons, draw up treaties, conduct war? How should the executive be removed, and for what causes? Who should succeed the executive if he were to be removed or die in office? Should there be restrictions on who could become the executive? What should they call the executive? All these and other questions faced the delegates as they gathered in Philadelphia to create a new executive and a new government.

The Cast of Characters

The first delegate to arrive in Philadelphia from out of town was James Madison, whose arrival on May 3, eleven days before the convention was scheduled to begin, betrayed the thirty-six-year-old Virginian's eagerness to begin the business at hand. His service in the Continental Congress during the early 1780s had convinced him of the need for a radical overhaul of American political institutions. Madison was appalled that the federal government was dependent on the states for raising, paying, and provisioning armies. Even worse, in Madison's view, the government had no way to compel states "to fulfill their federal engagements" (Rutland 1994, 266). After leaving Congress in 1783, he turned his penetrating intellect and extraordinary diligence to remedying "the vices of the political system of the United System." To aid in this endeavor he carried out an intense study of the history of confederacies and republics, ancient and modern, a task that was aided by two trunks full of books on history and politics that had been sent to him by his friend Thomas Jefferson, who was during this period stationed in Paris as minister to France. Madison's preparation for the Philadelphia convention impressed almost all observers. Georgia delegate William Pierce, who penned brief character sketches of each of the convention delegates, judged that "from a spirit

ﾉ and application which he possesses in a most eminent degree, he ﾉays comes forward the best informed Man of any point in debate. The affairs of the United States, he perhaps, has the most correct knowledge of, of any man in the Union" (Farrand 1937, 3:94).

Though the studious Virginian had thought long and hard about many of the political issues facing the new nation, executive power was not among these, as Madison himself readily conceded. Madison knew he did not like the weakness of the Virginia executive (it was, he wrote, "the worst part of a ba[d] Constitution") but had few positive ideas about what shape the executive should take. Asked in 1785 for his suggestions on a constitution for Kentucky (which at the time was still part of Virginia), Madison confessed his uncertainty about executive power:

> I have made up no final opinion whether the first Magistrate should be chosen by the Legislature or the people at large or whether the power should be vested in one man assisted by a council or in a council of which the President shall be only primus inter pares. There are examples of each in the U. States and probably advantages and disadvantages attending each. (Hutchinson et al. 1962–, 8:352)

Two years later Madison's ideas about the executive were still largely unformed. Writing to George Washington just two weeks before his arrival in Philadelphia, Madison allowed that "a national Executive must also be provided" but in the next breath admitted, "I have scarcely ventured as yet to form my own opinion either of the manner in which it ought to be constituted or of the authorities with which it ought to be cloathed" (9:385).

If Madison had few fixed ideas on the subject of executive power, his diagnosis of what plagued American politics propelled him in the direction of supporting a powerful executive. In Madison's view the primary source of the country's troubles lay in its unchecked legislatures, whose many and changeable laws he believed to be frequently unwise and unjust. Coming into the convention, Madison had hoped to persuade his fellow delegates to grant the national government "a negative *in all cases whatsoever* on the legislative acts of the States, as heretofore exercised by the Kingly prerogative" (9:383). Madison explained his p.an to Washington:

> The great desideratum which has not yet been found for Republican Governments, seems to be some disinterested & dispassionate umpire in disputes between different passions & interests in the State. The majority who alone have the right of decision, have frequently an interest real or supposed in abusing it. In Monarchies the sovereign is more neutral to the interests and views of different parties; but unfortunately he too often forms interests of his own repugnant to those of the whole. Might not the national prerogative here suggested [that is, the veto] be found sufficiently disinterested for the decision of local questions of policy, whilst it would itself be sufficiently restrained from the pursuit of interests adverse to those of the whole Society? (9:384)

Madison thought this absolute veto to be "absolutely necessary" (9:383; also Hobson 1979), but the idea proved far too radical for most of his fellow delegates. Though unable to mask his disappointment at the defeat of an idea that he regarded as one of the two main pillars upon which he had erected his plans for a new national system (the other was representation based on population in both houses of a bicameral legislature rather than, as in the unicameral Continental Congress, having each state equally represented), Madison was compelled to seek other, more acceptable means to check "vicious legislation" (9:353). Given his own quest for an impartial umpire above the contending "interests and views" of society, it is perhaps not surprising that the Virginian was attracted to the arguments advanced by others (especially the two Pennsylvanians, James Wilson and Gouverneur Morris) that a strong, independent executive could serve such a purpose and provide a useful check on the passions, interests, and factions of popular assemblies.

Madison's disappointments, though, were still in the future as the Virginia delegates worked together in the days leading up to the start of the convention to produce a set of resolutions—what became known as the Virginia Plan—that would form the basis for the convention's business. The tardiness of other state delegations delayed the start of the convention by almost two weeks (not until May 25 would there be a quorum of seven states) and had given the punctual Virginians (the last of whom, George Mason, arrived on May 17) precious time to craft a plan that enabled them to set the convention's agenda for the first month. Though Madison was far and away the best prepared of the seven-member Virginia delegation, he was not among its most distinguished members. Not only had Virginia sent Gen. George Washington, the most revered individual in the entire country, but it had also selected two distinguished jurists, George Wythe (the "Socrates of Virginia") and John Blair,[3] the sitting governor of the state, Edmund Randolph, and the leading architect of Virginia's 1776 constitution, George Mason. The only political nonentity of the bunch was Dr. James McClurg, who was chosen only after famed orator Patrick Henry and veteran political leader Richard Henry Lee had refused to attend the convention.

Reading the records of the federal convention might leave the impression that Washington was an unimportant player at the convention—a symbolic figurehead and little more. Apart from making some brief obligatory remarks on the opening day of the convention after he had been unanimously chosen as president of the convention and a short speech on the last day of the con-

---

3. Wythe, among the most distinguished men in Virginia, would almost certainly have played a major role but for the mortal illness of his wife, which forced him to leave the convention on June 4. Before he left he chaired a group that drew up the rules governing the convention's operations, including the all-important secrecy rule, which forbade delegates to speak about the convention's proceedings with anyone other than the delegates.

vention in support of a motion to lower the representation ratio in the House of Representatives from 40,000 to 1 to 30,000 to 1, Washington remained silent throughout the official proceedings. But his silence during debate is misleading, for no delegate's presence was more important; it "propelled the meeting forward as his agreement to be there had insured that it would be held" (Bradford 1984, 125). He is the only person of whom it can be said that his support for the Constitution was a necessary condition for its creation and ratification.

Washington's importance, moreover, went well beyond merely being there. Although Washington felt that his role as president of the convention "restrained him from offering his sentiments on questions" (Farrand 1937, 2:644), he never relinquished his vote, which he consistently cast in favor of a strong central government and a powerful, independent chief executive. Washington's position on these issues was no secret to the delegates (Farrand 1913, 65–66); he had after all been among the most prominent American advocates of a more energetic central government for the past decade. Unlike Madison, however, who was deeply invested in his favorite remedies (like the national negative on state laws), Washington assiduously avoided tying himself to any one particular plan, even when he thought the idea sound. Though on most questions he voted with Madison, Washington was a moderating influence within the convention and the Virginia delegation, siding on occasion with those he disagreed with in order to build wider political support for the Constitution. His support for lowering the ratio of representation was an example of the general's making concessions to political opponents in order to build greater support for the final product. Washington, moreover, was active outside the halls of the convention, socializing with delegates in taverns and private houses, using the occasions to forge personal bonds of trust and to counsel forbearance (Flexner 1969, 123–24). Perhaps it was this aspect of Washington's behavior that prompted William Pierce to observe that "like Peter the great [Washington] appears as the politician and the States-man" (Farrand 1937, 3:94). For Washington, the precise details of the Constitution were ultimately far less important than ensuring that the delegates and the people would support the system they created, a stance that is well captured in a letter he wrote to Jefferson two months after Virginia had ratified the Constitution. "For myself," he told his fellow Virginian, "I was ready to have embraced any tolerable compromise that was competent to save us from impending ruin" (Holcombe 1956, 326).

Washington's influence on the federal convention, and the presidency in particular, was felt in still another way. Since each of the delegates knew that Washington would almost certainly be the first man to assume the post of chief executive in the new government, it was virtually impossible to discuss presidential power without thinking of Washington. It was not so much the certain knowledge that Washington would be the first president that was so important. The framers after all were not naive; they knew that Washington would not be president forever and that they were devising a system that had to work not only for the virtuous but for the vicious and corrupt as well.[4] What was critical was that Washington helped revive the idea of virtuous, nonpartisan executive leadership, an ideal that had long been a central part of eighteenth-century Anglo-American political thought (Ketcham 1984). The Revolution had sublimated that tradition (in 1776 when Americans thought of executive power they thought of the tyranny of King George III), but inside the Philadelphia State House, with the dignified Washington presiding, it was possible to think of executive power again in more positive, virtuous terms. Washington seemed the embodiment of the "dispassionate umpire" that Madison sought, a "patriot king" who could rise above rival parties and interests and watch out for the good of the whole. In relinquishing his post as commander in chief of the Continental army at the close of the Revolutionary War and returning to his farm, Washington had proven not only that he could be trusted with great power but that great power need not corrupt. South Carolinian delegate Pierce Butler became convinced that the presidency's substantial powers (which, he conceded, were "greater than I was disposed to make them") would not "have been so great had not many of the members cast their eyes towards General Washington as President; and shaped their ideas of the Powers to be given to a President, by their opinions of his Virtue." Butler brooded ominously over the paradox that "the Man, who by his Patriotism and Virtue, Contributed largely to the Emancipation of his Country, may be the Innocent means of its being, when He is lay'd low, opress'd" (Farrand 1937, 3:302).

These dark fears of executive power were much on the minds of the two other delegates from Virginia who were to play an important role in the debates over the presidency: George Mason and Edmund Randolph. Next to Madison (who spoke 161 times on the floor of the convention) Mason was the most vocal (he spoke 136 times) and articulate member of the Virginia delegation. A fourth-generation Virginian who was widely celebrated for his role as the author of Virginia's Declaration of Rights, America's first bill of rights, Mason possessed a reputation within the state that was exceeded only by Washington's and possibly Jefferson's. Madison pronounced Mason "the soundest & clearest reasoner that he ever listened to"; Jefferson judged him "of the first order of wisdom among those who acted on the theater of the revolution, of expansive mind, profound judgment, cogent in argument"; and

---

4. Toward the beginning of the convention, for instance, Benjamin Franklin acknowledged that "the first man, put at the helm will be a good one," but warned that "no body knows what sort may come afterwards" (Farrand 1937, 1:103). That the first president would be virtuous and would relinquish power did not make him any less fearful of monarchy. "The Executive," Franklin predicted, "will be always increasing here, as elsewhere, till it ends in a monarchy."

Richard Henry Lee thought Mason "perhaps second to none in wisdom and virtue," noting that "many of the most renowned of his contemporaries ... regarded [him] as the wisest of them all" (Greene 1979, 32). Mason was admired not only for his penetrating intellect and wide learning but also for his probity and independence. Though he served as a representative in the Virginia House of Delegates between 1775 and 1781, Mason was not a political animal, preferring private life to the messy bargains and compromising evasions of the political world.

At sixty-one, Mason was the oldest Virginia delegate; Randolph was the youngest, only thirty-three when the convention opened. At the age of twenty-two, Randolph had been selected to the 1776 Virginia constitutional convention and despite being the youngest member of the convention was chosen to sit on the committee responsible for drafting the state's constitution. Prior to becoming the governor of Virginia in 1786, he had served as the state's attorney general for a decade and had also been elected to several terms in the Continental Congress. How did a person so young achieve positions of such prominence and responsibility? A handsome appearance, good manners, and impressive oratory helped. But more important was his name. Few delegates could boast a more distinguished pedigree: his legendary great-grandfather, William Randolph, was the original patriarch; his grandfather Sir John Randolph had been the first native Virginian to be knighted; his father, John Randolph, had been the Crown's attorney general; and his uncle Peyton Randolph (who left young Edmund everything when he died in 1775) had been Virginia's leading statesman and had been unanimously selected to be the first president of the Continental Congress.

In the end, both Mason and Randolph refused to sign the Constitution. The seasoned Mason knew his own mind, but the younger Randolph was far less certain of the position he had staked out. Mason, to be fair, had the luxury of holding no elective office and having no desire to reenter political life. Randolph, on the other hand, was not only a sitting governor but no doubt hoped for a political career as illustrious as his uncle's. Upon returning to Virginia after the convention, Randolph began to worry that he had backed the wrong horse. Perhaps not wanting to repeat the mistake of his father (who had gone to England in 1774 rather than take up arms against the Crown), Randolph succumbed to the urging of General Washington (Farrand 1937, 3:242) and others to support the Constitution at the Virginia ratifying convention. Randolph's "flip-flop" at the ratifying convention helped to build him a reputation as a political trimmer that haunted him for the rest of his political career (a career that came to a crashing end in 1795 when he was forced to resign as Washington's secretary of state amid allegations of dishonesty and disloyalty). Jefferson would call Randolph "the poorest chameleon I ever saw, having no color of his own, and reflecting that nearest him" (Bradford 1984, 169).

One delegate who could never be accused of being a chameleon was Alexander Hamilton, who as Washington's secretary of the Treasury would become Jefferson's chief nemesis. Whereas Randolph was the heir to a famous Virginia dynasty, Hamilton was an illegitimate child and an orphan by the age of eleven. Born on the Caribbean island of Nevis, Hamilton did not set foot in the United States until he was fifteen, when by a stroke of good fortune his precocious intelligence caught the eye of a Princeton-educated Presbyterian minister who considered it his calling to serve as a "patron who draws genius out of obscurity" (McDonald 1982, 10). The minister sent young Hamilton to a preparatory school in New Jersey with an eye to getting him admitted to the reverend's alma mater. Hamilton completed his preparations in less than a year and then took the audacious step of proposing to the president of Princeton that he should be admitted in whichever "of the classes to which his attainments would entitle him but with the understanding that he should be permitted to advance from Class to Class with as much rapidity as his exertions would enable him to do" (12). Princeton rejected the unorthodox plan but Hamilton, unfazed, persuaded New York's Columbia University (then called King's College) to accept him on these same terms. The coming of the Revolution prevented him from ever finishing his degree. While still a second-year student and barely eighteen years old, Hamilton wrote two important revolutionary tracts totaling about 60,000 words (13). By the beginning of his third year he was drawn increasingly into the fighting, and by the winter of 1776 he was captain of an artillery company; by the following winter he had become an aide to General Washington, who promoted him to lieutenant colonel. Six distinguished years in the army culminated in his leading a successful assault on Lord Cornwallis's forces that led directly to the English surrender at Yorktown in October 1781. War, far more than education, was to be the vehicle that would raise Hamilton from obscurity to the fame he so desperately sought.

Having achieved military glory at Yorktown, Hamilton resigned from the army to study law and within a year had gained admittance to the New York bar, helped by a special regulation that permitted war veterans to waive the customary three-year apprenticeship as a clerk (50–51). At the same time Hamilton's military fame and connections helped him secure an appointment to the Continental Congress. Hamilton was among Congress's most energetic advocates of a strengthened national government; the trouble with revolutionary America, as Hamilton explained in his widely read *Continentalist* essays published the previous summer, was its "extreme jealousy of power" (McDonald 1985, 2). As a representative in the New York legislature during the mid-1780s Hamilton played a vital role in getting New York to participate in the 1786 Annapolis Convention, which was designed to address pressing national problems such as the regulation of interstate commerce. A quorum never materialized in Annapolis, but Hamilton (along with Madison and

John Dickinson) helped snatch victory from the jaws of defeat by persuading the convention to issue an address to the states calling for a new and more sweeping convention the following May in Philadelphia that would be empowered to make changes "as shall appear to them necessary to render the constitution of the Federal government adequate to the exigencies of the Union" (Bradford 1984, 42).

Hamilton's important role in bringing about the convention stands in stark contrast to his relatively insignificant role at the convention. Though selected as one of New York's three delegates, the thirty-year-old Hamilton's influence within the New York delegation was limited by the fact that the two other members, Robert Yates and John Lansing, were both deeply suspicious of any efforts to limit state sovereignty. In their view, the convention was empowered only to augment the powers of the Continental Congress by amending the Articles of Confederation; the convention, they insisted, had no right to create a new national government. Lansing and Yates consistently voted against Hamilton, rendering the latter's vote essentially meaningless, since votes were cast by state in the convention. Hamilton grew increasingly frustrated at his colleagues' intransigence and left the convention on June 30 to attend to other matters in New York. On July 10 both Lansing and Yates quit the convention in protest over its direction, leaving New York without any representation for the remainder of the convention. Hamilton returned as a nonvoting delegate for a few days in mid-August and then returned for the duration on September 6, in time to be named to the five-member Committee of Style, which was charged with putting the finishing touches on the Constitution.

The New York delegation's absence from much of the convention and its strong opposition to the Constitution is particularly ironic, since it was New York's 1777 constitution that was probably the constitutional model that most directly shaped the delegates' conceptions of the presidential office. Neither Hamilton, Yates, nor Lansing had been involved in the writing of New York's constitution, but there was one delegate in Philadelphia who had been among the main authors of that document: the well-bred Gouverneur Morris, who represented Pennsylvania in the federal convention despite having spent most of his life in New York. Born into one of the great landed families of New York, Morris's attitudes toward the populace were very much those of his class. In 1774, as the Revolution got under way, a caustic Morris expressed the nervousness of the landed aristocracy: "The mob begin to think and reason. Poor reptiles! it is with them a vernal morning; they are struggling to cast off their winter's slough, they bask in the sunshine, and ere noon they will bite, depend on it" (Young 1980, 119). His estimation of the people had not improved greatly over the subsequent decade; at the federal convention, for instance, he pushed for property qualifications for the suffrage on the grounds that if people without property (whom he identified with the "ignorant & the dependent") were allowed to vote, "they will sell [their vote] to the rich" (Farrand 1937, 2:202).

Morris's attitudes toward the demos may have been conventional for a man of his class but there was little else typical about this remarkable individual. His wooden leg (he lost a leg in a carriage accident at the age of 28) and crippled arm (a scalding as a child had removed all the flesh from his right arm) may have helped him stand out in a crowd, but it was his rapier wit, infectious humor, and brilliant mind that set him apart and drew others—including most especially Hamilton—toward him. Despite being absent from the convention during much of June, Morris managed to speak more often (173 times) than any other delegate. Yet it was not the quantity of his speaking that impressed listeners but the dazzling way in which he delivered his sentiments. Pierce, who had little love for Morris, observed that the thirty-five-year-old Morris was

> one of those Genius's in whom every species of talents combine to render him conspicuous and flourishing in public debate:—He winds through all the mazes of rhetoric and throws around him such a glare that he charms, captivates, and leads away the senses of all who hear him. With an infinite stretch of fancy he brings to view things when he is engaged in deep argumentation, that render all the labor of reasoning easy and pleasing. (3:92)

That even his adversaries recognized his gifts with language is evident from the fact that Morris was chosen to prepare the final draft of the Constitution, and he has been credited for much of the final document's graceful, spare language. Among his most consequential contributions was the broad language of the vesting clause in the opening line of Article 2: "The executive Power shall be vested in a President of the United States of America."

The only delegate who had more influence than Morris on the shape of the presidency was Morris's fellow Pennsylvanian, James Wilson. Though Wilson and Morris generally voted together in their efforts to secure a powerful, independent presidency—both favored, for instance, giving the president an absolute veto over legislation and both opposed having the president elected by the legislature—their political philosophies, like their backgrounds, were decidedly different. Whereas Morris's father was a landed magnate, Wilson's was a yeoman farmer in a small Scottish village. Whereas Morris likened the people to reptiles, Wilson was the convention's most uncompromising proponent of popular sovereignty. He wanted not only the House to be popularly elected but also the Senate and the presidency, and he strongly opposed Morris's efforts to restrict the vote to property holders. Unlike Morris, who had a deeply pessimistic view of human nature, Wilson adhered to the Scottish moral philosophy he had learned at St. Andrews University, which held that every individual possessed an innate moral sense that enabled the common person to act as a responsible citizen. Morris had little patience with the abstractions of natural rights philosophy: "He who wishes to enjoy natural

Rights must establish himself where natural Rights are admitted. He must live alone" (Bradford 1984, 75). But for Wilson it was axiomatic that "all men are, by nature, free and equal" (89). The differences between Morris and Wilson are evident in the way they described the president they envisioned: for Wilson the president was to be "the man of the people" (Farrand 1937, 2:523), whereas the more hierarchical Morris spoke of the president as "the great protector of the Mass of the people" or as "the Guardian of the people" (2:52–53).

Wilson, however, was no radical democrat. Indeed in Pennsylvania politics he was a leader of the opposition to Pennsylvania's ultrademocratic 1776 constitution, which established a unicameral legislature, abolished the governor, and required that every act passed by the legislature be publicized throughout the state for direct consideration by the people and then repassed by the legislature at the following session. Moreover, Pennsylvania not only mandated annual elections, which was not uncommon in the lower houses established in other revolutionary state constitutions, but also required rotation in office for legislators, something that no other state had done. In Wilson's view, the Pennsylvania constitution was "the most detestable that ever was formed" (Bradford 1984, 89). Wilson's opposition to the 1776 constitution, coupled with his aloof, even haughty demeanor, made him one of the most hated figures in Pennsylvania politics. In 1779 a mob violently attacked his house (which became known thereafter as "Fort Wilson") and in 1788, shortly after Wilson had spearheaded the successful effort to induce Pennsylvania to ratify the Constitution, he was burned in effigy.

Wilson was not a particularly loveable person, but his peers at the convention recognized his impressive talents and deep learning; he had, as Max Farrand has written, "the respect of many but the affection of few" (1913, 21). Pierce's judgment was that Wilson "ranks among the foremost in legal and political knowledge." Government, Pierce noted, "seems to have been his peculiar Study, [and] all the political institutions of the World he knows in detail" (Farrand 1937, 3:91–92). Wilson's impressive erudition was frequently on display at the convention; he spoke 168 times, second only to Morris.[5] Though as loquacious as his fellow Pennsylvanian, Wilson lacked the biting wit and dazzling eloquence of Morris. As Pierce observed, "No man is more clear, copious and comprehensive than Mr. Wilson, yet he is no great Orator. He draws the attention not by the charm of his eloquence, but by the force of his reasoning." Wilson's commanding performance earned him a position on the vitally important five-member Committee of Detail, which was charged at the end of July with drawing up a first draft of a constitution that was "conformable to the Resolutions passed by the Convention" (2:106). Wilson, moreover, was the man the committee assigned the

---

5. On the subject of the presidency Wilson also spoke more often—fifty-six times—than every delegate but Morris, who spoke sixty-five times (DiClerico 1987, 303).

important task of knitting together the final strands into a finished draft (Farrand 1913, 125–26). Although not a member of the Committee of Style, Wilson was consulted by Morris as the latter put the finishing touches on the final document.

Although Wilson's influence on the creation of the Constitution, and especially the presidency, was enormous, Wilson was in many ways quite atypical of the framers, almost sui generis. In 1787 most Americans looked upon their state as the most important source of their political identity; they were Virginians or New Yorkers first, Americans second. It was commonplace for many to refer to their state as their "country."[6] Yet Wilson, perhaps because he did not even arrive in the United States until he was twenty-three, could cavalierly dismiss the states as "imaginary beings" (Farrand 1937, 2:483); it was individuals and not states, Wilson lectured the convention, who formed a government. Wilson was hardly alone in favoring a strong central government and a strong executive (Madison, Morris, Washington, and Hamilton all agreed on this), nor was he the only delegate to speak in a democratic accent; but no other delegate combined popular rule and a powerful presidency as Wilson did. If not representative of the framers, Wilson does come closest, as Robert McCloskey has emphasized, "to representing in his views what the United States was to become" (1967, 2:2; also see Bradford 1984, 88). In Wilson's understanding of the presidency can be seen most clearly our own modern conceptions of that office.

Wilson and Morris were the most important delegates from Pennsylvania, but the most famous was eighty-one-year-old philosopher, politician, and inventor, Benjamin Franklin.[7] Franklin, who suffered from severe gout, was

---

6. Pierce, for instance, writes of Gerry: he "cherishes as his first virtue, a love for his Country" (Farrand 1937, 3:88), by which Pierce meant Massachusetts. On the floor of the convention, Randolph declared that he would "not do justice to the Country which sent him" (that is, Virginia) if he failed to oppose the idea of a single executive (1:88). Also see the comments by Gorham on July 18 (2:41).

7. The other important Pennsylvania delegate was Robert Morris (no relation to Gouverneur Morris), who at the time of the convention was perhaps the wealthiest man in the United States. Franklin's fame was wider, but Robert Morris, a signer of both the Declaration of Independence and the Articles of Confederation, was the acknowledged leader of the Pennsylvania delegation. His most important contribution to the nation had been his enormously successful tenure as superintendent of finance (1781–1784), where he almost single-handedly brought order to the country's chaotic finances. When not serving as financier of the revolution, he was a forceful leader in the Pennsylvania legislature; "when he speaks in the Assembly of Pennsylvania" it was said that "he bears down all before him" (Farrand 1937, 3:91). Strangely for a man of his influence and talents, Morris was almost completely silent at the convention, perhaps because his views were already being forcefully expressed by his protègè and former assistant in the department of finance, Gouverneur Morris. The Morrises were in especially close contact throughout the convention since Gouverneur Morris along with George Washington, who was a close friend of both Morrises, stayed at Robert Morris's luxurious house all summer. Rounding out the large, eight-member Pennsylvania delegation were lawyer Jared Ingersoll, Thomas Mifflin, a former president of the Continental Congress, a rich Irish merchant, Thomas Fitzsimmons, and George Clymer, one of the signers of the Declaration of Independence.

carried to and from the convention each day in a sedan chair that was carried by four convicts from the city prison. At the convention, Franklin played a constructive role as conciliator,[8] but Pierce was correct that the elderly Franklin did "not shine much in public Council." Franklin had never been much of a speaker and his infirmity now prevented him from delivering long orations. Franklin's first "speech" to the convention, on June 2, was actually read aloud by James Wilson. In that speech Franklin proposed that the Executive should serve without pay, but no further discussion of the idea ensued. The idea, as Madison dryly observed, "was treated with great respect, but rather for the author of it, than from any apparent conviction of its expediency or practicability" (Farrand 1937, 1:85). Though the eventual Constitution, particularly in its creation of a strong presidency, ended up being far distant from Franklin's own ideas (Franklin himself was a leading supporter of the 1776 Pennsylvania constitution), Franklin never hesitated in pledging his full support for the Constitution. On the last day of the convention he made an eloquent plea (again read by Wilson) that he hoped would persuade the remaining holdouts to sign the Constitution.

> I confess that there are several parts of this constitution which I do not at present approve, but I am not sure I shall never approve them: For having lived long, I have experienced many instances of being obliged by better information or fuller consideration, to change opinions even on important subjects, which I once thought right, but found to be otherwise. It is therefore that the older I grow, the more apt I am to doubt my own judgment, and to pay more respect to the judgment of others. ... I cannot help expressing a wish that every member of the Convention who may still have objections to it, would with me, on this occasion doubt a little of his own infallibility—and to make manifest our unanimity, put his name to the instrument. (2:641–43)

Franklin's parting counsel was aimed primarily at the Virginians, Mason and Randolph, as well as Massachusetts's Elbridge Gerry. Today Gerry is best known as the source of the term "gerrymander," so called because in 1811, as Massachusetts governor, he presided over a redrawing of district lines designed to advantage his party in the upcoming elections, including one district that was so strangely shaped that it was said to resemble a salamander. At the time of the convention, though, Gerry was best known as a protégè of revolutionary leader Samuel Adams. Like his mentor, Gerry agitated for rebellion against the distant tyranny of the British, but he took a quite different view of rebellions closer to home. Shays' Rebellion, a rebellion of farmers in western Massachusetts in 1786 that had done so much to galva-

---

8. At one point during the debate over representation Franklin reminded his colleagues, "We are sent here to *consult,* not to *contend,* with each other; and declarations of a fixed opinion, and of determined resolution, never to change it, neither enlighten nor convince us. Positiveness and warmth on one side, naturally beget their like on the other" (Wright 1986, 341).

nize support for a constitutional convention, left a particularly deep impression on Gerry. "I am still a republican," he told his fellow delegates on May 31, "but I have been taught by experience the danger of the levelling spirit." The event had helped persuade Gerry that "the evils we experience flow from the excess of democracy" (1:48). Yet whereas other delegates, like Madison, saw Shays' Rebellion as an argument for a strong central government capable of intervening in the affairs of states, Gerry retained a vivid fear of central power[9] and rejected Madison's novel argument that liberty was safer in a large than a small republic. Ignoring Franklin's plea for unanimity, Gerry, who was one of only three delegates to have signed both the Declaration of Independence and the Articles of Confederation (the other two were Pennsylvania's Robert Morris and Connecticut's Roger Sherman), decided not to affix his signature to a document he believed was "full of vices." One colleague unkindly ascribed Gerry's opposition to his tendency to "object to everything he did not propose" (Charleton, Ferris, and Ryan 1986, 150), but Gerry's stated objections to the Constitution focused on the absence of a bill of rights and the destruction of the "Sovereignty or Liberty of the States" (Farrand 1937, 2:635). None of the three branches of government escaped his censure: the powers of Congress were "indefinite and dangerous," the judiciary would be "oppressive," and, finally, he worried that "the Executive is blended with and will have an undue influence over the Legislature" (Storing 1981, 2:6–7).

Throughout much of the convention, Gerry was at odds with the other members of the Massachusetts delegation, particularly Nathaniel Gorham and Rufus King.[10] The thirty-two-year-old King was deeply conservative and among the strongest supporters of a powerful presidency. An eloquent speaker, he was considered a rising star in American politics; Pierce ranked the young New Englander as "among the Luminaries of the present Age" (Farrand 1937, 3:87). King's name might be widely remembered today had

---

9. Gerry particularly feared a standing army, proposing at one point that the number of troops in time of peace be limited constitutionally (Farrand 1937, 2:330). Gerry's idea was summarily rejected and was alleged to have prompted Washington to quip that Gerry's motion should be amended to read that "no foreign enemy should invade the United States at any time, with more than three thousand troops" (Warren 1929, 483).

10. The fourth member of the delegation, Caleb Strong, voted with Gerry more often (most notably on the Connecticut Compromise), but, unlike Gerry, Strong vigorously supported the final product. Strong was unable to sign the Constitution because a family illness forced him to leave the convention in late August, but his support for the Constitution at the Massachusetts ratifying convention was critically important in achieving ratification. Though Strong spoke infrequently—he was a "feeble" speaker, observed Pierce (Farrand 1937, 3:88)—he was greatly respected and formed part of that unsung sensible center of the convention that did so much to steer the convention toward the compromises that enabled the Constitution to be realized. Despite not being a powerful speaker, Strong was a popular politician, serving eleven annual terms as governor between 1800 and 1816 (Bradford 1984, 13), during which time he never lost an election and always ran ahead of the ticket. The man he beat in five of those elections (1800, 1801, 1802, 1803, and 1812) was none other than Elbridge Gerry (10).

he not hitched his star to the fading Federalist political party. He was the Federalist candidate for president in 1816, the last year the party ran a national candidate, and the party's vice presidential nominee in both 1804 and 1808. Like most conservative New England Federalists, King was deeply skeptical of democracy and equality. "The great body of people," he wrote in the year prior to the Constitutional Convention, "are without virtue, and not governed by any restraints of conscience." Equality was "the arch enemy of the moral world," degrading all that was worthy. King was scathingly critical of utopian abstractions like "the rights of man"; "experience, not abstraction," he intoned, "ought to be our guide in practice and conduct" (Bradford 1984, 17). Though the forty-nine-year-old Gorham usually voted with King, his views were far less philosophical or ideological. A businessman of limited education, Gorham was more interested in the economic powers of the new government than in the structure of government. Gorham had been a fixture of Massachusetts politics since the Revolution, serving as a delegate to the provincial congress (1774–1775), a member of the Massachusetts Board of War (1778–1781), a delegate to his state's constitutional convention (1779–1780), a representative in the state legislature (1780–1787), and a speaker of the lower house for three years. He had also been a member of the Continental Congress in 1782–1783 and 1785–1787, including a recently completed six-month term as president of Congress. Gorham, like King, spoke often and participated actively at the Convention (Gorham served on the five-person Committee of Detail; King was placed on the Committee of Style).

Gerry, King, and Gorham, as well as the state's fourth delegate, Caleb Strong, were all well-respected politicians in Massachusetts but none came with a genuinely national reputation or outlook, and certainly none could match the intellectual brilliance or deep learning of Madison, Mason, Wilson, or Hamilton. The leading lights of Massachusetts were all absent. The state's preeminent citizen, John Adams, who had drafted the widely admired Massachusetts constitution of 1780, was in London as the U.S. minister to Great Britain, though his presence was felt at the convention through his just published book, *A Defense of the Constitution of the Government of the United States of America,* which mounted a lengthy defense of the principles—a bicameral legislature, checks and balances, and separation of powers—that had been institutionalized in the Massachusetts constitution.[11] Absent, too, were the renowned revolutionary radicals, Samuel Adams and John Hancock. Lacking its leading citizens and its brightest minds—like the future chief justice of the Massachusetts Supreme Court

---

11. Madison was nonplussed by Adams's new book. "Men of learning," he told Jefferson, will "find nothing in it. Men of taste [will] find many things to criticize. And men without either, not a few things, which they will not understand" (St. John 1987, 32).

Theophilus Parsons—the Massachusetts delegation never assumed the same leadership role in the creation of the Constitution that the state had occupied during the Revolution.

More influential in the convention's deliberations than Massachusetts was the impressive and generally cohesive delegation of its small neighbor to the north, Connecticut.[12] All three Connecticut delegates, Oliver Ellsworth, William Samuel Johnson, and Roger Sherman, were current or former judges. It was the Connecticut delegation, particularly Sherman, that was instrumental in creating and brokering the vitally important "Great Compromise" (or, as it is sometimes known, the "Connecticut Compromise" or "Sherman Compromise") by which representation in the House would be based on population and representation in the Senate would be based on states. Without that compromise, reached in the middle of July by a narrow 5 to 4 vote (Massachusetts was divided, King and Gorham against, Gerry and Strong in favor) and bitterly opposed by the likes of Madison and Wilson, it is difficult to see how the convention could have continued.

The eldest and perhaps most remarkable of the Connecticut delegation was the sixty-six-year-old Sherman, a self-made man who had started out life as a shoemaker. Without the benefit of family connections or formal education, Sherman slowly climbed to prominence in Connecticut politics through surveying, storekeeping, and law. A rustic, plain exterior belied a skilled and experienced politician who was judged "as cunning as the Devil" by one who knew him well (Bradford 1984, 21). His political career began in the 1750s as a justice of the peace and a representative in the Connecticut General Assembly. In 1766 he was elected to the upper house of the legislature (called the Governor's Council of Assistants), a post he held for almost two decades. This appointment by tradition also brought with it an appointment as a judge on the Connecticut Superior Court (Collier 1971, 58), where he remained until 1789.[13] From 1774 to 1781 and again between 1783 and 1784 he served in the Continental Congress; "Father Sherman," as he became known, was among the Congress's most dedicated and industrious members (Bradford 1984, 24). At the time of the convention he was also mayor of New Haven, a position he occupied until his death in 1793. Age had done little to slow the energetic Sherman. At the federal convention, Sherman was among the most active and frequently heard delegates, speaking around 140 times,

---

12. The remaining two New England states—Rhode Island and New Hampshire—played little or no role at the convention. Rhode Island was the lone state that refused to send any representatives to the convention. New Hampshire voted a delegation, but the legislature refused to fund the delegates' expenses. Only after one of the New Hampshire delegates, John Langdon, offered to pay the expenses out of his own pocket did two delegates from New Hampshire set out for Philadelphia. They arrived July 23, by which time the convention was more than half over.

13. Sherman had given up his seat on the council after the assembly had passed a law that no person could be a judge of the Superior Court and simultaneously hold any other high state or national office (Collier 1971, 218).

usually in opposition to the plans presented by Wilson, Morris, and Madison for a stronger executive and stronger central government.[14] Though Sherman had serious reservations about aspects of the Constitution, including the creation of the presidency, he supported the final Constitution and his backing of the Constitution at the Connecticut ratifying convention was pivotal to its ratification.

William Samuel Johnson, under whom Sherman had studied law in the early 1750s, was among the most widely respected and best loved of the delegates. Doctor Johnson, as he was universally addressed, was recognized as one of the best educated and most learned legal minds in the United States, with degrees (some of which were honorary) from Yale, Harvard, and Oxford. Johnson's father, a noted philosopher and Anglican minister, had been the first president of Columbia College, a position to which Johnson himself had been appointed just prior to the opening of the convention. At the convention, and throughout his life, Johnson was a voice of moderation. He distrusted philosophical battles of first principles: "While they serve to whet the wits of men," he warned, "they most surely sharpen their tempers toward each other" (30). Although the nearly sixty-year-old Johnson did not speak as often as either Sherman or Ellsworth, he played an important behind-the-scenes role in facilitating compromise. Johnson was particularly useful in forming bridges with many of the southern (particularly Carolina) delegates, who were "vastly fond" of the sweet-tempered and charming Johnson (32).[15] The high esteem in which the delegates held Johnson was manifest in his selection to chair the final Committee of Style.

At forty-two Ellsworth was the youngster of the Connecticut delegation, but like his two much admired elders he brought a judicious voice of moderation to the proceedings, including his work on the Committee of Detail. "Let not too much be attempted" (35) was his counsel to those who would push too far and end with nothing. A French observer described the future chief justice of the United Supreme Court as "a man simple in his manners, but wise and infinitely reasonable" (Collier 1971, 236), a description the Frenchman

---

14. Though of common origins and enormously popular in the state of Connecticut, Sherman was no radical democrat. "The people," he explained at the Constitutional Convention, "immediately should have as little to do as may be about the Government. They want information and are constantly liable to be misled" (Bradford 1984, 25).

15. Southerners' affinity and fondness for Johnson was in marked contrast to their attitudes toward Sherman, whom they found little short of baffling. Sherman, wrote Pierce, was "the oddest shaped character I ever remember. ... He is awkward ... and unaccountably strange in his manner. ... The oddity of his address, the vulgarisms that accompany his public speaking, and that strange New England cant which runs through his public as well as his private speaking make everything that is connected with him grotesque and laughable." Not that Pierce lacked respect for Sherman who, he believed, "deserves infinite praise—no Man has a better Heart or a clearer Head. ... In his train of thinking there is something regular, deep and comprehensive" (Farrand 1937, 3:88–89).

also said fit Sherman. The young Ellsworth greatly admired Sherman, whom he served with in the Continental Congress, Connecticut's Superior Court, and the Governor's Council during the late 1770s and early 1780s. But unlike Sherman, Ellsworth was the product of an old Connecticut family and had been schooled at Yale and Princeton (then called the College of New Jersey). He possessed, wrote a contemporary, a "tall, dignified and commanding" presence, though without any trace of "haughtiness and arrogance" (Fischer 1965, 288). An eloquent debater, Ellsworth spoke frequently at the convention (84 times) before having to leave in late August to attend to judicial duties. Although he did not get a chance to sign the Constitution, he was the primary defender of the Constitution during Connecticut's ratifying debates.

The Connecticut delegation had a kindred spirit in Delaware's John Dickinson, one of the three or four most prominent delegates to attend the convention. Ever since his emergence on the national stage during the Stamp Act Congress in 1765, the fifty-four-year-old Dickinson had played a leading role in virtually every defining moment in the republic's history. Like the Connecticut delegates, Dickinson was a powerful force for moderation and conciliation, though severe ill health, which forced him to miss much of July, prevented him from participating as fully in the proceedings as he would otherwise have done (McDonald and McDonald 1988, 99). A supporter of a strong national government (including a national veto on state laws), he cautioned his fellow nationalists that it was both "politic" and "unavoidable" that the states be left "a considerable agency in the System" (Farrand 1937, 1:136). After the intransigence of the larger states had led to the introduction of the New Jersey Plan, which envisioned a much weaker national government than was provided for in the Virginia Plan, he privately upbraided Madison for "pushing things too far" and jeopardizing the whole process by refusing to make concessions to the smaller states. Many of the small state representatives, he instructed the young Virginian, are "friends to a good National Government; but we would sooner submit to a foreign power, than submit to be deprived of an equality of suffrage, in both branches of the legislature, and thereby be thrown under the domination of the large States" (1:242; also Flower 1983, 243). In the opening weeks of the convention, Dickinson offered a principled rationale for the Great Compromise that would eventually unlock the convention's deadlock. Rejecting Wilson's argument that the people ought to be the sole source of the national government's authority, Dickinson suggested that the states (through the Senate) should also constitute a basis of the government's authority. Having different sources of authority, Dickinson maintained, would "produce that collision between the different authorities which should be wished for in order to check each other," much as in Britain the House of Lords and House of Commons served as mutual checks by drawing their powers from different sources (Farrand 1937, 1:153, 156). Only a national government so checked could safely be trusted with great powers.

Not all the Delaware delegates were as moderate or conciliatory as Dickinson. Gunning Bedford was the "stormy petrel" (Bradford 1984, 104) of the convention, insisting that "there was no middle way" between "a perfect consolidation" and a confederacy of equal states (Farrand 1937, 2:490). In perhaps the most intemperate speech of the convention he assailed the motives of the large state representatives and threatened them with mayhem—in the form of alliances with foreign powers—if they did not accede to the small states' demands. No less extreme in his way was the nationalist George Read. While Dickinson tried to navigate a middle way between the states and the nation, Read bluntly rebuked his colleague, "Too much attachment is betrayed to the State Govermts. We must look beyond their continuance. A national Govt. must soon of necessity swallow all of them up" (1:136). Read's views on executive power were equally extreme. For instance, in a discussion on how the Senate should be selected, Read proposed that "the Senate should be appointed by the Executive Magistrate" from a list of people nominated by the state legislatures, a proposal that not surprisingly was neither seconded nor supported (1:151). The remaining two Delaware delegates, Richard Bassett and Jacob Broom, were mercifully silent.

Neighboring Maryland sent one of the least distinguished delegations, in part because many of the state's leading men had declined appointments. The state's most vocal member was attorney general Luther Martin, whose fifty-three speeches, a number of them wandering and long-winded, and virtually all of them stridently oppositional, sorely tried the delegates' patience, even among those sympathetic to the cause of states' rights that Martin so vociferously championed. A late arrival (he came on June 9), Martin made an early exit, leaving the convention (together with fellow Maryland delegate John Francis Mercer, who did not arrive in Philadelphia until August 6) on September 4 in order to organize opposition to ratification. However, the delegates at the ratifying convention were spared Martin's "eternal volubility" (3:272; also 3:93) because an attack of laryngitis prevented him from speaking on the floor (Bradford 1984, 114).

One of the few delegates who seemed to be able to tolerate Martin and work constructively with him was his old college friend William Paterson, who came to Philadelphia as a delegate from New Jersey. Both Paterson and Martin were raised in New Jersey, attended the College of New Jersey, entered law, and became attorney general of their respective states (Martin having moved to Maryland immediately after graduating from college). But there the similarities ended. Whereas Martin seemed to choose the most inopportune times to deliver an impassioned harangue, Paterson was, as Pierce described him, "very happy in the choice of time and manner in engaging in a debate, and never speaks but when he understands his subject well." The smallest man in the convention, Paterson (who would later be selected by President Washington to serve as a justice on the U.S. Supreme Court) was also one of the most impressive; he was, wrote Pierce, "one of those kind of Men whose powers break in upon you, and create wonder and astonishment" (Farrand 1937, 3:90). Paterson was the motive power behind the New Jersey Plan, which he presented to the convention on June 15. Little is known about precisely how many hands were involved in penning the New Jersey Plan, which gave each state equal representation in a unicameral legislature, but it seems probable that Paterson was assisted by several others, including his old friend Martin as well as David Brearly, chief justice of the New Jersey Supreme Court (Bradford 1984, 61, 110). Brearly and Paterson were the only New Jersey delegates who spoke with any frequency. The rest of the delegation, Jonathan Dayton (at 26 the youngest delegate at the convention), William Churchill Houston (who was mortally ill with tuberculosis and attended the convention less than two weeks), and even the revered sixty-three-year-old William Livingston (who was New Jersey's first elected governor, a position he occupied continuously from 1776 until his death in 1790), virtually never spoke.

The New Jersey Plan was defeated on June 18, largely because it failed to secure the support of a single southern state. North Carolina, South Carolina, and Georgia all voted against it and stood firmly with Virginia in favor of Randolph's plan. Throughout the convention, the Carolinas and Georgia frequently voted together and thus often held the balance of power in their hands. Though an important voting bloc, neither the Georgia nor the North Carolina delegates exercised an important influence on the convention debates. Georgia's four delegates combined spoke no more than twenty times, and never on the subject of the executive. Of North Carolina's five delegates only the fifty-two-year-old Hugh Williamson (who spent the first forty years of his life as a resident of Pennsylvania) took to the floor with any frequency. The multitalented Williamson had been a preacher, professor of mathematics, physician, and scientist, and had studied and traveled extensively in Europe and the West Indies, all before the age of forty. During the Revolutionary War he was appointed surgeon general of North Carolina and used that post as a springboard into politics in 1782, when he was elected to the North Carolina legislature as well as to the Continental Congress. Perhaps Williamson's most important act at the convention was his deciding, along with William Davie and Alexander Martin, to back the Connecticut Compromise, thus making North Carolina the crucial fifth vote in favor of giving states equal voting strength in the Senate. "[Unless] we concede on both sides," the cosmopolitan Williamson cautioned, "our business must be at an end" (Bradford 1984, 177).

If the North Carolina and Georgia delegations were generally unremarkable, South Carolina was another matter. Its distinguished four-person delegation was among the most respected and most important to attend the Philadelphia convention. The undisputed head of the delegation was John Rutledge, considered by many the greatest political leader south of Virginia. He was a man of such enormous standing in South Carolina that in 1784, after a man had insulted one of Rutledge's domestic slaves, the state legislature made it "a crime, punishable by exile, to offend John Rutledge" (192). Rutledge had been South Carolina's first (and only) president under the 1776 constitution (a constitution he had helped draft[16]), but it was his role during the dark days of the Revolutionary War that made him an icon in South Carolina. In 1780, as the British overran South Carolina and occupied the capital city of Charleston (an event that did wonders to help remedy Rutledge's lingering Anglophilia), governor Rutledge fled to the north in an effort to mobilize the resources necessary to liberate the capital and the state. With the legislature and privy council unable to convene for well over a year, Rutledge exercised virtually absolute power over the state's politics. Greater still was the fame of "Dictator John," as he was affectionately known thereafter, when he relinquished his office shortly after the British had been driven out of South Carolina. Though always a popular leader, the imperious Rutledge would never be mistaken for a democrat. At the convention, he favored making wealth a condition of service for both the president and the two houses of Congress; he wanted the number of representatives each state received to be based on wealth and not population; and he pressed for even the House to be elected by the state legislatures. "If this Convention had been chosen by the people," he bluntly reminded the delegates, "it is not supposed that such proper characters would have been preferred" (192). That the convention rejected each of these particular ideas should not obscure his towering influence at the convention. Judicious and tactful, he was the convention's unanimous choice to chair the all-important Committee of Detail. In addition to having a leading hand in the first draft of the Constitution, Rutledge was a frequent speaker whose opinions and judgment carried great weight not only with his own delegation but with the other deep south states as well.

Second only to Rutledge in the esteem and affections of South Carolinians was Gen. Charles Cotesworth Pinckney, whose aristocratic views were virtu-

---

16. In important respects South Carolina's 1776 constitution was quite unlike the other state constitutions enacted in 1776 and 1777. It was, for example, the only revolutionary constitution explicitly to vest legislative authority in both the legislature and an executive (styled a "president"). It was also the only constitution created during this period that gave the executive an absolute veto over all bills (Thorpe 1909, 6:3244). Indeed no other state even gave the chief executive a qualified veto that could be overridden by the legislature. In 1778 South Carolina rewrote its constitution, bringing it more in line with the antiexecutive bias of the other revolutionary state constitutions. One of the most important changes made was to eliminate the president's veto power. Rutledge refused to sign the 1778 constitution; among his objections was that it would "annihilate one Branch of the Legislature" by depriving the governor of his veto (Haw 1997, 107). Rutledge also objected to the fact that a new popularly elected Senate was replacing the old Legislative Council, which under the 1776 constitution had been chosen by the lower house. These changes, Rutledge lamented, shifted South Carolina from a "compounded or mixed Government" to "a simple Democracy or one verging towards it" (108). Claiming the people were behind him, Rutledge abruptly resigned his office. Such was the respect in which Rutledge was held that the following year the legislature elected him governor under the new constitution.

ally identical to those of Rutledge, with whom he was connected through marriage (Rutledge's brother, Governor Edward Rutledge, was Pinckney's brother-in-law). John Adams's running mate in 1800 and the Federalist Party's presidential candidate in 1804 and 1808, Pinckney might be remembered today as our third or fourth president had the Federalist Party not disintegrated so rapidly after Washington left the presidency. During the Constitutional Convention, Pinckney played an unspectacular but vital role in making sure that the Constitution protected southern interests (particularly slavery) sufficiently that the southern states would be willing to ratify the document. But he was no intransigent; indeed he was one of the leading forces working toward compromise. It was the general, for instance, who proposed a committee of one member from each state be appointed to seek a compromise on the vexing question of representation in the Senate (Farrand 1937, 1:511), the committee out of which came the Connecticut Compromise. Though he spoke often enough and with authority on issues respecting slavery and legislative election and representation, Pinckney rarely spoke on other issues, including the presidency.

In the debate over the presidency the South Carolinian from whom the delegates heard most frequently was Pinckney's twenty-nine-year-old cousin, Charles Pinckney III. Not one to be overawed by his distinguished elders, the enterprising young Pinckney came to the convention with his own plan of government, which he laid before the convention on the same day (May 29) that the Virginia Plan was first put before the delegates. Pinckney's plan was conspicuously ignored by the other delegates, perhaps because the convention's elders felt the presumptuous Pinckney needed to be put in his place.[17]

---

17. Because Pinckney's original plan has not survived, it is impossible to know precisely what was in the plan. Some thirty years after the Constitutional Convention Pinckney sent a copy of what he claimed to be a draft of his plan to the secretary of state, John Quincy Adams, who was preparing the journal of the convention for publication. But as Madison realized (Farrand 1937, 3:504–5) and as Max Farrand subsequently reiterated, the document Pinckney sent Adams could not possibly have been the original Pinckney Plan. "Its provisions, in several important particulars," observes Farrand, "are directly at variance with Pinckney's opinions as expressed in the Convention." Moreover, "the document embodies several provisions that were only reached after weeks of bitter disputes—compromises and details, that it was impossible for any human being to have forecast accurately" (3:602). Based mainly on notes found in the possession of James Wilson (who drafted the final report of the Committee of Detail, to which the Pinckney Plan was referred), Farrand has reconstructed what the original plan probably looked like (3:604–9). It is clear from this reconstruction that the Pinckney Plan was far more specific about executive powers than was the original Virginia Plan, but the extent to which it shaped the Committee of Detail's work on the presidency is difficult to ascertain. Certainly it is possible to find parallels between Pinckney's plan and the Committee of Detail's report. For instance, both begin the section enumerating executive powers by specifying the president's duty to report to the legislature on the state of the nation. The Committee of Detail's final draft began, "He shall, from time to time, give information to the Legislature, of the state of the Union: he may recommend to their consideration such measures as he may judge necessary and expedient" (2:185); the Pinckney Plan's opening sentence reads, "It shall be his duty to inform the Legislature of the condition of

Unfazed by this snub, Pinckney proceeded to play an extraordinarily active role in debate. At least one delegate was most impressed. The young man, observed Pierce, possessed "a spirit of application and industry beyond most Men. He speaks with great neatness and perspicuity, and treats every subject as fully, without running into prolixity, as it requires" (3:96). The talents that Pierce spied blossomed as Pinckney became an important state political leader (including serving as governor of the state in three different decades), first of the Federalist Party and then, in the mid-1790s, of the emerging Jeffersonian party. In 1800 he managed Jefferson's presidential campaign in South Carolina and helped swing South Carolina into Jefferson's column and away from his distinguished cousin. Worse still, Pinckney began to advocate universal white manhood suffrage and press for legislative reapportionment that would more fairly represent the poorer backcountry areas. Pinckney's betrayal of class, party, and family earned him the Charleston elite's enduring enmity and the appellation of "Blackguard Charlie" (Bradford 1984, 202).

The only South Carolina delegate not born to the Charleston elite was Pierce Butler. Yet Butler was no democrat either. In fact he was the most genuine aristocrat in the convention, his father having been a baronet. Not being the eldest son, he was prevented from inheriting his father's estates and so he entered the military, a career path followed by countless other younger sons of the British aristocracy (Charleton, Ferris, and Ryan 1986, 132). While on military duty in the colonies, the Irish-born Butler married a wealthy Charleston heiress, resigned his military commission, and settled down to the life of a Charleston planter. Though he would become one of the richest planters in South Carolina, his views were never narrowly tied to his class.

---

the United States, so far as may respect his Department—to recommend Matters to their Consideration" (3:606). Since this idea had not been discussed at all on the convention floor and did not appear in an earlier draft of the committee's report compiled by Edmund Randolph, it seems very likely that Wilson was influenced by Pinckney's plan, though it must be noted that (1) Pinckney's wording was not his own but was lifted verbatim from section 19 of the New York constitution (Thorpe 1909, 5:2633), a constitution that Wilson and the rest of the committee also had before them, and (2) the phrasing of the committee report (which with minor modifications would become the opening sentence of Article 2, section 3) is substantially different and improved from Pinckney's wording. To take another example, the only report or resolution referred to the Committee of Detail that included the designation of commander in chief was the Pinckney Plan. Yet it is unlikely that the committee's final report, which made the president "the commander in chief of the Army and navy of the United States, and of the Militia of the several States," was influenced by Pinckney's provision. Before Wilson had begun drafting the committee's final report, committee chair John Rutledge had already inserted the commander in chief clause into Randolph's early draft (Farrand 1937, 2:145). Even if this were not the case, it needs to be emphasized that the "commander in chief" designation was a commonplace in the state constitutions and that there was never any doubt at the federal convention that the power of commander in chief would be vested in the chief executive. Far from showing the influence of the Pinckney Plan, then, the commander in chief clause helps illustrate Clinton Rossiter's judgment that the Pinckney Plan "was at best merely a source of familiar phrases for the members of the committee of detail" (1987, 171; but compare Collier and Collier 1986, 64–74).

During his time in the state legislature in the 1780s he took a leading role in advocating causes dear to the western parts of the state, including making representation in the legislature more equitable and relocating the state capital from Charleston to Columbia. Though not much of an orator, the independent and sometimes difficult Butler spoke frequently (roughly 50 times) on a wide range of subjects, including the presidency.

On Monday, September 17, Butler and the rest of the South Carolina delegation, together with thirty-four delegates from the other states, affixed their signatures to the new Constitution.[18] The framers then promptly dissolved the convention and returned to their home states to try to persuade a skeptical people that this new Constitution should be adopted. Nine states would need to ratify in order for the new union to take effect. A few states, like Delaware, Georgia, and New Jersey, would ratify promptly and with little debate. But in most states it would be necessary for proponents of the new Constitution to overcome vehement opposition to the framers' handiwork. The fights in Virginia and New York were particularly bitter, with both states ratifying by razor-thin margins and only then after the crucial ninth state—New Hampshire, the keystone state—had already voted to ratify. It would take three years before the thirteenth and last state, Rhode Island, finally ratified the Constitution and entered the union.

---

18. Before leaving the convention, Dickinson had asked George Read to sign his name, so although there were thirty-nine names affixed to the Constitution, only thirty-eight delegates physically signed the document.

I

Constituting the Executive

1

One President or Many?

The executive Power shall be vested in a President of the United States of America.

Article 2, section 1

On Friday, June 1, the delegates began their deliberations on the executive branch of government. Their starting point was the seventh resolution of the Virginia Plan, which had been presented to the convention by Virginia governor Edmund Randolph earlier in the week. The resolution proposed

> that a National Executive be instituted; to be chosen by the National Legislature for a term of ____ years, to receive punctually at stated times, a fixed compensation for the services rendered, in which no increase or diminution shall be made so as to affect the Magistracy, existing at the time of increase or diminution, and to be ineligible a second time; and that besides a general authority to execute the National laws, it ought to enjoy the Executive rights vested in Congress by the Confederation. (Farrand 1937, 1:21)

Modern readers may be surprised to find that the first motion to be considered on this day's discussion was James Wilson's proposal to make the executive a single person. Who, one might well wonder, would seriously prefer having two or three or more presidents?

Benjamin Franklin, for one. As a Pennsylvania delegate to the Second Continental Congress in 1775, the seventy-year-old Franklin had drafted a plan for an "Articles of Confederation and Perpetual Union." Franklin's plan included a twelve-person executive council empowered to carry out administrative and executive functions while Congress was in recess. Franklin's preference for a plural executive was also evident in his support for Pennsylvania's constitution of 1776,[1] which abolished the office of governor and

---

1. Franklin was president of the convention that drafted the constitution but it is not true, as Forrest McDonald writes, that the constitution was "authored mainly by Benjamin Franklin" (1994, 132). Franklin's role in the drafting of the constitution was in fact quite minor. See the editorial comment in Labaree et al. (1959–), 22:514–15.

vested executive power in a "supreme executive council." The Pennsylvania legislature was charged with selecting a president from among the twelve-person council, but other than serving as commander in chief the president had no more power than any other member of the council.[2] At the Constitutional Convention in 1787, Franklin continued to favor a plural executive in part because he believed government policy would thereby be less changeable and more predictable, something that was particularly important in foreign policy. A plural executive, Franklin maintained, also obviated the problems of succession, illness, or death that inescapably marred a single elected executive (1:102 n. 14).

John Dickinson, who attended the federal convention as a delegate from Delaware, was one of Franklin's longtime adversaries. Over the course of their political careers Dickinson and Franklin had clashed repeatedly. In the 1760s Franklin spearheaded the effort to transform Pennsylvania from a proprietary to a royal colony, while Dickinson, twenty-five years Franklin's junior, had led the opposition. In 1776 Dickinson refused to sign the Declaration of Independence that Franklin helped pen. So bitter was their enmity that Dickinson reportedly refused to put a lightning rod on his house (Wright 1986, 235). Yet on one thing these political enemies agreed: the desirability of a plural executive. The summer after Franklin had sketched his plan for union, the Continental Congress appointed a committee of thirteen (one member from each colony) to devise a plan of confederation. Dickinson was the Pennsylvania representative and the primary drafter of the plan that emerged from the committee in 1776. Dickinson's draft, like Franklin's, vested administrative powers in a council of state. Three years (1782–85) as president of Pennsylvania (and another year, in 1781, as president of Delaware) did nothing to shake Dickinson's belief in the efficacy of a plural executive. At the federal convention, Dickinson voted with the Delaware delegation to oppose Wilson's motion to make the executive a single person. In fact Dickinson drafted his own plan of government in the middle of June that would have created a three-headed executive, consisting of one person from the eastern states, another from the middle states, and a third from the southern states (Hutson 1987, 87). Their terms would be staggered and the one who had been in office the longest would be styled the president, but each of the three executives would have equal power. In Dickinson's view, lodging the executive in a single person was a massive mistake, since there was "no instance of its being ever done with safety" (96).

Franklin and Dickinson were not alone in their support for a plural executive. In addition to Delaware, two other states, New York and Maryland, op-

---

2. The only power given specifically to the president was that of "commander in chief of the forces of the state," but even this was qualified by provision that he "shall not command in person, except advised thereto by the council, and then only so long as they shall approve thereof" (Thorpe 1909, 5:3088).

posed Wilson's motion for a single executive when it came to a vote on June 4. Three of the seven delegates from Virginia (Randolph, John Blair, and George Mason) also opposed the motion. All told, at least a quarter of the delegates at the convention favored a plural executive.[3] In fact the idea had enough support that it resurfaced in the New Jersey Plan, submitted by William Paterson on June 15. The New Jersey Plan left unspecified the number of persons who would make up the federal executive, but it clearly anticipated that it would be more than one person. In the short debate over the New Jersey Plan, which was rejected on June 19, the only delegate to address the plural executive provision of the plan was James Wilson, who strongly opposed it. "In order to control the Legislative authority," Wilson instructed the convention, "you must divide it. In order to control the Executive you must unite it." Anticipating the argument of Hamilton in *Federalist* 70, Wilson insisted that "One man will be more responsible than three." Intrigue and violence, Wilson argued, would result from a plural executive. "Three will contend among themselves till one becomes the master of his colleagues. In the triumvirates of Rome first Caesar, then Augustus, are witnesses of this truth" (Farrand 1937, 1:254; also see McCloskey 1967, 1:293–94). A plural executive would be a house divided against itself and could not stand.

Those who favored a plural executive were unlikely to have been swayed by Wilson's reasoning (after all, they had not been persuaded earlier in the month when he and others offered similar arguments) but there was no further debate on this fundamental question at the convention. Did a plural executive have a realistic chance of succeeding at the convention? Probably not; certainly not with the personnel who attended. Arguably the plural executive was an idea whose time had passed. Even the revolutionary state constitutions, with the exception of Pennsylvania, had preserved the office of governor, even as they had sharply limited the office's power.[4] Most of the support for a plural executive at the convention came from the oldest delegates. Franklin was eighty-one, Dickinson fifty-four, Roger Sherman sixty-six, Daniel of St. Thomas Jenifer sixty-four, George Mason sixty-one. Among

---

3. McDonald (1985, 240–41 n. 48) rightly counts Sherman, Randolph, Mason, Blair, Franklin, Dickinson, Williamson, Jenifer, Lansing, and Yates as supporters of a plural executive. But in addition to these ten there must also have been at least two additional Delaware delegates (the five-person delegation included Bedford, Bassett, Broom, Read) who joined Dickinson in favoring a plural executive. McDonald counts two New Jersey delegates, Brearly and Houston, as having voted for a plural executive but in fact New Jersey did not vote on any motions that day or the previous session on June 2. The two were prevented from voting because their state's instructions required that three delegates be present for the state to take part in the proceedings (Farrand 1913, 178).

4. The only other revolutionary constitution to emulate Pennsylvania's plural executive was Vermont, which vested "supreme executive power" in a governor and council (Thorpe 1909, 6:3742). Vermont, though, would not be admitted as a state until 1791. In two state constitutions drafted in 1776, those of Delaware and South Carolina, the chief magistrate was designated as a "president" rather than a "governor," but neither state adopted a plural executive.

the ten delegates known to have voted against Wilson's motion on June 4 the average age was around fifty-five. In contrast, the five delegates who spoke in favor of Wilson's motion averaged forty-one years of age (the average age at the convention was close to 44).[5] The older delegates' views of executive power were colored by their battles against the royal governors; the younger delegates who had come of political age during the 1770s and 1780s had learned different lessons and were more worried about the weakness of executive power in the state constitutions and the Articles of Confederation. These younger delegates were generally much less worried that a single executive was, as Edmund Randolph warned, the "fetus of monarchy." For them it was possible to imagine an executive that was both unitary and republican.

1. The Federal Convention of 1787

These records are from Madison's notes of the convention, the standard and most reliable source we have of who said what and when at the convention. Before coming to Philadelphia, Madison had decided that he would keep a record of the convention's work, a decision born out of his own frustrations in researching the formation of past republics. As he explained many years later, "the curiousity I had felt during my researches into the History of the most distinguished Confederacies, particularly those of antiquity, and the deficiency I found in the means of satisfying it more especially in what related to the process, the principles—the reasons, & the anticipations, which prevailed in the formation of them, determined me to preserve as far as I could an exact account of what might pass in the Convention." Each day Madison took his seat directly below the president's chair, facing the other delegates and taking detailed notes of what was said, in "terms legible & in abbreviations & marks intelligible to myself" (Farrand 1937, 3:550). Every evening, he would laboriously write out the notes he had scribbled down during the day. It was a labor, he said, that almost killed him; yet it was also a labor that succeeded in bringing to life for subsequent generations the framers' deliberations.

Gaillard Hunt and James Brown Scott, eds., *The Debates in the Federal Convention of 1787 Which Framed the Constitution of the United States of America Reported by James Madison* (New York: Oxford University Press, 1920), 37–39, 48–51.

5. Those who spoke in favor of the unitary executive were Wilson (who was 44 years old), Pinckney (29), Rutledge (47), Butler (42), and Gerry (42). Those who we can say with virtual certainty voted against the proposal were Franklin (81), Sherman (66), Jenifer (64), Mason (61), Dickinson (54), Blair (55), Williamson (52), Yates (49), Randolph (33), and Lansing (33). Williamson's vote is inferred from a later speech (Farrand 1937, 2:100) opposing "unity in the executive." Mason was late that day and so missed the vote but Madison recorded him as "being no" (1:97). Though Delaware opposed Wilson's motion, it is not possible to ascertain which of the other delegates joined Dickinson.

June 1

The committee of the whole proceeded to Resolution 7. "that a national Executive be instituted, to be chosen by the national Legislature—for the term of ____ years, &c" ...

Mr. Wilson moved that the Executive consist of a single person.

Mr. Pinckney seconded the motion, so as to read "that a National Executive to consist of a single person, be instituted."

A considerable pause ensuing and the Chairman asking if he should put the question, Doctor Franklin observed that it was a point of great importance and wished that the gentlemen would deliver their sentiments on it before the question was put.

Mr. Rutledge animadverted on the shyness of gentlemen on this and other subjects. He said it looked as if they supposed themselves precluded by having frankly disclosed their opinions from afterwards changing them, which he did not take to be at all the case. He said he was for vesting the Executive power in a single person. ... A single man would feel the greatest responsibility and administer the public affairs best.

Mr. Sherman said he considered the Executive magistracy as nothing more than an institution for carrying the will of the Legislature into effect, that the person or persons ought to be appointed by and accountable to the Legislature only, which was the depositary of the supreme will of the society. As they were the best judges of the business which ought to be done by the Executive department, and consequently of the number necessary from time to time for doing it, he wished the number might not be fixed, but that the Legislature should be at liberty to appoint one or more as experience might dictate.

Mr. Wilson preferred a single magistrate, as giving most energy, dispatch and responsibility to the office. ...

Mr. Gerry favored the policy of annexing a council to the Executive in order to give weight and inspire confidence.

Mr. Randolph strenuously opposed a unity in the Executive magistracy. He regarded it as the fetus of monarchy. We had he said no motive to be governed by the British Government as our prototype. He did not mean however to throw censure on that excellent fabric. If we were in a situation to copy it he did not know that he should be opposed to it; but the ... genius of the people of America required a different form of Government. He could not see why the great requisites for the Executive department, vigor, despatch and responsibility, could not be found in three men as well as in one man. The Executive ought to be independent. It ought therefore in order to support its independence to consist of more than one.

Mr. Wilson said that unity in the Executive instead of being the fetus of monarchy would be the best safeguard against tyranny. He ... was not governed by the British Model which was inapplicable to the situation of this country; the extent of which was so great, and the manners so republican, that nothing but a great confederated Republic would do for it.

Mr. Wilson's motion for a single magistrate was postponed by common consent, the Committee seeming unprepared for any decision on it; and the first part of the clause agreed to, viz—"that a National Executive be instituted."

June 2

Mr. Rutledge and Mr. Pinckney moved that the blank for the number of persons in the Executive be filled with the words "one person." Mr. Pinckney supposed the reasons to be so obvious and conclusive in favor of one that no member would oppose the motion.

Mr. Randolph opposed it with great earnestness, declaring that he should not do justice to the Country which sent him if he were silently to suffer the establishment of a unity in the Executive department. He felt an opposition to it which he believed he should continue to feel as long as he lived. He urged 1. that the permanent temper of the people was adverse to the very semblance of monarchy. 2. that a unity was unnecessary; a plurality being equally competent to all the objects of the department. 3. that the necessary confidence would never be reposed in a single Magistrate. 4. that the appointments would generally be in favor of some inhabitant near the center of the Community, and consequently the remote parts would not be on an equal footing. He was in favor of three members of the Executive to be drawn from different portions of the Country.

Mr. Butler contended strongly for a single magistrate as most likely to answer the purpose of the remote parts. If one man should be appointed he would be responsible to the whole, and would be impartial to its interests. If three or more should be taken from as many districts, there would be constant struggle for local advantages. In military matters this would be particularly mischievous. He said his opinion on this point had been formed under the opportunity he had had of seeing the manner in which a plurality of military heads distracted Holland when threatened with invasion by the imperial troops. One man was for directing the force to the defence of this party, another to that part of the Country, just as he happened to be swayed by prejudice or interest.

June 4

The question was resumed on the motion of Mr. Pinckney. ...

Mr. Wilson was in favor of the motion. It had been opposed by [Mr. Randolph] but the arguments used had not convinced him. He observed that the objections of Mr. Randolph were levelled not so much against the measure itself, as against its unpopularity. If he could suppose that it would occasion a rejection of the plan of which it should form a part, though the part was an important one, yet he would give it up rather than lose the whole. On examination he could see no evidence of the alleged antipathy of the people. On the contrary, he was persuaded that it does not exist. All know that a single magistrate is not a King. One fact has great weight with him. All the 13 States, though agreeing in scarce any other instance, agree in placing a single magistrate at the head of the Government. The idea of three heads has taken place in none. The degree of power is indeed different; but there are no coordinate heads. In addition to his former reasons for preferring a unity, he would mention another. The tranquility not less than the vigor of the Government he thought would be favored by it. Among three equal members, he foresaw nothing but uncontrolled, continued, and violent animosities; which would not only interrupt the public administration but diffuse their poison through the other branches of Government, through the States, and at length through the people at large. If the members were to be unequal in power, the principle of the opposition to the unity was given up. If equal, the making them an odd number would not be a remedy. In Courts of Justice there are two sides only to a question. In the Legislative and Executive departments questions have commonly many sides. Each member therefore might espouse a separate one and no two agree.

Mr. Sherman. This matter is of great importance and ought to be well considered before it is determined. Mr. Wilson he said had observed that in each State a single magistrate was placed at the head of the Government. It was so he admitted, and properly so, and he wished the same policy to prevail in the federal Government. But then it should be also remarked that in all the States there was a council of advice, without which the first magistrate could not act. A council he thought necessary to make the establishment acceptable to the people. Even in Great Britain the King has a council; and though he appoints it himself, its advice has its weight with him, and attracts the confidence of the people.

Mr. Williamson asks Mr. Wilson whether he means to annex a council.

Mr. Wilson means to have no council, which oftener serves to cover, than prevent malpractices.

Mr. Gerry was at a loss to discover the policy of three members for the Executive. It would be extremely inconvenient in many instances, particularly in military matters, whether relating to the militia, an army, or a navy. It would be a general with three heads.

On the question for a single Executive it was agreed to [7 states yes; 3 states no].

2. George Mason, Draft of a Speech, June 4, 1787

Mason arrived at the convention late on June 4 and so missed the vote that took place earlier that day creating a one-person executive. The Virginian had prepared a long speech attacking unity in the executive and proposing a plural executive. But finding he had arrived too late to affect the vote, Mason instead focused his comments on the veto power, which the convention was then considering. Below is the speech Mason had originally planned to give.

It is not yet determined how the executive is to be regulated—Whether it is to act solely from its own judgment, or with the advice of others. Whether there is, or is not to be a council annexed to it; and if a council, how far their advice shall operate in controlling the judgment of the supreme magistracy. If there is no council of state, and the executive power be vested in a single person, what are the provisions for its proper operation, upon casual disability by sickness, or otherwise. These are subjects which must come under our consideration; and perhaps some of the most important objections would be obviated by placing the executive power in the hands of three, instead of one person.

It is proposed ... in the [Virginia] Plan ... that [a] Council of Revision [invested with a qualified veto over legislation] shall be formed out of the members of the judiciary ... joined with the executive; and I am inclined to think, when the subject shall be taken up, it may be demonstrated that this will be the wisest and safest mode of constituting this important Council of Revision. But the federal inferior courts of justice must, I presume, be fixed in the several respective states, and consequently most of them at a great distance from the seat of the federal government. The almost continual operation of the Council of Revision upon the acts of the national parliament ... will require that this Council should be easily and

George Mason, "Draft of a Speech on the Advantages of Vesting the Executive Power in Three Persons," in *The Papers of George Mason, 1725–1792,* ed. Robert A. Rutland, 3 vols. (Chapel Hill: University of North Carolina Press, 1970), 3:895–98. Used by permission of the publisher.

speedily convened; and consequently that only the judges of the supreme federal court, fixed near the seat of government, can be members of it; their number will be small. By placing the executive power in three persons, instead of one, we shall not only increase the number of the Council of Revision ... but by giving to each of the three a vote in the Council of Revision, we shall increase the strength of the executive, in that particular circumstance, in which it will most want strength—in the power of defending itself against the encroachments of the legislature. These, I must acknowledge, are with me, weighty considerations for vesting the executive rather in three than in one person.

The chief advantages which have been urged in favour of unity in the executive are the secrecy, the dispatch, the vigour and energy which the government will derive from it, especially in time of war. That these are great advantages, I shall most readily allow. They have been strongly insisted on by all monarchical writers—they have been acknowledged by the ablest and most candid defenders of republican government; and it can not be denied that a monarchy possesses them in a much greater degree than a republic. Yet perhaps a little reflection may incline us to doubt whether these advantages are not greater in theory than in practice—or lead us to enquire whether there is not some pervading principle in republican governments, which sets at naught, and tramples upon this boasted superiority—as has been experienced, to their cost, by most monarchies, which have been imprudent enough to invade or attack their republican neighbors. This invincible principle is to be found in the love, the affection, the attachment of the citizens to their laws, to their freedom, and to their country. Every husbandman will be quickly converted into a soldier when he knows and feels that he is to fight not in defence of the rights of a particular family, or a Prince; but for his own. ... It was this which, in ancient times, enabled the little cluster of Grecian republics to resist, and almost constantly to defeat the Persian monarch. It was this which supported the states of Holland against a body of veteran troops through a thirty years war with Spain, then the greatest monarchy in Europe, and finally rendered them victorious. It is this which preserves the freedom and independence of the Swiss cantons in the midst of the most powerful nations. And who that reflects seriously upon the situation of America, in the beginning of the late War—without arms—without soldiers—without trade, money, or credit—in a manner destitute of all resources, but must ascribe our success to this pervading, all-powerful principle?

We have not yet been able to define the powers of the executive; and however moderately some gentlemen may talk or think upon the subject, I believe there is a general tendency to a strong executive and I am inclined to think a strong executive necessary. If strong and extensive powers are vested in the executive, and that executive consists only of one person, the government will of course degenerate (for I will call it degeneracy) into a monarchy—a government so contrary to the genius of the people that they will reject even the appearance of it. ...

Have not the different parts of this extensive government, the several states of which it is composed, a right to expect an equal participation in the executive, as the best means of securing an equal attention to their interests? Should an insurrection, a rebellion or invasion happen in New Hampshire when the single supreme magistrate is a citizen of Georgia, would not the people of New Hampshire naturally ascribe any delay in defending them to such a circumstance and so vice versa? If the executive is vested in three persons, one chosen from the northern, one from the middle, and one from the southern states, will it not contribute to quiet minds of the people, and convince them that there will be proper attention paid to their respective concerns? Will not three men so chosen bring with them, into office, a more perfect and extensive knowledge of the real interests of this great Union? Will not such a

mode of appointment be the most effectual means of preventing cabals and intrigues between the legislature and the candidates for this office, especially with those candidates
who from their local situation, near the seat of the federal government, will have the greatest temptations and the greatest opportunities? Will it not be the most effectual means of
checking and counteracting the aspiring views of dangerous and ambitious men, and consequently the best security for the stability and duration of our government upon the invaluable principles of liberty? These, sir, are some of my motives for preferring an executive consisting of three persons rather than of one.

3. The Federal Farmer XIV, January 17, 1788

The letters of the Federal Farmer, of which there were eighteen in all, are generally considered to be among the most astute Anti-Federalist writings. Certainly they were among the most influential, being widely circulated in pamphlet form during the fall and winter of 1787. Long thought to be the work
of Virginian Richard Henry Lee, recent scholarship (Wood 1974; Webking
1987) has discredited this theory and shown that the author is more likely to
be Melancton Smith, a moderate New York Anti-Federalist who played a
leading role at his state's ratification convention. Whoever the author, the
measured tones of the Federal Farmer, praising some parts of the Constitution
and criticizing others, stand in marked contrast to some of the more whole-
sale condemnations issued by others who opposed the handiwork of the
Philadelphia convention. In this selection, the Federal Farmer offers up a defense of the Constitution's unitary executive.

Each state in the union has uniformly shown its preference for a single executive, and generally directed the first executive magistrate to act in certain cases by the advice of an executive council. Reason, and the experience of enlightened nations, seem justly to assign the
business of making laws to numerous assemblies, and the execution of them, principally, to
the direction and care of one man. Independent of practice, a single man seems to be peculiarly well circumstanced to superintend the execution of laws with discernment and decision,
with promptitude and uniformity. The people usually point out a first man—he is to be seen
in civilized as well as uncivilized nations, in republics as well as in other governments. In every
large collection of people there must be a visible point serving as a common center in the government, towards which to draw their eyes and attachments. The constitution must fix a man,
or a congress of men, superior in the opinion of the people to the most popular men in the
different parts of the community, else the people will be apt to divide and follow their respective leaders. Aspiring men, armies and navies, have not often been kept in tolerable order
by the decrees of a senate or an executive council. The advocates for lodging the executive

"Additional Number of Letters from the Federal Farmer to the Republican," in *Selected Americana from Sabin's Dictionary of Books relating to America* (Woodbridge, Conn.: Primary Source
Media, 1996), fiche 19,259, pp. 123–26.

power in the hands of a number of equals, as an executive council, say that much wisdom may be collected in such a council, and that it will be safe; but they agree that it cannot be so prompt and responsible as a single man—they admit that such a council will generally consist of the aristocracy, and not stand so indifferent between it and the people as a first magistrate. But the principal objection made to a single man is that when possessed of power he will be constantly struggling for more, disturbing the government, and encroaching on the rights of others. It must be admitted that men, from the monarch down to the porter, are constantly aiming at power and importance, and this propensity must be as constantly guarded against in the forms of the government. Adequate powers must be delegated to those who govern, and our security must be in limiting, defining, and guarding the exercise of them, so that those given shall not be abused, or made use of for openly or secretly seizing more. Why do we believe this abuse of power peculiar to a first magistrate? Is it because in the wars and contests of men, one man has often established his power over the rest? Or are men naturally fond of accumulating powers in the hands of one man? I do not see any similitude between the cases of those tyrants, who have sprung up in the midst of wars and tumults, and the cases of limited executives in established governments. Nor shall we, on a careful examination, discover much likeness between the executives in Sweden, Denmark, Holland, etc., which have, from time to time, increased their powers, and become more absolute, and the executives, whose powers are well ascertained and defined, and which remain, by the constitution, only for a short and limited period in the hands of any one man or family.

4. Alexander Hamilton, *Federalist* 70, March 15, 1788

The *Federalist* papers, written under the pseudonym "Publius," were initially conceived by Alexander Hamilton as a joint project involving himself, Madison, John Jay, and Gouverneur Morris. Morris refused and Jay became too ill to complete more than a few essays, which left Madison and Hamilton to carry the load. In a span of seven months, beginning in late October, the two men wrote eighty papers defending every aspect of the proposed constitution. The partnership ended in March when Madison left New York to campaign for a seat in the Virginia ratifying convention, leaving Hamilton to write the last twenty-one papers himself, including all eleven papers on the executive branch. The first of these eleven papers (*Federalist* 67) appeared on March 11, a week after Madison's departure, and the last (*Federalist* 77) on April 2, an impressive work rate of a paper every other day. In *Federalist* 70, which may be the most often cited of Hamilton's *Federalist* essays on the executive, Hamilton forcefully defends "the unity of the executive." In the first half of the essay, which is excerpted here, Hamilton zeroes in particularly on the dangers to the state that are posed by a plurality of coequal magistrates.

New York *Independent Journal*, March 15, 1788.

There is an idea, which is not without its advocates, that a vigorous executive is inconsistent with the genius of republican government. The enlightened well-wishers to this species of government must at least hope that the supposition is destitute of foundation, since they can never admit its truth without at the same time admitting the condemnation of their own principles. Energy in the executive is a leading character in the definition of good government. It is essential to the protection of the community against foreign attacks; it is not less essential to the steady administration of the laws; to the protection of property against those irregular and high-handed combinations which sometimes interrupt the ordinary course of justice; to the security of liberty against the enterprises and assaults of ambition, of faction, and of anarchy. Every man the least conversant in Roman history knows how often that republic was obliged to take refuge in the absolute power of a single man, under the formidable title of Dictator, [not only] against the intrigues of ambitious individuals who aspired to ... tyranny, and the seditions of whole classes of the community whose conduct threatened the existence of all government, [but also] against the invasions of external enemies who menaced the conquest and destruction of Rome.

There can be no need, however, to multiply argument or examples on this head. A feeble executive implies a feeble execution of the government. A feeble execution is but another phrase for a bad execution; and a government ill executed, whatever it may be in theory, must be, in practice, a bad government.

Taking it for granted, therefore, that all men of sense will agree in the necessity of an energetic executive, it will only remain to inquire, what are the ingredients which constitute this energy? How far can they be combined with those other ingredients which constitute safety in the republican sense? And how far does this combination characterize the plan which has been reported by the convention? ...

Those politicians and statesmen who have been the most celebrated for the soundness of their principles and for the justice of their views, have declared in favor of a single executive and a numerous legislature. They have, with great propriety, considered energy as the most necessary qualification of the former, and have regarded this as most applicable to power in a single hand; while they have, with equal propriety, considered the latter as best adapted to deliberation and wisdom, and best calculated to conciliate the confidence of the people and to secure their privileges and interests.

That unity is conducive to energy will not be disputed. Decision, activity, secrecy, and dispatch will generally characterize the proceedings of one man in a much more eminent degree than the proceedings of any greater number; and in proportion as the number is increased, these qualities will be diminished.

This unity may be destroyed in two ways: either by vesting the power in two or more magistrates of equal dignity and authority; or by vesting it ostensibly in one man, subject, in whole or in part, to the control and cooperation of others in the capacity of counsellors to him. Of the first, the two consuls of Rome may serve as an example; of the last, we shall find examples in the constitutions of several of the states. New York and New Jersey, if I recollect right, are the only states which have intrusted the executive authority wholly to single men.[6] Both these methods of destroying the unity of the executive have their partisans; but

---

6. Hamilton's recollection was a little faulty or at least incomplete. Although the New Jersey constitution vested the "the supreme executive power" in the governor, he was to be assisted "at all times" by "a privy-council" with whom he was required to "consult." The privy council was chosen from among the members of the upper house, styled the Legislative Council (Thorpe 1909, 5:2596).

the votaries of an executive council are the most numerous. They are both liable, if not to equal, to similar objections, and may in most lights be examined in conjunction.

The experience of other nations will afford little instruction on this head. As far, however, as it teaches anything, it teaches us not to be enamored of plurality in the executive. We have seen that the Achaeans, on an experiment of two praetors, were induced to abolish one. The Roman history records many instances of mischiefs to the republic from the dissensions between the consuls, and between the military tribunes, who were at times substituted for the consuls. But it gives us no specimens of any peculiar advantages derived to the state from the circumstance of the plurality of those magistrates. That the dissensions between them were not more frequent or more fatal is [a] matter of astonishment until we advert to the singular position in which the republic was almost continually placed and to the prudent policy pointed out by the circumstances of the state, and pursued by the consuls, of making a division of the government between them. The patricians engaged in a perpetual struggle with the plebeians for the preservation of their ancient authorities and dignities; the consuls, who were generally chosen out of the former body, were commonly united by the personal interest they had in the defence of the privileges of their order. In addition to this motive of union, after the arms of the republic had considerably expanded the bounds of its empire, it became an established custom with the consuls to divide the administration between themselves by lot—one of them remaining at Rome to govern the city and its environs, the other taking the command in the more distant provinces. This expedient must, no doubt, have had great influence in preventing those collisions and rivalships which might otherwise have embroiled the peace of the republic.

But quitting the dim light of historical research, attaching ourselves purely to the dictates of reason and good sense, we shall discover much greater cause to reject than to approve the idea of plurality in the executive, under any modification whatever.

Wherever two or more persons are engaged in any common enterprise or pursuit, there is always danger of difference of opinion. If it be a public trust or office, in which they are clothed with equal dignity and authority, there is peculiar danger of personal emulation and even animosity. From either, and especially from all these causes, the most bitter dissensions are apt to spring. Whenever these happen, they lessen the respectability, weaken the authority, and distract the plans and operation of those whom they divide. If they should unfortunately assail the supreme executive magistracy of a country, consisting of a plurality of persons, they might impede or frustrate the most important measures of the government, in the most critical emergencies of the state. And what is still worse, they might split the community into the most violent and irreconcilable factions, adhering differently to the different individuals who composed the magistracy.

Men often oppose a thing merely because they have had no agency in planning it, or because it may have been planned by those whom they dislike. But if they have been consulted, and have happened to disapprove, opposition then becomes, in their estimation, an indispensable duty of self-love. They seem to think themselves bound in honor, and by all the motives of personal infallibility, to defeat the success of what has been resolved upon contrary to their sentiments. Men of upright, benevolent tempers have too many opportunities of remarking, with horror, to what desperate lengths this disposition is sometimes carried, and how often the great interests of society are sacrificed to the vanity, to the conceit, and to the obstinacy of individuals who have credit enough to make their passions and their caprices interesting to mankind. Perhaps the question now before the public may, in its consequences, afford melancholy proofs of the effects of this despicable frailty, or rather detestable vice, in the human character.

Upon the principles of a free government, inconveniences from the source just mentioned must necessarily be submitted to in the formation of the legislature; but it is unnecessary, and therefore unwise, to introduce them into the constitution of the executive. It is here too that they may be most pernicious. In the legislature, promptitude of decision is oftener an evil than a benefit. The differences of opinion, and the jarrings of parties in that department of the government, though they may sometimes obstruct salutary plans, yet often promote deliberation and circumspection, and serve to check excesses in the majority. When a resolution too is once taken, the opposition must be at an end. That resolution is a law, and resistance to it punishable. But no favorable circumstances palliate or atone for the disadvantages of dissension in the executive department. Here they are pure and unmixed. There is no point at which they cease to operate. They serve to embarrass and weaken the execution of the plan or measure to which they relate, from the first step to the final conclusion of it. They constantly counteract those qualities in the executive which are the most necessary ingredients in its composition—vigor and expedition—and this without any counterbalancing good. In the conduct of war, in which the energy of the executive is the bulwark of the national security, everything would be to be apprehended from its plurality.

Questions for Discussion

1. How would American politics and history be different if Mason, Dickinson, and other proponents of a plural executive had prevailed at the convention and succeeded in creating a three-person presidency? How, for instance, might a plural executive have impacted the coming of the Civil War?

2. Is a plural executive a good idea? Are there circumstances in which a plural executive might improve the performance of the political system? What are the circumstances under which it might promote discord?

2

An Executive Council?

The President ... may require the Opinion, in writing, of the principal Officer in each of the executive Departments, upon any Subject relating to the Duties of the respective Offices.

Article 2, section 2

Having decided that the executive power would be vested in a single person, the convention still needed to determine whether to establish a council to advise the president. That the framers of the Constitution rejected a plural executive was perhaps predictable; that they would reject a council was more surprising. During the revolutionary period no other state had followed Pennsylvania's lead in abolishing the governor and vesting the executive power in a council, but every state constitution had established a council of some kind to advise the governor. It was against this backdrop that George Mason blasted the Constitution for not including an executive council. The absence of a council, he observed, was "a thing unknown in any safe and regular government."

In Mason's own state of Virginia, the constitution mandated that the governor could exercise no executive functions without the advice of an eight-member privy council, or council of state. The council was selected by joint ballot of the two legislative assemblies, and its advice and proceedings were to be "entered on record, and signed by the members present (to any part whereof, any member may enter his dissent) to be laid before the General Assembly, when called for by them" (Thorpe 1909, 5:3816–17). Nor was Virginia's constitution unusual. Similar provisions existed in the state constitutions of Delaware (1776), Maryland (1776), Massachusetts (1780), New Hampshire (1784), and North Carolina (1776) (1:563–64, 3:1695; 1904, 4:2465–66, 5:2791).

Even New York, which had established the strongest, most independent governor of all the revolutionary state constitutions, did not allow the governor to act without a council in the matters of appointments and the veto. Although New York's 1777 constitution avoided the sort of privy council or council of state common in the other states, it curtailed the governor's power of appointment by establishing a four-member council (to be chosen by the assembly from among the senators) empowered to fill most important state offices. The governor presided over the council of appointment, but as president he was to have only "a casting voice, but no other vote" (Thorpe 5:2633). Similarly, the veto power (absent in all the other states, except for two brief years in South Carolina) was given to a council of revision made up of the governor and the judges of the state supreme court (5:2628–29).

The idea of a council of state to advise and to check the chief executive had deep roots in colonial history. Each colony possessed an executive council, whose consent the governor needed on many important matters, including appointments. The members of the council were generally appointed by the crown from a list of names nominated by the governor. Governors were instructed to nominate councillors who were men "of good life, well-affected to our government, of good estates and abilities, and not necessitous people" (Main 1967, 3; Greene [1898] 1966, 73). Though governors generally tried to select councillors whose support they could count on, they were often compelled to choose councillors whose backing they needed in order to govern the colony effectively. In Virginia, for instance, the council was made up of the colony's most powerful families because, as historian Jackson Turner Main observes, "the executive could not function without their support" (1967, 44; also see Greene [1898] 1966, 86). Further strengthening the hand of the council was that most served a life tenure, although technically they served at the pleasure of the king (or proprietor). A change in governors thus did not bring a change in councillors.

Americans who lived in the 1770s and 1780s, in short, were thoroughly accustomed to the idea of an executive council. Indeed, judging by the revolutionary state constitutions drafted between 1776 and 1784, they could barely imagine a chief executive exercising important executive powers without the advice and consent of an executive council. New York came closest to breaking out of this mold, but even here the idea of a council was preserved for the power of appointment and the veto. Yet for all this rich history and precedent, all that remained of the council in the federal constitution was a provision allowing the president to "require the Opinion, in writing, of the principal Officer in each of the executive Departments, upon any subject relating to the Duties of their respective Offices." And this clause, as Alexander Hamilton pointed out in *Federalist* 74, is "a mere redundancy in the plan; as the right for which it provides would result of itself from the office."

Not that the framers of the convention left the chief executive untrammeled. Instead, the advice and consent function that had previously been exercised by an executive council was now given to a legislative body, the United States Senate. To us the transfer of such powers from an executive to a legislative body may seem surprising, but Americans of the founding period would have found this more comprehensible because they would not have differentiated as sharply between a senate and a council. Colonial councils typically combined executive and legislative (as well as judicial) functions. They not only advised the governor but also sat as the upper house of the legislature (as well as serving as the highest court of appeals in civil cases). Most revolutionary state constitutions stripped the executive council of its legislative (and judicial) role, but a few did not. In Georgia's 1777 constitution, for instance, the executive council doubled as a quasi-legislative body to which all laws and ordinances passed by the assembly were to be sent for "perusal and advice" (Thorpe 1909, 2:779). Georgia's governor was forbidden from presiding in the executive council when it was meeting in its legislative capacity, a proscription that had become commonplace in the late colonial period (2:781; also see Main 1967, 247 n. 5). In two constitutions—those of Delaware and South Carolina—the upper house was styled a council, though the advice and consent functions were lodged in a separate privy council.

The framers' decision to lodge the advice and consent function in the Senate may be understandable given this historical background, but the absence of a council clearly troubled many of the convention delegates. On September 7, in the closing days of the convention, Mason raised the issue again. Moreover, his proposal to instruct the drafting committee to prepare a clause establishing a council of state was supported not only by Franklin and Dickinson, both of whom, like Mason, had favored a plural executive from the outset, but also by Madison and James Wilson, both of whom had consistently supported a powerful, unitary executive. At this late date in the convention few delegates had the stomach for tackling such a contentious question. But Mason's motion failed (only Georgia, Maryland, and South Carolina supported it) less from principled opposition to an executive council (most delegates in fact probably supported the idea) than from a fear, as James Iredell frankly acknowledged at the North Carolina ratifying convention, that the problem of selecting a council would raise the same questions of representation that had bedeviled the convention as they created the legislature and the presidency. Which states would be represented on the council? How were the interests of large and small states, northern and southern states, to be balanced? Little wonder that a majority of the delegates preferred to leave well enough alone and keep the advice and consent function in the Senate.

Whatever the reasons for not including an executive council, the framers' decision was a momentous one for American political development. In eighteenth-century Britain the power of the king's privy council was waning, and in its place the cabinet was emerging as the center of power. By rejecting a council, as Iredell pointed out, the framers ensured that "the President must be personally responsible for everything," a doctrine that stands in stark contrast to the idea of the collective responsibility of the cabinet that would emerge in Britain in the nineteenth century. In Philadelphia, the framers not only created a new office, the American presidency, but they also changed in important respects the way Americans thought about executive power. Prior to 1787, a council of state was widely seen as essential to making executive power safe and accountable; after 1787 a council became seen as an anachronism. Five states—Delaware, Georgia, New Hampshire, Pennsylvania, and South Carolina—drafted new constitutions within five years of the federal convention and each abolished its executive council, closely modeling their executive branch on the model the framers of the Constitution had established.

5. The Federal Convention of 1787

As the hot Philadelphia summer wore on, convention delegates grew increasingly anxious to finish up their business. Speeches became briefer, and an exhausted Madison's notes grew less detailed. Instead of contentious issues being debated on the floor of the convention, motions and proposals were promptly handed over to smaller committees in hopes that an agreement could be brokered quickly and quietly. Such was the fate of several calls for an executive council made in late August. Connecticut's Oliver Ellsworth was the first to rise to remind the delegates that they had not yet made provision for an executive council to advise the president.

August 18

Mr. Ellsworth observed that a Council had not yet been provided for the President. He conceived there ought to be one. His proposition was that it should be composed of the President of the Senate, the Chief Justice, and the ministers as they might be established for the departments of foreign and domestic affairs, war, finance and marine, who should advise but not conclude the President.

Mr. Pinckney wished the proposition to lie over, as notice had been given for a like purpose by Mr. Govr. Morris who was not then on the floor. His own idea was that the President should be authorized to call for advice or not as he might choose. Give him an able Council and it will thwart him; a weak one and he will shelter himself under their sanction.

Mr. Gerry was against letting the heads of the departments, particularly of finance, have anything to do in business connected with legislation. He mentioned the Chief Justice also

Gaillard Hunt and James Brown Scott, eds., *The Debates in the Federal Convention of 1787 Which Framed the Constitution of the United States of America Reported by James Madison* (New York: Oxford University Press, 1920), 423, 428–29, 506, 508, 531–32. The August 22 entry is from the Journal of the Federal Convention, in Jonathan Elliot, ed., *The Debates in the Several State Constitutions on the Adoption of the Federal Constitution* (New York: Burt Franklin, 1888), 1:256–57.

as particularly exceptionable. These men will also be so taken up with other matters as to neglect their own proper duties.

Mr. Dickinson urged that the great appointments should be made by the Legislature, in which case they might properly be consulted by the Executive, but not if made by the Executive himself—This subject by general consent lay over.

August 20

Mr. Govr. Morris seconded by Mr. Pinckney submitted the following propositions which were in like manner referred to the Committee of Detail.

"To assist the President in conducting the public affairs there shall be a Council of State composed of the following officers—1. The Chief Justice of the Supreme Court, who shall from time to time recommend such alterations of and additions to the laws of the U.S. as may in his opinion, be necessary to the due administration of Justice, and such as may promote useful learning and inculcate sound morality throughout the Union: He shall be President of the Council in the absence of the President

2. The Secretary of Domestic Affairs who shall be appointed by the President and hold his office during pleasure. It shall be his duty to attend to matters of general police, the state of agriculture and manufactures, the opening of roads and navigations, and the facilitating communications through the United States; and he shall from time to time recommend such measures and establishments as may tend to promote those objects.

3. The Secretary of Commerce and Finance who shall also be appointed by the President during pleasure. It shall be his duty to superintend all matters relating to the public finances, to prepare and report plans of revenue and for the regulation of expenditures, and also to recommend such things as may in his judgment promote the commercial interests of the U.S.

4. The Secretary of Foreign Affairs who shall also be appointed by the President during pleasure. It shall be his duty to correspond with all foreign ministers, prepare plans of treaties, and consider such as may be transmitted from abroad; and generally to attend to the interests of the U.S. in their connections with foreign powers.

5. The Secretary of War who shall also be appointed by the President during pleasure. It shall be his duty to superintend everything relating to the War Department, such as the raising and equipping of troops, the care of military stores, public fortifications, arsenals and the like—also in time of war to prepare and recommend plans of offence and defence.

6. The Secretary of the Marine who shall also be appointed during pleasure—It shall be his duty to superintend everything relating to the Marine Department, the public ships, dock yards, naval stores and arsenals—also in time of war, to prepare and recommend plans of offence and defence.

The President shall also appoint a Secretary of State to hold his office during pleasure; who shall be Secretary to the Council of State, and also public Secretary to the President. It shall be his duty to prepare all public despatches from the President which he shall countersign.

The President may from time to time submit any matter to the discussion of the Council of State, and he may require the written opinions of any one or more of the members. But he shall in all cases exercise his own judgment, and either conform to such opinions or not as he may think proper; and every officer above mentioned shall be responsible for his opinion on the affairs relating to his particular department."

August 22

Mr. Rutledge, from the Committee to whom were referred on the ... 20th ... the propositions of Mr. [Morris] and Mr. Pinckney, ... reports that ... the following additions should be made to the report now before the Convention, namely: ...

"The President of the United States shall have a privy council, which shall consist of the president of the senate, the speaker of the house of representatives, the chief justice of the supreme court, and the principal officer in the respective departments of foreign affairs, domestic affairs, war, marine, and finance, as such departments of office shall from time to time be established, whose duty it shall be to advise him in matters respecting the execution of his office, which he shall think proper to lay before them: but their advice shall not conclude him, nor affect his responsibility for the measures which he shall adopt."

September 4

Mr. Brearly from the Committee of Eleven made a further partial report as follows. ...

(8) ... [I]n section 2, article 10, add "and may require the opinion in writing of the principal Officer in each of the Executive Departments, upon any subject relating to the duties of their respective offices."

September 7

"and may require the opinion in writing of the principal Officer in each of the Executive Departments, upon any subject relating to the duties of their respective offices," being before the House.

Col. Mason said that in rejecting a Council to the President we were about to try an experiment on which the most despotic Governments had never ventured. The Grand Signor himself had his Divan. He moved to postpone the consideration of the clause in order to take up the following:

"That it be an instruction to the Committee of the States to prepare a clause or clauses for establishing an Executive Council, as a Council of State, for the President of the United States, to consist of six members, two of which from the Eastern, two from the middle, and two from the Southern States, with a Rotation and duration of office similar to those of the Senate; such Council to be appointed by the Legislature or by the Senate."

Doctor Franklin seconded the motion. We seemed he said too much to fear cabals in appointments by a number, and to have too much confidence in those of single persons. Experience showed that caprice, the intrigues of favorites and mistresses, etc. were nevertheless the means most prevalent in monarchies. Among instances of abuse in such modes of appointment, he mentioned the many bad Governors appointed in Great Britain for the Colonies. He thought a Council would not only be a check on a bad President but be a relief to a good one.

Mr. Govr. Morris. The question of a Council was considered in the Committee [of Eleven], where it was judged that the President, by persuading his Council to concur in his wrong measures, would acquire their protection for them.

Mr. Wilson approved of a Council in preference to making the Senate a party to appointments.

Mr. Dickinson was for a Council. It would be a singular thing if the measures of the Executive were not to undergo some previous discussion before the President.

Mr. Madison was in favor of the instruction to the Committee proposed by Col. Mason. The motion of Mr. Mason was negatived [3 yes; 8 no].

On the question, "authorizing the President to call for the opinions of the Heads of Departments, in writing": it passed in the affirmative, New Hampshire only being no.

6. George Mason, "Objections to the Constitution," October 7, 1787

Mason initially wrote his "Objections to the Constitution" on the back of his copy of the Committee of Style's report. He evidently intended to deliver them to the convention as a way of explaining his refusal to sign the Constitution but, as he told Jefferson, was "discouraged from doing so, by the precipitate, & intemperate, not to say indecent Manner, in which the Business was conducted, during the last Week of the Convention" (Rutland 1970, 3:1045). Upon returning to Virginia, Mason elaborated on his objections and sent a copy to his old friend and neighbor, George Washington. "My objections are not numerous," he tried to reassure the general, "tho' in my mind, some of them are capital ones." Even these objections, he chided, might have been removed with "a little Moderation and Temper, in the latter End of the Convention" (3:1001–2). Mason's chief concern was the absence of a declaration of rights, and, indeed, had the delegates heeded Mason's counsel, they might not only have secured Mason's support but made ratification of the Constitution much easier. Yet reading Mason's "Objections," Washington could have been forgiven for wondering where was the moderation or temper in his friend's missive. Far from being few in number, Mason's complaints extended to almost every aspect of the new government. Each of the branches came in for strong criticism: the national judiciary would "absorb and destroy" the state courts, the House of Representatives was "not the Substance, but the Shadow only of Representation," the Senate was an aristocratic body that "will destroy any Balance in the Government and enable them to accomplish what Usurpations they please upon the Rights and Libertys of the People," and the President's "unrestrained Power of granting Pardons" would allow him to cover up his own high crimes. He ended with a dire prediction: "the Government will commence in a moderate Aristocracy; it is at present impossible to foresee whether it will, in it's Operation, produce a Monarchy, or a corrupt oppres-

---

John P. Kaminski and Gaspare Saladino, eds., *The Documentary History of the Ratification of the Constitution* (Madison: State Historical Society of Wisconsin, 1988), 8:44. Used with permission of the State Historical Society.

sive Aristocracy; it will most probably vibrate some years between the two, and then terminate in the one or the other" (Jensen, Kaminski, and Saladino 1976-, 8:4345–46). Mason's vehement opposition to the Constitution permanently fractured his long friendship with Washington, who put Mason's opposition down to the "pride" and "want of manly candor" of his "quondam friend" (Flexner 1969, 135; Rutland 1961, 103). The following selection is from the version of his "Objections" that he sent to Washington.

The President of the United States has no constitutional Council (a thing unknown in any safe and regular Government). He will therefore be unsupported by proper Information and Advice; and will generally be directed by Minions and Favorites—or He will become a Tool to the Senate—or a Council of State will grow out of the principal Officers of the great Departments, the worst and most dangerous of all Ingredients for such a Council, in a free Country; for they may be induced to join in any dangerous or oppressive Measures; to shelter themselves and prevent an Inquiry into their own Misconduct in Office. Whereas had a constitutional Council been formed (as was proposed) of six Members ... two from the Eastern, two from the Middle, and two from the Southern States, to be appointed by Vote of the States in the House of Representatives, with the same Duration and Rotation of Office as the Senate, the Executive would always have had safe and proper Information and Advice. The President of such a Council might have acted as Vice President of the United States, pro tempore, upon any Vacancy or Disability of the chief Magistrate; and long continued Sessions of the Senate would in a great Measure have been prevented.

From this fatal Defect of a constitutional Council has arisen the improper Power of the Senate in the Appointment of public Officers, and the alarming Dependence and Connection between that Branch of the Legislature and the supreme Executive. Hence also sprung that unnecessary and dangerous Officer the Vice President, who for want of other Employment is made President of the Senate, thereby dangerously blending the executive and legislative Powers, besides always giving to some one of the States an unnecessary and unjust Preeminence over the others.

7. Marcus [James Iredell],
"Answers to Mr. Mason's *Objections*
to the New Constitution," February 27, 1788

Mason's "Objections to the Constitution" were circulated widely in the months following the convention. The fame of the author made them a natural target for Federalist writers who were justly concerned of the impact they might have on wavering minds. Among the best replies to Mason was by James Iredell who, writing under the pseudonym "Marcus," provided a detailed refutation of each of Mason's objections. Iredell was a highly respected

Norfolk and Portsmouth Journal, February 27, 1788.

North Carolina lawyer and judge who in 1787 was appointed by the assembly to compile and revise the state's laws, an assignment he finished in 1791, the year after President Washington elevated him to the United States Supreme Court. What follows is Iredell's answer to Mason's objection to the absence of a "constitutional Council."

Mr. Mason here reprobates the omission of a particular Council for the President as a thing contrary to the example of all safe and regular governments. ... I think I cannot do better than to select for the subject of our inquiry in this particular, a government which must be universally acknowledged to be the most safe and regular of any considerable government now in being (though I hope America will soon be able to dispute that preeminence). Everybody must know I speak of Great Britain; and in this I think I give Mr. Mason all possible advantage since, in my opinion, it is most probable he had Great Britain principally in his eye when he made this remark. And in the very height of our quarrel with that country, so wedded were our ideas to the institution of a Council that the practice was generally if not universally followed at the formation of our governments, though we instituted councils of a quite different nature; and so far as the little experience of the writer goes, have very little benefited by it. ...

By the laws of England the King is said to have four Councils. 1. The High Court of Parliament. 2. The Peers of the Realm. 3. His Judges. 4. His Privy Council. By the first, I presume, is meant in regard to the making of laws, because the usual introductory expressions in most acts of Parliament, viz. "By the King's Most Excellent Majesty, by and with the advice and consent of the Lords Spiritual and Temporal, and Commons, &c." show that, in a constitutional sense, they are deemed the King's laws, after a ratification in Parliament. The Peers of the Realm are, by their birth, hereditary Counsellors of the Crown, and may be called upon for their advice either in time of Parliament, or when no Parliament is in being. They are called in some law books, Magnum Concilium Regis (The King's Great Council). It is also considered the privilege of every particular Peer to demand an audience of the King, and to lay before him anything he may deem of public importance. The Judges, I presume, are called "A Council of the King" upon the same principle that the Parliament is, because the administration of justice is in his name, and the Judges are considered as his instruments in the distribution of it. We come now to the Privy Council, which I imagine, if Mr. Mason had any particular view towards England when he made this objection, was the one he intended as an example of a Constitutional Council in that kingdom. The Privy Council in that country is undoubtedly of very ancient institution, but it has one fixed property invariably annexed to it: that it is a mere creature of the Crown, dependent on its will both for number and duration, since the King may, whenever he thinks proper, discharge any particular Member, or the whole of it, and appoint another. ...

So far as precedents in England apply, the Peers being constitutionally the Great Council of the King, though also a part of the Legislature, we have reason to hope that there is by no means such gross impropriety as has been suggested in giving the Senate, though a branch of the Legislature, a strong control over the Executive. The only difference in the two cases is that the Crown may or may not give this consequence to the Peers at [the Crown's] own pleasure; and accordingly we find, that for a long time past, this Great Council has been very seldom consulted. Under our Constitution, the President is allowed no option in respect to certain points, wherein he cannot act without the Senate's concurrence. But we cannot infer from any example in England that a concurrence between the Executive and a part of the Legislature is contrary to the maxims of their government, since their government allows of such a concurrence whenever the Executive pleases. The rule therefore from the example of the freest government in Europe, that the Legislative and Executive powers must be altogether distinct, is liable to exceptions. It does not mean that the Executive shall not form a part of the Legislature (for the King, who has the whole Executive authority, is one entire branch of the Legislature; and this, Montesquieu, who recognizes the general principle, declares is necessary). Neither can it mean (as the example above evinces) that the Crown must consult neither house as to any exercise of its Executive power. But its meaning must be that one power shall not include both authorities. The King, for instance, shall not have the sole Executive and sole Legislative authority also. He may have the former, but must participate in the latter with the two Houses of Parliament. The rule also would be infringed were the three branches of the Legislature to share jointly the Executive power. But so long as the people's Representatives are altogether distinct from the Executive authority, the liberties of the people may be deemed secure. And in this point surely there can be no manner of comparison between the provisions by which the independence of our House of Representatives is guarded, and the condition in which the British House of Commons is left exposed to every species of corruption.

But Mr. Mason says, for want of a Council the President may become "a tool to the Senate." Why? Because he cannot act without their concurrence. Would not the same reason hold for his being "a tool to the Council" if he could not act without their concurrence, supposing a Council was to be imposed upon him without his own nomination (according to Mr. Mason's plan)? As great care is taken to make him independent of the Senate as I believe human precaution can provide. Whether the President will be a tool to any persons will depend upon the man; and the same weakness of mind which would make him pliable to one body of control would certainly attend him with another.

But Mr. Mason objects, if he is not directed by minions and favorites, nor becomes a tool of the Senate, "A Council of State will grow out of the principal officers of the great departments, the worst and most dangerous of all ingredients for such a Council, in a free country; for they may be induced to join in any dangerous or oppressive measures to shelter themselves, and prevent an inquiry into their own misconduct in office." I beg leave again to carry him to my old authority, England, and ask him what efficient Council they have there, but one formed of their great officers? Notwithstanding their important constitutional Council, everybody knows that the whole movements of their government, where a Council is consulted at all, are directed by their Cabinet Council, composed entirely of the principal officers of the great departments. That when a Privy Council is called, it is scarcely ever for any other purpose than to give a formal sanction to the previous determinations of the [cabinet council], so much so that it is notorious that not one time in a thousand one Member of the Privy Council, except a known adherent of administration, is summoned to it. But though the President, under our Constitution, may have the aid of the "principal officers of the great departments," he is to have this aid, I think, in the most unexceptionable manner possible. He is not to be assisted by a Council, summoned to a jovial dinner perhaps and giving their opinions according to the nod of the President—but the opinion is to be given with the utmost solemnity, in writing. No after equivocation can explain it away. It must forever afterwards speak for itself, and commit the character of the writer in lasting colors either of fame or infamy, or neutral insignificance, to future ages as well as the present. From those written reasons, weighed with care, surely the President can form as good a judgment as if they had been given by a dozen formal characters, carelessly met together on a slight appointment.

And this further advantage would be derived from the proposed system (which would be wanting if he had constitutional advice to screen him) that the President must be personally responsible for everything. For though an ingenious gentleman has proposed that a Council should be formed, who should be responsible for their opinions? ... I am persuaded it will in general be thought infinitely more safe, as well as more just, that the President who acts should be responsible for his conduct, following advice at his peril, than that there should be a danger of punishing any man for an erroneous opinion which might possibly be sincere. Besides the morality of this scheme, which may well be questioned, its inexpediency is glaring, since it would be so plausible an excuse, and the insincerity of it so difficult to detect. The hopes of impunity this avenue to escape would afford would nearly take away all dread of punishment. As to the temptations mentioned to the officers joining in dangerous or oppressive measures to shelter themselves, and prevent an enquiry into their own misconduct in office, this proceeds upon a supposition that the President and the great officers may form a very wicked combination to injure their country; a combination that in the first place it is utterly improbable, in a strong respectable government, should be formed for that purpose; and in the next, with such a government as this Constitution would give us, could have little chance of being successful, on account of the great superior strength, and natural and jealous vigilance of one at least, if not both of the two weighty branches of Legislation. This evil, however, of the possible depravity of all public officers is one that can admit of no cure, since in every institution of government, the same danger in some degree or other must be risked. It can only be guarded against by strong checks, and I believe it would be difficult for the objectors to our new Constitution to provide stronger ones against any abuse of the Executive authority than will exist in that. ...

I am concerned to see among Mr. Mason's other reasons so trivial a one as the little advantage one State might accidentally gain by a Vice-President of their country having a seat, with merely a casting vote in the Senate. Such a reason is utterly unworthy of that spirit of amity, and rejection of local views, which can alone save us from destruction. It was the glory of the late Convention that by discarding such, they formed a general government upon principles that did as much honor to their hearts as to their understandings. God grant that in all our deliberations we may consider America as one body, and not divert our attention from so noble a prospect to small considerations of partial jealousy and distrust. It is in vain to expect upon any system to secure an exact equilibrium of power for all the States. Some will occasionally have an advantage from the superior abilities of its Members; the field of emulation is however open to all. Suppose any one should now object to the superior influence of Virginia ... on account of the high character of General Washington, confessedly the greatest man of the present age, and perhaps equal to any that has existed in any period of time. Would this be a reason for refusing a union with her, though the other States can scarcely hope for the consolation of ever producing his equal?

8. James Iredell, North Carolina Ratifying Convention, July 28, 1788

Nowhere except Rhode Island did the Constitution meet greater resistance than in North Carolina. By the time the ratifying convention was finally convened on July 21, all the other states except Rhode Island and New York (which rat-

Jonathan Elliot, ed., *The Debates in the Several State Constitutions on the Adoption of the Federal Constitution* (New York: Burt Franklin, 1888), 4:108–10.

ified five days later, on July 26) had already met and ratified the Constitution. Those who did not know North Carolina well might have expected the state to accede to the inevitable, but on August 2 North Carolina voted overwhelmingly (180 to 80) to reject the Constitution. For those who followed North Carolina politics closely, the result could not have been a surprise. Among the delegates, those opposed to the Constitution outnumbered friends of the Constitution by better than a 2 to 1 margin. The debate changed no minds or votes. Anti-Federalist spokesman Timothy Bloodworth spoke for many when he declared that the "many words ... spoken ... have gone in at one ear, and out at the other" (Lienesch 1989, 349; Elliot 1888, 4:143). Though the Constitution's opponents controlled the votes, the debate was dominated by the Federalists, the most vocal of whom was James Iredell. In the following selection, Iredell elaborates on his reasons for thinking that the president will act more responsibly and with greater wisdom without a council than with one.

The next part, which says "that he may require the opinion in writing of the principal officers," is, in some degree, substituted for a council. He is only to consult them if he thinks proper. Their opinion is to be given him in writing. By this means he will be aided by their intelligence; and the necessity of their opinions being in writing, will render them more cautious in giving them, and make them responsible should they give advice manifestly improper. This does not diminish the responsibility of the President himself.

They might otherwise have colluded, and opinions have been given too much under his influence.

It has been the opinion of many gentlemen that the President should have a council. This opinion, probably, has been derived from the example in England. It would be very proper for every gentleman to consider attentively whether that example ought to be imitated by us. Although it be a respectable example, yet, in my opinion, very satisfactory reasons can be assigned for a departure from it in this Constitution.

It was very difficult, immediately on our separation from Great Britain, to disengage ourselves entirely from ideas of government we had been used to. We had been accustomed to a council under the old government, and took it for granted we ought to have one under the new. But examples ought not to be implicitly followed; and the reasons which prevail in Great Britain for a council do not apply equally to us. In that country, the executive authority is vested in a magistrate who holds it by birthright. He has great powers and prerogatives, and it is a constitutional maxim that he can do no wrong. We have experienced that he can do wrong, yet no man can say so in his own country. There are no courts to try him for any high crimes; nor is there any constitutional method of depriving him of his throne. If he loses it, it must be by a general resistance of his people, contrary to forms of law, as at the [Glorious] Revolution which took place about a hundred years ago. It is, therefore, of the utmost moment in that country that whoever is the instrument of any act of government should be personally responsible for it, since the king is not; and, for the same reason, that no act of government should be exercised but by the instrumentality of some person who can be accountable for it. Everything, therefore, that the king does must be by some advice, and the adviser of course answerable. Under our Constitution we are much happier.

No man has an authority to injure another with impunity. No man is better than his fellow citizens, nor can pretend to any superiority over the meanest man in the country. If the President does a single act by which the people are prejudiced, he is punishable himself, and no other man merely to screen him. If he commits any misdemeanor in office, he is impeachable, removable from office and incapacitated to hold any office of honor, trust or profit. If he commits any crime, he is punishable by the laws of his country, and in capital cases may be deprived of his life. This being the case, there is not the same reason here for having a council which exists in England. It is, however, much to be desired that a man who has such extensive and important business to perform should have the means of some assistance to enable him to discharge his arduous employment. The advice of the principal executive officers, which he can at all times command, will, in my opinion, answer this valuable purpose. He can at no time want advice, if he desires it, as the principal officers will always be on the spot. Those officers, from their abilities and experience, will probably be able to give as good, if not better, advice than any counsellors would do; and the solemnity of the advice in writing, which must be preserved, would be a great check upon them.

Besides these considerations, it was difficult for the Convention to prepare a council that would be unexceptionable. That jealousy which naturally exists between the different states enhanced this difficulty. If a few counsellors were to be chosen from the Northern, Southern, or Middle States, or from a few states only, undue preference might be given to those particular states from which they should come. If, to avoid this difficulty, one counsellor should be sent from each state, this would require great expense, which is a consideration, at this time, of much moment, especially as it is probable that, by the method proposed, the President may be equally well advised without any expense at all.

We ought also to consider that had he a council by whose advice he was bound to act, his responsibility, in all such cases, must be destroyed. You surely would not oblige him to follow their advice, and punish him for obeying it. If called upon on any occasion of dislike, it would be natural for him to say, "You know my council are men of integrity and ability: I could not act against their opinions, though I confess my own was contrary to theirs." This, sir, would be pernicious. In such a situation, he might easily combine with his council, and it might be impossible to fix a fact upon him. It would be difficult often to know whether the President or counsellors were most to blame. A thousand plausible excuses might be made, which would escape detection. But the method proposed in the Constitution creates no such embarrassment. It is plain and open. And the President will personally have the credit of good, or the censure of bad measures since, though he may ask advice, he is to use his own judgment in following or rejecting it. For all these reasons, I am clearly of the opinion that the clause is better as it stands than if the President were to have a council. I think every good that can be derived from the institution of a council may be expected from the advice of these officers, without its being liable to the disadvantages to which, it appears to me, the institution of a council would be.

9. Alexander Hamilton, *Federalist* 70, March 15, 1788

Having devoted the opening half of *Federalist* 70 to the dangers to be apprehended from a plural executive, Hamilton moves in the latter half of the

---

New York *Independent Journal*, March 15, 1788.

paper to analyze why even an executive council would be detrimental to the republic. However compelling his argument against "a plurality of magistrates of equal dignity and authority," Hamilton readily conceded that this was a scheme "the advocates for which are not likely to form a numerous sect." The tougher task was to show that the same ill effects would result from "a council whose concurrence is made constitutionally necessary."

It must be confessed that these observations apply with principal weight to the [idea of a plurality of coequal magistrates] ... but they apply, though not with equal yet with considerable weight to the project of a council whose concurrence is made constitutionally necessary to the operations of the ostensible executive. An artful cabal in that council would be able to distract and to enervate the whole system of administration. If no such cabal should exist, the mere diversity of views and opinions would alone be sufficient to tincture the exercise of the executive authority with a spirit of habitual feebleness and dilatoriness.

But one of the weightiest objections to a plurality in the executive, and which lies as much against the last as the first plan, is that it tends to conceal faults and destroy responsibility. Responsibility is of two kinds—to censure and to punishment. The first is the more important of the two especially in an elective office. Man, in public trust, will much oftener act in such a manner as to render him unworthy of being any longer trusted than in such a manner as to make him obnoxious to legal punishment. But the multiplication of the executive adds to the difficulty of detection in either case. It often becomes impossible, amidst mutual accusations, to determine on whom the blame or the punishment of a pernicious measure, or series of pernicious measures, ought really to fall. It is shifted from one to another with so much dexterity, and under such plausible appearances, that the public opinion is left in suspense about the real author. The circumstances which may have led to any national miscarriage or misfortune are sometimes so complicated that, where there are a number of actors who may have had different degrees and kinds of agency, though we may clearly see upon the whole that there has been mismanagement, yet it may be impracticable to pronounce to whose account the evil which may have been incurred is truly chargeable.

"I was overruled by my council. The council were so divided in their opinions that it was impossible to obtain any better resolution on the point." These and similar pretexts are constantly at hand, whether true or false. And who is there that will either take the trouble or incur the odium, of a strict scrutiny into the secret springs of transaction? Should there be found a citizen zealous enough to undertake the unpromising task, if there happen to be collusion between the parties concerned, how easy it is to clothe the circumstances with so much ambiguity, as to render it uncertain what was the precise conduct of any of those parties?

In the single instance in which the governor of this state [New York] is coupled with a council—that is, in the appointment to offices, we have seen the mischiefs of it in the view now under consideration. Scandalous appointments to important offices have been made. Some cases, indeed, have been so flagrant that all parties have agreed in the impropriety of the thing. When inquiry has been made, the blame has been laid by the governor on the members of the council, who, on their part, have charged it upon his nomination; while the people remain altogether at a loss to determine by whose influence their interests have been committed to hands so unqualified and so manifestly improper. ...

It is evident from these considerations that the plurality of the executive tends to deprive the people of the two greatest securities they can have for the faithful exercise of any delegated power: first, the restraints of public opinion, which lose their efficacy, as well on account of the division of the censure attendant on bad measures among a number, as on account of the uncertainty on whom it ought to fall; and, secondly, the opportunity of discovering with facility and clearness the misconduct of the persons they trust, in order either to their removal from office, or to their actual punishment in cases which admit of it.

In England, the king is a perpetual magistrate, and it is a maxim which has obtained for the sake of the public peace that he is unaccountable for his administration, and his person sacred. Nothing, therefore, can be wiser in that kingdom than to annex to the king a constitutional council, who may be responsible to the nation for the advice they give. Without this, there would be no responsibility whatever in the executive department—an idea inadmissible in a free government. But even there the king is not bound by the resolutions of his council, though they are answerable for the advice they give. He is the absolute master of his own conduct in the exercise of his office, and may observe or disregard the counsel given to him at his sole discretion.

But in a republic, where every magistrate ought to be personally responsible for his behavior in office, the reason which in the British Constitution dictates the propriety of a council, not only ceases to apply, but turns against the institution. In the monarchy of Great Britain, it furnishes a substitute for the prohibited responsibility of the chief magistrate, which serves in some degree as a hostage to the national justice for his good behavior. In the American republic, it would serve to destroy, or would greatly diminish, the intended and necessary responsibility of the chief magistrate himself.

The idea of a council to the executive, which has so generally obtained in the state constitutions, has been derived from that maxim of republican jealousy which considers power as safer in the hands of a number of men than of a single man. If the maxim should be admitted to be applicable to the case, I should contend that the advantage on that side would not counterbalance the numerous disadvantages on the opposite side. But I do not think the rule at all applicable to the executive power. I clearly concur in opinion ... with [Jean Louis de Lolme] ... that "the executive power is more easily confined when it is one";[1] that it is far more safe there should be a single object for the jealousy and watchfulness of the people; and, in a word, that all multiplication of the executive is rather dangerous than friendly to liberty.

A little consideration will satisfy us that the species of security sought for in the multiplication of the executive is unattainable. Numbers must be so great as to render combination difficult, or they are rather a source of danger than of security. The united credit and influence of several individuals must be more formidable to liberty than the credit and influence of either of them separately. When power, therefore, is placed in the hands of so small a number of men as to admit of their interests and views being easily combined in a common enterprise by an artful leader, it becomes more liable to abuse, and more dangerous when abused, than if it be lodged in the hands of one man who, from the very circumstance of his being alone, will be more narrowly watched and more readily suspected and who cannot unite so great a mass of influence as when he is associated with others. The Decemvirs of Rome, whose name denotes their number [i.e., ten], were more to be dreaded in their usurpation than any one of them would have been. No person would think of proposing an executive much more numerous than that body; from six to a dozen have been suggested for the number of the council. The extreme of these numbers is not too great for an easy combination; and from such a combination America would have more to fear than

---

1. Students interested in de Lolme and his book, *The Constitution of England*, should consult the useful summary in McDonald (1994, 61–65).

from the ambition of any single individual. A council to a magistrate, who is himself responsible for what he does, are generally nothing better than a clog upon his good intentions, are often the instruments and accomplices of his bad, and are almost always a cloak to his faults. ...

I will only add that prior to the appearance of the Constitution I rarely met with an intelligent man from any of the states, who did not admit, as the result of experience, that the unity of the executive of this state was one of the best of the distinguishing features of our Constitution.

Questions for Discussion

1. If you had been a delegate at the constitutional convention, would you have preferred the Committee of Detail's August 22 proposal of a Privy Council or would you have preferred the Brearly Committee's recommendation issued on September 4? Had the convention adopted the former provision what difference, if any, would it have made in the development of the presidency?

2. Evaluate George Mason's proposal for a six-member Council of State in which different regions of the nation would be represented. What would be the benefits and also the costs of such a plan?

II

Selecting
the President

3

The Long and Tortuous Debate

Americans take bloodless presidential elections largely for granted. That the loser steps down upon defeat is rarely remarked upon; it is accepted as part of the natural order of things. But the framers inhabited a far different political universe in which the possibility of armed conflict upon the defeat of a head of state seemed vividly real.[1] Fear of such conflict led famed British legal commentator William Blackstone to conclude that although "an elective monarchy seems to be the most obvious, and best suited of any to the rational principles of government," in practice a hereditary monarchy is preferable because elections "in the present state of human nature ... are too frequently brought about by influence, partiality and artifice: and, even where the case is otherwise, these practices will be often suspected, and as constantly charged upon the successful, by a splenetic disappointed minority." A hereditary monarchy, Blackstone explained, had been established in Great Britain, as in most other countries, "in order to prevent that periodical bloodshed and misery, which the history of antient imperial Rome, and the more modern experience of Poland and Germany, may shew us are the consequences of elective kingdoms" ([1783] 1978, 1:192–93). The challenge for the American framers was how to construct an elective chief executive without the "periodic bloodshed and misery" that had marred past efforts to make the head of state elective.

The problem of presidential selection was the most vexing issue faced by the delegates at the constitutional convention. James Wilson was far from the only delegate to testify that "the convention ... were perplexed with no part of this plan so much as with the mode of choosing the President of the United States" (Elliot 1888, 2:511). Over the last two months of the convention no fewer than ten days were given up in whole or in large part to the issue.

---

1. The writers of Georgia's 1777 constitution thought the issue important enough that as part of his oath of office the governor had to "solemnly promise and swear that I will peaceably and quietly resign the government to which I have been elected" at the expiration of the term of office (Thorpe 1909, 2:781).

Moreover, since the delegates had difficulty agreeing on the scope of the president's powers before they had settled on an acceptable system of selection, the issue proved a bottleneck. Not until they settled how the president was to be selected (by whom, for how long, and whether he would eligible for re-election) would they be able to agree on the powers that could be safely vested in the presidency.

Why did the framers have so much difficulty devising a scheme to select the president? The short answer is that there were thirteen states and only one president. How the president was selected would determine which states would exercise the greatest power over the nation's most important political office. If the president was elected directly by the people, as James Wilson advocated, the most populous states stood to benefit. Pennsylvania had ten times the number of people as Delaware. The three most populous states had nearly as many white inhabitants as the other ten states combined (Farrand 1937, 1:573). But far more than naked state interests were at stake in this debate. There was a widely shared feeling among the delegates that the people in a nation as vast as the United States would not be in a position to evaluate the merits and demerits of national political leaders. As George Mason pungently put the point: "It would be as un-natural to refer the choice of a proper character for chief Magistrate to the people, as it would, to refer a trial of colours to a blind man" (July 17). Popular choice would inevitably be ill-informed and parochial.

The obvious alternative to popular election was selection by the national legislature, as the Virginia Plan proposed at the outset. Throughout most of the convention this seemed the only realistic option to the great majority of the delegates. The New Jersey Plan, offered as the small states' substitute to the Virginia Plan, was identical to the Virginia Plan in its provisions for presidential selection. The only other convention plan to be referred to the Committee of Detail, the Pinckney Plan, also called for election by the national legislature. Contributing to the delegates' bias toward legislative selection was the fact that at the state level most governors were chosen by the state legislatures. Of the twelve states at the convention, only four (Connecticut, Massachusetts, New York, and New Hampshire) had any experience with a popularly elected chief executive. In every southern state the chief executive was selected by the legislature.[2]

But selection by the legislature also was perceived to have serious drawbacks, none more so than the way it threatened to undermine the independence of the executive. If the president relied on the legislature for his appointment, how could he be expected to act as an effective check on the

---

2. The Pinckney Plan differed from the other two plans, however, in calling specifically for the vote to be by joint ballot of the two houses (Farrand 1937, 3:606). Also unlike the other two plans, Pinckney's plan evidently did not make the executive ineligible for reelection.

legislative branch? If the legislature was to select the president, most of the delegates agreed, executive independence could only be secured by a relatively long term of office and especially by making the executive ineligible for a second term. Only a president who had no hope of reelection would have the will to defend executive prerogatives against legislature encroachments. Legislative selection raised another problem as well, especially for those who were more fearful of executive power than they were concerned to safeguard executive independence. An executive selected by the legislature and eligible for reelection might use the powers of his office (particularly the appointive power) to corrupt the legislature by buying legislators' support. Without a bar to reeligibility, Mason worried, there would be too great a "temptation on the side of the Executive to intrigue with the Legislature for re-appointment" (June 1). These twin concerns—maintaining executive independence from the legislature and avoiding corruption of the legislature—were so acute that on July 17, four of the ten states present (Pennsylvania, Virginia, Delaware, and New Jersey) voted in favor of allowing the president to serve "during good behavior" rather than have him be made eligible for reelection. Over the next ten days the delegates considered a range of alternative proposals but made no headway. At the end of July they found themselves back where they had been at the beginning of June: an executive selected by the legislature, serving a seven-year term, and ineligible for reelection.

And yet doubts lingered. Many delegates disliked making the executive ineligible for reelection. If the president was doing a good job, why should he not be retained? No rotation in office was required of national legislators, so why should rotation exist for the executive, where there was arguably greater need for continuity, experience, and stability? If the president was made, as James Madison put it, the "tenant of an unrenewable lease," might it not take away "one powerful motive to a faithful & useful administration" ("Observations on Jefferson's Draft of a Constitution for Virginia," October 15, 1788, Hutchinson 1962–, 11:289)? Was it wise for the nation to tie its hands so that at some critical juncture it might be unable to choose a chief executive deemed to be "essential to the public safety"? More ominously still, would a chief executive who was denied a legitimate means for his political ambitions be tempted to seek violent and unconstitutional means to maintain himself in power? "Shut the Civil road to Glory," Gouverneur Morris warned the convention, "and he may be compelled to seek it by the sword" (July 19).

When the convention returned to the issue of presidential selection toward the end of August, these philosophical doubts mixed potently with state interests to stymie the convention once again. It was all very well to agree that the legislature should select the president, but that formulation left out how the legislature should select the president. If the president were to be selected by joint ballot of the two houses of Congress, the advantage would go to the larger states. If, on the other hand, each house was granted a negative on the vote of the other house, or if the legislature cast votes by state rather than by individuals, then the smaller states would be advantaged. It was this raw clash of state interests that forced the convention to hand the matter over to the Committee on Postponed Matters, out of which emerged the most original part of the founders' handiwork, the electoral college.

10. The Federal Convention of 1787

In devising a scheme of presidential selection, the framers confronted three questions: (1) who should select the president? (2) how long should be the term of office? and (3) should the president be eligible for reelection? Because the delegates saw the answers to these three questions as closely interrelated (if the legislature did the selecting then the term should be long and the president ineligible for a second term; if the legislature did not do the selecting then the term could be shorter and the president reeligible), it is necessary to read the convention debates on presidential selection chronologically. To try to separate the debate over the presidential term of office from the debate over who was to select the president would be to render the deliberations almost incomprehensible. The convention debate over presidential selection can be usefully separated into four periods: (1) preliminary skirmishes (June 1, 2, and 9), (2) quagmire (July 17–26), (3) crisis (August 24), and (4) resolution (September 4–6).

Preliminary Skirmishes, June 1–9

The Virginia Plan, presented to the convention on May 29, called for the executive to be "chosen by the National Legislature ... and to be ineligible a second time." The plan left blank the length of the term of office. On the first day of debate over this clause (June 1) the convention filled in the blank with the term of seven years. Two alternative election schemes were considered and easily rejected in these opening days. The first, offered by James Wilson, proposed the president be elected by electors chosen by the people. Only two states, Pennsylvania and Maryland (at the time of the vote represented by a single delegate, Daniel of St. Thomas Jenifer), supported this electoral scheme. Even less support was found for Elbridge Gerry's idea of having the state governors select the national executive. These early deliberations gave only the barest of hints of the difficulty this issue would later give the delegates. If bookmakers

Gaillard Hunt and James Brown Scott, eds., *The Debates in the Federal Convention of 1787 Which Framed the Constitution of the United States of America Reported by James Madison* (New York: Oxford University Press, 1920), 40–43, 79–80, 267–74, 282–89, 310–23, 324–26, 461–63, 506–11, 514–25.

had been taking bets in the opening days of the convention, the odds would have been strongly stacked in favor of legislative election; only a desperate gambler would have placed money on popular election of some form.

June 1

The next clause in Resolution 7, relating to the mode of appointing and the duration of the Executive, being under consideration.

Mr. Wilson said he was almost unwilling to declare the mode which he wished to take place, being apprehensive that it might appear chimerical. He would say however at least that in theory he was for an election by the people. Experience, particularly in New York and Massachusetts, showed that an election of the first magistrate by the people at large was both a convenient and successful mode. The objects of choice in such cases must be persons whose merits have general notoriety.

Mr. Sherman was for the appointment by the Legislature, and for making him absolutely dependent on that body, as it was the will of that which was to be executed. An independence of the Executive [from] the supreme Legislature was in his opinion the very essence of tyranny if there was any such thing.

Mr. Wilson moves that the blank for the term of duration should be filled with three years, observing at the same time that he preferred this short period on the supposition that a reeligibility would be provided for.

Mr. Pinckney moves for seven years.

Mr. Sherman was for three years, and against the doctrine of rotation as throwing out of office the men best qualified to execute its duties.

Mr. Mason was for seven years at least, and for prohibiting a reeligibility as the best expedient both for preventing the effect of a false complaisance on the side of the Legislature towards unfit characters; and a temptation on the side of the Executive to intrigue with the Legislature for a re-appointment.

Mr. Bedford was strongly opposed to so long a term as seven years. He begged the committee to consider what the situation of the Country would be in case the first magistrate should be saddled on it for such a period and it should be found on trial that he did not possess the qualifications ascribed to him, or should lose them after his appointment. An impeachment he said would be no cure for this evil, as an impeachment would reach misfeasance only, not incapacity. He was for a triennial election, and for an ineligibility after a period of nine years.

On the question for seven years [5 yes; 4 no; 1 divided].

The mode of appointing the Executive was the next question.

Mr. Wilson renewed his declarations in favor of an appointment by the people. He wished to derive not only both branches of the Legislature from the people, without the intervention of the State Legislatures, but the Executive also; in order to make them as independent as possible of each other as well as of the States.

Col. Mason favors the idea, but thinks it impracticable. He wishes however that Mr. Wilson might have time to digest it into his own form—the clause "to be chosen by the National Legislature"—was accordingly postponed.

Mr. Rutledge suggests an election of the Executive by the second branch only of the national Legislature.

June 2

Mr. Wilson made the following motion, to be substituted for the mode proposed by Mr. Randolph's resolution, "that the Executive Magistracy shall be elected in the following manner: That the States be divided into ____ districts: and that the persons qualified to vote in each district for members of the first branch of the national Legislature elect ____ members for their respective districts to be electors of the Executive magistracy, that the said Electors of the Executive magistracy meet at ____ and they or any ____ of them so met shall proceed to elect by ballot, but not out of their own body ____ person(s) in whom the Executive authority of the national Government shall be vested."

Mr. Wilson repeated his arguments in favor of an election without the intervention of the States. He supposed too that this mode would produce more confidence among the people in the first magistrate than an election by the national Legislature.

Mr. Gerry opposed the election by the national legislature. There would be a constant intrigue kept up for the appointment. The Legislature and the candidates would bargain and play into one another's hands, votes would be given by the former under promises or expectations from the latter, of recompensing them by services to members of the Legislature or to their friends. He liked the principle of Mr. Wilson's motion, but fears it would alarm and give a handle to the State partisans, as tending to supersede altogether the State authorities. ... He was not clear that the people ought to act directly even in the choice of electors, being too little informed of personal characters in large districts, and liable to deceptions.

Mr. Williamson could see no advantage in the introduction of Electors chosen by the people who would stand in the same relation to them as the State Legislatures, whilst the expedient would be attended with great trouble and expense.

On the question for agreeing to Mr. Wilson's substitute, it was negatived [2 yes; 8 no].

On the question for electing the Executive by the national Legislature for the term of seven years, it was agreed to [8 yes; 2 no].

June 9

Mr. Gerry ... moved "that the National Executive should be elected by the Executives of the States whose proportion of votes should be the same with that allowed to the States in the election of the Senate." If the appointment should be made by the National Legislature, it would lessen that independence of the Executive which ought to prevail, would give birth to intrigue and corruption between the Executive and Legislature previous to the election, and to partiality in the Executive afterwards to the friends who promoted him. Some other mode therefore appeared to him necessary. He proposed that of appointing by the State Executives as most analogous to the principle observed in electing the other branches of the National Government; the first branch being chosen by the people of the States, and the second by the Legislatures of the States; he did not see any objection against letting the Executive be appointed by the Executives of the States. He supposed the Executives would be most likely to select the fittest men, and that it would be [in] their interest to support the man of their own choice.

Mr. Randolph urged strongly the inexpediency of Mr. Gerry's mode of appointing the National Executive. The confidence of the people would not be secured by it to the National magistrate. The small States would lose all chance of an appointment from within themselves. Bad appointments would be made; the Executives of the States being little conversant with characters not within their own small spheres. The State Executives, too, notwithstanding their constitutional independence, being in fact dependent on the State Legislature, will generally be guided by the views of the latter and prefer either favorites within the States or such as it may be expected will be most partial to the interests of the State. A National Executive thus chosen will not be likely to defend with becoming vigilance and firmness the National rights against State encroachments. ... He could not suppose either that the Executives would feel the interest in supporting the National Executive which has been imagined. They will not cherish the great oak which is to reduce them to paltry shrubs.

On the question for referring the appointment of the National Executive to the State Executives as proposed by Mr. Gerry [0 yes; 10 no].

Quagmire, July 17–26

On July 16, the convention agreed to give each state equal representation in the Senate, a decision that ended weeks of acrimonious debate and allowed the convention to move on to other matters. The day after reaching this momentous decision, the delegates turned their attention to presidential selection, a subject that proved if anything even more difficult to resolve. From July 17 until the convention's adjournment on July 26, the convention went round and round in a debate that is at times as frustrating and repetitive to read as it must have been for the delegates to hear. The convention seemed on the verge of a major breakthrough on July 19 when the delegates approved Oliver Ellsworth's plan for an electoral college chosen by state legislatures, but the six-state coalition (Virginia, Pennsylvania, Connecticut, Maryland, New Jersey, and Delaware) that backed this plan fell apart over the practical question of how many electors each state should be assigned. After several abortive efforts to devise a satisfactory formula, the issue was revisited on July 24. The coalition's two least populous states, New Jersey and Delaware, reversed themselves and now swung their support back to congressional election. Saddled again with legislative selection and ineligibility, delegates fired off new proposals: Elbridge Gerry offered a modified version of his earlier call for election by state executives; James Wilson proposed having the president selected by a small number of legislators chosen "by lot," a plan that he said would combat both the problems of dependence and intrigue; John Dickinson proposed that the people of each state nominate its "best citizen" and that either the national legislature or electors chosen by the legislature select a president from this list of thirteen names. Ellsworth himself offered a new scheme by which election would remain in the hands of the national legislature but reelection of the chief executive would be handled by electors chosen by the state legislatures. Only the last of these proposals gained any substantial support, but even that fell well short of majority support. After ten days of searching debate and alternative proposals the delegates referred to the Committee of Detail the same scheme of presidential selection that they had endorsed at the outset of the convention. Despite the lack of progress made during this period the debates remain worth reading for at least two reasons. First, these debates sparked some of the most penetrating and revealing speeches about the framers' understanding of the executive's place in the political system. Second, only by wading through these "tedious and reiterated discussions" (Madison to Jefferson, October 24, 1787, Hutchinson 1962–, 10:208) can one grasp just how difficult the framers found it to devise a satisfactory scheme of presidential selection.

July 17

[The next clause] "To be chosen by the National Legislature" [being considered].

Mr. Govr. Morris was pointedly against his being so chosen. He will be the mere creature of the Legislature if appointed and impeachable by that body. He ought to be elected by the people at large, by the freeholders of the Country. That difficulties attend this mode, he admits. But they have been found superable in New York and in Connecticut, and would he believed be found so in the case of an Executive for the United States. If the people should elect, they will never fail to prefer some man of distinguished character or services; some man, if he might so speak, of continental reputation. If the Legislature elect, it will be the work of intrigue, of cabal, and of faction; it will be like the election of a pope by a conclave of cardinals; real merit will rarely be the title to the appointment. He moved to strike out "National Legislature" and insert "Citizens of U.S."

Mr. Sherman thought that the sense of the Nation would be better expressed by the Legislature than by the people at large. The latter will never be sufficiently informed of characters, and besides will never give a majority of votes to any one man. They will generally vote for some man in their own State, and the largest State will have the best chance for the appointment. If the choice be made by the Legislature a majority of voices may be made necessary to constitute an election.

Mr. Wilson. Two arguments have been urged against an election of the Executive Magistrate by the people. 1. The example of Poland where an Election of the supreme Magistrate is attended with the most dangerous commotions. The cases he observed were totally dissimilar. The Polish nobles have resources and dependents which enable them to appear in force and to threaten the Republic as well as each other. In the next place the electors all assemble in one place, which would not be the case with us. 2. The second argument is that a majority of the people would never concur. It might be answered that the concurrence of a majority of people is not a necessary principle of election, nor required as such in any of the States. But allowing the objection all its force, it may be obviated by the expedient used in Massachusetts, where the Legislature by majority of voices decide in case a majority of people do not concur in favor of one of the candidates. This would restrain the choice to a good nomination at least, and prevent in a great degree intrigue and cabal. A particular objection with him against an absolute election by the Legislature was that the Executive in that case would be too dependent to stand the mediator between the intrigues and sinister views of the Representatives and the general liberties and interests of the people.

Mr. Pinckney did not expect this question would again have been brought forward; an election by the people being liable to the most obvious and striking objections. They will be led by a few active and designing men. The most populous States by combining in favor of the same individual will be able to carry their points. The National Legislature being most immediately interested in the laws made by themselves will be most attentive to the choice of a fit man to carry them properly into execution.

Mr. Govr. Morris. It is said that in case of an election by the people the populous States will combine and elect whom they please. Just the reverse. The people of such States cannot combine. If there be any combination it must be among their representatives in the Legislature. It is said the people will be led by a few designing men. This might happen in a small district. It can never happen throughout the continent. In the election of a Governor of New York, it sometimes is the case in particular spots that the activity and intrigues of little partisans are successful, but the general voice of the State is never influenced by such artifices. It is said the multitude will be uninformed. It is true they would be uninformed of what passed in the Legislative Conclave if the election were to be made there; but they will not be uninformed of those great and illustrious characters which have merited their esteem and confidence. If the executive be chosen by the National Legislature he will not be independent of it; and if not independent, usurpation and tyranny on the part of the Legislature will be the consequence. This was the case in England in the last century. It has been the case in Holland, where their Senates have engrossed all power. It has been the case everywhere. He was surprised that an election by the people at large should ever have been likened to the Polish election of the first Magistrate. An election by the Legislature will bear a real likeness to the election by the Diet of Poland. The great must be the electors in both cases, and the corruption and cabal which are known to characterize the one would soon find their way into the other. Appointments made by numerous bodies are always worse than those made by single responsible individuals or by the people at large.

Col. Mason. It is curious to remark the different language held at different times. At one moment we are told that the Legislature is entitled to thorough confidence, and to indefinite power. At another, that it will be governed by intrigue and corruption, and cannot be trusted at all. But not to dwell on this inconsistency he would observe that a Government which is to last ought at least to be practicable. Would this be the case if the proposed election should be left to the people at large? He conceived it would be as unnatural to refer the choice of a proper character for chief Magistrate to the people, as it would to refer a trial of colors to a blind man. The extent of the Country renders it impossible that the people can have the requisite capacity to judge of the respective pretensions of the candidates.

Mr. Wilson could not see the contrariety stated [by Col. Mason]. The Legislature might deserve confidence in some respects, and distrust in others. In acts which were to affect them and their constituents precisely alike, confidence was due. In others jealousy was warranted. In the appointment to great offices, where the Legislature might feel many motives not common to the public, confidence was surely misplaced. This branch of business it was notorious was most corruptly managed of any that had been committed to legislative bodies.

Mr. Williamson conceived that in this case there was the same difference between an election by the people and by the legislature as between an appointment by lot and by choice. There are at present distinguished characters, who are known perhaps to almost every man. This will not always be the case. The people will be sure to vote for some man in their own State, and the largest State will be sure to succeed. This will not be Virginia however. Her slaves will have no suffrage.[3] As the salary of the Executive will be fixed and he will not be eligible a second time, there will not be such a dependence on the Legislature as has been imagined.

Question on an election by the people instead of the Legislature which passed in the negative [1 yes; 9 no].

Mr. L. Martin moved that the Executive be chosen by Electors appointed by the several Legislatures of the individual States.

Mr. Broom seconds.

On the question, it passed in the negative [2 yes; 8 no].

On the question on the words "to be chosen by the National Legislature" it passed unanimously in the affirmative. ...

"to be ineligible a second time"—Mr. Houston moved to strike out this clause.

Mr. Sherman seconds the motion.

Mr. Govr. Morris espoused the motion. The ineligibility proposed by the clause as it stood tended to destroy the great motive to good behavior, the hope of being rewarded by a reappointment. It was saying to him, make hay while the sun shines.

On the question for striking out as moved by Mr. Houston, it passed in the affirmative [6 yes; 4 no].

"For the term of 7 years" resumed.

Mr. Broom was for a shorter term since the Executive Magistrate was now to be re-eligible. Had he remained ineligible a second time, he should have preferred a longer term.

Docr. McClurg moved to strike out 7 years, and insert "during good behavior." By striking out the words declaring him not re-eligible he was put into a situation that would keep him dependent forever on the Legislature; and he conceived the independence of the Executive to be equally essential with that of the Judiciary department.

Mr. Govr. Morris seconded the motion. He expressed great pleasure in hearing it. This was the way to get a good Government. His fear that so valuable an ingredient would not be attained had led him to take the part he had done. He was indifferent how the Executive should be chosen, provided he held his place by this tenure.

Mr. Broom highly approved the motion. It obviated all his difficulties.

Mr. Sherman considered such a tenure as by no means safe or admissible. As the Executive Magistrate is now reeligible, he will be on good behavior as far as will be necessary. If he behaves well he will be continued; if otherwise, displaced, on a succeeding election.

Mr. Madison. If it be essential to the preservation of liberty that the Legislative, Executive and Judiciary powers be separate, it is essential to a maintenance of the separation that they should be independent of each other. The Executive could not be independent of the Legis-

---

3. Direct popular election, as Williamson intimates, would advantage large northern states with no slave populations and disadvantage southern states with large slave populations, since slaves could not vote. The Connecticut Compromise had helped slave states by counting slaves as three-fifths of a person for the purposes of representation in the House of Representatives, and so the choice between popular election and legislative election was in part a clash of interests between slave states and free states. Under the three-fifths clause Virginia would have by far the largest delegation in the House of Representatives, but in a direct popular election of the president, in which only white inhabitants would matter, Virginia would plummet to the third largest state. Similar steep declines in influence would have affected Maryland and the Carolinas. One of the great political attractions of the electoral college that the delegates eventually agreed on was that it preserved the three-fifths compromise for the purposes of the presidential selection process.

lature if dependent on the pleasure of that branch for a reappointment. Why was it determined that the Judges should not hold their places by such a tenure? Because they might be tempted to cultivate the Legislature, by an undue complaisance, and thus render the Legislature the virtual expositor, as well the maker of the laws. In like manner, a dependence of the Executive on the Legislature would render it the Executor as well as the maker of laws; and then, according to the observation of Montesquieu, tyrannical laws may be made that they may be executed in a tyrannical manner. There was an analogy between the Executive and Judiciary departments in several respects. The latter executed the laws in certain cases as the former did in others. The former expounded and applied them for certain purposes, as the latter did for others. The difference between them seemed to consist chiefly in two circumstances: 1. the collective interest and security were much more in the power belonging to the Executive than to the Judiciary department. 2. in the administration of the former much greater latitude is left to opinion and discretion than in the administration of the latter. But if the second consideration proves that it will be more difficult to establish a rule sufficiently precise for trying the Executive than the Judges, and forms an objection to the same tenure of office, both considerations prove that it might be more dangerous to suffer a union between the Executive and Legislative powers, than between the Judiciary and Legislative powers. He conceived it to be absolutely necessary to a well-constituted republic that the two first should be kept distinct and independent of each other. Whether the plan proposed by the motion was a proper one was another question, as it depended on the practicability of instituting a tribunal for impeachments as certain and as adequate in the one case as in the other. On the other hand, respect for the mover entitled his proposition to a fair hearing and discussion, until a less objectionable expedient should be applied for guarding against a dangerous union of the Legislative and Executive departments.

Col. Mason. ... He considered an Executive during good behavior as a softer name only for an Executive for life. And that the next would be an easy step to hereditary Monarchy. If the motion should finally succeed, he might himself live to see such a Revolution. If he did not it was probable his children or grandchildren would. He trusted there were few men in that House who wished for it. No state he was sure had so far revolted from Republican principles as to have the least bias in its favor.

Mr. Madison was not apprehensive of being thought to favor any step towards monarchy. The real object with him was to prevent its introduction. Experience had proved a tendency in our governments to throw all power into the Legislative vortex. The Executives of the States are in general little more than Cyphers; the legislatures omnipotent. If no effectual check be devised for restraining the instability and encroachments of the latter, a revolution of some kind or other would be inevitable. The preservation of Republican Government therefore required some expedient for the purpose, but required evidently at the same time that in devising it the genuine principles of that form should be kept in view.

Mr. Govr. Morris was as little a friend to monarchy as any gentleman. He concurred in the opinion that the way to keep out monarchial Government was to establish such a Republican Government as would make the people happy and prevent a desire of change.

Docr. McClurg was not so much afraid of the shadow of monarchy as to be unwilling to approach it; nor so wedded to Republican Government as not to be sensible of the tyrannies that had been and may be exercised under that form. It was an essential object with him to make the Executive independent of the Legislature; and the only mode left for effecting it, after the vote destroying his ineligibility a second time, was to appoint him during good behavior.

On the question for inserting "during good behavior" in place of 7 years with a reeligibility it passed in the negative [4 yes; 6 no].

On the motion "to strike out seven years" it passed in the negative [4 yes; 6 no].

It was now unanimously agreed that the vote which had struck out the words "to be ineligible a second time" should be reconsidered tomorrow.

July 19

On reconsideration of the vote rendering the Executive reeligible a second time, Mr. L. Martin moved to reinstate the words, "to be ineligible a second time."

Mr. Govr. Morris. It is necessary to take into one view all that relates to the establishment of the Executive; on the due formation of which must depend the efficacy and utility of the Union among the present and future States. It has been a maxim in Political Science that Republican Government is not adapted to a large extent of the Country, because the energy of the Executive Magistracy can not reach the extreme parts of it. Our Country is an extensive one. We must either then renounce the blessings of the Union, or provide an Executive with sufficient vigor to pervade every part of it. This subject was of so much importance that he hoped to be indulged in an extensive view of it.

One great object of the Executive is to control the Legislature. [Members of] the Legislature will continually seek to aggrandize and perpetuate themselves, and will seize those critical moments produced by war, invasion or convulsion for that purpose. It is necessary then that the Executive Magistrate should be the guardian of the people, even of the lower classes, against Legislative tyranny, against the Great and the wealthy who in the course of things will necessarily compose the Legislative body. Wealth tends to corrupt the mind and to nourish its love of power, and to stimulate it to oppression. History proves this to be the spirit of the opulent. ... The Executive therefore ought to be so constituted as to be the great protector of the Mass of the people.

It is the duty of the Executive to appoint the officers and to command the forces of the Republic, [as well as] to appoint ministerial officers for the administration of public affairs [and] officers for the dispensation of Justice. Who will be the best judges whether these appointments be well made? The people at large, who will know, will see, will feel the effects of them. Again who can judge so well of the discharge of military duties for the protection and security of the people, as the people themselves who are to be protected and secured?....

The Executive is not to be reeligible. What effect will this have? In the first place, it will destroy the great incitement to merit public esteem by taking away the hope of being rewarded with a reappointment. It may give a dangerous turn to one of the strongest passions in the human breast. The love of fame is the great spring to noble and illustrious actions. Shut the Civil road to Glory and he may be compelled to seek it by the sword. In the second place, it will tempt him to make the most of the short space of time allotted him, to accumulate wealth and provide for his friends. In the third place, it will produce violations of the very constitution it is meant to secure. In moments of pressing danger the tried abilities and established character of a favorite Magistrate will prevail over respect for the forms of the Constitution. ...

These then are the faults of the Executive establishment as now proposed. Can no better establishment be devised? If he is to be the Guardian of the people let him be appointed by the people. Let him be of short duration that he may with propriety be reeligible. It has been said that the candidates for this office will not be known to the people. If they be known to the Legislature, they must have such a notoriety and eminence of Character that they cannot possibly be unknown to the people at large. It cannot be possible that a man shall have sufficiently distinguished himself to merit this high trust without having his character proclaimed by fame throughout the Empire. ... He suggested a biennial election of the Executive at the time of electing the first branch. ... An election by the people at large throughout so great an extent of country could not be influenced by those little combinations and those momentary lies which often decide popular elections within a narrow sphere. ... He saw no alternative for making the Executive independent of the Legislature but either to give him his office for life or make him eligible by the people. ... It might be objected that two years would be too short a duration, but he believes that as long as he should behave himself well he would be continued in his place. The extent of the Country would secure his reelection against the factions and discontents of particular States. It deserved consideration also that such an ingredient in the plan would render it extremely palatable to the people. ...

Mr. Randolph urged the motion of Mr. L. Martin for restoring the words making the Executive ineligible a second time. If he ought to be independent, he should not be left under a temptation to court a reappointment. If he should be reappointable by the Legislature, he will be no check on it. His revisionary [i.e., veto] power will be of no avail. He had always thought and contended ... that the danger apprehended by the little States was chimerical, but those who thought otherwise ought to be peculiarly anxious for the motion. If the Executive be appointed ... by the Legislature, he will probably be appointed either by joint ballot of both houses, or be nominated by the first and appointed by the second branch. In either case the large States will preponderate. If he is to court the same influence for his reappointment, will he not make his revisionary power, and all the other functions of his administration, subservient to the views of the large States. ... It has been said that a constitutional bar to reappointment will inspire unconstitutional endeavors to perpetuate himself. It may be answered that his endeavors can have no effect unless the people be corrupt to such a degree as to render all precautions hopeless: to which may be added that this argument supposes him to be more powerful and dangerous than other arguments which have been used admit, and consequently calls for stronger fetters on his authority. He thought an election by the Legislature with an incapacity to be elected a second time would be more acceptable to the people that the plan suggested by Mr. Govr. Morris.

Mr. King did not like the ineligibility. He thought there was great force in the remark of Mr. Sherman that he who has proved himself to be most fit for an office ought not to be excluded by the constitution from holding it. He would therefore prefer any other reasonable plan that could be substituted. He was much disposed to think that in such cases the people at large would choose wisely. There was indeed some difficulty arising from the improbability of a general concurrence of the people in favor of any one man. On the whole he was of the opinion that an appointment by electors chosen by the people for the purpose, would be liable to fewest objections.

Mr. Paterson's ideas nearly coincided he said with those of Mr. King. He proposed that the Executive should be appointed by Electors to be chosen by the States in a ratio that would allow one elector to the smallest and three to the largest States.

Mr. Wilson. It seems to be the unanimous sense that the Executive should not be appointed by the Legislature unless he be rendered ineligible a second time. He perceived with pleasure that the idea was gaining ground of an election mediately or immediately by the people.

Mr. Madison. If it be a fundamental principle of free Government that the Legislative, Executive and Judiciary powers should be separately exercised, it is equally so that they be independently exercised. There is the same and perhaps greater reason why the Executive should be independent of the Legislature than why the Judiciary should. A coalition of the two former powers would be more immediately and certainly dangerous to public liberty. It is essential then that the appointment of the Executive should either be drawn from some source, or held by some tenure, that will give him a free agency with regard to the Legislature. This could not be if he was to be appointable from time to time by the Legislature. It was not clear that an appointment in the first instance even with an ineligibility afterwards would not establish an improper connection between the two departments. Certain it was that the appointment would be attended with intrigues and contentions that ought not to be unnecessarily admitted. He was disposed for these reasons to refer the appointment to some other source. The people at large was in his opinion the fittest in itself. It would be as likely as any that could be devised to produce an Executive Magistrate of distinguished Character. The people generally could only know and vote for some Citizen whose merits had rendered him an object of general attention and esteem. There was one difficulty however of a serious nature attending an immediate choice by the people. The right of suffrage was much more diffusive in the Northern than the Southern States, and the latter could have no influence in the election on the score of the Negroes. The substitution of electors obviated this difficulty and seemed on the whole to be liable to fewest objections.

Mr. Gerry. If the Executive is to be elected by the Legislature he certainly ought not to be reeligible. This would make him absolutely dependent. He was against a popular election. The people are uninformed and would be misled by a few designing men. He urged the expediency of an appointment of the Executive by Electors to be chosen by the State Executives. The people of the states will then choose the first branch; the legislatures of the States, the second branch of the National Legislature; and the Executives of the States, the National Executive. This he thought would form a strong attachment in the States to the National System. The popular mode of electing the chief Magistrate would certainly be the worst of all. If he should be so elected and should do his duty, he will be turned out for it like Governor Bowdoin in Massachusetts and President Sullivan in New Hampshire. ...

Mr. Ellsworth moved to strike out the appointment by the National Legislature, and insert "to be chosen by electors appointed by the Legislatures of the States in the following ratio; to wit—one for each State not exceeding [100,000] inhabitants, two for each [State] above [that] number and not exceeding 300,000, and three for each State exceeding 300,000." Mr. Broom seconded the motion.

Mr. Rutledge was opposed to all the modes except the appointment by the National Legislature. He will be sufficiently independent if he be not reeligible.

Mr. Gerry preferred the motion of Mr. Ellsworth to an appointment by the National Legislature, or by the people; though not to an appointment by the State Executives. ...

The question as moved by Mr. Ellsworth being divided; On the first part, shall [the] National Executive be appointed by Electors? [6 yes (Conn., N.J., Pa., Del., Md., Va.); 3 no (N.C., S.C., Ga.); 1 divided (Mass.)] On the second part, shall the Electors be chosen by State Legislatures? [8 yes; 2 no].

The part relating to the ratio in which the States should choose electors was postponed.

Mr. L. Martin moved that the Executive be ineligible a second time.

Mr. Williamson seconds the motion. He had no great confidence in the Electors to be chosen for the special purpose. They would not be the most respectable citizens, but persons not occupied in the high offices of Government. They would be liable to undue influence, which might the more readily be practiced as some of them will probably be in appointment 6 or 8 months before the object of it comes on.

Mr. Ellsworth supposed any persons might be appointed Electors excepting solely members of the National Legislature.

On the question, shall he be ineligible a second time? [2 yes; 8 no].

On the question, shall the executive continue for 7 years? [3 yes; 5 no; 2 divided].

Mr. King was afraid we should shorten the term too much.

Mr. Govr. Morris was for a short term, in order to avoid impeachments which would be otherwise necessary.

Mr. Butler was against [the] frequency of the elections. Georgia and South Carolina were too distant to send electors often.

Mr. Ellsworth was for 6 years. If the elections be too frequent the Executive will not be firm enough. There must be duties which will make him unpopular for the moment. There will be outs as well as ins. His administration therefore will be attacked and misrepresented.

Mr. Williamson was for 6 years. The expense will be considerable and ought not to be unnecessarily repeated. If the elections are too frequent, the best men will not undertake the service and those of an inferior character will be liable to be corrupted.

On question for 6 years [9 yes; 1 no].

July 20

The postponed Ratio of Electors for appointing the Executive, to wit 1 for each State whose inhabitants do not exceed 100,000 etc, being taken up.

Mr. Madison observed that this would make in time all or nearly all the States equal. Since there were few that would not in time contain the number of inhabitants entitling them to 3 Electors ... this ratio ought either to be made temporary, or so varied as that it would adjust itself to the growing population of the States.

Mr. Gerry moved that in the first instance the Electors should be allotted to the States in the following ratio: to N.H. 1. Mass. 3. R.I. 1. Conn. 2. N.Y. 2. N.J. 2. Pa. 3. Del. 1. Md. 2. Va. 3. N.C. 2. S.C. 2. Ga. 1.

On the question to postpone in order to take up this motion of Mr. Gerry. It passed in the affirmative [6 yes; 4 no].

Mr. Ellsworth moved that 2 electors be allotted to New Hampshire. Some rule ought to be pursued, and New Hampshire has more than 100,000 inhabitants. He thought it would be proper also to allot 2 to Georgia.

Mr. Broom and Mr. Martin moved to postpone Mr. Gerry's allotment of Electors, leaving a fit ratio to be reported by the Committee to be appointed for detailing the Resolutions.

On this motion [3 yes; 7 no].

Mr. Houston seconded the motion of Mr. Ellsworth to add another Elector to New Hampshire and Georgia. On the question [3 yes; 7 no].

Mr. Williamson moved as an amendment to Mr. Gerry's allotment of Electors in the first instance that in future elections of the National executive, the number of Electors to be appointed by the several States shall be regulated by their respective numbers of Representatives in the first branch pursuing as nearly as may be the present proportions.

On [the] question on Mr. Gerry's ratio of Electors [6 yes (Mass., Conn., Pa., Va., S.C., N.C.); 4 no (N.J., Del., Ga., Md.)].

Mr. Gerry and Mr. Govr. Morris moved "that the Electors of the Executive shall not be members of the National Legislature, nor officers of the United States, nor shall the Electors themselves be eligible to the supreme magistracy." Agreed to nem. con. [that is, without disagreement].

July 23

Mr. Houston and Mr. Spaight moved "that the appointment of the Executive by Electors chosen by the Legislatures of the States, be reconsidered." Mr. Houston urged the extreme inconveniency and the considerable expense of drawing together men from all the States for the single purpose of electing the Chief Magistrate.

On the question which was put without any debate [7 yes; 3 no].

July 24

The appointment of the Executive by Electors reconsidered.

Mr. Houston moved that he be appointed by the "National Legislature" instead of "Electors appointed by the State Legislatures." ... He dwelt chiefly on the improbability that capable men would undertake the service of Electors from the more distant States.

Mr. Spaight seconded the motion.

Mr. Gerry opposed it. He thought there was no ground to apprehend the danger urged by Mr. Houston. The election of the Executive Magistrate will be considered as of vast importance and will excite great earnestness. The best men, the Governors of the States, will not hold it derogatory from their character to be the electors. If the motion should be agreed to it will be necessary to make the Executive ineligible a second time in order to render him independent of the Legislature, which was an idea extremely repugnant to his way of thinking.

Mr. Strong supposed that there would be no necessity, if the Executive should be appointed by the Legislature, to make him ineligible a second time, as new elections of the Legislature will have intervened and he will not depend for his second appointment on the same set of men as his first was received from. It had been suggested that gratitude for his past appointment would produce the same effect as dependence for his future appointment. He thought very differently. Besides this objection would lie against the Electors who would be objects of gratitude as well as the Legislature. It was of great importance not to make the Government too complex which would be the case if a new set of men like the Electors should be introduced into it. He thought also that the first characters in the States would not feel sufficient motives to undertake the office of Electors.

Mr. Williamson was for going back to the original ground: to elect the Executive for 7 years and render him ineligible a second time. The proposed Electors would certainly not be men of the first nor even of the second grade in the States. These would all prefer a seat either in the Senate or in the other branch of the Legislature. He did not like the Unity in the Executive. He had wished the Executive power to be lodged in three men taken from three districts into which the States should be divided. As the executive is to have a kind of veto on the laws, and there is an essential difference of interests between the Northern and Southern States, particularly in the carrying trade, the power will be dangerous, if the Executive is to be taken from part of the Union, to the part from which he is not taken. The case is different here from what it is in England, where there is a sameness of interests throughout the Kingdom. Another objection against a single Magistrate is that he will be an elective King, and will feel the spirit of one. He will spare no pains to keep himself in for life, and will then lay a train for the succession of his children. It was pretty certain he thought that we should at some time or other have a King, but he wished no precaution to be omitted that might postpone the event as long as possible. Ineligibility a second time appeared to him to be the best precaution. With this precaution he had no objection to a longer term than 7 years. He would go as far as 10 or 12 years.

Mr. Gerry moved that the Legislatures of the States should vote by ballot for the Executive in the same proportions as it had been proposed they should choose electors; and that in case a majority of the votes would not center on the same person, the first branch of the National Legislature should choose two out of the four candidates having most votes, and out of these two, the second branch should choose the Executive.

Mr. King seconded the motion. On the Question to postpone in order to take [Gerry's motion] into consideration, the nays were so predominant that the States were not counted.

Question on Mr. Houston's motion that the Executive be appointed by the National Legislature [7 yes (N.H., Mass., N.J., Del., N.C., S.C., Ga.); 4 no (Conn., Pa., Md., Va.)].

Mr. L. Martin and Mr. Gerry moved to reinstate the ineligibility of the Executive a second time.

Mr. Ellsworth. With many this appears a natural consequence of his being elected by the Legislature. It was not the case with him. The Executive he thought should be reelected if his conduct proved him worthy of it. And he will be more likely to render himself worthy of it if he be rewardable with it. The most eminent characters also will be more willing to accept the trust under this condition than if they foresee a necessary degradation at a fixed period.

Mr. Gerry. That the Executive should be independent of the Legislature is a clear point. The longer the duration of his appointment the more will his dependence be diminished. It will be better then for him to continue 10, 15, or even 20 years and be ineligible afterwards.

Mr. King was for making him reeligible. This is too great an advantage to be given up for the small effect it will have on his dependence. ...

Mr. L. Martin, suspending his motion as to the ineligibility, moved "that the appointment of the Executive shall continue for eleven years."

Mr. Gerry suggested fifteen years.

Mr. King twenty years. This is the medium life of princes.[4]

Mr. Davie eight years.

Mr. Wilson. The difficulties and perplexities into which the House is thrown proceed from the election by the Legislature, which he was sorry had been reinstated. The inconveniency of this mode was such that he would agree to almost any length of time in order to get rid of the dependence which must result from it. He was persuaded that the longest term would not be equivalent to a proper mode of election unless indeed it should be during good behavior. It seemed to be supposed that at a certain advance of life a continuance in office would cease to be agreeable to the officer as well as desirable to the public. Experience had shown in a variety of instances that both a capacity and inclination for public service existed in very advanced states. He mentioned the instance of a Doge of Venice who was elected after he was 80 years of age. The popes have generally been elected at very advanced

---

4. Madison added a footnote that "this might possibly be meant as a caricature of the previous motions in order to defeat the object of them."

periods, and yet in no case had a more steady or a better concerted policy been pursued than in the Court of Rome. If the Executive should come into office at 35 years of age, which he presumes may happen, and his continuance should be fixed at 15 years, at the age of 50 in the very prime of life, and with all the aid of experience, he must be cast aside like a useless hulk. ... Notwithstanding what had been done he could not but hope that a better mode of election would yet be adopted; and one that would be more agreeable to the general sense of the House. ...

Mr. Gerry. We seem to be entirely at a loss on this head. He would suggest whether it would not be advisable to refer the clause relating to the Executive to the Committee of Detail to be appointed. Perhaps they will be able to hit on something that may unite the various opinions which have been thrown out.

Mr. Wilson. As the great difficulty seems to spring from the mode of election, he would suggest a mode which had not been mentioned. It was that the Executive be elected for 6 years by a small number, not more than 15 of the National Legislature, to be drawn from it not by ballot but by lot, and who should retire immediately and make the election without separating. By this mode intrigue would be avoided in the first instance, and the dependence would be diminished. This was not he said a digested idea and might be liable to strong objections.

Mr. Govr. Morris. Of all possible modes of appointment that by the Legislature is the worst. If the Legislature is to appoint, and impeach or to influence the impeachment, the Executive will be the mere creature of it. ... He had been charged heretofore [by Col. Mason] with inconsistency in pleading for confidence in the Legislature on some occasions, and urging a distrust on others. The charge was not well founded. The Legislature is worthy of unbounded confidence in some respects, and liable to equal distrust in others. When their interest coincides precisely with that of their Constituents, as happens in many of their Acts, no abuse of trust is to be apprehended. When a strong personal interest happens to be opposed to the general interest, the Legislature can not be too much distrusted. In all public bodies there are two parties. The Executive will necessarily be more connected with one than with the other. There will be a personal interest therefore in one of the parties to oppose as well as in the other to support him. Much had been said of the intrigues that will be practiced by the Executive to get into office. Nothing had been said on the other side of the intrigues to get him out of office. Some leader of party will always covet his seat, will perplex his administration, will cabal with the Legislature till he succeeds in supplanting him. This was the way in which the King of England was got out; he meant the real King, the Minister. This was the way in which Pitt forced himself into place. Fox was for pushing the matter still farther. If he had carried his India bill, which he was very near doing, he would have made the Minister the King in form almost as well as in substance.[5] Our President will be the British Minister, yet we are about to make him appointable by the Legislature. Something had been said of the danger of Monarchy. If a good government should not now be formed, if a good organization of the Executive should not be provided, he doubted whether we should not have something worse than a limited Monarchy. In order to get rid of the dependence of the Executive on the Legislature, the expedient of making him ineligible a second time had been devised. This was as much as to say we should give him the benefit of experience and then

---

5. In 1783, Charles James Fox (1749–1806) introduced a bill for reorganizing the government of India. Over King George III's objections the House of Commons passed the bill by a 2 to 1 margin. The bill was defeated in the House of Lords by thirteen votes only after the king made it clear that he would regard any peer voting for the bill as a personal enemy (Cooke 1961, 486).

deprive ourselves of the use of it. But make him ineligible a second time, and prolong his duration even to 15 years, will he by any wonderful interposition of providence at that period cease to be a man? No, he will be unwilling to quit his exaltation. The road to his object through the Constitution will be shut. He will be in possession of the sword, a civil war will ensue, and the Commander of the victorious army ... will be the despot of America. This consideration renders him particularly anxious that the Executive should be properly constituted. The vice here would not, as in some other parts of the system, be curable. It is the most difficult of all rightly to balance the executive. Make him too weak: The Legislature will usurp his powers. Make him too strong: He will usurp on the Legislature. He preferred a short period, a reeligibility, but a different mode of election. A long period would prevent an adoption of the plan: it ought to do so. He should himself be afraid to trust it. He was not prepared to decide on Mr. Wilson's mode of election just hinted by him. He thought it deserved consideration. It would be better that chance should decide than intrigue. ...

Mr. Wilson then moved that the Executive be chosen every "____ years by ____ Electors to be taken by lot from the National Legislature who shall proceed immediately to the choice of the Executive and not separate until it be made."

Mr. Carroll seconds the motion.

Mr. Gerry. This is committing too much to chance. If the lot should fall on a set of unworthy men, an unworthy Executive must be saddled on the Country. He thought it had been demonstrated that no possible mode of electing by the Legislature could be a good one.

Mr. King. The lot might fall on a majority from the same State which would ensure the election of a man from that State. We ought to be governed by reason, not by chance. As nobody seemed to be satisfied he wished the matter to be postponed.

Mr. Wilson did not move this as the best mode. His opinion remained unshaken that we ought to resort to the people for the election. He seconded the postponement. ...

On the question of postponement it was agreed to nem. con.

July 25

Mr. Ellsworth moved "that the Executive be appointed by the Legislature, except when the magistrate last chosen shall have continued in office the whole term for which he was chosen, and be reeligible, in which case the choice shall be by Electors appointed by the Legislatures of the States for that purpose." By this means a deserving magistrate may be reelected without making him dependent on the Legislature.

Mr. Gerry repeated his remark that an election at all by the National Legislature was radically and incurably wrong; and moved that the Executive be appointed by the Governors and Presidents of the States with advice of their Councils, and where there are no Councils by Electors chosen by the Legislatures. ...

Mr. Madison. There are objections against every mode that has been or perhaps can be proposed. The election must be made either by some existing authority under the National or State constitutions, or by some special authority derived from the people, or by the people themselves. The two existing authorities under the National Constitution would be the Legislative and Judiciary. The latter he presumed was out of the question. The former was in his judgment liable to insuperable objections. Besides the general influence of that mode on the independence of the Executive, 1. the election of the Chief Magistrate would agitate and divide the legislature so much that the public interest would materially suffer by it. Public bodies are always apt to be thrown into contentions, but into more violent ones by such occasions than by any others. 2. The candidate would intrigue with the Legislature, would derive his appointment from the predominant faction, and be apt to render his administration subservient to its views. 3. The Ministers of foreign powers would have and make use of the opportunity to mix their intrigues and influence with the election. Limited as the powers of the Executive are, it will be an object of great moment with the great rival powers of Europe who have American possessions, to have at the head of our Government a man attached to their respective politics and interests. No pains, nor perhaps expense, will be spared, to gain from the Legislature an appointment favorable to their wishes. Germany and Poland are witnesses of this danger. In the former, the election of the Head of the Empire, till it became in a manner hereditary, interested all Europe, and was much influenced by foreign interference. In the latter, although the elective Magistrate has very little real power, his election has at all times produced the most eager interference of foreign princes, and has in fact at length slid entirely into foreign hands.

The existing authorities in the States are the Legislative, Executive and Judiciary. The appointment of the National Executive by the first was objectionable in many points of view, some of which had been already mentioned. He would mention one which of itself would decide his opinion. The Legislatures of the States had betrayed a strong propensity to a variety of pernicious measures. One object of the National Legislature was to control this propensity. One object of the National Executive, so far as it would have a negative on the laws, was to control the National Legislature, so far as it might be infected with a similar propensity. Refer the appointment of the National Executive to the State Legislatures, and this controlling purpose may be defeated. The Legislatures can and will act with some kind of regular plan, and will promote the appointment of a man who will not oppose himself to a favorite object. Should a majority of the Legislatures at the time of election have the same object, or different objects of the same kind, the National Executive would be rendered subservient to them. An appointment by the State Executives was liable among other objections to this insuperable one, that being standing bodies, they could and would be courted, and intrigued with by the Candidates, by their partisans, and by the Ministers of foreign powers. The State Judiciaries had not and he presumed would not be proposed as a proper source of appointment.

The option before us then lay between an appointment by Electors chosen by the people and an immediate appointment by the people. He thought the former mode free from many of the objections which had been urged against it, and greatly preferable to an appointment by the National Legislature. As the electors would be chosen for the occasion, would meet at once, and proceed immediately to an appointment, there would be very little opportunity for cabal or corruption. As a farther precaution, it might be required that they should meet at some place distinct from the seat of Government, and even that no person within a certain distance of the place at the time should be eligible. This mode however had been rejected so recently and by so great a majority that it probably would not be proposed anew. The remaining mode was an election by the people or rather by the qualified part of them. ... With all its imperfections he liked this best. He would not repeat either the general arguments for or the objections against this mode. He would only take notice of two difficulties which he admitted to have weight. The first arose from the disposition in the people to prefer a Citizen of their own State, and the disadvantage this would throw on the smaller States. Great as this objection might be he did not think it equal to such as lay against every other mode which had been proposed. He thought too that some expedient might be hit upon that would obviate it. The second difficulty arose from the disproportion of qualified voters in the Northern and Southern States, and the disadvantages which this mode would throw on the latter. The answer to this objection was: 1. That this disproportion would be continually decreasing under the influence of the Republican laws introduced in the Southern States, and the more rapid increase of their population. 2. That local considerations must give way to the general interest. As an individual from the Southern States he was willing to make the sacrifice.

Mr. Ellsworth. The objection drawn from the different sizes of the States is unanswerable. The Citizens of the largest States would invariably prefer the Candidate within the State, and the largest States would invariably have the man.

Question on Mr. Ellsworth's motion as above [4 yes; 7 no].

Mr. Pinckney moved that the election by the Legislature be qualified with a proviso that no person be eligible for more than 6 years in any twelve years. He thought this would have all the advantage and at the same time avoid in some degree the inconvenience of an absolute ineligibility a second time.

Col. Mason approved the idea. It had the sanction of experience in the instance of Congress and some of the Executives of the States. It rendered the Executive as effectually independent as an ineligibility after his first election, and opened the way at the same time for the advantage of his future services. He preferred on the whole the election by the National Legislature, though candor obliged him to admit that there was great danger of foreign influence, as had been suggested. This was the most serious objection with him that had been urged.

Mr. Butler. The two great evils to be avoided are cabal at home and influence from abroad. It will be difficult to avoid either if the election be made by the National Legislature. On the other hand, the Government should not be made so complex and unwieldy as to disgust the States. This would be the case if the election should be referred to the people. He liked best an election by Electors chosen by the Legislatures of the States. He was against a reeligibility at all events. He was also against a ratio of votes in the States. An equality should prevail in this case. The reasons for departing from it do not hold in the case of the Executive as in that of the Legislature.

Mr. Gerry approved of Mr. Pinckney's motion as lessening the evil.

Mr. Govr. Morris was against a rotation in every case. ... The evils to be guarded against in this case are: 1. the undue influence of the Legislature; 2. instability of Councils; 3. misconduct in office. To guard against the first, we run into the second evil. We adopt a rotation which produces instability of Councils. ... A change of men is ever followed by a change of measures. We see this fully exemplified in the vicissitudes among ourselves, particularly in the State of Pennsylvania. ... A victorious party scorns to tread in the paths of their predecessors. ... Rotation in office will not prevent intrigue and dependence on the Legislature. The man in office will look forward to the period at which he will become reeligible. The distance of the period, the improbability of such a protraction of his life, will be no obstacle. Such is the nature of man, formed by his benevolent author no doubt for wise ends, that although he knows his existence to be limited to a span, he takes his measures as if he were to live forever. ... To avoid the third evil, impeachments will be essential, and hence an additional reason against an election by the Legislature. He considered an election by the people as the best, by the Legislature as the worst, mode. ...

Mr. Williamson was sensible that strong objections lay against an election of the Executive by the Legislature, and that it opened a door for foreign influence. The principal objection against an election by the people seemed to be the disadvantage under which it would place the smaller States. He suggested as a cure for this difficulty that each man should vote for 3 candidates. One of these he observed would be probably of his own State, the other 2 of some other States, and as probably of a small as a large one.

Mr. Govr. Morris liked the idea, suggesting as an amendment that each man should vote for two persons one of whom at least should not be of his own State.

Mr. Madison also thought something valuable might be made of the suggestion with the proposed amendment of it. The second best man in this case would probably be the first in fact. The only objection which occurred was that each Citizen, after having given his vote for his favorite fellow Citizen, would throw away his second on some obscure Citizen of another State in order to ensure the object of his first choice. But it could hardly be supposed that the Citizens of many States would be so sanguine of having their favorite elected as not to give their second vote with sincerity to the next object of their choice. It might moreover be provided in favor of the smaller States that the Executive should not be eligible more than ____ times in ____ years from the same State.

Mr. Gerry. A popular election in this case is radically vicious. The ignorance of the people would put it in the power of some one set of men dispersed through the Union and acting in concert to delude them into any appointment. He observed that such a Society of men existed in the Order of the Cincinnati.[6] They are respectable, united, and influential. They will in fact elect the chief Magistrate in every instance if the election be referred to the people. His respect for the characters composing this Society could not blind him to the danger and impropriety of throwing such a power into their hands.

Mr. Dickinson. As far as he could judge from the discussions which had taken place during his attendance, insuperable objections lay against an election of the Executive by the National Legislature; as also by the Legislatures or Executives of the States. He had long leaned towards an election by the people which he regarded as the best and purest source. Objections he was aware lay against this mode, but not so great he thought as against the other modes. The greatest difficulty in the opinion of the House seemed to arise from the partiality of the States to their respective Citizens. But, might not this very partiality be turned to a useful purpose. Let the people of each State choose its best Citizen. The people will know the most eminent characters of their own States, and the people of different States will feel an emulation in selecting those of which they will have the greatest reason to be proud. Out of the thirteen names thus selected, an Executive Magistrate may be chosen either by the National Legislature or by Electors appointed by it.

On a Question which was moved for postponing Mr. Pinckney's motion in order to make way for some such proposition as had been hinted by Mr. Williamson and others, it passed in the negative [5 yes; 6 no].

---

6. The Society of the Cincinnati, a fraternal order of officers who had served during the Revolutionary War, was a frequent target of republican denunciations during the period prior to the Constitution. Its exclusivity, hereditary membership (repealed in 1784 at Washington's urging), and military complexion all combined to raise republican fears of aristocracy and conspiracy. Gerry's comments must have discomfited Washington, who was not only close friends with many of his former officers but had been president of the society during the previous year. In fact Washington's initial reluctance to attend the Philadelphia convention was in part related to the fact that he had previously turned down an invitation to attend a meeting of the Cincinnati, which was to occur in the same city at roughly the same time. Washington worried that having declined the Cincinnati invitation, citing personal reasons, he could not accept the invitation to attend the Constitutional Convention without offending his former comrades and tarnishing his reputation (Phelps 1993, 93).

On Mr. Pinckney's motion that no person shall serve in the Executive more than 6 years in 12 years, it passed in the negative [5 yes; 6 no].

July 26

Col. Mason. In every stage of the question relative to the Executive, the difficulty of the subject and the diversity of the opinions concerning it have appeared. Nor have any of the modes of constituting that department been satisfactory. 1. It has been proposed that the election should be made by the people at large; that is that an act which ought to be performed by those who know most of eminent characters and qualifications should be performed by those who know least. 2. That the election should be made by the Legislatures of the States [or] 3. by the Executives of the States. Against these modes also strong objections have been urged. 4. It has been proposed that the election should be made by Electors chosen by the people for that purpose. This was at first agreed to, but on further consideration has been rejected. 5. Since which, the mode of Mr. Williamson requiring each freeholder to vote for several candidates has been proposed. This seemed, like many other propositions, to carry a plausible face, but on closer inspection is liable to fatal objections. A popular election in any form, as Mr. Gerry has observed, would throw the appointment into the hands of the Cincinnati, a Society for the members of which he had a great respect, but which he never wished to have a preponderant influence on the Government. 6. Another expedient was proposed by Mr. Dickinson, which is liable to so palpable and material an inconvenience that he had little doubt of its being by this time rejected by himself. It would exclude every man who happened not to be popular within his own State, though the causes of his local unpopularity might be of such a nature as to recommend him to the States at large. 7. Among other expedients, a lottery has been introduced. But as the tickets do not appear to be in much demand it will probably not be carried on and nothing therefore need be said on that subject. After reviewing all these various modes, he was led to conclude that an election by the National Legislature as originally proposed was the best. If it was liable to objections, it was liable to fewer than any other. He conceived at the same time that a second election ought to be absolutely prohibited. Having for his primary object, for the pole star of his political conduct, the preservation of the rights of the people, he held it as an essential point, as the very palladium of Civil liberty, that the great officers of State, and particularly the Executive, should at fixed periods return to that mass from which they were at first taken, in order that they may feel and respect those rights and interests which are again to be personally valuable to them. He concluded with moving that the constitution of the Executive as reported by the Committee of the whole be reinstated, namely, "that the Executive be appointed for seven years, and be ineligible a second time."

Mr. Davie seconded the motion.

Docr. Franklin. It seems to have been imagined by some that the returning to the mass of the people was degrading the magistrate. This he thought was contrary to republican principles. In free Governments the rulers are the servants, and the people their superiors and sovereigns. For the former therefore to return among the latter was not to degrade but to promote them. And it would be imposing an unreasonable burden on them, to keep them always in a state of servitude, and not allow them to become again one of the masters.

Question on Col. Mason's motion as above, which passed in the affirmative [7 yes; 3 no; 1 absent].

Mr. Govr. Morris was now against the whole paragraph. In answer to Col. Mason's position that a periodical return of the great officers of the State into the mass of the people was the palladium of Civil liberty, he would observe that on the same principle the Judiciary ought to be periodically degraded. Certain it was that the Legislature ought to be periodically degraded ... yet no one had proposed or conceived that the members of it should not be reeligible. In answer to Docr. Franklin that a return into the mass of the people would be a promotion instead of a degradation, he had no doubt that our Executive like most others would have too much patriotism to shrink from the burden of his office, and too much modesty not to be willing to decline the promotion. ...

On the question ... as amended in the words following—"that a National Executive be instituted—to consist of a single person—to be chosen by the National legislature—for the term of seven years—to be ineligible a second time" [6 yes; 3 no; 1 divided; 1 absent].

The Crisis Comes to a Head, August 24

As the Committee of Detail (John Rutledge, James Wilson, Oliver Ellsworth, Edmund Randolph, and Nathaniel Gorham) began its work on July 27, it knew the convention desired that the president be selected by the legislature, serve a seven-year term, and be ineligible for reelection. But the convention offered no guidance as to the mechanics by which the legislature would select the president: would the selection, for instance, be by joint ballot of the two houses or would each house have a veto over the choice of the other? This was presumably the sort of detail that the committee was expected to provide. Yet the committee's report to the convention on August 6 included no provision for how the legislature should choose the president. We know this omission was no oversight, since Randolph's first draft of the committee's work included an emendation, in Rutledge's handwriting, that called for "each House [to] hav[e] a Negative on the other" in the choice of the president (Farrand 1937, 2:145), as well as a crossed-out emendation calling for election by a joint ballot of the two houses. Giving each house a veto would help the least populous states because the Senate, in which each state was equally represented, would have a veto over the selection; a joint ballot would help the more populous states, since there were to be far more representatives than senators. No records were kept of the committee's deliberations, so it is not possible to know why or how these emendations were excised from the committee's final report presented to the convention on August 6. We do know that James Wilson was responsible for writing the final report, and it seems likely that Wilson, who was the convention's leading opponent of having representation in the Senate based on states rather than population, as well as the leading exponent of popular election of the president, would have strongly resisted the idea of giving the Senate a veto over the choice of president. Moreover, Wilson would have found strong allies in Randolph and especially Gorham, both of whom (like Wilson) represented the union's most populous states and both of whom had opposed the Connecticut Compromise that had given each state equal representation in the Senate. Whatever the reason, the committee opted to leave the divisive question of how the legislature should select the president to the whole convention.

August 24

Article X, section 1. ... "The President ... shall be elected by ballot by the Legislature. He shall hold his office during the term of seven years; but shall not be elected a second time." ...

Mr. Rutledge moved to insert "joint" before the word "ballot," as the most convenient mode of electing.

Mr. Sherman objected to it as depriving the States represented in the Senate of the negative intended them in that house.

Mr. Gorham said it was wrong to be considering at every turn whom the Senate would represent. The public good was the true object to be kept in view. Great delay and confusion would ensue if the two Houses should vote separately, each having a negative on the choice of the other.

Mr. Dayton. It might be well for those not to consider how the Senate was constituted, whose interest it was to keep it out of sight. If the amendment should be agreed to, a joint ballot would in fact give the appointment to one House. He could never agree to the clause with such an amendment. There could be no doubt of the two Houses separately concurring in the same person for President. The importance and necessity of the case would ensure a concurrence.

Mr. Carroll moved to strike out "by the Legislature" and insert "by the people." Mr. Wilson seconded him and on the question [2 yes; 9 no].

Mr. Brearly was opposed to the motion for inserting the word "joint." The argument that the small States should not put their hands into the pockets of the large ones did not apply in this case.[7]

Mr. Wilson urged the reasonableness of giving the larger States a larger share of the appointment, and the danger of delay from a disagreement of the two Houses. He remarked also that the Senate had peculiar powers balancing the advantage given by a joint ballot in this case to the other branch of the Legislature.

Mr. Langdon. This general officer ought to be elected by the joint and general voice. In New Hampshire the mode of separate votes by the two Houses was productive of great difficulties. The negative of the Senate would hurt the feelings of the man elected by the votes of the other branch. He was for inserting "joint," though unfavorable to New Hampshire as a small State. ...

Mr. Madison. If the amendment be agreed to, the rule of voting will give to the largest State, compared with the smallest, an influence as 4 to 1 only, although the population is as 10 to 1. This surely can not be unreasonable as the President is to act for the people not for the States. ...

---

7. Brearly here is making reference to the earlier Connecticut Compromise by which money bills were to originate only in the House, on the grounds that such bills more directly affected the larger and wealthier states. Echoing Pierce Butler's comments on July 25, Brearly argues that small states have as great an interest in who becomes president as the larger states.

On the question for inserting "joint," it passed in the affirmative [7 yes; 4 no].

Mr. Dayton then moved to insert, after the word "Legislatures," the words "each State having one vote." Mr. Brearly seconded him, and on the question it passed in the negative [5 yes; 6 no].

Mr. Pinckney moved to insert after the word "Legislature" the words "to which election a majority of the votes of the members present shall be required" and on this question, it passed in the affirmative [10 yes; 1 no].

Mr. Govr. Morris opposed the election of the President by the Legislature. He dwelt on the danger of rendering the Executive uninterested in maintaining the rights of his Station, as leading to Legislative tyranny. If [members of] the Legislature have the Executive dependent on them, they can perpetuate and support their usurpation by the influence of tax-gatherers and other officers, by fleets, armies, etc. Cabal and corruption are attached to that mode of election; so also is ineligibility a second time. Hence the Executive is interested in courting popularity in the Legislature by sacrificing his Executive Rights and then he can go into that Body, after the expiration of his Executive office, and enjoy there the fruits of his policy. To these considerations he added that rivals would be continually intriguing to oust the President from his place. To guard against all these evils he moved that the President "shall be chosen by Electors to be chosen by the People of the several States."

Mr. Carroll seconded him and on the question it passed in the negative [5 yes; 6 no].

Mr. Dayton moved to postpone the consideration [of these clauses] of Section 1, article X, which was disagreed to without a count of the States.

Mr. Broom moved to refer [these] clauses to a committee of a member from each State, and on the question, it failed, the states being equally divided [5 yes; 5 no; 1 divided].

On the question taken on the first part of Mr. Govr. Morris's motion, to wit, "shall be chosen by electors" as an abstract question, it failed, the States being equally divided [4 yes; 4 no; 2 divided; 1 absent].

The consideration of the remaining clauses of Section 1, article X was then postponed till tomorrow at the instance of the deputies of New Jersey.

Resolution, September 4–6

Although Rutledge's proposal to have the president selected by a joint ballot of the legislature had passed, the issue of how the president was to be selected had nonetheless brought the convention to an impasse. Dayton's motion to grant each state an equal vote in the process had failed by only a single vote, and it had divided the convention along lines that were strikingly similar to the division between small and large states in the debate over representation in the Senate. In both cases, the prime movers for giving each state an equal voice were the smaller states of New Jersey, Connecticut, Maryland, and Delaware; and in both votes it was the states of Virginia, Pennsylvania, and South Carolina that anchored the opposition. The series of closely divided votes that ensued indicated that the convention was nowhere close to a consensus on the issue. It was getting late in the convention and the delegates were clearly anxious to push ahead and not put off the issue. But the intensity of feeling on the part of those delegates who were opposed to Rutledge's motion as well as the closely divided subsequent votes made it clear that this was not a viable strategy. On August 31 the convention agreed to refer the matter to a Committee on Postponed Matters, made up of a member from each state, just as Delaware's Jacob Broom had unsuccessfully proposed on August 24. With Brearly installed as chair, and with a representative from each state (Roger Sherman [Conn.], Nicholas Gilman [N.H.], Rufus King [Mass.], Gouverneur Morris [Pa.], John Dickinson [Del.], Daniel Carroll [Md.], James Madison [Va.], Hugh Williamson [N.C.], Pierce Butler [S.C.], and Abraham Baldwin [Ga.]), the interests of the smaller states were in much better hands than they had been in the five-person Committee of Detail. We know even less about the deliberations within the Brearly Committee than we do of the Committee of Detail, so it is impossible to know who played what role in creating the electoral college. The idea of an electoral college of some sort was not, of course, new to the convention. Various versions of the idea had been floated on at least five previous occasions: first back on June 2 when James Wilson proposed an electoral college selected by the people, next when Alexander Hamilton proposed a similar plan in his long speech to the convention on June 18, then again on July 17 when Luther Martin proposed an electoral college selected by the state legislatures and on July 19 when Ellsworth's plan, identical to Martin's, was accepted by the convention, albeit only for a few days. Finally, on August 24, Gouverneur Morris's proposal for an electoral college chosen by the people was narrowly defeated. The contribution of the Committee on Postponed Matters was not to provide fresh ideas so much as to work out a compromise over the mechanics that would be acceptable both to large and small states. This they did, first, by providing a formula for electors (the number of representatives plus the number of senators) that advantaged the more populous states and, second, by allowing that in the event that no candidate had a majority (and most assumed this would be most of the time) the election would be decided by the Senate, thereby advantaging the smaller states. It was this artful political compromise that the convention immediately took up after hearing the Brearly Committee report on September 4.

September 4

Mr. Brearly from the Committee of Eleven made a further partial Report as follows.

"The Committee of Eleven, to whom sundry resolutions were referred on the 31st of August, report that in their opinion the following additions and alterations should be made to the Report before the Convention." ...

In section 1, article 10, to be inserted "He shall hold his office during the term of four years, and together with the vice-President, chosen for the same term, be elected in the following manner, viz. Each State shall appoint in such manner as its Legislature may direct, a number of electors equal to the whole number of Senators and members of the House of

Representatives to which the State may be entitled in the Legislature. The Electors shall meet in their respective States, and vote by ballot for two persons, of whom one at least shall not be an inhabitant of the same State with themselves; and they shall make a list of all the persons voted for, and of the number of votes for each, which list they shall sign and certify and transmit sealed to the Seat of the General Government, directed to the President of the Senate. The President of the Senate shall in that House open all the certificates; and the votes shall be then and there counted. The Person having the greatest number of votes shall be the President, if such number be a majority of that of the electors; and if there be more than one who have such majority, and have an equal number of votes, then the Senate shall immediately choose by ballot one of them for President: but if no person have a majority, then from the five highest on the list, the Senate shall immediately choose by ballot the President. And in every case after the choice of the President, the person having the greatest number of votes shall be vice-president: but if there should remain two or more who have equal votes, the Senate shall choose from them the vice-President. The Legislature may determine the time of choosing and assembling the Electors, and the manner of certifying and transmitting their votes." ...

Mr. Gorham disapproved of making the next highest after the President, the vice-President, without referring the decision to the Senate in case the next highest should have less than a majority of votes. As the regulation stands a very obscure man with very few votes may arrive at that appointment.

Mr. Sherman said the object of this clause of the report of the Committee was to get rid of the ineligibility, which was attached to the mode of election by the Legislature, and to render the Executive independent of the Legislature. As the choice of the President was to be made out of the five highest, obscure characters were sufficiently guarded against in that case; and he had no objection to requiring the vice-President to be chosen in like manner, where the choice was not decided by a majority in the first instance.

Mr. Madison was apprehensive that by requiring both the President and vice-President to be chosen out of the five highest candidates, the attention of the electors would be turned too much to making candidates instead of giving their votes in order to a definitive choice. Should this turn be given to the business, the election would in fact be consigned to the Senate altogether. It would have the effect at the same time, he observed, of giving the nomination of the candidates to the largest States.

Mr. Govr. Morris concurred in ... the remarks of Mr. Madison.

Mr. Randolph and Mr. Pinckney wished for a particular explanation and discussion of the reasons for changing the mode of electing the Executive.

Mr. Govr. Morris said he would give the reasons of the Committee and his own. 1. The first was the danger of intrigue and faction if the appointment should be made by the Legislature. 2. The inconvenience of an ineligibility required by that mode in order to lessen its evils. 3. The difficulty of establishing a Court of Impeachments other than the Senate, which would not be so proper for the trial, nor the other branch for the impeachment of the President, if appointed by the Legislature. 4. Nobody had appeared to be satisfied with an appointment by the Legislature. 5. Many were anxious even for an immediate choice by the people. 6. The indispensable necessity of making the Executive independent of the Legislature.—As the Electors would vote at the same time throughout the U.S. and at so great a distance from each other, the great evil of cabal was avoided. It would be impossible also to corrupt them. ...

Col. Mason confessed that the plan of the Committee had removed some capital objections, particularly the danger of cabal and corruption. It was liable however to this strong objection that nineteen times in twenty the President would be chosen by the Senate, an improper body for the purpose.

Mr. Butler thought the mode not free from objections, but much more so than an election by the Legislature where, as in elective monarchies, cabal, faction and violence would be sure to prevail.

Mr. Pinckney stated as objections to the mode: 1. That it threw the whole appointment in fact into the hands of the Senate. 2. The Electors will be strangers to the several candidates and of course unable to decide on their comparative merits. 3. It makes the Executive reeligible which will endanger the public liberty. 4. It makes the same body of men which will in fact elect the President his Judges in case of an impeachment.

Mr. Williamson had great doubts whether the advantages of reeligibility would balance the objection to such a dependence of the President on the Senate for his reappointment. He thought at least the Senate ought to be restrained to the two highest on the list.

Mr. Govr. Morris said the principal advantage aimed at was that of taking away the opportunity for cabal. The President may be made, if thought necessary, ineligible on this as well as on any other mode of election. Other inconveniences may be no less redressed on this plan than any other.

Mr. Baldwin thought the plan not so objectionable when well considered, as at first view. The increasing intercourse among the people of the States would render important characters less and less unknown, and the Senate would consequently be less and less likely to have the eventual appointment thrown into their hands.

Mr. Wilson. This subject has greatly divided the House and will also divide people out of doors. It is in truth the most difficult of all on which we have had to decide. He had never made up an opinion on it entirely to his own satisfaction. He thought the plan on the whole a valuable improvement on the former. It gets rid of one great evil, that of cabal and corruption; and Continental Characters will multiply as we more and more coalesce, so as to enable the electors in every part of the Union to know and judge of them. It clears the way also for a discussion of the question of reeligibility on its own merits, which the former mode of election seemed to forbid. He thought it might be better however to refer the eventual appointment to the Legislature than to the Senate, and to confine it to a smaller number than five of the Candidates. The eventual election by the Legislature would not open cabal anew, as it would be restrained to certain designated objects of choice. ... And if the election be made as it ought, as soon as the votes of the electors are opened ... there can be little danger of corruption. Another reason for preferring the Legislature to the Senate in this business was that the House of Representatives will be so often changed as to be free from the influence and faction to which the permanence of the Senate may subject that branch.

Mr. Randolph preferred the former mode of constituting the Executive, but if the change was to be made he wished to know why the eventual election was referred to the Senate and not to the Legislature? He saw no necessity for this and many objections to it. He was apprehensive also that the advantage of the eventual appointment would fall into the hands of the States near the Seat of Government.

Mr. Govr. Morris said the Senate was preferred because fewer could then say to the President, you owe your appointment to us. He thought the President would not depend so much on the Senate for his reappointment as on his general good conduct.

The further consideration of the Report was postponed that each member might take a copy of the remainder of it.

September 5

The Report made yesterday as to the appointment of the Executive being taken up. Mr. Pinckney renewed his opposition to the mode arguing: 1. That the electors will not have sufficient knowledge of the fittest men, and will be swayed by an attachment to the eminent men of their respective States. 2. Hence ... the dispersion of the votes would leave the appointment with the Senate, and as the President's reappointment will thus depend on the Senate he will be the mere creature of that body. 3. He will combine with the Senate against the House of Representatives. 4. This change in the mode of election was meant to get rid of the ineligibility of the President a second time, whereby he will become fixed for life under the auspices of the Senate.

Mr. Gerry did not object to this plan of constituting the Executive in itself, but should be governed in his final vote by the powers that may be given to the President.

Mr. Rutledge was much opposed to the plan reported by the Committee. It would throw the whole power into the Senate. He was also against a reeligibility. He moved to postpone the Report under consideration and take up the original plan of appointment by the Legislature, to wit. "He shall be elected by joint ballot by the Legislature to which election a majority of the votes of the members present shall be required. He shall hold his office during the term of seven years; but shall not be elected a second time."

On this motion to postpone [2 yes; 8 no; 1 divided].

Col. Mason admitted that there were objections to an appointment by the Legislature as originally planned. He had not yet made up his mind, but would state his objections to the mode proposed by the Committee. 1. It puts the appointment in fact into the hands of the Senate, as it will rarely happen that a majority of the whole votes will fall on any one candidate. And as the existing President will always be one of the five highest, his reappointment will of course depend on the Senate. 2. Considering the powers of the President and those of the Senate, if a coalition should be established between these two branches, they will be able to subvert the Constitution. The great objection with him would be removed by depriving the Senate of the eventual election. He accordingly moved to strike out the words "if such number be a majority of that of the electors."

Mr. Williamson seconded the motion. He could not agree to the clause without some such modification. He preferred making the highest though not having a majority of the votes, President, to a reference of the matter to the Senate. Referring the appointment to the Senate lays a certain foundation for corruption and aristocracy.

Mr. Govr. Morris thought the point of less consequence than it was supposed on both sides. It is probable that a majority of votes will fall on the same man. As each elector is to give two votes, more than $1/4$ will give a majority. Besides as one vote is to be given to a man out of the State, and as this vote will not be thrown away, $1/2$ the votes will fall on characters eminent and generally known. Again if the President shall have given satisfaction the votes will turn on him of course, and a majority of them will reappoint him without resort to the Senate. If he should be disliked, all disliking him would take care to unite their votes so as to ensure his being supplanted.

Col. Mason. Those who think there is no danger of there not being majority for the same person in the first instance ought to give up the point to those who think otherwise.

Mr. Sherman reminded the opponents of the new mode proposed that if the small states had the advantage in the Senate's deciding among the five highest candidates, the large States would have in fact the nomination of these candidates.

On the motion of Col. Mason [2 yes; 9 no].

Mr. Wilson moved to strike out "Senate" and insert the word "Legislature."

Mr. Madison considered it as a primary object to render an eventual resort to any part of the Legislature improbable. He was apprehensive that the proposed alteration would turn the attention of the large States too much to the appointment of candidates instead of aiming at an effectual appointment of the officer, as the large States would predominate in the Legislature which would have the final choice out of the Candidates. Whereas if the Senate in which the small States predominate should have this final choice, the concerted effort of the large States would be to make the appointment in the first instance conclusive.

Mr. Randolph. We have in some revolutions of this plan made a bold stroke for Monarchy. We are now doing the same for an aristocracy. He dwelt on the tendency of such an influence in the Senate over the election of the President, in addition to [the Senate's] other powers, to convert that body into a real and dangerous Aristocracy.

Mr. Dickinson was in favor of giving the eventual election to the Legislature instead of the Senate. It was too much influence to be superadded to that body.

On the question moved by Mr. Wilson [3 yes; 7 no; 1 divided].

Mr. Madison and Mr. Williamson moved to strike out the word "majority" and insert "one-third" so that the eventual power might not be exercised if less than a majority, but not less than $1/3$ of the electors should vote for the same person.

Mr. Gerry objected that this would put it in the power of three or four States to put in whom they pleased.

Mr. Williamson. There are seven States which do not contain one-third of the people. If the Senate are to appoint, less than one-sixth of the people will have the power.

On the question [2 yes; 9 no].

Col. Mason moved to strike out the word "five" and insert the word "three" as the highest candidates for the Senate to choose out of.

Mr. Gerry seconded the motion.

Mr. Sherman would sooner give up the plan. He would prefer seven or thirteen.

On the question moved by Col. Mason and Mr. Gerry [2 yes; 9 no].

Mr. Spaight and Mr. Rutledge moved to strike out "five" and insert "thirteen," to which all the States disagreed except North Carolina and South Carolina.

Mr. Madison and Mr. Williamson moved to insert after "Electors" the words "who shall have balloted" so that the non-voting electors not being counted might not increase the number necessary as a majority of the whole to decide the choice without the agency of the Senate.

On this question [4 yes; 7 no].

Col. Mason. As the mode of appointment is now regulated he could not forbear expressing his opinion that it is utterly inadmissible. He would prefer the Government of Prussia to one which will put all power into the hands of seven or eight men, and fix an Aristocracy worse than absolute monarchy.

September 6

Mr. King and Mr. Gerry moved to insert ... after the words "may be entitled in the Legislature" the words following—"But no person shall be appointed an elector who is a member of the Legislature of the U.S. or who holds any office of profit or trust under the U.S." which passed nem. con.

Mr. Gerry proposed, as the President was to be elected by the Senate out of the five high-est candidates, that if he should not at the end of his term be reelected by a majority, the eventual election should be made by the Legislature. This he said would relieve the President from his particular dependence on the Senate for his continuance in office.

Mr. King liked the idea as calculated to satisfy particular members and promote unanim-ity, and as likely to operate but seldom.

Mr. Read opposed it, remarking that if individual members were to be indulged, alterations would be necessary to satisfy most of them.

Mr. Williamson espoused it as a reasonable precaution against the undue influence of the Senate.

Mr. Sherman liked the arrangement as it stood, though he should not be adverse to some amendments. He thought ... that if the Legislature were to have the eventual appointment instead of the Senate, it ought to vote ... by States, in favor of the small States, as the large States would have so great an advantage in nominating the candidates.

Mr. Govr. Morris thought favorably of Mr. Gerry's proposition. It would free the Presi-dent from being tempted [in making appointments to office] to conform to the will of the Senate. ...

Mr. Wilson said that he had weighed carefully the report of the Committee for remodel-ling the constitution of the Executive; and on combining it with other parts of the plan, he was obliged to consider the whole as having a dangerous tendency to aristocracy, as throw-ing a dangerous power into the hands of the Senate. [Senators] will have in fact the ap-pointment of the President, and through his dependence on them, the virtual appointment to offices, among others the offices of the Judiciary Department. They are to make Treaties, and they are to try all impeachments. In allowing them thus to make the Executive and Ju-diciary appointments, to be the Court of impeachments, and to make Treaties which are to be laws of the land, the Legislative, Executive and Judiciary powers are all blended in one branch of the Government. ... According to the plan as it now stands, the President will not be the man of the people as he ought to be, but the Minion of the Senate. He cannot even appoint a tide-waiter without the Senate. ... The Senate, will moreover in all probability be in constant Session. They will have high salaries. And with all those powers, and the Presi-dent in their interest, they will depress the other branch of the Legislature and aggrandize themselves in proportion. Add to all this that the Senate, sitting in conclave, can by holding up to their respective States various and improbable candidates contrive so to scatter their votes as to bring the appointment of the President ultimately before themselves. Upon the whole he thought the new mode of appointing the President with some amendments a valu-able improvement, but he could never agree to purchase it at the price of the ensuing parts of the Report nor befriend a system of which they make a part.

Mr. Govr. Morris expressed his wonder at the observations of Mr. Wilson so far as they preferred the plan in the printed Report to the new modification of it before the House, and entered into a comparative view of the two, with an eye to the nature of Mr. Wilson's objections to the last. By the first the Senate ... had a voice in appointing the President out of all the Citizens of the United States. By this they were limited to five candidates previously nominated to them, with a probability of being barred altogether by the suc-cessful ballot of the Electors. Here surely was no increase of power. They are now to ap-point Judges nominated to them by the President. Before they had the appointment with-out any agency whatever of the president. Here again was surely no additional power. If they are to make Treaties as the plan now stands, the power was the same in the printed plan. If they are to try impeachments, the Judges must have been triable by them before. Wherein then lay the dangerous tendency of the innovations to establish an aristocracy in the Senate? ...

Mr. Williamson, replying to Mr. Morris, observed that the aristocratic complexion proceeds from the change in the mode of appointing the president which makes him dependent on the Senate. ...

Mr. Hamilton said that he had been restrained from entering into the discussions by his dislike of the scheme of Government in general but as he meant to support the plan to be recommended, as better than nothing, he wished in this place to offer a few remarks. He liked the new modification, on the whole, better than that in the printed Report. In this the President was a Monster elected for seven years and ineligible afterwards; having great powers in appointments to office and continually tempted by this constitutional disqualification to abuse them in order to subvert the Government. Although he should be made reeligible, still if appointed by the Legislature he would be tempted to make use of corrupt influence to be continued in office. It seemed peculiarly desirable therefore that some other mode of election should be devised. Considering the different views of different States, and the different districts, Northern, Middle and Southern, he concurred with those who thought that the votes would not be concentered, and that the appointment would consequently in the present mode devolve on the Senate. The nomination to offices will give great weight to the President. Here then is a mutual connection and influence that will perpetuate the President and aggrandize both him and the Senate. What is to be the remedy? He saw none better than to let the highest number of ballots, whether majority or not, appoint the President. What was the objection to this? Merely that too small a number might appoint. But as the plan stands, the Senate may take the candidate having the smallest number of votes and make him President.

Mr. Spaight and Mr. Williamson moved to insert "seven" instead of "four" years for the term of the President.

On this motion [3 yes; 8 no].

Mr. Spaight and Mr. Williamson then moved to insert "six" instead of "four."

On which motion [2 yes; 9 no].

On the term "four" all the States were ay, except North Carolina.

On the question ... for appointing the President by electors—down to the words—"entitled in the Legislature" inclusive [9 yes; 2 no].

Mr. Spaight said if the election by Electors is to be crammed down, he would prefer their meeting all together and deciding finally without any reference to the Senate, and moved "That the Electors meet at the seat of the General Government."

Mr. Williamson seconded the motion, on which all the States were in the negative except North Carolina.

On motion, the words "But the election shall be on the same day throughout the United States," were added after the words "transmitting their votes" [8 yes; 3 no].

Mr. Madison made a motion requiring $^2/_3$ at least of the Senate to be present at the choice of a President. Mr. Pinckney seconded the motion. ...

On the question moved by Mr. Madison and Mr. Pinckney [6 yes; 4 no; 1 absent].

Mr. Williamson suggested as better than an eventual choice by the Senate that this choice should be made by the Legislature, voting by States and not per capita.

Mr. Sherman suggested the House of Representatives as preferable to the Legislature, and moved, accordingly, to strike out the words "The Senate shall immediately choose ..." and in-

sert "The House of Representatives shall immediately choose by ballot one of them for President, the members from each State having one vote."

Col. Mason liked the latter mode best as lessening the aristocratic influence of the Senate.
On the motion of Mr. Sherman [10 yes; 1 no].

Questions for Discussion

1. Which of the convention delegates do you find most persuasive on the
topic of presidential selection? What makes that person's argument persuasive?

2. Why did the convention delegates eventually give up on legislative selection of the president? How would the presidency look different today had
the delegates decided to stick with the plan reported out by the Committee of
Detail on August 6 in which the legislature was to select the president for a
term of seven years and the president was to be ineligible for a second term?

3. Imagine you had been a delegate at the federal convention on September 4, the day the Brearly Committee reported out its plan for presidential selection. Compose a speech that you think might have swayed the delegates to
rethink their plan for an electoral college.

4

Term of Office and Reeligibility

[The President] shall hold his Office during the Term of Four Years.

Article 2, section 1

In the debate over ratification, by far the most frequently criticized part of the convention's plan for presidential selection was the absence of a bar on reeligibility. A president eligible to be reelected, it was widely feared, would become a president for life, an "elective monarchy." Almost every important Anti-Federalist writer, including the Federal Farmer and Cato, as well as a host of lesser lights, from Agrippa to the Columbia Patriot, targeted the renewable four-year term as among the dangerous parts of the proposed new government.[1] This fear, moreover, was expressed not only by opponents of the Constitution but also by its supporters. Writing from Paris in February 1788, a concerned Thomas Jefferson confided to a close friend his "strong dislike" for "the perpetual re-eligibility of the President." It would, Jefferson predicted, "be productive of cruel distress to our country even in your day and mine" (Boyd 1950–, 12:571). Why did so many regard the renewable four-year term with such apprehension and even dread?

To understand the source of these fears, it helps to contrast the federal provisions for presidential tenure with the state provisions for executive term and reeligibility. At the state level the norm was annual terms. In fact only three of the thirteen states had terms for the chief executive that were longer than one year: in South Carolina the governor served a two-year term, and New York and Delaware specified three-year terms for the chief executive. Both Delaware and South Carolina, moreover, required rotation in office. In Delaware the chief magistrate was ineligible for three years after the expira-

---

1. See Luther Martin, "The Genuine Information," Letters of Cato IV, Letters from the Federal Farmer, Letters of Agrippa XVI, A Friend to the Rights of the People, A Columbian Patriot, Essay by a Farmer and Planter, Essays by Cato I [South Carolina], in Storing 1981, 2:65–66, 114, 312–13, 4:112, 236–37, 278, 5:76–77, 139–41.

tion of his three-year term, and in South Carolina the governor had to wait four years after serving a two-year term to be eligible for the office again. Even many of the states that had annual terms provided for rotation: in Virginia and Maryland a governor who had served three one-year terms had to wait four years before serving again; in North Carolina the governor could not serve more than three years in six; and in Georgia the governor was ineligible for two years after one year in office.[2] Only New York, then, with its renewable three-year term, had constitutional provisions for executive tenure that resembled those in the proposed federal constitution. The framers had established a system that, although not without precedent, was vastly different from what most Americans were familiar with. Considering the contrast between federal and state practice, the interesting question perhaps becomes not why the Anti-Federalists objected so strongly to this provision but why they didn't object more vociferously.

But there was more to gubernatorial tenure than constitutional provisions. To understand why critics of the Constitution felt certain that reeligibility would mean perpetual reelection it helps to examine the experience of those states that did not mandate rotation in office. New York had the same governor, George Clinton, ever since the state's constitution was adopted in 1777. Clinton had been handily reelected in 1780, 1783, 1786; after the Constitution was adopted he would be reelected another two times before his retirement in 1795. Even state governors who faced annual elections had remarkable records of longevity. At the time of the Constitutional Convention, New Jersey, like New York, had only known one governor, William Livingston, since establishing its revolutionary constitution in 1776. In addition to serving as a delegate to the Constitutional Convention, the venerable Livingston served fourteen consecutive one-year terms as governor of New Jersey between 1776 and 1790. In Connecticut, annual elections had not prevented Jonathan Trumbull from serving as governor continuously from 1769 to 1786. The first governor of Massachusetts under its 1780 constitution, John Hancock, served for all but two of the state's first thirteen years, and he was never defeated in an election, having resigned because of ill health in 1785 and then dying in office in 1793. Little wonder, then, that so many Americans worried that reeligibility would mean a president for life.

Nor were these worries without substance. Certainly George Washington could have been president for life had he so desired. Nor is it difficult to imagine Thomas Jefferson, given his stature in the country as well as the

---

2. Pennsylvania's president, like the executive council from which he was selected, was limited to serving three years in seven. The counsellors served three-year terms (one-third of the council to be elected each year), but the president was selected annually. The aims of this rotation in office, the Pennsylvania constitution explained, were to prevent "the danger of establishing an inconvenient aristocracy" and to help "more men [to] be trained to public business" (Thorpe 1909, 5:3087).

weakness of the opposition Federalist Party, being perpetually elected president. And given Jefferson's longevity (he died in 1826 at the age of 83), a Jefferson presidency could easily have spanned more than two decades. Anti-Federalist worries about a president who would serve for life, then, were anything but far-fetched. If they appear somewhat exaggerated today it is in part because of subsequent contingencies that the founding generation could not or did not foresee. First and foremost was Washington's fateful decision to bow out after eight years on the job, helping to establish, even if unintentionally, the two-term precedent that no president until Franklin Roosevelt would dare violate.[3] But the two-term tradition owed as much or more to the fears of the followers as to the self-abnegation of leaders. The followers' fears structured an incentive system that meant the road to fame for a Washington lay not in amassing power but in relinquishing it (Schwartz 1987). Jefferson's retirement after two terms, moreover, came about not in spite of Anti-Federalist fears of perpetual election but because Jefferson fully shared those fears that the presidency might degenerate into a hereditary monarchy (Stein 1943, 31–38).

The other unforeseen development that worked to undercut the danger of perpetual reelection was the rise of organized political parties at the presidential level. The rise of political parties, especially by the 1830s, meant not only that all presidential elections would be hotly contested but also that the president would resemble less a patriot king above party (as Washington had appeared) than he would a prime minister at the head of a party. Yet even with political parties contesting presidential elections, incumbent presidents have the visibility and political resources that, with skill and luck, can be parlayed into tenures well beyond two terms, as Franklin Roosevelt's four terms demonstrated. Roosevelt's wartime tenure was certainly extraordinary, but Dwight Eisenhower undoubtedly could have beaten John Kennedy in 1960 had he run a third time, and in all likelihood Ronald Reagan could have won a third term in 1988 had he been allowed to run again.

The Twenty-second Amendment (see appendix 5), limiting presidents to two terms, does not go nearly as far as some Anti-Federalists would have wished. "Agrippa," for instance, recommended to the Massachusetts ratifying convention that the Constitution be amended so that "the president shall be chosen annually and shall serve but one year, and shall be chosen successively from the different states, changing each year" (Storing 1981, 4:112). But most Anti-Federalists would surely see the Twenty-second Amendment as a vindication of their concerns. If we do not need to fear, as one Anti-Federalist did, that "a four-years President will be, in time, a King for life,

---

3. In fact throughout much of the nineteenth century there was a robust one-term tradition. In the decades prior to the Civil War many presidential candidates of both parties pledged that if elected they would serve only a single term.

and after him, his son" (Storing 1981, 5:76–77), we do perhaps still need to worry that unpopular policies may hide behind a popular president. People often elect a president for reasons (the state of the economy, presidential character) that have little to do with his specific policies. Strong arguments exist on both sides of this question, and we are no closer to consensus today than we were in 1787.

11. George Mason and Edmund Randolph, Virginia Ratifying Convention, June 17, 1788

Opposition to reeligibility of the executive tended to be most intense in the south. Every chief executive in the southern states faced some sort of limitation on his reeligibility, and many in the south viewed the absence of rotation in office as a peculiarly (and dangerously) northern notion. The debate in the Virginia convention was particularly charged because Edmund Randolph, like George Mason, had strongly and publicly objected to the reeligibility of the president (Storing 1981, 2:97). By the time the Virginia ratifying convention met in June, Randolph had been persuaded to back the Constitution. What follows is a tense exchange between Mason, who charges the president "will be continued in office for life," and Randolph, who attempts to explain why he no longer feels a constitutional amendment restricting the president's reeligibility is necessary.

Mr. George Mason. Mr. Chairman, there is not a more important article in the Constitution than this. The great fundamental principle of responsibility in republicanism is here sapped. The President is elected without rotation. It may be said that a new election may remove him, and place another in his stead. If we judge from the experience of all other countries, and even our own, we may conclude that as the President of the United States may be re-elected so he will. How is it in every government where rotation is not required? Is there a single instance of a great man not being reelected? Our governor is obliged to return, after a given period, to a private station. It is so in most of the states. This President will be elected time after time: he will be continued in office for life. If we wish to change him, the great powers in Europe will not allow us.

The honorable gentleman, my colleague in the late federal Convention [Edmund Randolph], mentions with applause those parts of which he had expressed his approbation; but when he comes to those parts of which he had expressed his disapprobation, he says not a word. If I am mistaken, let me be put right. I shall not make use of his name; but, in the course of this investigation, I shall use the arguments of that gentleman against it.

Jonathan Elliot, ed., *The Debates in the Several State Constitutions on the Adoption of the Federal Constitution* (New York: Burt Franklin, 1888), 3:483–86.

Will not the great powers of Europe, as France and Great Britain, be interested in having a friend in the President of the United States? And will they not be more interested in his election than in that of the king of Poland? The people of Poland have a right to displace their king. But do they ever do it? No. Prussia and Russia, and other European powers, would not suffer it. This clause will open a door to the dangers and misfortunes which the people of Poland undergo. The powers of Europe will interpose, and we shall have a civil war in the bowels of our country, and be subject to all the horrors and calamities of an elective monarchy. ... The electors, who are to meet in each state to vote for him, may be easily influenced. To prevent the certain evils of attempting to elect a new President, it will be necessary to continue the old one. The only way to alter this would be to render him ineligible after a certain number of years, and then no foreign nation would interfere to keep in a man who was utterly ineligible.

Nothing is so essential to the preservation of a republican government as a periodical rotation. Nothing so strongly impels a man to regard the interest of his constituents as the certainty of returning to the general mass of the people, from whence he was taken, where he must participate in their burdens. ... Some stated time ought to be fixed when the President ought to be reduced to a private station. I should be contented that he might be elected for eight years, but I would wish him to be capable of holding the office only eight years out of twelve or sixteen years. But, as it now stands, he may continue in office for life; or, in other words, it will be an elective monarchy.

Gov. Randolph. Mr. Chairman, the honorable gentleman last up says that I do not mention the parts to which I object. I have hitherto mentioned my objections with freedom and candor. But, sir, I considered that our critical situation rendered adoption necessary, were it even more defective than it is. ... Every gentleman who has turned his thoughts to the subject of politics, and has considered the most eligible mode of republican government, agrees that the greatest difficulty arises from the executive—as to the time of his election, mode of his election, quantum of power, etc. I will acknowledge that, at one stage of this business, I had embraced the idea of the honorable gentleman that the reeligibility of the President was improper. But I will acknowledge that on a further consideration of the subject, and attention to the lights which were thrown upon it by others, I altered my opinion of the limitation of his eligibility. When we consider the advantages arising to us from it, we cannot object to it. That which has produced my opinion against the limitation of his eligibility is this: that it renders him more independent in his place and more solicitous of promoting the interest of his constituents; for, unless you put it in his power to be reelected, instead of being attentive to their interests he will lean to the augmentation of his private emoluments. This subject will admit of high coloring and plausible arguments but, on considering it attentively and coolly, I believe it will be found less exceptionable than any other mode. The mode of election here excludes that faction which is productive of those hostilities and confusion in Poland. It renders it unnecessary and impossible for foreign force or aid to interpose. The electors must be elected by the people at large. To procure his reelection, his influence must be coextensive with the continent. And there can be no combination between the electors, as they elect him on the same day in every state. When this is the case, how can foreign influence or intrigue enter? There is no reason to conclude from the experience of these states that he will be continually reelected. There have been several instances where officers have been displaced where they were reeligible. This has been the case with the executive of Massachusetts, and I believe of New Hampshire. It happens from the mutation of sentiments, though the officers be good.

12. The Federal Farmer XIV, January 17, 1788

The Federal Farmer was generally approving of the electoral college, which he regarded as on the whole "a judicious combination of principles and precautions." Though he expressed concerns about the possible corruption of electors, he was persuaded that "be the electors more or less democratic the president will be one of the very few of the most elevated characters" (Storing 1981, 2:310). But that did not mean that he approved of the renewable four-year term, as he makes clear in no uncertain terms in the excerpt below.

The convention, it seems, first agreed that the president should be chosen for seven years, and never after to be eligible. Whether seven years is a period too long or not is rather [a] matter of opinion, but clear it is that this mode is infinitely preferable to the one finally adopted. When a man shall get the chair, who may be reelected ... for life, his greatest object will be to keep it; to gain friends and votes, at any rate; to associate some favorite son with himself, to take the office after him. Whenever he shall have any prospect of continuing the office in himself and family, he will spare no artifice, no address, and no exertions, to increase the powers and importance of it. The servile supporters of his wishes will be placed in all offices, and tools constantly employed to aid his views and sound his praise. ... If we reason at all on the subject, we must irresistibly conclude that this will be the case with nine–tenths of the presidents. We may have, for the first president, and, perhaps, one in a century or two afterwards ... a great and good man, governed by superior motives, but these are not events to be calculated upon in the present state of human nature.

A man chosen to this important office for a limited period, and always afterwards rendered ... ineligible, will be governed by very different considerations. He can have no rational hopes or expectations of retaining his office after the expiration of a known limited time, or of continuing the office in his family, as by the constitution there must be a constant transfer of it from one man to another, and consequently from one family to another. No man will wish to be a mere cipher at the head of the government. The great object of each president then will be to render his government a glorious period in the annals of his country. When a man constitutionally retires from office, he retires without pain; he is sensible he retires because the laws direct it, and not from the success of his rivals, nor with that public disapprobation which being left out, when eligible, implies. ...

On the whole, it would be, in my opinion, almost as well to create a limited monarchy at once, and give some family permanent power and interest in the community, and let it have something valuable to itself to lose in convulsions in the state, and in attempts of usurpation, as to make a first magistrate eligible for life, and to create hopes and expectations in him and his family of obtaining what they have not. In the latter case, we actually tempt them to disturb the state, to ferment struggles and contests, by laying before them the flattering prospect of gaining much in them without risking anything.

"Additional Number of Letters from the Federal Farmer to the Republican," in *Selected Americana from Sabin's Dictionary of Books relating to America* (Woodbridge, Conn.: Primary Source Media, 1996), fiche 19,259, pp. 126–28.

13. Alexander Hamilton,
Federalist 71, March 18, 1788

On June 18 Alexander Hamilton delivered a roughly five-hour speech to the delegates at the Philadelphia Convention. At the close of the marathon speech Hamilton outlined his plan of government, which included a call for a "Governour to be elected during good behaviour" (Farrand 1937, 1:292). The Constitution's four-year term fell well short of what Hamilton felt was necessary to ensure the requisite "stability of the system of administration," but he nonetheless defended it in *Federalist* 71 because he recognized that the four-year renewable term was the best the convention could do and the most the nation would accept. Not that Hamilton disguises his own vision of the presidency altogether in *Federalist* 71; in fact, it is in this paper that Hamilton perhaps most clearly reveals his own conception of the presidency. The president, he writes, should not show "an unqualified complaisance to every sudden breeze of passion, or to every transient impulse which the people may receive from the arts of men, who flatter their prejudices to betray their interests." On the theory that the best defense is a good offense, Hamilton also launches a frontal assault on the legislature: "The representatives of the people, in a popular assembly, seem sometimes to fancy that they are the people themselves." Although a revealing statement of Hamilton's own views, *Federalist* 71 was less useful as a rebuttal to Anti–Federalist objections, since few opponents of the Constitution objected to the four-year term itself. Most critics of the presidential term would have gladly settled for a longer term of six or seven years in exchange for a bar on reeligibility.

Duration in office [is] the second requisite to the energy of the executive authority.[4] This has relation to two objects: to the personal firmness of the executive magistrate in the employment of his constitutional powers, and to the stability of the system of administration which may have been adopted under his auspices. With regard to the first, it must be evident that the longer the duration in office, the greater will be the probability of obtaining so important an advantage. ...

There are some who would be inclined to regard the servile pliancy of the executive to a prevailing current, either in the community or in the legislature, as its best recommendation. But such men entertain very crude notions ... of the purposes for which government was instituted, [as well] as of the true means by which the public happiness may be promoted. The republican principle demands that the deliberate sense of the community should govern the conduct of those to whom they intrust the management of their affairs, but it does not require an unqualified complaisance to every sudden breeze of passion, or to every transient

---

New-York Packet, March 18, 1788.
    4. The first requisite is unity, the theme of *Federalist* 70.

impulse which the people may receive from the arts of men, who flatter their prejudices to betray their interests. It is a just observation that the people commonly intend the public good. This often applies to their very errors. But their good sense would despise the adulator who should pretend that they always reason right about the means of promoting it. They know from experience that they sometimes err; and the wonder is that they so seldom err as they do, beset, as they continually are, by the wiles of parasites and sycophants, by the snares of the ambitious, the avaricious, the desperate, by the artifices of men who possess their confidence more than they deserve it, and of those who seek to possess rather than to deserve it. When occasions present themselves in which the interests of the people are at variance with their inclinations, it is the duty of the persons whom they have appointed to be the guardians of those interests, to withstand the temporary delusion in order to give them time and opportunity for more cool and sedate reflection. Instances might be cited in which a conduct of this kind has saved the people from very fatal consequences of their own mistakes, and has procured lasting monuments of their gratitude to the men who had courage and magnanimity enough to serve them at the peril of their displeasure.

But however inclined we might be to insist upon an unbounded complaisance in the executive to the inclinations of the people, we can with no propriety contend for a like complaisance to the humors of the legislature. The latter may sometimes stand in opposition to the former, and at other times the people may be entirely neutral. In either supposition, it is certainly desirable that the executive should be in a situation to dare to act his own opinion with vigor and decision.

The same rule which teaches the propriety of a partition between the various branches of power teaches us likewise that this partition ought to be so contrived as to render the one independent of the other. To what purpose separate the executive or the judiciary from the legislative, if both the executive and the judiciary are so constituted as to be at the absolute devotion of the legislative? ... In governments purely republican [the tendency of the legislative authority to absorb every other] is almost irresistible. The representatives of the people, in a popular assembly, seem sometimes to fancy that they are the people themselves, and betray strong symptoms of impatience and disgust at the least sign of opposition from any other quarter; as if the exercise of its rights, by either the executive or judiciary, were a breach of their privilege and an outrage to their dignity. They often appear disposed to exert an imperious control over the other departments; and as they commonly have the people on their side, they always act with such momentum as to make it very difficult for the other members of the government to maintain the balance of the Constitution.

It may perhaps be asked, how the shortness of the duration in office can affect the independence of the executive [from] the legislature, unless the one were possessed of the power of appointing or displacing the other. One answer to this inquiry may be drawn from the principle ... that ... a man is apt to take ... slender interest ... in a short-lived advantage, and ... it affords him ... little inducement ... to expose himself, on account of it, to any considerable inconvenience or hazard. Another answer, perhaps more obvious, though not more conclusive, will result from the consideration of the influence of the legislative body over the people, which might be employed to prevent the reelection of a man who by an upright resistance to any sinister project of that body should have made himself obnoxious to its resentment.

It may be asked also, whether a duration of four years would answer the end proposed; and if it would not, whether a less period, which would at least be recommended by greater security against ambitious designs, would not, for that reason, be preferable to a longer period, which was, at the same time, too short for the purpose of inspiring the desired firmness and independence of the magistrate.

It cannot be affirmed that a duration of four years, or any other limited duration, would completely answer the end proposed; but it would contribute towards it in a degree which would have a material influence upon the spirit and character of the government. Between the commencement and termination of such a period, there would always be a considerable interval in which the prospect of annihilation would be sufficiently remote not to have an improper effect upon the conduct of a man endued with a tolerable portion of fortitude; and in which he might reasonably promise himself that there would be time enough before it arrived to make the community sensible of the propriety of the measures he might incline to pursue. Though it be probable that as he approached the moment when the public were, by a new election, to signify their sense of his conduct, his confidence, and with it his firmness, would decline, yet both the one and the other would derive support from the opportunities which his previous continuance in the station had afforded him of establishing himself in the esteem and good will of his constituents. He might, then, hazard with safety, in proportion to the proofs he had given of his wisdom and integrity, and to the title he had acquired to the respect and attachment of his fellow citizens. As, on the one hand, a duration of four years will contribute to the firmness of the executive in a sufficient degree to render it a very valuable ingredient in the composition; so, on the other, it is not enough to justify any alarm for the public liberty.

14. Alexander Hamilton, *Federalist* 72, March 19, 1788

Federalist 72 begins by completing the unfinished business of the previous paper. Returning to the point raised in the opening sentences of *Federalist* 71, Hamilton explains the contribution that duration in office makes to "stability of the system of administration." After this brief prelude in the opening paragraph Hamilton then launches his case against reeligibility. Here at last Hamilton directly and systematically engages the Anti–Federalists' main complaint against the Constitution's plan for presidential selection.

The administration of government, in its largest sense, comprehends all the operations of the body politic, whether legislative, executive or judiciary; but in its most usual and perhaps in its most precise signification, it is limited to executive details, and falls peculiarly within the province of the executive department. The actual conduct of foreign negotiations, the preparatory plans of finance, the application and disbursement of the public moneys in conformity to the general appropriations of the legislature, the arrangement of the army and navy, the direction of the operations of war—these, and other matters of a like nature, constitute what seems to be most properly understood by the administration of government. The persons, therefore, to whose immediate management these different matters are committed,

New York *Independent Journal*, March 19, 1788.

ought to be considered as the assistants or deputies of the chief magistrate, and on this account, they ought to derive their offices from his appointment, at least from his nomination, and ought to be subject to his superintendence. This view of the subject will at once suggest to us the intimate connection between the duration of the executive magistrate in office and the stability of the system of administration. To reverse and undo what has been done by a predecessor is very often considered by a successor as the best proof he can give of his own capacity and desert; and in addition to this propensity, where the alteration has been the result of public choice, the person substituted is warranted in supposing that the dismissal of his predecessor has proceeded from a dislike to his measures, and that the less he resembles him the more he will recommend himself to the favor of his constituents. These considerations, and the influence of personal confidences and attachments, would be likely to induce every new president to promote a change of men to fill the subordinate stations, and these causes together could not fail to occasion a disgraceful and ruinous mutability in the administration of the government.

With a positive duration of considerable extent, I connect the circumstance of reeligibility. The first is necessary to give to the officer himself the inclination and the resolution to act his part well, and to the community time and leisure to observe the tendency of his measures, and thence to form an experimental estimate of their merits. The last is necessary to enable the people, when they see reason to approve of his conduct, to continue him in his station in order to prolong the utility of his talents and virtues, and to secure to the government the advantage of permanency in a wise system of administration.

Nothing appears more plausible at first sight, nor more ill-founded upon close inspection, than a scheme which in relation to the present point has had some respectable advocates. I mean that of continuing the chief magistrate in office for a certain time, and then excluding him from it, either for a limited period or forever after. This exclusion, whether temporary or perpetual, would have nearly the same effects, and these effects would be for the most part rather pernicious than salutary.

One ill effect of the exclusion would be a diminution of the inducements to good behavior. There are few men who would not feel much less zeal in the discharge of a duty, when they were permitted to entertain a hope of obtaining, by meriting, a continuance of them. This position will not be disputed so long as it is admitted that the desire of reward is one of the strongest incentives of human conduct, or that the best security for the fidelity of mankind is to make their interest coincide with their duty. Even the love of fame, the ruling passion of the noblest minds—which would prompt a man to plan and undertake extensive and arduous enterprises for the public benefit, requiring considerable time to mature and perfect them, if he could flatter himself with the prospect of being allowed to finish what he had begun—would, on the contrary, deter him from the undertaking, when he foresaw that he must quit the scene before he could accomplish the work, and must commit that, together with his own reputation, to hands which might be unequal or unfriendly to the task. The most to be expected from the generality of men, in such a situation, is the negative merit of not doing harm, instead of the positive merit of doing good.

Another ill effect of the exclusion would be the temptation to sordid views, to peculation, and, in some instances, to usurpation. An avaricious man, who might happen to fill the office, looking forward to a time when he must at all events yield up the emoluments he enjoyed, would feel a propensity, not easy to be resisted by such a man, to make the best use of the opportunity he enjoyed while it lasted, and might not scruple to have recourse to the most corrupt expedients to make the harvest as abundant as it was transitory;

though the same man, probably with a different prospect before him, might content himself with the regular perquisites of his situation, and might even be unwilling to risk the consequences of an abuse of his opportunities. His avarice might be a guard upon his avarice. Add to this that the same man might be vain or ambitious, as well as avaricious. And if he could expect to prolong his honors by his good conduct, he might hesitate to sacrifice his appetite for them to his appetite for gain. But with the prospect before him of approaching an inevitable annihilation, his avarice would be likely to get the victory over his caution, his vanity, or his ambition.

An ambitious man, too, when he found himself seated on the summit of his country's honors, when he looked forward to the time at which he must descend from the exalted eminence forever, and reflected that no exertion of merit on his part could save him from the unwelcome reverse; such a man, in such a situation, would be much more violently tempted to embrace a favorable conjuncture for attempting the prolongation of his power, at every personal hazard, than if he had the probability of answering the same end by doing his duty.

Would it promote the peace of the community, or the stability of the government to have half a dozen men who had had credit enough to be raised to the seat of the supreme magistracy, wandering among the people like discontented ghosts, and sighing for a place which they were destined never more to possess?

A third ill effect of the exclusion would be the depriving the community of the advantage of the experience gained by the chief magistrate in the exercise of his office. That experience is the parent of wisdom is an adage the truth of which is recognized by the wisest as well as the simplest of mankind. What more desirable or more essential than this quality in the governors of nations? Where more desirable or more essential than in the first magistrate of a nation? Can it be wise to put this desirable and essential quality under the ban of the Constitution, and to declare that the moment it is acquired, its possessor shall be compelled to abandon the station in which it was acquired and to which it is adapted? This, nevertheless, is the precise import of all those regulations which exclude men from serving their country, by the choice of their fellow citizens, after they have by a course of service fitted themselves for doing it with a greater degree of utility.

A fourth ill effect of the exclusion would be the banishing men from stations in which, in certain emergencies of the state, their presence might be of the greatest moment to the public interest or safety. There is no nation which has not, at one period or another, experienced an absolute necessity of the services of particular men in particular situations; perhaps it would not be too strong to say, to the preservation of its political existence. How unwise, therefore, must be every such self-denying ordinance as serves to prohibit a nation from making use of its own citizens in the manner best suited to its exigencies and circumstances! Without supposing the personal essentiality of the man, it is evident that a change of the chief magistrate, at the breaking out of a war or at any similar crisis, for another, even of equal merit, would at all times be detrimental to the community, inasmuch as it would substitute inexperience to experience, and would tend to unhinge and set afloat the already settled train of the administration.

A fifth ill effect of the exclusion would be that it would operate as a constitutional interdiction of stability in the administration. By necessitating a change of men in the first office of the nation, it would necessitate a mutability of measures. It is not generally to be expected that men will vary and measures remain uniform. The contrary is the usual course of things. And we need not be apprehensive that there will be too much stability, while there is even the option of changing; nor need we desire to prohibit the people from continuing their confidence where they think it may be safely placed, and where, by constancy on their part, they may obviate the fatal inconveniences of fluctuating councils and a variable policy.

These are some of the disadvantages which would flow from the principle of exclusion. They apply most forcibly to the scheme of a perpetual exclusion; but when we consider that even a partial exclusion would always render the readmission of the person a remote and precarious object, the observations which have been made will apply nearly as fully to one case as to the other.

What are the advantages promised to counterbalance these disadvantages? They are represented to be: 1st, greater independence in the magistrate; 2nd, greater security to the people. Unless the exclusion be perpetual, there will be no pretence to infer the first advantage. But even in that case, may he have no object beyond his present station to which he may sacrifice his independence? May he have no connections, no friends, for whom he may sacrifice it? May he not be less willing, by a firm conduct, to make personal enemies, when he acts under the impression that a time is fast approaching, on the arrival of which he not only may, but must, be exposed to their resentments, upon an equal, perhaps upon an inferior, footing? It is not an easy point to determine whether his independence would be most promoted or impaired by such an arrangement.

As to the second supposed advantage, there is still greater reason to entertain doubts concerning it. If the exclusion were to be perpetual, a man of irregular ambition, of whom alone there could be reason in any case to entertain apprehension, would, with infinite reluctance, yield to the necessity of taking his leave forever of a post in which his passion for power and preeminence had acquired the force of habit. And if he had been fortunate or adroit enough to conciliate the good will of the people, he might induce them to consider as a very odious and unjustifiable restraint upon themselves, a provision which was calculated to debar them of the right of giving a fresh proof of their attachment to a favorite. There may be conceived circumstances in which this disgust of the people, seconding the thwarted ambition of such a favorite, might occasion greater danger to liberty than could ever reasonably be dreaded from the possibility of a perpetuation in office by the voluntary suffrages of the community, exercising a constitutional privilege.

There is an excess of refinement in the idea of disabling the people to continue in office men who had entitled themselves, in their opinion, to approbation and confidence; the advantages of which are at best speculative and equivocal, and are overbalanced by disadvantages far more certain and decisive.

Questions for Discussion

1. Something like two hundred constitutional amendments have been proposed that would limit the president to a single nonrenewable term of six or seven years. A number of former presidents, including Thomas Jefferson, Lyndon Johnson, and Jimmy Carter, have supported the idea. What would be the advantages of having a president serve a longer term and be ineligible for reelection? The disadvantages? Would you vote for such amendment to the Constitution?

2. If the framers desired the president to rise above party and to resist "every sudden breeze of passion," would they have been better off giving the president a nonrenewable seven-year term? Was a renewable four-year term necessarily at odds with a vision of the presidency remaining above partisan and popular passions?

3. Should the Twenty-second Amendment be repealed? Why should we have term limits for the president when we don't have them for Congress?

5

The Electoral College

Few aspects of the American political system are more regularly or bitterly assailed than the electoral college. Historian Morton Borden, for instance, dismisses the electoral college as "a useless relic" and "the least successful of all the political devices created by the founding fathers" (1965, 207). Political scientist Lawrence Longley is no kinder, indicting the electoral college as a "deplorable" institution with "multiple flaws, possible grave consequences, and inherent gross inequalities" (1994, 200; 1998, 93). Over the first two hundred years of the republic, approximately seven hundred proposals to change the electoral college were introduced in Congress (Slonim 1986, 35). To the critics, the electoral college is plainly undemocratic as well as too complex.

The harshness with which the electoral college is criticized today contrasts markedly with the kind reception the institution received in 1787. Noah Webster, in one of the first published defenses of the Constitution, identified the mode of presidential selection to be "a capital improvement on the best governments" because it "excludes the danger of faction and corruption" (Ford [1888] 1968, 64–65).[1] Alexander Hamilton thought that the electoral college was "almost the only part of the system, of any consequence, which has escaped without severe censure, or which has received the slightest mark of approbation from its opponents" (*Federalist* 68). The Federal Farmer, though strongly critical of presidential reeligibility, judged the electoral college itself "a judicious combination of principles and precautions." Most members of the federal convention were proud of their "perfectly novel" invention (Farrand 1937, 3:403), feeling that it admirably balanced rival state interests while ensuring executive independence and protecting against intrigue and corruption, especially by a foreign power.

---

1. Over a decade later Webster, like almost all the framers, was forced to revise his view. In the margins of his own copy of the pamphlet, which he had originally published in October 1787, he now scribbled, "This proves how little dependence can be placed on theory. Twelve years experience, or four elections demonstrates the contrary" (McCormick 1982, 41; Ford [1888] 1968, 65).

For most of the framers' handiwork there are clear precedents in either colonial government, the state constitutions, or the Articles of Confederation, each of which served as models in the crafting of the federal Constitution. "Experience must be our only guide," John Dickinson instructed the delegates. "Reason may mislead us" (Farrand 1937, 2:278). But experience proved an insufficient guide when it came to devising an acceptable mode of selecting the president, and so the delegates were forced to rely on reason and imagination. Most Americans in 1787 had little more than a decade's experience with electing a chief executive. During the colonial period the governor was generally appointed by the Crown,[2] and the monarch was of course hereditary. Since the Revolution Americans had tried out, at the state level, both direct popular election and legislative election of the governor. Since neither of these options were deemed satisfactory for the president, the delegates were left to conjure up a new set of institutional arrangements.[3]

If the electoral college itself was novel, the idea of having the legislature make the selection in case no candidate received a majority of votes was not. This provision was modeled on the state constitutions of Massachusetts and New Hampshire, both of which provided that the legislature would make the choice from among the top four vote getters if no candidate for governor received a majority of the popular vote.[4] But the mode of presidential selection owed far less to state precedent than it did to the convention's own deliberations. The Brearly Committee, which reported the electoral college on September 4, was less like a magician pulling a rabbit out of a hat than a producer putting together a movie from rejected outtakes scattered across the cutting room floor. The idea of an electoral college of some sort had been proposed and rejected many times in the course of the convention: Wilson's electoral

---

2. The only colonies that elected their own governors were Rhode Island and Connecticut, both of which were self-governing corporate colonies. In the proprietary colonies of Maryland, Pennsylvania, and Delaware the governor was selected by the proprietor, though by the 1760s even this appointment had become "subject to confirmation by the crown" (Greene [1898] 1966, 46). The remaining eight colonies were royal governments in which the governor was selected directly by the Crown.

3. The closest parallel to the electoral college was in the state of Maryland, in which eligible voters selected electors who in turn elected the fifteen-member senate (Thorpe 1909, 3:1693–94). At the Massachusetts ratifying convention, Gov. James Bowdoin (who was not a delegate at the Philadelphia Convention) claimed that the electoral college was "probably taken from the manner of choosing senators under the constitution of Maryland" (Elliot 1888, 2:127–28), but there is no evidence from either the debates at the federal convention or the delegates' correspondence to support Bowdoin's claim.

4. To be more precise, the House of Representatives chose two from the top four vote getters, and the Senate chose the governor from these two. In 1855 Massachusetts amended its constitution, abolishing the legislature's role in the election process and making a plurality of the popular vote sufficient for election (Thorpe 1909, 3:1917). In 1792 New Hampshire rewrote its constitution so that if a candidate failed to get a majority of votes, the two houses by joint ballot would choose a governor from the two highest vote getters (4:2481). In Connecticut too the legislature chose the governor if no candidate received a majority of the popular vote (Purcell 1918, 180).

college proposal was rejected on June 2 by an 8 to 2 margin, Hamilton's plan of June 18 was never even brought to a vote, Luther Martin's July 17 proposal was defeated 8 to 2, Oliver Ellsworth's plan was accepted on July 19 and then reversed on July 24 by a 7 to 4 vote, and Gouverneur Morris's proposal on August 24 was defeated by 6 to 5 and then thwarted by a deadlocked 4 to 4 vote with three states either divided or abstaining. But the Brearly Committee did more than just borrow the general idea of having electors select a president. They also borrowed from the convention proceedings in constructing some of the important details. Most notably, the provision requiring that each elector vote for two persons, only one of whom could be from the elector's state, was lifted directly from a suggestion made on July 25 by Hugh Williamson and Gouverneur Morris, both of whom served on the Brearly Committee.

It is often said that the framers expected that except in rare circumstances the electoral college would essentially be a nominating device, with the final selection left to the legislature (Pious 1996, 31; Rakove 1996, 265–66). George Mason's estimate that nineteen times in twenty the legislature would make the selection is frequently taken as representative of the thinking of the framers (Roche 1961, 811). But a close reading of the convention debates suggests that opinion on this question was in fact sharply divided.[5] Those who agreed with Mason that the electoral college would rarely make the final selection believed that the voting for president would almost invariably be highly fragmented because electors would vote for their own state's favorite son. But Mason's view was strongly challenged on the floor by members of the Brearly Committee. Georgia's representative on the committee, Abraham Baldwin, countered that "increasing intercourse among the people of the States" would make national figures better known and thus make it increasingly likely that a candidate would gain a majority in the electoral college. The primary spokesman for the Brearly Committee on the convention floor, Gouverneur Morris, pointed out that the requirement that electors vote for two candidates, only one of whom could be from the elector's own state, made it probable that the election would be settled in the electoral college. Virginia's representative on the committee, James Madison, defended the committee's decision to vest the contingent election in the Senate on the grounds that since the small states predominated in the Senate the large states would have a strong incentive to avoid the contingency election and make

---

5. The evidence from the states was also mixed. Massachusetts had yet to use its runoff procedure in the contest for governor, as every winner had received a majority of the popular vote, usually a decisive majority. In 1780, for instance, John Hancock polled almost 90 percent of the votes, and in 1787 Hancock beat his opponent by a 3 to 1 margin (Allan 1948, 295, 323). New Hampshire, though, was a different story. In two of the first four elections, in 1785 and 1787, no candidate received a majority of popular votes, forcing the decision into the legislature. In both cases the Senate passed over the leading vote getter and selected as president the candidate who had received the second most popular votes (Turner 1984, 64–65).

sure the selection was made by the electoral college. If the contingent election was to be made by the legislature as a whole, as Pennsylvania's James Wilson proposed, this incentive would be eroded and selection by the legislature would become more likely. Though Madison would have preferred to see the committee go further to realize the goal of "render[ing] an eventual resort to any part of the Legislature improbable" (September 5),[6] he would never have supported the electoral college had he believed it to be, as Mason charged, a de facto legislative election. Nor would he, as he did in the closing days of the convention, have described the president as being "elected by the people" (Farrand 1937, 2:587).

The creation of the electoral college was a mixed motive game. Delegates from large states could support it in the knowledge that they would dominate the electoral college, which they had sound reasons to expect would make the final selection.[7] Small state representatives could support it in the plausible hope that elections would frequently be thrown into the Senate (or, as it was amended on the floor, in the House of Representatives with each state possessing an equal vote). It was a compromise made possible by the uncertainty that inevitably accompanied an institution with which no delegate had any practical experience. For instance, the provision that electors must cast two votes could be seen as helping candidates from the smaller states since, as Hugh Williamson explained, the second vote would be "as probably of a small as a large [state]" (July 25), but a case could also be made that it would advantage the large states since, as Morris emphasized (September 5), it would make it less likely that the selection would be thrown into the legislature. Theories and reasons abounded, but in truth no one really had a clear sense

---

6. Hence the proposals Madison (along with Williamson) made on the floor of the convention, first, to make one-third rather than a majority of the electoral votes sufficient for victory and, second, to exclude nonvoting electors in computing what constituted a majority of the electoral votes. Both motions, offered on September 5, were defeated.

7. Historian Shlomo Slonim emphasizes that the distribution of electors was itself a concession to the small states, since every state, no matter its size, received three electoral votes. In the electoral college, the ratio between Delaware and Virginia, the smallest and the largest state in the union, was 1 to 4, whereas had population alone been the criterion the ratio would have been more like 1 to 10 (1986, 52; also see Farrand 1937, 2:403). But though small states certainly were overrepresented in the electoral college, small state representatives did not seem to view this aspect of the Brearly report as a concession to them. Indeed an earlier proposal (July 20) to establish a ratio of 1 to 3 electors between the smallest and largest states had been supported by each of the largest states and opposed by the smaller states of Delaware, New Jersey, Maryland, and Georgia. Moreover, at the time the Brearly committee offered its scheme to make the number of electors each state received equal to the number of representatives and senators, the alternative before the convention was legislative election and not direct popular election, so there was no reason for the small states to see the ratio established in the electoral college as a net gain for them. The attraction of the Brearly committee's scheme allocating electors based on representation in Congress was primarily that it provided a simple, workable formula that allowed the delegates to avoid a messy fight over which states would get how many electors and how that ratio would change in the future to accommodate shifts in population.

of how this novel creation would actually work, which probably explains why critics and defenders alike did such a poor job of anticipating the problems the electoral college would generate, problems that would become apparent to the framers almost immediately.

Even before the first presidential election had been held, concerns about the mechanics of the electoral college began to surface. Less than a year after stoutly defending the electoral college in *Federalist* 68, Hamilton confided to James Wilson his fear that the system might malfunction. "Every body," he wrote Wilson, "is aware of that defect in the constitution which renders it possible that the man intended for Vice President may in fact turn up President. Every body sees that unanimity in [John] Adams as Vice President and a few votes insidiously witheld [sic] from Washington might substitute the former to the latter" (Syrett 1961–1987, 5:248). Such a result was possible because the Constitution required electors to vote for two persons but did not establish separate ballots for president and vice president. The development of political parties in the 1790s exacerbated this hypothetical problem because now, even if no votes were "insidiously withheld," the winning party's presidential and vice presidential candidates would receive an equal number of votes and the election would be thrown into the House of Representatives. In an attempt to avoid this scenario the Federalists in the 1796 election arranged to withhold votes from their party's vice presidential candidate, Thomas Pinckney, so that he and the Federalist presidential candidate, John Adams, would not end up with the same number of votes. But the Federalists miscalculated, withholding enough votes from Pinckney that the opposition party's presidential candidate, Thomas Jefferson, became vice president. Trying to avoid a repeat of the 1796 fiasco, the parties ran into a far greater calamity in 1800. Thomas Jefferson, the Republican presidential candidate, received the same number of votes as the party's vice presidential candidate, Aaron Burr, throwing the election into the House of Representatives. After thirty-six ballots and much cynical maneuvering by the defeated Federalists, who tried to throw the House election to Burr, Jefferson finally received a majority of the votes and became president. The crisis had been averted but the harrowing experience prompted the nation to pass the Twelfth Amendment (see appendix 5), which remedied the problem by setting up separate ballots for president and vice president.[8]

How could the framers have made such an elementary and colossal blunder? No less puzzling, why did opponents of the Constitution, who were generally so eager to seize on the document's weaknesses, never once expose this basic flaw in the mechanics of the electoral college? The short answer is that neither supporters nor opponents of the Constitution anticipated the formation of organized national political parties. The framers hoped and even ex-

---

8. The Twelfth Amendment also limited the House to the top three rather than the top five vote getters in those cases in which no candidate received a majority of the electoral votes.

pected elections to be nonpartisan affairs in which the most revered man in the country would be selected president and the next most respected man would be chosen vice president. But once political parties fielded a ticket made up of a presidential and a vice presidential candidate, as they began to do in 1796, the electoral college broke down almost completely. Ironically it was the creation of the presidency, an office the framers hoped would be above parties and factions, that was probably the greatest stimulus to the national party organization that destroyed the framers' plan of presidential selection.

Yet to paint the electoral college as an unmitigated failure is too harsh a judgment. After all, the electoral college, as amended, continues to function to this day. To be sure, it operates in ways that little resemble the plan envisioned by the framers. The framers imagined that the electors would exercise a meaningful choice but the emergence of political parties quickly turned electors into automatons, mere adding devices for recording the views of the state's voters. Though few voters may understand the electoral college, many political scientists maintain that the college serves a number of important ends. Its winner-take-all system, it is argued, fosters moderation and coalition building by encouraging candidates to focus their attention on highly competitive, large states, states that typically possess extremely diverse populations. Defenders of the electoral college also point out that the alternative of a direct popular election would require either an expensive runoff between the top two candidates or accepting a president who had only achieved the support of a minority of the population. The latter option is particularly troubling because in a crowded field a candidate could win by mobilizing an intense minority, thus promoting a politics of division rather than the compromise and coalition building that are privileged under the current system. If the electoral college violates popular sovereignty (by allotting electors based not only on population but on states), it is no worse a violation than the Senate itself, which gives every state, no matter its population, the same number of representatives. The electoral college, as the founders intended, preserves a role in our democracy for the states.[9] On the other hand, should an election be thrown into the House of Representatives (as happened in 1824) or should a candidate win the popular vote but not triumph in the electoral vote (as happened in 1876 and 1888) Americans can be expected to give the electoral college a long, hard second look.

---

9. "The executive power," Madison explained in *Federalist* 39, "will be derived from a very compound source. The immediate election of the President is to be made by the States in their political characters. The votes allotted to them are in a compound ratio, which considers them partly as distinct and coequal societies, partly as unequal members of the same society. The eventual election, again, is to be made by that branch of the legislature which consists of the national representatives; but in this particular act they are to be thrown into the form of individual delegations from so many distinct and co-equal bodies politic. From this aspect of the government it appears to be of a mixed character, presenting at least as many federal as national features" (*Federalist* 39; also see Madison to Henry Lee, January 14, 1825, in Farrand 1937, 3:464).

15. William Grayson,
George Mason, and James Madison,
Virginia Ratifying Convention, June 18, 1788

Among the most frequently expressed worries about the electoral college today is what hypothetically might happen. A person could win the presidency, it is sometimes pointed out, and yet carry, even by paper-thin margins, only eleven of the fifty states. Or a razor-close election could be decided by a single "faithless elector" casting his vote for someone other than the person he was pledged to support. One of the few Anti-Federalist critics to focus on such hypothetical possibilities was William Grayson at the Virginia ratifying convention. In an argument that retains its cogency today, Grayson zeroes in on the undemocratic possibilities that could occur if the election were to be thrown into the House. Much like defenders of the electoral college today, Madison answers Grayson by insisting that "a bare calculation of possibility ought [not] to govern us." Madison also responds to the criticisms of George Mason who scores the electoral college as a "mere deception" since only one time in fifty (up from his 1 in 20 estimate at the federal convention) would the contest be decided by the people in the electoral college. For Mason, like Grayson, the problem is not the electoral college itself but the contingency election in the legislature.

Mr. Grayson. The executive ... is to be elected by a number of electors in the country, but the principle is changed when no person has a majority of the whole number of electors appointed or when more than one have such a majority and have an equal number of votes, for then the lower house is to vote by states. ... It seems rather founded on accident than any principle of government I ever heard of. ... I have an extreme objection to the mode of his election. I presume the seven eastern States will always elect him. As he is vested with the power of making treaties, and as there is a material distinction between the carrying and productive states, the former will be disposed to have him to themselves. He will accommodate himself to their interests in forming treaties, and they will continue him perpetually in office. Thus mutual interest will lead them reciprocally to support one another. It will be a government of a faction, and this observation will apply to every part of it; for, having a majority, they may do what they please. I have made an estimate which shows with what facility they will be able to reelect him. The number of electors is equal to the number of representatives and senators: ninety-one. They are to vote for two persons. They give, therefore, one hundred and eighty-two votes. Let there be forty-five votes for four different candidates, and two for the President. He is one of the five highest if he have but two votes, which he may easily purchase. In this case ... the election is to be by the representatives, according to

Jonathan Elliot, ed., *The Debates in the Several State Constitutions on the Adoption of the Federal Constitution* (New York: Burt Franklin, 1888), 3:490–95.

states. Let New Hampshire be for him, a majority of its 3 representatives is 2, a majority of Rhode Island's 1 representative is 1, Connecticut's 5 representatives is 3, New Jersey's 4 representatives is 3, Delaware's 1 representative is 1, Georgia's 3 representatives is 2, and North Carolina's 5 representatives is 3. Thus the majority of seven states is but 15, while the minority amounts to 50. The total number of voices (91 electors and 65 representatives) is 156, [but the] voices in favor of the President are 2 state electors and 15 representatives. So that the President may be reelected by the voices of 17 against 139.

It may be said that this is an extravagant case and will never happen. In my opinion, it will often happen. A person who is a favorite of Congress, if he gets but two votes of electors, may, by the subsequent choice of 15 representatives, be elected President. Surely the possibility of such a case ought to be excluded. I shall postpone mentioning in what manner he ought to be elected till we come to offer amendments.

Mr. Mason contended that this mode of election was a mere deception ... on the American people ... thrown out to make them believe they were to choose him; whereas it would not be once out of fifty times that he would be chosen by them in the first instance. ... If the localities of the states were considered, and the probable diversity of the opinions of the people attended to, he thought it would be found that so many persons would be voted for that there seldom or never could be a majority in favor of one, except one great name [George Washington], who, he believed, would be unanimously elected. He then continued thus:—A majority of the whole number of electors is necessary to elect the President. It is not the greatest number of votes that is required, but a majority of the whole number of electors. If there be more than one having such majority, and an equal number, one of them is to be chosen by ballot of the House of Representatives. But if no one have a majority of the actual number of electors appointed, how is he to be chosen? From the five highest on the list, by ballot of the lower house, and the votes to be taken by states. I conceive he ought to be chosen from the two highest on the list. This would be simple and easy; then, indeed, the people would have some agency in the election. But when it is extended to the five highest, a person having a very small number of votes may be elected. This will almost constantly happen. The states may choose the man in whom they have most confidence. This, in my opinion, is a very considerable defect. The people will, in reality, have no hand in the election.

Mr. Madison. ... It was found difficult in the Convention, and will be found so by any gentleman who will take the liberty of delineating a mode of electing the President that would exclude those inconveniences which they apprehend. I would not contend against some of the principles laid down by some gentlemen, if the interests of some states only were to be consulted. But there is a great diversity of interests. The choice of the people ought to be attended to. I have found no better way of selecting the man in whom they place the highest confidence than that delineated in the plan of the Convention, nor has the gentleman told us. Perhaps it will be found impracticable to elect him by the immediate suffrages of the people. Difficulties would arise from the extent and population of the states. Instead of this, the people choose the electors.

This can be done with ease and convenience, and will render the choice more judicious. As to the eventual voting by states, it has my approbation. The lesser states, and some large states, will be generally pleased by that mode. The deputies from the small states argued (and there is some force in their reasoning) that when the people voted the large states evidently had the advantage over the rest, and, without varying the mode, the interest of the little states might be neglected or sacrificed. Here is a compromise; for in the eventual election, the small states will have the advantage. In so extensive a country, it is probable that many persons will be voted for, and the lowest of the five highest on the list may not be so inconsiderable as he supposes. With respect to the possibility that a small number of votes may decide his election, I do not know how, nor do I think that a bare calculation of possibility ought to govern us. One honorable gentleman has said that the Eastern States may, in the eventual election, choose him. But, in the extravagant calculation he has made, he has been obliged to associate North Carolina and Georgia with the five smallest Northern States. There can be no union of interest or sentiments between states so differently situated.

16. North Carolina Ratifying Convention, July 26, 1788

This brief exchange at the North Carolina convention touches on a critically important question that had been artfully elided by the Brearly Committee: who would select the electors and how. In the early days of the convention James Wilson had proposed having electors popularly elected by congressional districts, and in the middle of July Oliver Ellsworth briefly gained support for his idea of electors selected by state legislatures. By opting to leave each state to appoint electors "in such manner as the Legislature thereof may direct," the framers avoided a convention floor fight over this issue, leaving it to the state legislatures to contest and experiment. And experiment they did. Massachusetts altered its system of selecting electors no fewer than seven times in the first ten presidential elections, often to suit short-term partisan interests. Massachusetts may have been extreme but it was hardly unusual. Speaking on the floor of the Senate in 1818, New Jersey's Mahlon Dickerson lamented that "the discordant systems adopted by the different states are the subject of constant fluctuation and change—of frequent, hasty and rash experiment—established, altered, abolished, re-established, according to the dictates of the interest, ambition, the whim or caprice, of party and faction" (Peirce and Longley 1981, 44). Although there were a variety of hybrid systems tried in the early republic, the three main systems used were legislative selection, popular election by district, and popular election under a general ticket system in which the electors were chosen on a winner-take-all statewide basis. Through the first quarter century of the republic about half the states used legislative election, a quarter picked electors by district, and a quarter used the general ticket method. After 1820, though, the general ticket method began to win out. The spread of democratic ideas eroded the practice of legislative selection, which by 1832 existed in only one state, South Car-

---

Jonathan Elliot, ed., *The Debates in the Several State Constitutions on the Adoption of the Federal Constitution* (New York: Burt Franklin, 1888), 4:105

olina. The district system, favored by many of the leading statesmen of the founding generation, including Madison, Jefferson, and Hamilton, also rapidly withered after 1824 as states found that dividing their votes diluted their influence. After 1832 every state but South Carolina used statewide popular election to select electors.[10]

Gov. Johnston expressed doubts with respect to the persons by whom the electors were to be appointed. Some, he said, were of [the] opinion that the people at large were to choose them, and others thought the state legislatures were to appoint them.

Mr. Iredell was of the opinion that it could not be done with propriety by the state legislatures, because, as they were to direct the manner of appointing, a law would look very awkward which should say, "They gave the power of such appointments to themselves."

Mr. Maclaine thought the state legislatures might direct the electors to be chosen in what manner they thought proper, and they might direct it to be done by the people at large.

Mr. Davie was of the opinion that it was left to the wisdom of the legislatures to direct their election in whatever manner they thought proper.

17. Republicus, February 16 and March 1, 1788

Among the more common Anti-Federalist criticisms of the electoral college was that it created an intermediate body separating the president from the people. Mercy Otis Warren, writing under the pseudonym "A Columbian Patriot," complained that the electoral college was "nearly tantamount to the exclusion of the voice of the people in the choice of their first magistrate. It is vesting the choice solely in an aristocratic junto" (Storing 1981, 4:278). Cato similarly objected to the indirect procedure by which the president "arrives to this office at the fourth or fifth hand," insisting that "the representative of the people should be of their immediate choice" (2:115; also 5:87). In the selection below, Republicus develops the case against the electoral college as a violation of the simple democratic principle of one person one vote. Taking democracy seriously, for Republicus, meant opposing not only the electoral college but also the Senate, which he scores as violating democracy both in how it was to be selected (by state legislatures) and whom it represented (states rather than the people).

Kentucke Gazette, February 16, 1788; March 1, 1788.

10. South Carolina finally abandoned legislative election of electors during the Civil War. Colorado used legislative election of electors in the 1876 election (on a one-time-only basis) because the election followed so closely on the heels of its having been admitted to the Union (Berns 1992, 9). In the 1960s Maine adopted a district system of election, and Nebraska also currently selects electors by district. Other states occasionally consider switching to the district system (Glennon 1992, 74) but invariably pull back for fear that splitting their state's electoral votes would diminish the attention the state would receive in the campaign and diminish the state's influence in the selection process.

Civil government originates ... with the people. ... They form the compact, they prescribe the rules and they also enact them or delegate others to do it for them. [Public officials] are ... in the proper sense of the word their servants and accountable to them and to them only how they execute those trusts; as really so as the man whom I employ for daily wages is accountable to me and to me only how he performs my business. [Public officials] are therefore to be chosen by them, and that in a way perfectly consistent with the equality of [the people's] right; because if they have an equal natural right to legislative and executive power in all their different branches, which takes in all the powers that can exist in a state, none can have a right to exercise any of those powers but by appointment or delegation. Consequently those who are thus chose by them to the executive department are as really their representatives, as those similarly chosen to the legislature. ...

It is a well-known maxim that the simpler a machine is ... the more perfect [it is]. The reason on which it is grounded is obvious; namely, because it is the less liable to disorder, the disorder more easily discovered, and when discovered, more easily repaired, and in no instance is this maxim more applicable than in the great machine of government. ...

I go now to Article 2, Section 1, which vests the supreme continental executive power in a president: in order to the choice of whom, the legislative body of each state is empowered to point out to their constituents some mode of choice, or (to save trouble) may choose themselves a certain number of electors, who shall meet in their respective states, and vote by ballot, for two persons, one of whom, at least, shall not be an inhabitant of the same state with themselves. Or in other words, they shall vote for two, one or both of whom they know nothing of. An extraordinary refinement this, on the plain simple business of election; and of which the grand convention have certainly the honor of being the first inventors; and that for an officer too of so much importance as a president, invested with legislative and executive powers, who is to be commander in chief of the army, navy, militia, etc., grant reprieves and pardons, have a temporary negative on all bills and resolves, convene and adjourn both houses of congress, be supreme conservator of laws, commission all officers, make treaties, etc. etc., and who is to continue four years, and is only removable on conviction of treason or bribery. And trial be only by the senate, who are to be his own council [and] whose interest in every instance runs parallel with his own, and who are neither the officers of the people nor accountable to them. Is it then become necessary that a free people should first resign their right of suffrage into other hands besides their own, and then, secondly, that they to whom they resign it, should be compelled to choose men, whose persons, characters, manners, or principles they know nothing of; and after all ... to intrust Congress with the final decision at last? Is it necessary, is it rational that the sacred rights of mankind should thus dwindle down to electors, of electors, and those again electors of other electors. ...

I would ask (considering how prone mankind are to engross power and then to abuse it), is it not probable, at least possible, that the president who is to be vested with all this demi-omnipotence, who is not chosen by the community and who consequently as to them is irresponsible and independent; that he ... by a few artful and dependent emissaries in congress may not only perpetuate his own personal administration, but also make it hereditary. ...

To conclude, I can think of but one source of right to government, or any branch of it; and that is the people. They, and only they, have a right to determine whether they will make laws, or execute them, or do both in a collective body, or by a delegated authority. Delegation is a positive actual investiture. Therefore if any people are subjected to an authority which they have not thus actually chosen, even though they may have tamely submitted to it, yet it is not their legitimate government. They are wholly passive and, as far as they are so, are in a state of slavery. Thank heaven we are not yet arrived at that state; and while we continue to have sense enough to discover and detect, and virtue enough to detest and oppose every attempt, either of force or fraud, either from without or within, to bring us into it, we never will.

18. Alexander Hamilton, *Federalist* 68, March 12, 1788

Political scientists wanting to understand the meaning of the Constitution frequently turn to the *Federalist* papers. Often these essays are a useful guide to what the framers thought they were doing, but at other times they can be quite misleading. Nowhere is a reliance on *The Federalist* more problematic than in the case of the electoral college. Generations of students of the presidency have cited Hamilton's *Federalist* 68 as evidence that the electoral college was designed as an undemocratic device to wrest the power of choosing the president out of the hands of the many and to place it in the more reliable hands of a discerning few. "A small number of citizens, selected by their fellow citizens from the general mass," writes Hamilton, "will be most likely to possess the information and discernment requisite to such complicated investigations." Although this passage tells us a good deal about Hamilton, it reveals relatively little about the origins of the electoral college. To begin with, there was little agreement about what sorts of people would likely be selected as electors. Hugh Williamson felt sure the electors would "not be men of the 1st. nor even of the 2d. grade in the States"; the best men "would all prefer a seat either in the Senate or in the other branch of the Legislature" (July 24; also see July 19). Pinckney too thought the electors would be relatively parochial and thus "strangers to the several candidates and of course unable to decide on their comparative merits" (September 4). Since the choice of electors would be exercised in many cases by the state legislatures (not until 1828 did Hamilton's state of New York abandon legislative selection of electors), it is highly improbable that framers like Hamilton and Madison, both of whom were deeply skeptical of the wisdom and integrity of state legislatures, could have been particularly confident that electors would regularly be made up of the state's enlightened elite.[11] Moreover, at the federal convention no proponent of the electoral college argued that it would refine popular opinion; in fact most of those who advocated a system of electors, including Wilson, Morris, and Madison,

---

New York *Independent Journal*, March 12, 1788.
    11. Though Madison preferred electors to be popularly elected by district, he recognized that the state legislatures "must in all cases have a great share in [the president's] appointment, and will perhaps in most cases of themselves determine it" (*Federalist* 45).

preferred direct popular election of the president. The electoral college owed relatively little to elitism and a great deal to political concerns about who benefits. "The principle objection against an election by the people," as Williamson stated it, "seemed to be, the disadvantage under which it would place the smaller States" (July 25). By allotting each state the same number of electors as it had senators and representatives, the electoral college allowed the framers to settle the dispute between small states and large states, slave states and non-slave states, using the same principles and mechanisms they had used to settle their disagreements over representation in the legislature.

The mode of appointment of the chief magistrate of the United State is almost the only part of the system, of any consequence, which has escaped without severe censure, or which has received the slightest mark of approbation from its opponents. The most plausible of these who has appeared in print [the Federal Farmer] has even deigned to admit that the election of the president is pretty well guarded. I venture somewhat further, and hesitate not to affirm that if the manner of it be not perfect it is at least excellent. ...

It was desirable that the sense of the people should operate in the choice of the person to whom so important a trust was to be confided. This end will be answered by committing the right of making it not to any pre-established body but to men, chosen by the people for the special purpose, and at the particular conjuncture.

It was equally desirable that the immediate election should be made by men most capable of analyzing the qualities adapted to the station, and acting under circumstances favorable to deliberation and to a judicious combination of all the reasons and inducements which were proper to govern their choice. A small number of persons, selected by their fellow citizens from the general mass, will be most likely to possess the information and discernment requisite to such complicated investigations.

It was also peculiarly desirable to afford as little opportunity as possible to tumult and disorder. This evil was not least to be dreaded in the election of a magistrate who was to have so important an agency in the administration of the government as the president of the United States. But the precautions which have been so happily concerted in the system under consideration promise an effectual security against this mischief. The choice of several to form an intermediate body of electors will be much less apt to convulse the community with any extraordinary or violent movements than the choice of one who was himself to be the final object of the public wishes. And as the electors, chosen in each state, are to assemble and vote in the state in which they are chosen, this detached and divided situation will expose them much less to heats and ferments, which might be communicated from them to the people, than if they were all to be convened at one time, in one place.

Nothing was more to be desired than that every practicable obstacle should be opposed to cabal, intrigue and corruption. These most deadly adversaries of republican government might naturally have been expected to make their approaches from more than one quarter, but chiefly from the desire in foreign powers to gain an improper ascendance in our councils. How could they better gratify this, than by raising a creature of their own to the chief magistracy of the union? But the convention have guarded against all danger of this sort with the most provident and judicious attention. They have not made the appointment of the president to depend on any pre-existing bodies of men who might be tampered with beforehand to prostitute their votes; but they have referred it in the first instance to an immediate act of the people of America, to be exerted in the choice of persons for the temporary and sole purpose of making the appointment. And they have excluded from eligibility to this trust all those who from situation might be suspected of too great devotion to the president in office. No senator, representative, or other person holding a place of trust or profit under the United States, can be of the number of the electors. Thus, without corrupting the body of the people, the immediate agents in the election will at least enter upon the task free from any sinister bias. Their transient existence and their detached situation ... afford a satisfactory prospect of their continuing so, to the conclusion of it. ...

Another and no less important desideratum was that the executive should be independent for his continuance in office on all but the people themselves. He might otherwise be tempted to sacrifice his duty to his complaisance for those whose favor was necessary to the duration of his official consequence. This advantage will also be secured by making his reelection to depend on a special body of representatives, deputed by the society for the single purpose of making the important choice.

All these advantages will be happily combined in the plan devised by the convention. ... This process of election affords a moral certainty that the office of president will never fall to the lot of any man who is not in an eminent degree endowed with the requisite qualifications. Talents for low intrigue and the little arts of popularity may alone suffice to elevate a man to the first honors in a single state, but it will require other talents and a different kind of merit to establish him in the esteem and confidence of the whole union, or of so considerable a portion of it as would be necessary to make him a successful candidate for the distinguished office of president of the United States. It will not be too strong to say that there will be a constant probability of seeing the station filled by characters preeminent for ability and virtue. And this will be thought no inconsiderable recommendation of the constitution by those who are able to estimate the share which the executive in every government must necessarily have in its good or ill administration. Though we cannot acquiesce in the political heresy of the poet who says—

"For forms of government let facts contest
That which is best administered is best."

—yet we may safely pronounce, that the true test of a good government is its aptitude and tendency to produce a good administration.

19. James Madison to George Hay, August 23, 1823

Passage of the Twelfth Amendment (see appendix 5) did not put an end to dissatisfaction with the electoral college nor did it end efforts to fix its perceived failings. Even "the father of the Constitution" himself, James Madison, entered into the game toward the end of his life. In this letter, written several years after he had left the presidency, Madison offers his diagnosis of the electoral college's failings and his prescription for change.

Gaillard Hunt, ed., *The Writings of James Madison* (New York: Putnam's, 1906), 9:147–54.

I have received your letter of the 11th ... containing your remarks on the present mode of electing a President, and your proposed remedy for its defects. ... The difficulty of finding an unexceptionable process for appointing the Executive Organ of a Government such as that of the U.S. was deeply felt by the Convention; and as the final arrangement of it took place in the latter stage of the Session, it was not exempt from a degree of the hurrying influence produced by fatigue and impatience in all such Bodies, though the degree was much less than usually prevails in them.

The part of the arrangement which casts the eventual appointment on the House of Representatives voting by States was, as you presume, an accommodation to the anxiety of the smaller States for their sovereign equality, and to the jealousy of the larger towards the cumulative functions of the Senate. The agency of the House of Representatives was thought safer also than that of the Senate on account of the greater number of its members. It might indeed happen that the event would turn on one or two States having one or two Representatives only; but even in that case, the representations of most of the States being numerous, the House would present greater obstacles to corruption than the Senate with its paucity of members. It may be observed also that although for a certain period the evil of State votes given by one or two individuals would be extended by the introduction of new States, it would be rapidly diminished by growing populations within extensive territories. At the present period, the evil is at its maximum. Another Census will leave none of the States existing or in embryo, in the numerical rank of Rhode Island and Delaware. ...

But with all possible abatements the present rule of voting for President by the House of Representatives is so great a departure from the Republican principle of numerical equality, and even from the federal rule which qualifies the numerical by a State equality, and is so pregnant also with a mischievous tendency in practice, that an amendment of the Constitution on this point is justly called for by all its considerate and best friends.

I agree entirely with you in thinking that the election of Presidential Electors by districts is an amendment very proper to be brought forward at the same time with that relating to the eventual choice of President by the House of Representatives.[12] The district mode was mostly, if not exclusively in view when the Constitution was framed and adopted; and was exchanged from the general ticket and the legislative election as the only expedient for baffling the policy of the particular States which had set the example. A constitutional establishment of that mode will doubtless aid in reconciling the smaller States to the other change which they will regard as a concession on their part. And it may not be without a value in another important respect. The States when voting for President by general tickets or by their Legislatures, are a string of beads; when they make their elections by districts, some of these differing in sentiment from others, and sympathizing with that of districts in other States, they are so knit together as to break the force of those geographical and other noxious parties. ...

Of the different remedies you propose for the failure of a majority of Electoral votes for any one candidate, I like best that which refers the final choice to a joint vote of the two Houses of Congress, restricted to the two highest names on the Electoral lists. It might be a

---

12. Such an amendment had come close to congressional passage just a few years earlier. In 1820 an amendment calling for selection of electors by district passed the Senate by a better than two-thirds margin, but a similarly worded amendment in the House fell a few votes shy of the two-thirds majority necessary to send the amendment to the states for ratification (Peirce and Longley 1981, 133)

question whether the three instead of the two highest names might not be put within the choice of Congress, inasmuch as it not infrequently happens that the candidate third on the list of votes would in a question with either of the two first outvote him, and, consequently be the real preference of the voters. But this advantage of opening a wider door and a better chance to merit may be outweighed by an increased difficulty in obtaining a prompt and quiet decision by Congress with three candidates before them, supported by three parties, no one of them making a majority of the whole.

The mode which you seem to approve, of making a *plurality* of Electoral votes a definitive appointment, would have the merit of avoiding the Legislative agency in appointing the Executive; but might it not, by multiplying hopes and chances, stimulate intrigue and exertion, as well as incur too great a risk of success to a very inferior candidate? Next to the propriety of having a President the real choice of a majority of his constituents, it is desirable that he should inspire respect and acquiescence. ...

Having thus made the remarks to which your communication led, with a frankness which I am sure you will not disapprove, whatever errors you may find in them, I will sketch for your consideration a substitute which has occurred to myself for the faulty part of the Constitution in question.

"The Electors to be chosen in districts ... and the arrangement of the districts not to be alterable within the period of _____ previous to the election of President. Each Elector to give two votes, one naming his first choice, the other his next choice. If there be a majority of all the votes on the first list for the same person, he of course to be President; if not, and there be a majority (which may well happen) on the other list for the same person, he then to be the final choice; if there be no such majority on either list, then a choice to be made by joint ballot of the two Houses of Congress, from the two names having the greatest number of votes on the two lists taken together." Such a process would avoid the inconvenience of a second resort to the electors; and furnish a double chance of avoiding an eventual resort to Congress.

Questions for Discussion

1. Many of the founding generation, including Madison, Jefferson, and Hamilton, preferred that electors be selected using the district system. Had the Constitution required electors to be selected by district how might the course of American politics have been changed?

2. Is the electoral college an archaic, outdated institution that should be abolished in favor of direct election of the president? How would moving to direct election likely affect candidate strategies, political parties, and the political system?

3. At the federal convention George Mason wanted the president to be elected by the national legislature not the people, saying that "it would be as unnatural to refer the choice of a proper character for chief Magistrate to the people, as it would, to refer a trial of colours to a blind man." Yet at the Virginia ratifying convention Mason criticized the electoral college's contin-

gency arrangement by which the president would be selected by the legislature, complaining that "the people will, in reality, have no hand in the election." Is it possible to find consistency in these two positions?

4. If a second constitutional convention were held today, what changes would likely be made to the mode of presidential selection? Which changes do you think should be made?

III

Empowering
the President

6

To Veto or Not to Veto

Every Bill which shall have passed the House of Representatives and the Senate, shall, before it becomes a Law, be presented to the President of the United States; If he approve he shall sign it, but if not he shall return it, with his Objections to that House in which it shall have originated, who shall enter the objections at large on their Journal, and proceed to reconsider it. If after such Reconsideration two thirds of that House shall agree to pass the Bill, it shall be sent, together with the Objections, to the other House ... and if approved by two thirds of that House, it shall become a Law.

Article 1, section 7

When the colonists drew up their list of grievances against King George III in the Declaration of Independence, their first complaint was that "he has refused his Assent to Laws, the most wholesome and necessary for the public good." When new state constitutions were drawn up in 1776 and 1777, only South Carolina vested the power to veto legislation in a governor, and that decision was quickly reversed by the South Carolinians in their revised constitution of 1778. Yet a decade later the framers at the federal convention decided, with little disagreement, to vest a qualified veto in the president. The debate over the veto power at the convention focused not on whether to give the president a veto but whether the power should be absolute or qualified, and if qualified whether the override should be two-thirds or three-fourths. There was also a persistent minority, headed by James Madison, who favored giving the veto power to a council of revision consisting of the president and several members of the national judiciary.[1]

---

1. This provision was so important to Madison and his allies that the idea was proposed on no less than four separate occasions. Debate on the eighth resolution of the Virginia Plan commenced on June 4; after its defeat it was proposed again by James Wilson two days later but met with the same fate. Unfazed, Wilson reintroduced the idea on July 21 only to see it defeated once more. Finally Madison floated a modified version of the proposal one last time on August 15, but with the same unsuccessful result.

The model for the idea of a council of revision was the New York constitution of 1777, which gave a qualified veto power (subject to a two-thirds
override) to a council composed of the governor, the state's Supreme Court
justices, and the chancellor of the court of chancery. Drafted by the likes of
Gouverneur Morris, John Jay, and Robert Livingston, the New York constitution explained that the aim of granting a veto power was to remedy those situations in which the legislature "hastily and unadvisedly passed ... laws inconsistent with the spirit of this constitution, or with the public good" (Thorpe
1909, 5:2628). The council was not shy about using its veto power, negating
ten bills in its first three years, and fifty-eight bills in the first decade of its
existence (Spitzer 1988, 9).[2]

Madison was among those who were greatly impressed with the operation
of New York's Council of Revision as a "security against fluctuating & in-
degested laws" (Hutchinson et al. 1962–, 8:351). He recommended such a
council when asked in 1785 for his ideas for a constitution for the state of
Kentucky (8:351), and when offering his thoughts for a new government to
both Randolph and Washington in the spring of 1787 he again proposed "a
council of revision" composed of "the great ministerial officers" (9:370, 385).
An elaborated version of Madison's suggestion became the eighth resolution
of the Virginia Plan, which called for a council of revision consisting of "the
Executive and a convenient number of the National Judiciary," with a qualified veto over national legislation (the percentage required for overriding the
veto was left unspecified).[3]

The other model of executive veto power that the delegates had before
them was the Massachusetts constitution of 1780, which vested a qualified
veto power (again subject to a two-thirds legislative override[4]) in the governor alone. Why did Madison prefer New York's council of revision to the
Massachusetts model? Far from indicating a fear of executive power, Madison's preference for the New York plan seems to have been motivated by a

---

2. The Council of Revision existed until 1821, when New York wrote a new constitution that
gave the veto power to the governor alone (Spitzer 1988, 153 n. 3).

3. One suspects that Madison's thought about lodging the veto in "the great ministerial officers" may have run afoul of fellow Virginian George Mason. In notes for a speech he planned to
deliver on June 4, Mason recorded his belief that the council of revision as constituted in the
Virginia Plan was "the wisest and safest mode of constituting this important Council of Revision" but that the idea of forming such a council out of "the principal Officers of the State" (an
idea, he said, which had "been suggested, either within or without doors") was a terrible mistake.
"We can hardly find," intoned Mason, "worse Materials out of which to create a Council of Revision; or more improper or unsafe Hands in which to place the Power of a Negative upon our
Laws" (Farrand 1937, 1:111).

4. John Adams's original draft of the Massachusetts constitution had given the governor an
absolute veto, but the convention later amended the provision, substituting a two-thirds override. To a skeptical Elbridge Gerry, Adams defended the absolute veto: "The executive ... ought
to be the reservoir of wisdom as the legislature is of liberty. Without this weapon of defense [the
veto power] he will be run down like a hare before the hounds" (Smith 1962, 1:442).

concern that a single executive would be reluctant to use the veto power. For confirmation of this fear Madison needed only to look to Massachusetts, where, in stark contrast to New York, only one bill was vetoed in the first decade of the constitution's existence (Spitzer 1988, 10). Only if the executive was joined with the judiciary, Madison believed, would the veto power serve as an effective check upon the will of the legislature.

At the convention the Virginia Plan's eighth resolution quickly ran into strong and insurmountable opposition, mainly from those who felt such a council violated the separation of powers by giving judges a role in the legislative process. The opposition, spearheaded by three Massachusetts delegates, Elbridge Gerry, Nathaniel Gorham, and Rufus King, managed to persuade the convention that having judges share in the veto power was unsound principle and bad policy. Judges, noted Gorham, "are not to be presumed to possess any peculiar knowledge of the mere policy of public measures." An 8 to 2 vote in the opening week of the convention (with only Maryland and Connecticut dissenting[5]) lodged a qualified veto power in the hands of the executive alone. Despite Madison's and James Wilson's persistent efforts—they proposed to reinstate a council of revision on three separate occasions—they failed to get more than three states at any one time to support them.[6]

If most delegates preferred giving the veto power to the president acting alone, few wanted to give the president an absolute veto. The proposal to do so, made by Wilson and Alexander Hamilton, failed spectacularly, with not a single state supporting it. Given the delegates' suspicions of executive power, and of the British monarchy in particular, this thunderous rejection hardly seems surprising. Yet it is worth emphasizing that the idea of a qualified veto, though widely accepted at the convention, was still relatively new. In the colonial period, the governor had an absolute veto over legislative enactments, and the king's veto over colonial acts was absolute, as was the Crown's veto over acts of Parliament.[7] South Carolina's short-lived 1776 constitution had followed in this tradition, giving the governor an absolute veto. New York's and Massachusetts's provisions for a two-thirds override mechanism were thus a historical novelty, a novelty that the framers built upon in their creation of the presidential veto.

---

5. Connecticut's three delegates—Oliver Ellsworth, Roger Sherman, and William Samuel Johnson—were, perhaps not coincidentally, all judges themselves. Maryland's only delegate at the time of the June 4 vote was Daniel of St. Thomas Jenifer; the state's other delegates, Luther Martin, Daniel Carroll, and John Francis Mercer, were yet to arrive, and James McHenry had already come and gone.

6. On June 6, Connecticut, Virginia, and New York supported the council of revision; on July 21 the votes in favor came from Connecticut, Maryland, and Virginia; on August 15 support came from Delaware, Maryland, and Virginia. The closest the idea came to passing was the vote on July 21, when in addition to the three yes votes, two states (Pennsylvania and Georgia) were divided and one absent (New Jersey), leaving only four states (Delaware, Massachusetts, South Carolina, North Carolina) to sustain the executive veto.

7. The last monarch to veto an act of Parliament was Queen Anne, in 1707, though the royal veto was frequently used to negate colonial legislation.

How often did the framers expect the veto to be used and what were considered legitimate reasons for its use? In the decades prior to the Civil War this question would be bitterly contested by the two political parties. On the one hand, many Whigs agreed with Zachary Taylor that the veto was properly understood "as an extreme measure, to be resorted to only in extraordinary cases, as where it may become necessary to defend the executive against the encroachments of the legislative power or to prevent hasty and inconsiderate or unconstitutional legislation" (Spitzer 1988, 55). Some Whigs drew the circle even more narrowly, insisting that only a bill deemed unconstitutional or that encroached on executive authority could be vetoed. Jacksonian Democrats generally took a more expansive view of the veto power, arguing that it was a legitimate way for the president to act when he disagreed with the political judgment of Congress, though even Jacksonian presidents often lathered their veto messages with constitutional reasoning to lend them greater legitimacy. So bitter was Whig opposition to the use of the veto, particularly as used by Andrew Jackson and John Tyler, that in a ten-year period between 1833 and 1842 there were no fewer than nine constitutional amendments proposed that would have allowed Congress to override the veto with a simple majority (38). After the Civil War, the debate gradually faded as people began to accept the veto as a regular instrument in the president's arsenal. Today we might disagree with a president's decision to veto a particular piece of legislation but none doubt his authority to do so.[8]

So who is closer to the framers' intent: modern-day Americans or the defeated Whigs? The evidence from the convention debates and the framers' correspondence, as well as early usage of the presidential veto, is clearly at odds with the Whig view that the presidential negative should be limited only to those cases in which a bill is judged unconstitutional or it encroaches on a president's power. James Madison and George Mason disagreed about the desirability of the new government, but both agreed that the veto's purpose was to check not just unconstitutional but also "unjust and pernicious laws" (Farrand 1937, 2:78; also 4:81). Moreover, the message that accompanied President Washington's second and final veto, which rejected legislation that would have reduced the size of the army by two dragoons, contained no constitutional arguments. Washington simply thought the bill bad policy. Similarly, President Madison vetoed a bill that would have revived the national bank, even though he explicitly conceded in the message that the bank was constitutional. But if the framers were no Whigs, they would probably have found equally strange our modern acceptance of the veto as a weapon for all seasons.

---

8. Debate today has focused on whether the president can constitutionally exercise a line-item veto, that is, veto a part or parts of a bill he disagrees with. A few enterprising if misguided legal scholars have argued that the Constitution grants the president such a power, but this theory, as Spitzer (1997) shows, is completely fanciful. When Congress passed legislation in 1996 giving the president a modified version of the line-item veto, the Supreme Court was quick to strike down the law as unconstitutional.

The framers' understanding of the veto is nicely captured in an opinion offered in 1791 by Secretary of State Jefferson in which he urged President Washington to veto a bill that would establish a national bank. "The negative of the President," Jefferson wrote, "is the shield provided by the constitution to protect against the invasions of the legislature." But it was not alone "the right of the Executive" that needed presidential protection against legislative encroachment but also the rights "of the Judiciary [and] of the States and State legislatures." Since the incorporation of a bank was "a right remaining exclusively with the States" it was necessary for the president to veto the bill to protect the states from the national legislature. Having made his case for the veto, Jefferson ended on a cautionary note:

> Unless the president's mind on ... every thing which is urged for and against this bill, is tolerably clear that it is unauthorised by the constitution, if the pro and con hang so even as to balance his judgment, a just respect for the wisdom of legislature would naturally decide the balance in favor of their opinion. It is chiefly for cases where they are clearly misled by error, ambition, or interest that the constitution has placed a check in the negative of the President. (Boyd 1950–, 19:280)

Although Washington rejected Jefferson's advice to veto the bank bill (a bill to which he was sympathetic on policy grounds), he shared Jefferson's view of the need for restraint in exercising the veto. To Edmund Pendleton, Washington explained that "from motives of respect to the Legislature ... I give my Signature to many Bills with which my Judgment is at variance." To negative a bill "can only be justified upon the clear and obvious grounds of propriety; and I never had such confidence in my own faculty of judging as to be over tenacious of the opinions I may have imbibed in doubtful cases" (Spitzer 1988, 29). This philosophy of restraint is reflected in the infrequency with which early presidents resorted to the veto. Jefferson himself never cast a veto as president, though given his personal influence in the legislature, relatively little passed Congress with which he disagreed. During the first six presidencies, spanning forty years, there were only ten vetoes, and seven of those came during Madison's two terms.

This is not to say that were the framers alive today they would advocate scaling back the veto power. The framers hoped, as Hamilton emphasized in *Federalist* 73, that the veto would promote "due deliberation" by slowing down the legislative process and encouraging the legislature to scrutinize its work more closely. Given the huge increase in the numbers of laws passed by Congress today, it is reasonable to suppose that the framers might see frequent use of the "revisionary power" (as the veto power was often called) to be a sensible and necessary adjustment to changing circumstances. Overuse of the veto, after all, was generally of less concern to the framers than was the possibility that the president's veto, like the king's negative, would not be used at all. After three years of Washington's first term had slipped by without a veto, a concerned Jefferson cautioned the president that the "non-use of [your] negative begins already to excite a belief that no President will ever venture to use it" (Spitzer 1988, 28). Whereupon Washington promptly vetoed his first bill. Still it is hard to imagine the framers mustering much sympathy or understanding for the partisan veto of today. In one year most presidents today will veto almost as many bills as were vetoed in the first forty years of the republic. Even Hamilton could not have imagined a president vetoing 635 bills, as Franklin D. Roosevelt did during his thirteen years in the presidency. If the framers could neither have conceived nor have approved of the partisan veto, that is largely because the president they had created was to be a man above parties. If the veto is used more often and with different purposes than the framers envisioned, that is because the presidency and the political system are far different today than they were in 1789.

20. The Federal Convention of 1787

The Virginia Plan specifically granted the executive only one power, the power to veto legislation, and even this power could only be exercised with the consent of a council drawn from the judiciary and could be overriden by an unspecified portion of the legislature. For those delegates who desired a strong presidency, like James Wilson and Alexander Hamilton, the Virginia Plan's veto provision did not go nearly far enough to establish a vigorous, independent executive. For those who wanted a weak executive, like the backers of the New Jersey Plan, which provided for no executive veto at all, the Virginia Plan's veto provision went too far. As soon as the delegates took up the question of the veto power on June 4, the stark differences between them were immediately exposed.

June 4

First Clause of Proposition 8 relating to a Council of Revision taken into consideration.

Mr. Gerry doubts whether the Judiciary ought to form a part of it, as they will have a sufficient check against encroachments on their own department by their exposition of the laws, which involved a power of deciding on their constitutionality. In some States the Judges had actually set aside laws as being against the Constitution. This was done too with general approbation. It was quite foreign from the nature of the office to make them judges of the policy of public measures. He moves to postpone the clause in order to propose "that the National Executive shall have a right to negative any Legislative act which shall not be afterwards passed by ____ parts of each branch of the national Legislature."

Gaillard Hunt and James Brown Scott, eds., *The Debates in the Federal Convention of 1787 Which Framed the Constitution of the United States of America Reported by James Madison* (New York: Oxford University Press, 1920), 51–56, 67–69, 294–300, 405–8, 554–56.

Mr. King seconds the motion, observing that the Judges ought to be able to expound the law as it should come before them, free from the bias of having participated in its formation.

Mr. Wilson thinks neither the original proposition nor the amendment go far enough. If the Legislative, Executive and Judiciary ought to be distinct and independent, the Executive ought to have an absolute negative. Without such a self-defence the Legislature can at any moment sink it into non-existence. He was for varying the proposition in such a manner as to give the Executive and Judiciary jointly an absolute negative.

On the question to postpone in order to take Mr. Gerry's proposition into consideration it was agreed to [6 yes; 4 no].

Mr. Gerry's proposition being now before Committee, Mr. Wilson and Mr. Hamilton move that the last part of it ["which should not be afterwards passed unless by ___ parts of each branch of the national Legislature"] be struck out, so as to give the Executive an absolute negative on the laws. There was no danger they thought of such a power being too much exercised. It was mentioned by Col. Hamilton that the King of Great Britain had not exerted his negative since the Revolution [of 1688].

Mr. Gerry sees no necessity for so great a control over the legislature as the best men in the community would be comprised in the two branches of it.

Docr. Franklin said he was sorry to differ from his colleague for whom he had a very great respect ... but he could not help it on this. He had had some experience of this check in the Executive on the Legislature, under the proprietary Government of Pennsylvania. The negative of the Governor was constantly made use of to extort money. No good law whatever could be passed without a private bargain with him. An increase of his salary, or some donation, was always made a condition; till at last it became the regular practice to have orders in his favor on the Treasury presented along with the bills to be signed, so that he might actually receive the former before he should sign the latter. When the Indians were scalping the western people, and notice of it arrived, the concurrence of the Governor in the means of self-defence could not be got, till it was agreed that his estate should be exempted from taxation; so that the people were to fight for the security of his property, whilst he was to bear no share of the burden. This was a mischievous sort of check. If the Executive was to have a Council, such a power would be less objectionable. It was true the King of Great Britain had not, as was said, exerted his negative since the Revolution, but that matter was easily explained. The bribes and emoluments now given to the members of parliament rendered it unnecessary, everything being done according to the will of the Ministers. He was afraid, if a negative should be given as proposed, that more power and money would be demanded, till at last enough would be gotten to influence and bribe the Legislature into a complete subjection to the will of the Executive.

Mr. Sherman was against enabling any one man to stop the will of the whole. No one man could be found so far above all the rest in wisdom. He thought we ought to avail ourselves of his wisdom in revising the laws, but not permit him to overrule the decided and cool opinions of the Legislature.

Mr. Madison supposed that if a proper proportion of each branch should be required to overrule the objections of the Executive, it would answer the same purpose as an absolute negative. It would rarely if ever happen that the Executive, constituted as ours is proposed to be, would have firmness enough to resist the legislature, unless backed by a certain part of the body itself. The King of Great Britain with all his splendid attributes would not be able to withstand the unanimous and eager wishes of both houses of Parliament. To give such a prerogative would certainly be obnoxious to the temper of this Country, its present temper at least.

Mr. Wilson believed as others did that this power would seldom be used. The Legislature would know that such a power existed and would refrain from such laws as [the veto] would be sure to defeat. Its silent operation would therefore preserve harmony and prevent mischief. The case of Pennsylvania formerly was very different from its present case. The Executive was not then as now to be appointed by the people. It will not in this case as in the one cited be supported by the head of a Great Empire, actuated by a different and sometimes opposite interest. ... The requiring a large proportion of each House to overrule the Executive check might do in peaceable times, but there might be tempestuous moments in which animosities may run high between the Executive and Legislative branches, and in which the former ought to be able to defend itself.

Mr. Butler had been in favor of a single Executive Magistrate; but could he have entertained an idea that a complete negative on the laws was to be given him he certainly should have acted very differently. It had been observed that in all countries the Executive power is in a constant course of increase. This was certainly the case in Great Britain. Gentlemen seemed to think that we had nothing to apprehend from an abuse of the Executive power. But why might not a Cataline or a Cromwell arise in this Country as well as in others?

Mr. Bedford was opposed to every check on the Legislative, even the Council of Revision first proposed. He thought it would be sufficient to mark out in the Constitution the boundaries to the Legislative Authority, which would give all the requisite security to the rights of the other departments. The Representatives of the people were the best judges of what was for their interest, and ought to be under no external control whatever. The two branches would produce a sufficient control within the Legislature itself.

Col. Mason. ... The probable abuses of a negative had been well explained by Dr. Franklin as proved by experience, the best of all tests. Will not the same door be opened here? The Executive may refuse its assent to necessary measures till new appointments shall be referred to him; and having by degrees engrossed all these into his own hands, the American Executive, like the British, will by bribery and influence, save himself the trouble and odium of exerting his negative afterwards. We are ... going very far in this business. We are not indeed constituting a British Government, but a more dangerous monarchy, an elective one. ... Do gentlemen mean to pave the way to hereditary Monarchy? Do they flatter themselves that the people will ever consent to such an innovation? If they do I venture to tell them, they are mistaken. The people never will consent. ... Notwithstanding the oppressions and injustice experienced among us from democracy, the genius of the people is in favor of it and the genius of the people must be consulted. ... He hoped that nothing like a Monarchy would ever be attempted in this Country. A hatred to its oppressions had carried the people through the late Revolution. Will it not be enough to enable the Executive to suspend offensive laws, till they shall be coolly revised and the objections to them overruled by a greater majority than was required in the first instance? He never could agree to give up all the rights of the people to a single Magistrate. If more than one had been fixed on, greater powers might have been entrusted to the Executive. ...

On the question for striking out so as to give Executive an absolute negative [0 yes; 10 no].

Mr. Butler moved that the Resolution be altered so as to read—"Resolved that the National Executive have a power to suspend any Legislative act for the term of _____."

Doctr. Franklin seconds the motion.

Mr. Gerry observed that a power of suspending might do all the mischief dreaded from the negative of useful laws, without answering the salutary purpose of checking unjust or unwise ones.

On [the] question "for giving this suspending power" all the States ... were No.

On a question for enabling two thirds of each branch of the Legislature to overrule the revisionary check, it passed in the affirmative ... and was inserted in the blank of Mr. Gerry's motion.

On the question on Mr. Gerry's motion which gave the Executive alone without the Judiciary the revisionary control on the laws unless overruled by 2/3 of each branch [8 yes; 2 no].

June 6

Mr. Wilson moved to reconsider the vote excluding the Judiciary from a share in the revision of the laws, and to add after "National Executive" the words "with a convenient number of the national Judiciary." ...

Mr. Madison seconded the motion. He observed that the great difficulty in rendering the Executive competent to its own defence arose from the nature of Republican Government which could not give to an individual citizen that settled preeminence in the eyes of the rest, that weight of property, that personal interest against betraying the national interest, which appertain to an hereditary magistrate. In a Republic personal merit alone could be the ground of political exaltation, but it would rarely happen that this merit would be so preeminent as to produce universal acquiescence. The Executive Magistrate would be envied and assailed by disappointed competitors. His firmness therefore would need support. He would not possess those great emoluments from his station, nor that permanent stake in the public interest which would place him out of the reach of foreign corruption. He would stand in need therefore of being controlled as well as supported. An association of the Judges in his revisionary function would both double the advantage and diminish the danger. It would also enable the Judiciary Department the better to defend itself against Legislative encroachments. Two objections had been made: First, that the Judges ought not to be subject to the bias which a participation in the making of laws might give in the exposition of them. Second, that the Judiciary Department ought to be separate and distinct from the other great Departments. The first objection had some weight, but it was much diminished by reflecting that a small proportion of the laws coming in question before a Judge would be such wherein he had been consulted; that a small part of this proportion would be so ambiguous as to leave room for his prepossessions; and that but a few cases would probably arise in the life of a Judge under such ambiguous passages. How much good on the other hand would proceed from the perspicuity, the conciseness, and the systematic character which the Code of laws would receive from the Judiciary talents? As to the second objection, it either had no weight, or it applied with equal weight to the Executive and to the Judiciary revision of the laws. The maxim on which the objection was founded required a separation of the Executive as well as of the Judiciary from the Legislature and from each other. There would in truth however be no improper mixture of these distinct powers in the present case. In England, whence the maxim itself had been drawn, the Executive had an absolute negative on the laws; and the supreme tribunal of Justice [the House of Lords] formed one of the other branches of the Legislature. In short whether the object of the revisionary power was to restrain the Legislature from encroaching on the other co-ordinate Departments or on the rights of the people at large, or from passing laws unwise in their principle or incorrect in their form, the utility of annexing the wisdom and weight of the Judiciary to the Executive seemed incontestable.

Mr. Gerry thought the Executive, whilst standing alone, would be more impartial than when he could be covered by the sanction and seduced by the sophistry of the Judges.

Mr. King. If the Unity of the Executive was preferred for the sake of responsibility, the policy of it is as applicable to the revisionary as to the Executive power.

Mr. Pinckney had been at first in favor of joining the heads of the principal departments—the Secretary of War, of foreign affairs, etc.—in the council of revision. He had however relinquished the idea from a consideration that these could be called in by the Executive Magistrate whenever he pleased to consult them. He was opposed to an introduction of the Judges into the business.

Col. Mason was for giving all possible weight to the revisionary institution. The Executive power ought to be well secured against Legislative usurpations on it. The purse and the sword ought never to get into the same hands, whether Legislative or Executive.

Mr. Dickinson. Secrecy, vigor and despatch are not the principal properties required in the Executive. Important as these are that of responsibility is more so, which can only be preserved by leaving it singly to discharge its functions. He thought too a junction of the Judiciary to it involved an improper mixture of powers. ...

On the question for joining the Judges to the Executive in the revisionary business [3 yes; 8 no].

July 21

Mr. Wilson moved ... that "the supreme National Judiciary should be associated with the Executive in the Revisionary power." This proposition had been before made and failed but he was so confirmed by reflection in the opinion of its utility that he thought it incumbent on him to make another effort. The Judiciary ought to have an opportunity of remonstrating against projected encroachments on the people as well as on themselves. It had been said that the Judges, as expositors of the Laws, would have an opportunity of defending their constitutional rights. There was weight in this observation, but this power of the Judges did not go far enough. Laws may be unjust, may be unwise, may be dangerous, may be destructive, and yet may not be so unconstitutional as to justify the Judges in refusing to give them effect. Let them have a share in the Revisionary power, and they will have an opportunity of taking notice of these characters of a law, and of counteracting, by the weight of their opinions, the improper views of the Legislature.

Mr. Madison seconded the motion.

Mr. Gorham did not see the advantage of employing the Judges in this way. As Judges they are not to be presumed to possess any peculiar knowledge of the mere policy of public measures. Nor can it be necessary as a security for their constitutional rights. The Judges in England have no such additional provision for their defence, yet their jurisdiction is not invaded. He thought it would be best to let the Executive alone be responsible, and at most to authorize him to call on Judges for their opinions.

Mr. Ellsworth approved heartily of the motion. The aid of the Judges will give more wisdom and firmness to the Executive. They will possess a systematic and accurate knowledge of the Laws, which the Executive can not be expected always to possess. The law of Nations also will frequently come into question. Of this the Judges alone will have competent information

Mr. Madison considered the object of the motion as of great importance to the meditated Constitution. It would be useful to the Judiciary department by giving it an additional opportunity of defending itself against Legislative encroachments. It would be useful to the Executive by inspiring additional confidence and firmness in exerting the revisionary power. It would be useful to the Legislature by the valuable assistance it would give in preserving a consistency, conciseness, perspicuity and technical propriety in the laws, qualities peculiarly necessary and yet shamefully wanting in our republican Codes. It would moreover be useful to the Community at large as an additional check against a pursuit of those unwise and unjust measures which constituted so great a portion of our calamities. If any solid objection could be urged against the motion, it must be on the supposition that it tended to give too much strength either to the Executive or Judiciary. He did not think there was the least ground for this apprehension. It was much more to be apprehended that notwithstanding this co-operation of the two departments, the Legislature would still be an overmatch for them. Experience in all the States had evinced a powerful tendency in the Legislature to absorb all power into its vortex. This was the real source of danger to the American constitutions and suggested the necessity of giving every defensive authority to the other departments that was consistent with republican principles.

Mr. Mason said he had always been a friend to this provision. It would give a confidence to the Executive, which he would not otherwise have, and without which the Revisionary power would be of little avail.

Mr. Gerry did not expect to see this point, which had undergone full discussion, again revived. The object he conceived of the Revisionary power was merely to secure the Executive department against legislative encroachment. The Executive therefore who will best know and be ready to defend his rights ought alone to have the defence of them. The motion was liable to strong objections. It was combining and mixing together the Legislative and Judiciary departments. It was making Statesmen of the Judges, and setting them up as the guardians of the Rights of the people. He relied for his part on the Representatives of the people as the guardians of their rights and interests. It was making the Expositors of the Laws the Legislators, which ought never to be done. A better expedient for correcting the laws would be to appoint, as had been done in Pennsylvania, a person or persons of proper skill to draw bills for the Legislature.

Mr. Strong thought with Mr. Gerry that the power of making ought to be kept distinct from that of expounding the laws. No maxim was better established. The Judges in exercising the function of expositors might be influenced by the part they had taken in framing the laws.

Mr. Govr. Morris. Some check being necessary on the Legislature, the question is in what hands it should be lodged. On one side it was contended that the Executive alone ought to exercise it. He did not think that an Executive appointed for 6 years, and impeachable whilst in office, would be a very effectual check. On the other side it was urged that he ought to be reinforced by the Judiciary departments. Against this it was objected that Expositors of laws ought to have no hand in making them, and arguments in favor of this had been drawn from England. What weight was due to them might be easily determined by an attention to facts. The truth was that the Judges in England had a great share in ... Legislation. They are consulted in difficult and doubtful cases. They may be and some of them are members of the Legislature. They are or may be members of the privy Council, and can there advise the Executive as they will do with us if the motion succeeds. The influence the English Judges may have in the latter capacity in strengthening the Executive check can not be ascertained, as the King by his influence in a manner dictates the laws.

There is one difference in the two cases however which disconcerts all reasoning from the British to our proposed Constitution. The British Executive has so great an interest in his prerogatives and such powerful means of defending them that he will never yield any part of them. The interest of our Executive is so inconsiderable and so transitory, and his means of defending it so feeble, that there is the justest ground to fear his want of firmness in resisting encroachments. He was extremely apprehensive that the auxiliary firmness and weight of the Judiciary would not supply the deficiency.

He concurred in thinking the public liberty in greater danger from Legislative usurpations than from any other source. It had been said that the Legislature ought to be relied on as the proper Guardians of liberty. The answer was short and conclusive. Either bad laws will be pushed or not. On the latter supposition no check will be wanted. On the former a strong check will be necessary. And this is the proper supposition. Emissions of paper money, largesses to the people, a remission of debts and similar measures, will at some times be popular, and will be pushed for that reason. At other times such measures will coincide with the interests of the Legislature themselves, and that will be a reason not less cogent for pushing them. It may be thought that the people will not be deluded and misled in the latter case. But experience teaches another lesson. The press is indeed a great means of diminishing the evil, yet it is found to be unable to prevent it altogether.

Mr. L. Martin considered the association of the Judges with the Executive as a dangerous innovation, as well as one which could not produce the particular advantage expected from it. A knowledge of Mankind and of Legislative affairs cannot be presumed to belong in a higher degree to the Judges than to the Legislature. And as to the constitutionality of laws, that point will come before the Judges in their proper official character. In this character they have a negative on the laws. Join them with the Executive in the Revision and they will have a double negative. It is necessary that the Supreme Judiciary should have the confidence of the people. This will soon be lost if they are employed in the task of remonstrating against popular measures of the Legislature. Besides in what mode and proportion are they to vote in the Council of Revision?

Mr. Madison could not discover in the proposed association of the Judges with the Executive in the Revisionary check on the Legislature any violation of the maxim which requires the great departments of power to be kept separate and distinct. On the contrary he thought it an auxiliary precaution in favor of the maxim. If a Constitutional discrimination of the departments on paper were a sufficient security to each against encroachments of the others, all further provisions would indeed be superfluous. But experience had taught us a distrust of that security, and that it is necessary to introduce such a balance of powers and interests as will guarantee the provisions on paper. Instead therefore of contenting ourselves with laying down the theory in the Constitution that each department ought to be separate and distinct, it was proposed to add a defensive power to each which should maintain the theory in practice. In so doing we did not blend the departments together. We erected effectual barriers for keeping them separate. The most regular example of this theory was in the British Constitution. Yet it was not only the practice there to admit the Judges to a seat in the legislature and in the Executive Councils, and to submit to their previous examination all laws of a certain description, but it was a part of their Constitution that the Executive might negative any law whatever, a part of their Constitution which had been universally regarded as calculated for the preservation of the whole. The objection against a union of the Judiciary and Executive branches in the revision of the laws had either no foundation or was not carried far enough. If such a Union was an improper mixture of powers, or such a Judiciary check on the laws was inconsistent with the theory of a free Constitution, it was equally so to admit the Executive to any participation in the making of laws, and the revisionary plan ought to be discarded altogether.

Col. Mason observed that the defence of the Executive was not the sole object of the Revisionary power. He expected even greater advantages from it. Notwithstanding the precautions taken in the constitution of the Legislature, it would still so much resemble that of the individual States that it must be expected frequently to pass unjust and pernicious laws. This restraining power was therefore essentially necessary. It would have the effect not only of hindering the final passage of such laws, but would discourage demagogues from attempting to get them passed. It had been said [by Mr. L. Martin] that if the Judges were joined in this check on the laws, they would have a double negative, since in their expository capacity of Judges they would have one negative. He would reply that in this capacity they could impede in one case only, the operation of laws. They could declare an unconstitutional law void. But with regard to every law, however unjust, oppressive or pernicious, which did not come plainly under this description, they would be under the necessity as Judges to give it a free course. He wished the further use to be made of the Judges, of giving aid in preventing every improper law. Their aid will be the more valuable as they are in the habit and practice of considering laws in their true principles, and in all their consequences.

Mr. Wilson. The separation of the departments does not require that they should have separate objects but that they should act separately though on the same objects. It is necessary that the two branches of the Legislature should be separate and distinct, yet they are both to act precisely on the same object.

Mr. Gerry had rather give the Executive an absolute negative for its own defence than thus to blend together the Judiciary and Executive departments. It will bind them together in an offensive and defensive alliance against the Legislature, and render the latter unwilling to enter into a contest with them.

Mr. Govr. Morris was surprised that any defensive provision for securing the effectual separation of the departments should be considered as an improper mixture of them. Suppose that the three powers were to be vested in three persons, by compact among themselves; that one was to have the power of making, another of executing, and a third of judging, the laws. Would it not be very natural for the two latter, after having settled the partition on paper, to observe (and would not candor oblige the former to admit?) that as a security against legislative acts of the former which might easily be so framed as to undermine the powers of the two others, the two others ought to be armed with a veto for their own defence, or at least to have an opportunity of stating their objections against acts of encroachment? And would any one pretend that such a right tended to blend and confound powers that ought to be separately exercised? As well might it be said that if three neighbors had three distinct farms, a right in each to defend his farm against his neighbors tended to blend the farms together.

Mr. Gorham. All agree that a check on the Legislature is necessary. But there are two objections against admitting the Judges to share in it which no observations on the other side seem to obviate. The first is that the Judges ought to carry into the exposition of the laws no prepossessions with regard to them. Second, that as the Judges will outnumber the Executive, the revisionary check would be thrown entirely out of the Executive hands and, instead of enabling him to defend himself, would enable the Judges to sacrifice him.

Mr. Wilson. The proposition is certainly not liable to all the objections which have been urged against it. According [to Mr. Gerry] it will unite the Executive and Judiciary in an offensive and defensive alliance against the Legislature. According to Mr. Gorham it will lead to a subversion of the Executive by the Judiciary influence. To the first gentleman the answer was obvious: that the joint weight of the two departments was necessary to balance the single weight of the Legislature. To the first objection stated by the other gentleman it might be answered that supposing the prepossession to mix itself with the exposition, the evil would be overbalanced by the advantages promised by the expedient. To the second objection, that such a rule of voting might be provided in the detail as would guard against it.

Mr. Rutledge thought ... Judges, of all men, the most unfit to be concerned in the revisionary Council. The Judges ought never to give their opinion on a law till it comes before them. He thought it equally unnecessary. The Executive could advise with the officers of State, as of war, finance, etc., and avail himself of their information and opinions.

On the question of Mr. Wilson's motion for joining the Judiciary in the Revision of laws it passed in the negative [3 yes; 4 no; 2 divided].

August 15

Mr. Madison moved that all acts before they become laws should be submitted both to the Executive and Supreme Judiciary Departments, that if either of these should object $2/3$ of each House, if both should object, $3/4$ of each House, should be necessary to overrule the objections and give to the acts the force of law. ...

Mr. Wilson seconds the motion.

Mr. Pinckney opposed the interference of the Judges in the Legislative business. It will involve them in parties, and give a previous tincture to their opinions. ...

Mr. Gerry. This motion comes to the same thing with what has been already negatived. Question on the motion of Mr. Madison [3 yes; 8 no].

Mr. Govr. Morris regretted that something like the proposed check could not be agreed to. He dwelt on the importance of public credit, and the difficulty of supporting it without some strong barrier against the instability of legislative assemblies. He suggested the idea of requiring three fourths of each house to repeal laws where the President should not concur. He had no great reliance on the revisionary power as the Executive was now to be constituted [that is, elected by the Congress]. The legislature will contrive to soften down the President. He recited the history of paper emissions, and the perseverance of the legislative assemblies in repeating them, with all the distressing effects of such measures before their eyes. Were the national Legislature formed, and a war was now to break out, this ruinous expedient would be again resorted to if not guarded against. The requiring $3/4$ to repeal would, though not a complete remedy, prevent the hasty passage of laws and the frequency of those repeals which destroy faith in the public and which are among our greatest calamities. ...

Mr. Govr. Morris suggested the expedient of an absolute negative in the Executive. ... A control over the legislature might have its inconveniences, but view the danger on the other side. The most virtuous Citizens will often as members of a legislative body concur in measures which afterwards in their private capacity they will be ashamed of. Encroachments of the popular branch of the Government ought to be guarded against. ... If the Executive be overturned by the popular branch, as happened in England [in the mid-seventeenth century under Oliver Cromwell], the tyranny of one man will ensue. ... [He] wished the section to be postponed in order to consider of some more effectual check than requiring $2/3$ only to overrule the negative of the Executive.

Mr. Sherman. Can one man be trusted better than all the others if they all agree? This was neither wise nor safe. He disapproved of Judges meddling in politics and parties. We have gone far enough in forming the negative as it now stands.

Mr. Carroll. ... He thought the controlling power ... of the Executive could not be well decided till it was seen how the formation of that department would be finally regulated. He wished the consideration of the matter to be postponed.

Mr. Gorham saw no end to these difficulties and postponements. Some could not agree to the form of Government before the powers were defined. Others could not agree to the powers till it was seen how the Government was to be formed.

Mr. Wilson ... was most apprehensive of a dissolution of the Government from the legislature swallowing up all the other powers. He remarked that the prejudices against the Executive resulted from a misapplication of the adage that the parliament was the palladium of liberty. Where the Executive was really formidable, King and Tyrant were naturally associated in the minds of people; not legislature and tyranny. But where the Executive was not formidable, the two last were most properly associated. After the destruction of the King in Great Britain, a more pure and unmixed tyranny sprang up in the parliament than had been exercised by the monarch. He insisted that we had not guarded against the danger on this side by a sufficient self-defensive power either to the Executive or Judiciary department.

Mr. Rutledge was strenuous against postponing, and complained much of the tediousness of the proceedings.

Mr. Ellsworth held the same language. We grow more and more skeptical as we proceed. If we do not decide soon, we shall be unable to come to any decision.

The question for postponement passed in the negative: Delaware and Maryland only being in the affirmative.

Mr. Williamson moved to change "⅔ of each House" into "¾" as requisite to overrule the dissent of the President. He saw no danger in this, and preferred giving the power to the President alone to admitting the Judges into the business of legislation.

Mr. Wilson seconded the motion. ...

On this motion for ¾ instead of two thirds; it passed in the affirmative [6 yes; 4 no; 1 divided].

September 12

Mr. Williamson moved to reconsider the clause requiring three fourths of each House to overrule the negative of the President, in order to strike out ¾ and insert ⅔. He had he remarked himself proposed ¾ instead of ⅔, but he had since been convinced that the latter proportion was the best. The former puts too much in the power of the President.

Mr. Sherman was of the same opinion, adding that the States would not like to see so small a minority and the President prevailing over the general voice. In making laws regard should be had to the sense of the people, who are to be bound by them, and it was more probable that a single man should mistake or betray this sense than the Legislature.

Mr. Govr. Morris. Considering the difference between the two proportions numerically, it amounts in one House to two members only and in the other to not more than five, according to the numbers of which the Legislature is at first to be composed. It is the interest moreover of the distant States to prefer ¾ as they will be oftenest absent and need the interposing check of the President. The excess rather than the deficiency of laws was to be dreaded. The example of New York shows that ⅔ is not sufficient to answer the purpose.

Mr. Hamilton added his testimony to the fact that ⅔ in New York had been ineffectual either where a popular object or a legislative faction operated. ...

Mr. Gerry. It is necessary to consider the danger on the other side also. ⅔ will be a considerable, perhaps a proper security. ¾ puts too much in the power of a few men. The primary object of the revisionary check of the President is not to protect the general interest but to defend his own department. If ¾ be required a few Senators, having hopes from the nomination of the President to offices, will combine with him and impede proper laws. ...

Mr. Williamson was less afraid of too few than of too many laws. He was most of all afraid that the repeal of bad laws might be rendered too difficult by requiring ¾ to overcome the dissent of the President.

Col. Mason had always considered this as one of the most exceptionable parts of the System. As to the numerical argument of Mr. Govr. Morris, little arithmetic was necessary to understand that ¾ was more than ⅔, whatever the numbers of the Legislature might be. The example of New York depended on the real merits of the laws. The gentlemen citing it had no doubt given their own opinions. But perhaps there were others of opposite opinions who could equally paint the abuses on the other side. His leading view was to guard against too great an impediment to the repeal of laws.

Mr. Govr. Morris dwelt on the danger to the public interest from the instability of laws. ... On the other side there could be little danger. If one man in office will not consent where he ought, every fourth year another can be substituted. This term was not too long for fair experiments. Many good laws are not tried long enough to prove their merit. This is often the case with new laws opposed to old habits. ...

Mr. Pinckney was warmly in opposition to ¾ as putting a dangerous power in the hands of a few Senators headed by the President.

Mr. Madison. When ¾ was agreed to, the President was to be elected by the Legislature and for seven years. He is now to be elected by the people and for four years. The object of the revisionary power is twofold. 1. to defend the Executive Rights. 2. to prevent popular or factious injustice. It was important principle in this and in the State constitutions to check legislative injustice and encroachments. The Experience of the States had demonstrated that their checks are insufficient. We must compare the danger from the weakness of ⅔ with the danger from the strength of ¾. He thought on the whole the former was the greater. As to the difficulty of repeals, it was probable that in doubtful cases the policy would soon take place of limiting the duration of laws so as to require renewal instead of repeal.

The reconsideration being agreed to. On the question to insert ⅔ in place of ¾ [6 yes; 4 no; 1 divided].

21. Luther Martin, "The Genuine Information," 1788

After walking out of the federal convention in early September, Martin headed back to Maryland to sound the alarm over what was transpiring in Philadel-

---

"The Genuine Information, Delivered to the Legislature of the State of Maryland, Relative to the Proceedings of the General Convention, Held at Philadelphia, in 1787, by Luther Martin," in Jonathan Elliot, ed., *The Debates in the Several State Constitutions on the Adoption of the Federal Constitution* (New York: Burt Franklin, 1888), 1:367.

phia. In November the Maryland legislature invited Martin to report to them on the convention's proceedings. He delivered a (characteristically) long oration that blended detailed description of the convention's proceedings with a spirited assault on the proposed government. Martin's speech was then revised and published as a widely read pamphlet, "The Genuine Information." Although Martin's central concern was the failure of the proposed government to preserve and safeguard the sovereignty of the states, he left no clause unturned as he laboriously worked his way through the document. In the excerpt below Martin offers his version of the debate that took place over the veto power. Readers should keep in mind that because Martin arrived at the convention on June 9 and left on September 4, he was only present for two (July 21 and August 15) of the six days during which the veto power was discussed.

There were also objections to that part ... which relates to the negative of the President. There were some who thought no good reason could be assigned for giving the President a negative of any kind. Upon the principle of a check to the proceedings of the legislature, it was said to be unnecessary; that the two branches having a control over each other's proceedings, and the Senate being chosen by the state legislatures, and being composed of members from the different States, there would always be a sufficient guard against measures being hastily or rashly adopted; that the President was not likely to have more wisdom or integrity than the senators or any of them, or to better know or consult the interest of the states than any member of the Senate, so as to be entitled to a negative on that principle; and as to the precedent from the British constitution (for we were eternally troubled with arguments and precedents from the British government) it was said it would not apply. The king of Great Britain there composed one of the three estates of the kingdom; he was possessed of rights and privileges as such, distinct from the Lords and Commons, rights and privileges which descended to his heirs and were inheritable by them; that, for the preservation of these, it was necessary he should have a negative, but that this was not the case with the President of the United States who was no more than an officer of the government; the sovereignty was not in him, but in the legislature. And it was further urged, even if he was allowed a negative, it ought not to be of so great extent as that given by the system, since his single voice is to countervail the whole of either branch, and any number less than two-thirds of the other. However, a majority of the convention was of a different opinion, and adopted it as it now makes a part of the system.

22. The Impartial Examiner IV, June 11, 1788

This essay, the fourth of five written by the Impartial Examiner, appeared in the *Virginia Independent Chronicle* on the tenth day of the Virginia ratifying

John P. Kaminski and Gaspare Saladino, eds., *The Documentary History of the Ratification of the Constitution* (Madison: State Historical Society of Wisconsin, 1993), 10:1609–12. Used with the permission of the State Historical Society.

convention. The veto power was not a focus of debate in the Virginia convention (or indeed in any other state ratifying convention), but the Impartial
Examiner zeroes in on the presidential veto as among the most inappropriate
and dangerous of the Constitution's features. Although conceding that the
veto may be appropriate for Great Britain, the Impartial Examiner insists that
this royal prerogative has no place in a republican form of government. Like
so many Anti-Federalist writings opposing the Constitution, the author remains unknown.

Although ... it seems to be the spirit of the proposed plan of government that [the Senate
and House of Representatives] should be considered as the grand deputation of America—
the great aggregate body to whom shall be delegated the important trust of representing the
whole nation, the august, puissant assembly in whom shall reside the full majesty of the
people—yet it seems too these alone shall not be sufficient to exercise the powers of legislation. It is ordained as a necessary expedient in the federal government that a president of
the United States (who is to hold the supreme executive power) should also concur in passing every law.

In monarchy, where the established maxim is that the king should be respected as a great
and transcendent personage who knows no equal—who in his royal political capacity can
commit no wrong—to whom no evil can be ascribed—in whom exists the height of perfection—who is supreme above all and accountable to no earthly being, it is consistent with
such a maxim that the prince should form a constituent branch of the legislature and that
his power of rejecting whatever has been passed by the other branches should be distinct
and coextensive with that of either of those branches in rejecting what has been proposed
and consented to by the other. It is necessary that the fundamental laws of the realm should
ascribe to the king those high and eminent attributes, that he should possess in himself the
sovereignty of the nation, and that the regal dignity should distinguish him as superior to all
his subjects, and in his political character endowed with certain inherent qualities which
cannot be supposed to reside in any other individual within the kingdom. Otherwise that
constitutional independence, which the laws meant peculiarly to establish in his person,
would not be preserved. To this end the king of England is invested with the sole executive
authority, and a branch of legislative jurisdiction so far as to pass his negative on all proceedings of the other two branches, or to confirm them by his assent.

This secures to him the intended superiority in the constitution and gives him the ascen-
dancy in government, else his sovereignty would become a shadow—whilst that doctrine,
whereby he is declared to be the head ... of the great body politic, would prove to be nothing more than mere sound. This twofold jurisdiction established in the British monarch being
founded on maxims extremely different from those which prevail in the American States, the
writer hereof is inclined to hope that he will not be thought singular if he conceives an impropriety in assimilating the component parts of the American government to those of the
British. And as the reasons which [induced] the founders of the British constitution ... to give
the executive a control over the legislative are so far from existing in this country that every
principle of that kind is generally, if not universally, exploded; so it should appear that the
same public spirit which pervades the nation would proclaim the doctrine of prerogative and
other peculiar properties of the royal character as incompatible with the view of these states
when they are settling the form of a republican government. Is it not therefore sufficient

that every branch in the proposed system be distinct and independent of each other, that no one branch might receive any accession of power (by taking part of another) which would tend to overturn the balance and thereby endanger the very being of the constitution? Whilst the king of England enjoys all the regalia which are annexed to his crown—whilst he exercises a transcendent dominion over his subjects, the existence whereof is coeval with the first rudiments of their constitution—let the free citizens of America, consulting their true national happiness, wish for no innovation but what is regulated according to the scale of equal liberty, or which may not destroy that liberty by too great a share of power being lodged in any particular hands. Let this collateral jurisdiction, which constitutes the royal negative, be held by kings alone, since with kings it first originated. Let this remain in its native soil as most congenial to it. There it will cumber less, and be more productive; here it will be an exotic, and may poison the stock in which it may be engrafted.

It will be said, perhaps, that the power granted the president of approving or disapproving the proceedings which have passed the senate and house of representatives will not be so decisive in its nature as the king's negative. True it is, this power of rejecting does not extend so far as ... to produce an entire overthrow of any law which has passed those two houses, but it may be expected that in many instances this negative will amount to a final and conclusive rejection. For as a law which has been once disapproved by the president cannot be repassed without the agreement of two-thirds of both houses, there can be no doubt it will frequently happen that this concurrence of two thirds cannot be obtained. The law must then fall, and thus the president, although he has not the power of resolving originally and enacting any laws independent of those two houses, has nevertheless in this legislative scale of government a weight almost equal to that of two thirds of the whole Congress. ...

When the spirit of America becomes such as to ascribe to their president all those extraordinary qualities which the subjects of kingly governments ascribe to their princes, then ... and not till then, he may consistently be invested with a power similar to theirs.

23. The Federal Farmer XIV, January 17, 1788

Unlike the Impartial Examiner, which rejected the veto power as inconsistent with republican government, the Federal Farmer acknowledges the legitimacy and value of the veto power but suggests the framers would have done better to follow New York's model of vesting the veto in a council of revision, much as the Virginia Plan had originally called for.

The [veto] may answer three valuable purposes, (1) to impede in their passage hasty and intemperate laws, (2) occasionally to assist the senate or people, and (3) to prevent the legislature from encroaching upon the executive or judiciary. In Great Britain the king has a complete negative upon all laws, but he very seldom exercises it. This may be well lodged in him,

---

"Additional Number of Letters from the Federal Farmer to the Republican," in *Selected Americana from Sabin's Dictionary of Books relating to America* (Woodbridge, Conn.: Primary Source Media, 1996), fiche 19,259, pp. 129–30.

who possesses strength to support it, and whose family has independent and hereditary interests and powers, rights and prerogatives ... to defend; but in a country where the first executive officer is elective, and has no rights, but in common with the people, a partial negative in legislation, as in Massachusetts and New-York, is, in my opinion, clearly best. In the former state ... it is lodged in the governor alone; in the latter, in the governor, chancellor, and judges of the supreme court. ... [The veto] is simply a branch of legislative power, and has in itself no relation to executive or judicial powers. The question is, in what hands ought it to be lodged to answer the three purposes mentioned the most advantageously? The prevailing opinion seems to be in favour of vesting it in the hands of the first executive magistrate. I will not say this opinion is ill founded. The negative, in [the first] case, is intended to prevent hasty laws; ... in the second, it is to aid the weaker branch; and in the third, to defend the executive and judiciary. To answer these ends, there ought, therefore, to be collected in the hands which hold this negative, firmness, wisdom, and strength. ... By lodging it in the executive magistrate, we give him a share in making the laws, which he must execute; by associating the judges with him, as in New York, we give them a share in making the laws, upon which they must decide as judicial magistrates. This may be a reason for excluding the judges; however, the negative in New York is certainly well calculated to answer its great purposes: the governor and judges united must possess more firmness and strength, more wisdom and information, than either alone, and also more of the confidence of the people. And as to the balance among the departments, why should the executive alone hold the scales, and the judicial be left defenseless? I think the negative in New York is found best in practice. We see it there frequently and wisely put upon the measures of the two branches, whereas in Massachusetts it is hardly ever exercised, and the governor, I believe, has often permitted laws to pass to which he had substantial objections, but did not make them.

24. James Wilson, Pennsylvania Ratifying Convention, December 1, 1787

Pennsylvania, host to the Constitutional Convention, was the first state to call a ratifying convention and the first to convene a ratification meeting. Opening on November 20, the Pennsylvania convention vigorously debated the Constitution for three weeks before ratifying the new government on December 12 by a 2 to 1 margin. Wilson was the primary spokesman for the friends of the Constitution. In the following excerpt Wilson defends the veto power against arguments that it constitutes a dangerous concentration of power that threatens liberty. The qualified negative of the president, Wilson counters, will increase deliberation and thus improve the quality while decreasing the quantity of legislation. Liberty will be safer with fewer and less changeable laws. Moreover, Wilson contends, it is a mistake to think of the president in

Jonathan Elliot, ed., *The Debates in the Several State Constitutions on the Adoption of the Federal Constitution* (New York: Burt Franklin, 1888), 2:447–48.

terms of a king because the president will be "THE MAN OF THE PEOPLE." Yet Wilson immediately betrays the continuing sway of older modes of thought when he speaks, in the very same sentence, of the president as "watch[ing] over the whole with paternal care and affection." The presidency, for Wilson, is a singular blend of populism and paternalism.

I believe, sir, that the observation which I am now going to make will apply to mankind in every situation; they will act with more caution, and perhaps more integrity, if their proceedings are to be under the inspection and control of another than when they are not. From this principle, the proceedings of Congress will be conducted with a degree of circumspection not common in single bodies, where nothing more is necessary to be done than to carry the business through amongst themselves, whether it be right or wrong. In compound legislatures, every object must be submitted to a distinct body, not influenced by the arguments or warped by the prejudices of the other. And, I believe, that the persons who will form the Congress will be cautious in running the risk, with a bare majority, of having the negative of the President put on their proceedings. As there will be more circumspection in forming the laws, so there will be more stability in the laws when made. Indeed one is the consequence of the other; for what has been well considered, and founded in good sense, will, in practice, be useful and salutary, and of consequence will not be liable to be soon repealed. Though two bodies may not possess more wisdom or patriotism than what may be found in a single body, yet they will necessarily introduce a greater degree of precision. An indigested and inaccurate code of laws is one of the most dangerous things that can be introduced into any government. The force of this observation is well-known by every gentleman that has attended to the laws of this state. ...

I will proceed now to take some notice of a still further restraint upon the legislature—I mean the qualified negative of the President. I think this will be attended with very important advantages, for the security and happiness of the people of the United States. The President, sir, will not be a stranger to our country, to our laws, or to our wishes. He will, under this Constitution, be placed in office as the President of the whole Union, and will be chosen in such a manner that he may be justly styled THE MAN OF THE PEOPLE; being elected by the different parts of the United States, he will consider himself as not particularly interested for any one of them, but will watch over the whole with paternal care and affection. This will be the natural conduct to recommend himself to those who placed him in that high chair, and I consider it as a very important advantage that such a man must have every law presented to him before it can become binding upon the United States. He will have before him the fullest information of our situation; he will avail himself not only of records and official communications, foreign and domestic, but he will have also the advice of the executive officers in the different departments of the general government.

If in consequence of this information and advice, he exercises the authority given to him, the effect will not be lost—he returns his objections, together with the bill, and unless two-thirds of both branches of the legislature are now found to approve it, it does not become a law. But even if his objections do not prevent its passing into a law, they will not be useless; they will be kept together with the law, and, in the archives of Congress, will be valuable and practical materials to form the minds of posterity for legislation. If it is found that the law operates inconveniently, or oppressively, the people may discover in the President's objections the source of that inconvenience or oppression.

25. Alexander Hamilton,
Federalist 73, March 21, 1788

The *Federalist* papers were meant to persuade people to support the Constitution. To sell the Constitution Hamilton often had to defend parts of the new government that he had opposed at the convention. So, for instance, in *Federalist* 73 we find him defending the qualified veto as superior to an absolute veto, despite having argued the reverse in Philadelphia the previous summer. In the federal convention, on June 4, Hamilton had proposed an absolute negative, arguing that "there was no danger ... of such a power being too much exercised." After all, Hamilton tried to reassure the delegates, the king of Great Britain had not exercised the same power in almost a century. In *Federalist* 73 Hamilton reverses himself, arguing now that the qualified veto was preferable precisely because it would be used more: it "is a power which would be much more readily exercised than the [absolute veto]. A man who might be afraid to defeat a law by his single veto, might not scruple to return it for reconsideration." Was Hamilton really persuaded that the qualified veto was better than an absolute veto? Perhaps, but it is more likely he realized that this was the best the nation could do, and he determined to use his formidable talents as a lawyer to marshall the best arguments he could to help his client, the Constitution.

The propensity of the legislative department to intrude upon the rights and to absorb the powers of the other departments has been already suggested and repeated; the insufficiency of a mere parchment delineation of the boundaries of each has also been remarked upon; and the necessity of furnishing each with constitutional arms for its own defence has been inferred and proved. From these clear and indubitable principles results the propriety of a negative, either absolute or qualified, in the executive, upon the acts of the legislative branches. Without the one or the other, the [executive] would be absolutely unable to defend himself against the depredations of the [legislature]. He might gradually be stripped of his authorities by successive resolutions, or annihilated by a single vote. And in the one mode or the other, the legislative and executive powers might speedily come to be blended in the same hands. If even no propensity had ever discovered itself in the legislative body to invade the rights of the executive, the rules of just reasoning and theoretic propriety would of themselves teach us that the one ought not to be left to the mercy of the other but ought to possess a constitutional and effectual power of self-defence.

But the power in question has a further use. It not only serves as a shield to the executive, but it furnishes an additional security against the enaction of improper laws. It establishes a salutary check upon the legislative body, calculated to guard the community against the effects of faction, precipitancy, or of any impulse unfriendly to the public good which may happen to influence a majority of that body.

New York *Independent Journal*, March 21, 1788.

The propriety of a negative has, upon some occasions, been combated by an observation that it was not to be presumed a single man would possess more virtue and wisdom than a number of men, and that unless this presumption should be entertained it would be improper to give the executive magistrate any species of control over the legislative body.

But this observation, when examined, will appear rather specious than solid. The propriety of the thing does not turn upon the supposition of superior wisdom or virtue in the executive, but upon the supposition that the legislature will not be infallible; that the love of power may sometimes betray it into a disposition to encroach upon the rights of other members of the government; that a spirit of faction may sometimes pervert its deliberations; that impressions of the moment may sometimes hurry it into measures which itself, on maturer reflection, would condemn. The primary inducement to conferring the power in question upon the executive is to enable him to defend himself; the secondary one is to increase the chances in favor of the community against the passing of bad laws through haste, inadvertence, or design. The oftener the measure is brought under examination, the greater the diversity in the situations of those who are to examine it, the less must be the danger of those errors which flow from want of due deliberation or of those missteps which proceed from the contagion of some common passion or interest. It is far less probable that culpable views of any kind should infect all the parts of the government at the same moment and in relation to the same object than that they should by turns govern and mislead every one of them.

It may perhaps be said that the power of preventing bad laws includes that of preventing good ones, and may be used to the one purpose as well as to the other. But this objection will have little weight with those who can properly estimate the mischiefs of that inconstancy and mutability in the laws, which form the greatest blemish in the character and genius of our governments. They will consider every institution calculated to restrain the excess of law-making and to keep things in the same state in which they happen to be at any given period as much more likely to do good than harm, because it is favorable to greater stability in the system of legislation. The injury which may possibly be done by defeating a few good laws will be amply compensated by the advantage of preventing a number of bad ones.

Nor is this all. The superior weight and influence of the legislative body in a free government, and the hazard to the executive in a trial of strength with that body, afford a satisfactory security that the negative would generally be employed with great caution and there would oftener be room for a charge of timidity than of rashness in the exercise of it. A king of Great Britain, with all his train of sovereign attributes, and with all the influence he draws from a thousand sources, would, at this day, hesitate to put a negative upon the joint resolutions of the two houses of Parliament. He would not fail to exert the utmost resources of that influence to strangle a measure disagreeable to him ... to avoid being reduced to the dilemma of permitting it to take effect or of risking the displeasure of the nation by an opposition to the sense of the legislative body. Nor is it probable that he would ultimately venture to exert his prerogatives but in a case of manifest propriety or extreme necessity. All well-informed men in that kingdom will accede to the justness of this remark. A very considerable period has elapsed since the negative of the crown has been exercised.

If a magistrate so powerful and so well fortified as a British monarch would have scruples about the exercise of the power under consideration, how much greater caution may be reasonably expected in a president of the United States, clothed for the short period of four years with the executive authority of a government wholly and purely republican?

It is evident that there would be greater danger of his not using his power when necessary than of his using it too often or too much. An argument, indeed, against its expediency has been drawn from this very source. It has been represented, on this account, as a power odious in appearance, useless in practice. But it will not follow that because it might be rarely exercised, it would never be exercised. In the case for which it is chiefly designed, that of an immediate attack upon the constitutional rights of the executive, or in a case in which the public good was evidently and palpably sacrificed, a man of tolerable firmness would avail himself of his constitutional means of defence, and would listen to the admonitions of duty and responsibility. In the former supposition, his fortitude would be stimulated by his immediate interest in the power of his office; in the latter, by the probability of the sanction of his constituents, who, though they would naturally incline to the legislative body in a doubtful case, would hardly suffer their partiality to delude them in a very plain case. I speak now with an eye to a magistrate possessing only a common share of firmness. There are men who, under any circumstances, will have the courage to do their duty at every hazard.

But the convention have pursued a mean in this business, which will both facilitate the exercise of the power vested in this respect in the executive magistrate and make its efficacy to depend on the sense of a considerable part of the legislative body. Instead of an absolute negative, it is proposed to give the executive the qualified negative already described. This is a power which would be much more readily exercised than the other. A man who might be afraid to defeat a law by his single VETO might not scruple to return it for reconsideration, subject to being finally rejected only in the event of more than one third of each house concurring in the sufficiency of his objections. He would be encouraged by the reflection that if his opposition should prevail, it would embark in it a very respectable proportion of the legislative body, whose influence would be united with his in supporting the propriety of his conduct in the public opinion. A direct and categorical negative has something in the appearance of it more harsh, and more apt to irritate, than the mere suggestion of argumentative objections to be approved or disapproved by those to whom they are addressed. In proportion as it would be less apt to offend, it would be more apt to be exercised; and for this very reason, it may in practice be found more effectual. It is to be hoped that it will not often happen that improper views will govern so large a proportion as two thirds of both branches of the legislature at the same time; and this, too, in spite of the counterpoising weight of the executive. It is at any rate far less probable that this should be the case than that such views should taint the resolutions and conduct of a bare majority. A power of this nature in the executive will often have a silent and unperceived, though forcible, operation. When men, engaged in unjustifiable pursuits, are aware that obstructions may come from a quarter which they cannot control, they will often be restrained by the bare apprehension of opposition from doing what they would with eagerness rush into if no such external impediments were to be feared.

This qualified negative ... is in this state vested in a council, consisting of the governor, with the chancellor and judges and the Supreme Court, or any two of them. It has been freely employed upon a variety of occasions, and frequently with success. And its utility has become so apparent that persons who, in compiling the Constitution, were violent opposers of it, have from experience become its declared admirers. ... In the formation of this part of their plan, [the convention] had departed from the model of the constitution of this state, in favor of that of Massachusetts. Two strong reasons may be imagined for this preference. One is that the judges, who are to be the interpreters of the law, might receive an improper bias from having given a previous opinion in their revisionary capacities. The other is that by being often associated with the executive, [judges] might be induced to embark too far in the political views of that magistrate, and thus a dangerous combination might by degrees be cemented between the executive and judiciary departments. It is impossible to keep the judges too distinct from every other avocation than that of expounding the laws. It is peculiarly dangerous to place them in a situation to be either corrupted or influenced by the executive.

Questions for Discussion

1. How would American politics be different today if Hamilton and Wilson had successfully carried their motion of June 4 to establish an absolute veto? Had the absolute veto been agreed to would we see fewer presidential vetoes, as Hamilton predicted?

2. What is your opinion of the council of revision proposed in the Virginia Plan? Would we better off if some subset of the Supreme Court, and the president, working together, were granted the power to veto laws, subject to a legislative override? What would be the benefits of such a scheme? What would be the costs?

3. How consequential for American politics was the decision taken late in the convention to change the veto override required from three-fourths to two-thirds of both houses of Congress?

4. How does Martin's account of the convention's debate over the veto power compare with the debate over the veto power in Madison's notes?

5. Imagine that the supporters and critics of the Constitution could be brought back to life: Which if any of them would approve of the way the veto power is exercised today? Which ones would disapprove? Who would feel that their views had been vindicated? Who would feel the greatest need to revise their thinking about the veto power?

6. How do the views of the Federal Farmer on the veto power compare with those expressed by Madison, Wilson, and Morris at the Constitutional Convention?

7

War and Peace

The Congress shall have Power ... [t]o declare War, grant Letters of Marque and Reprisal, and make Rules concerning Captures on Land and Water; To raise and support Armies ... To provide and maintain a Navy; To make Rules for the Government and Regulation of the land and naval forces; To provide for calling forth the Militia to execute the Laws of the Union, suppress Insurrections and repel Invasions; To provide for organizing, arming, and disciplining, Militia, and for governing such part of them as may be employed in the Service of the United States.

Article 1, section 8

The President shall be Commander in Chief of the Army and Navy of the United States, and of the Militia of the several States, when called into the actual Service of the United States

He shall have Power, by and with the Advice and Consent of the Senate, to make Treaties, provided two thirds of the Senators present concur.

Article 2, section 2

[The President] shall receive Ambassadors and other public Ministers.

Article 2, section 3

To whom belong the powers of war and peace? The question has divided Americans from almost the moment the Constitution was ratified. In 1793 Alexander Hamilton and James Madison, erstwhile allies and collaborators, divided bitterly over whether the president or Congress had the power to declare neutrality. A century later, Senators John Spooner and Augustus Bacon clashed in a famous debate triggered by President Theodore Roosevelt's foreign policy, with Spooner taking the Hamiltonian ground that "the conduct of our foreign relations is vested by the Constitution in the President" (Corwin 1957, 428) and Bacon adopting the Madisonian position that "Congress and not the President is supreme under the Constitution in the control of foreign affairs" (Wormuth and Firmage 1986, 184). More recently, the 1973 War Powers Resolution, which attempted to limit the president's power to send troops abroad, has been drenched in acrimonious controversy. Presidents from Richard Nixon on have refused to comply fully with the law because they see it as an unconstitutional infringement of presidential power. The law's defenders see it as a long overdue effort to return to the framers' original intent, which in Thomas Jefferson words was to chain "the dog of war by transferring the power of letting him loose from the executive to the legislative body" (Pious 1996, 442).[1] The federal courts have generally refrained from joining this dispute, usually judging it to be a "political question" best decided by the president and Congress. The courts have thus implicitly agreed with political scientist Edward S. Corwin's famous remark that "the Constitution ... is an invitation to struggle for the privilege of directing American foreign policy" (1957, 171).

The power to direct war and peace never fit neatly into the tripartite division of executive, legislative, and judicial powers that the framers used to order the political world. Writing in the late seventeenth century, English political theorist John Locke drew attention to the peculiar status of the "Power of War and Peace, Leagues and Alliances, and all the Transactions with all Persons and Communities without the Commonwealth." Noting that these powers were neither executive nor legislative, Locke coined the term "federative" to denote these powers. Yet for Locke, though the executive and federative powers were "distinct in themselves," the two powers could "hardly ... be separated, and placed, at the same time, in the hands of distinct persons." To place the executive and federative powers in "Persons that might act separately, whereby the Force of the Publick would be under different Commands[,] would be apt ... to cause disorder and ruine." So although federative power was analytically distinct from executive power, it was necessary as a practical matter to lodge both powers, as England did, in the hands of the monarch (1965, 411–12).

More commonly in the eighteenth century, however, legal commentators and political philosophers understood Locke's federative power as a subset or species of executive power. Massachusetts lawyer Theophilus Parsons, writing in 1778, subdivided the executive power into "the external executive and internal executive." The external executive, explained Parsons, "comprehends

---

1. The most controversial aspect of the War Powers Resolution has been the requirement that the president must withdraw American troops if within sixty days Congress has not "declared a war or ... enacted a specific authorization for such use." Presidents and their defenders have attacked this provision as an unconstitutional encroachment on presidential power, but others have attacked it for the opposite reason—that giving a president carte blanche to send troops anywhere in the world, even if for only sixty days, represents "an unconstitutional delegation of congressional war power to the president" (Wormuth and Firmage 1986, 187; also Adler 1989b, 142–43). More recently, Clinton administration officials have embraced the logic of these critics' position to support assertions of presidential hegemony. "The structure of the War Powers Resolution," Clinton's lawyers suggested in a letter to congressional Republicans, "recognized and presupposes the unilateral Presidential authority to deploy armed forces 'into hostilities' or imminent hostilities" (Pious 1996, 464).

war, peace, the sending and receiving ambassadors, and whatever concerns the transactions of the state with any other independent state," whereas the internal executive was that power "which is employed in the peace, security and protection of the subject and his property" (Handlin and Handlin 1966, 337). Montesquieu too subdivided executive power into two categories: domestic ("things that depend on the civil laws") and foreign ("things dependent on the law of nations"). By virtue of the latter species of executive power the prince or magistrate "makes peace or war, sends or receives embassies, establishes the public security, and provides against invasions" (1977, 201).[2] Having classified the power to make peace or war as an executive power, Montesquieu followed his commitment to a strict separation of powers to arrive at the conclusion that such power must be vested in a monarch or executive magistrate. Place executive power in the hands of a legislature, Montesquieu warned, and "there would be an end then of liberty" (207). The reasoning was different from Locke's but Montesquieu ended up affirming, as Locke had, the wisdom of the English constitution for placing the power of war and peace in the hands of the monarch rather than in Parliament.

In England the power of war and peace had long been a central pillar of the royal prerogative. In the nation's "intercourse with foreign nations," William Blackstone explained, the king is "considered as the delegate or representative of his people" ([1783] 1978, 1:261). From this principle follows the king's "sole prerogative of making war and peace" (1:257), "sending ambassadors to other states, and receiving ambassadors at home" (1:253), and "mak[ing] treaties, leagues, and alliances with foreign states and princes" (1:257). Parliament had no power to reject a treaty, declare war, or make peace, though it could use the "check of parliamentary impeachment" (1:258) to "call the king's advisers to a just and severe account ... for improper or inglorious conduct in beginning, conducting, or concluding a national war" (1:252, 258), or for advising the king to conclude a treaty that "shall afterwards be judged to derogate from the honour and interest of the nation" (1:257). Impeachment, in Blackstone's view, was "in general sufficient to restrain the ministers of the crown from a wanton or injurious exertion of this great prerogative" (1:258).[3]

---

2. Although Montesquieu begins with this division of the executive power into domestic and foreign, he muddies the issue by immediately reformulating the division in such a way that the domestic executive disappears altogether. The "executive [power] in regard to things that depend on the civil laws" becomes restated as the power to punish crimes and determine disputes that arise between individuals, which he terms the "judiciary power." Thus the executive power, in Montesquieu's reformulation, becomes equated entirely with the powers of foreign relations and commander in chief, and the domestic function of the executive as one who executes the laws drops out. On Montesquieu's conception of the executive see Mansfield 1989, chapter 9, esp. 216, 233–34, 239.

3. Blackstone's *Commentaries*, which were first published in 1765, were enormously influential in colonial America. The first American edition, published in 1771–1772, had an advance subscription of 1,587 sets (Marston 1987, 327; also see Lutz 1984). For Blackstone's influence on Hamilton, see Stourzh 1970.

The king's prerogative in the nation's "own domestic government and civil polity" (1:252) included the power to direct "the united strength of the community" so as to fulfill "the great end of society," which was "to protect the weakness of individuals." Thus the king, Blackstone explained, is considered "the generalissimo or the first in military command, within the kingdom" (1:262). It was "in this capacity [as] general of the kingdom," Blackstone argued, that the king possessed "the sole power of raising and regulating fleets and armies" as well as the "sole prerogative ... of erecting ... manning and governing ... all forts and other places of strength, within the realm" (1:262–63). Protection again external enemies and internal disorders was, as Scottish political philosopher Adam Ferguson simply put it, "the office of the executive power" (Marston 1987, 28).

King George III's declaration of war on the colonies rudely compelled Americans to rethink this commonplace assumption of eighteenth-century Anglo-American political thought. After all, far from providing protection from external enemies, the king was now himself the enemy. The newly constituted American government did away with the executive altogether and conferred upon the Continental Congress "the sole and exclusive right of determining on peace and war ... of sending and receiving ambassadors, [of] entering into treaties and alliances ... [and] of granting letters of marque and reprisal in times of peace." George Washington was made "General and Commander in Chief" of the army, and he was instructed "punctually to observe and follow such orders and directions, from time to time, as you shall receive from this or a future Congress of these United Colonies, or committees of Congress" (Wormuth and Firmage 1986, 106). Nor did Congress shy away from issuing detailed directives to Washington: to intercept specific British vessels, to send a force into Nova Scotia, to send General Gates to assume command in Canada. Congress even issued directives about troop movements to Washington's subordinates without consulting the commander in chief (106–7). Washington, moreover, was dependent on the Continental Congress and the state governments to raise armies and supplies.

Since the Continental Congress claimed for itself the exclusive power of foreign relations, the state constitutions generally said little about the power to make war and peace. An exception was South Carolina's 1776 constitution, which expressly declared that the state's chief executive "shall have no power to make war or peace, or enter into any final treaty, without the consent of the general assembly and legislative council" (Thorpe 1909, 6:3247). The clause was retained in the revised 1778 constitution, with the only modification in the prohibition being that "commence war, or conclude peace" was substituted for "make war or peace" (6:3255). Though the state constitutions generally ignored what the Essex Result called the "external executive" power, they all made provision for the "internal executive power ... to marshall and command [the state's] militia and armies for her defense" (Handlin and Handlin 1966, 337). All the state constitutions placed the governor or president at the head of the state's military forces, and all but Maryland and Virginia entitled this person "commander in chief."[4] Given the importance American presidents since Lincoln have attached to the commander in chief clause in the Constitution, as well as the complete absence of any debate about this clause at the federal Constitutional Convention, it is worth examining briefly the history of the designation "commander in chief."

The term, Francis Wormuth tells us, was introduced into English law in 1639 by Charles I, who raised an army to fight the Scots and then appointed the Earl of Arundel commander in chief of that army, instructing him to "withstand all Invasions, Tumults, [and] Seditious Conspiracies" (Wormuth and Firmage 1986, 105). The designation continued to be used into the eighteenth century to designate military commanders in the army and navy (each fleet had a separate commander in chief), but the post was always placed under the command of a political superior. "The commander in chief," complained the Duke of Wellington, "cannot move a Corporal's Guard from one station to another, without a Route countersigned by the Secretary of War" (105–6). Washington's appointment as commander in chief of the continental army was very much in this tradition.

In the colonies it had also become the practice, though, to designate each royal governor as commander in chief, a title that brought with it the power "to nominate and appoint all the colony's military establishment; raise, arm

---

4. Only the Massachusetts constitution of 1780 (and the 1784 New Hampshire constitution, which copied the relevant sections in the Massachusetts document) specified what the state expected from its commander in chief. The governor, the constitution declared, "shall have full power, by himself, or by any commander, or other officer, from time to time, to train, instruct, exercise, and govern the militia and navy; and, for the special defense and safety of the commonwealth to assemble in martial array and put in warlike posture, the inhabitants thereof, and to lead and conduct them and with them to encounter, resist, expel, and pursue, by force of arms, as well by sea as by land, within or without the limits of this commonwealth, and also to kill, slay, and destroy, if necessary, and conquer, by all fitting ways, enterprises, and means whatsoever, all and every such person and persons as shall, at any time hereafter, in a hostile manner, attempt or enterprise the destruction, invasion, detriment, or annoyance of this commonwealth; and to use and exercise, over the army and navy, and over the militia in actual service, the law-martial, in time of war or invasion, and also in time of rebellion, *declared by the legislature to exist,* as occasion shall necessarily require; and to take and surprise, by all ways and means whatsoever, all and every such person or persons, with their ships, arms, ammunition, and other goods, as shall, in a hostile matter, invade, or attempt the invading, conquering, or annoying this commonwealth; that the governor be intrusted with all these and other powers, incident to the offices of captain-general and commander-in-chief, and admiral, to be exercised agreeably to the rules and regulations of the constitution, and the laws of the land, and not otherwise.

Provided, that the said governor shall not, at any time hereafter ... transport any of the inhabitants of this commonwealth, or oblige them to march out of the limits of the same, *without their free and voluntary consent, or the consent of the [legislature];* except so far as may be necessary to march or transport them by land or water, for the defense of such part of the state to which they cannot otherwise conveniently have access" (Thorpe 1909, 3:1901; emphasis added). This last provision was modeled on the Massachusetts colonial charter, which forbade the governor's transporting troops out of the province without the consent of the legislature (Greene [1898] 1966, 100).

and command the provincial troops; and employ such troops wherever necessary to repel invasions, execute the commands of the Crown, or put down insurrections" (Greene 1963, 297). The colonial governor's power as commander in chief was not nearly as impressive as it appeared on paper, however, since colonial assemblies, like the House of Commons in England, used their power of the purse to limit the executive's control over the military. Without money the governor could raise no troops, a fact that gave the legislature leverage over the shape of military policy and, on occasion in the colonies at least, appointments. In appropriating money for the military, the assemblies typically tried to minimize executive discretion by stipulating "the purpose of the appropriation; the number of men and officers to be raised; their distribution and organization, rates of pay, and place and period of service; and the apportionment of supplies" (303; Greene [1898] 1966, 99–103). Despite these limitations, the colonial governor's power as commander in chief was clearly modeled on the king's domestic prerogative as "the generalissimo or first in command." Even on the most liberal construction of the commander in chief clause, however, it is clear that this power was never conceived of as encompassing the external power of commencing war or concluding peace (Wormuth and Firmage 1986, 105). By explicitly vesting the raising and regulating of military forces in the Congress, the Constitution also signaled that the president's power as commander in chief would be more limited than the formal powers exercised by the "generalissimo or first in command" in either colonial America or England.

The absence of any debate in the federal convention over the commander in chief clause is arguably further evidence that the framers did not imagine it to be an expansive grant of power but rather saw presidential command of military operations as a narrow but necessary instrument to secure civilian control over the military and achieve an effective direction of military forces once war had been "authorized or begun" (Adler 1989b, 128–29). The ruling assumption seemed to be that since "the means of carrying on the war would not be in the hands of the President but of the Legislature," as Nathaniel Gorham told the convention on September 7, then making the president commander in chief of the army and navy posed no real threat to liberty. The revolutionary experience of governors serving as commanders in chief served as important evidence in favor of the safety of making the chief executive commander in chief. Left unanswered and even unasked at the convention, however, was whether or to what extent the president, as commander in chief, should take directions from Congress. Was the president as commander in chief to be like General Washington or the Earl or Arundel or even the colonial governors, all of whom were subordinate to a higher civilian authority? Or was the president's authority as commander in chief more akin to the king's authority as "generalissimo" (shorn, of course, of those powers that were specifically granted to Congress in Article 1, section 8), in which case the president had powers that went beyond carrying out legislative directions and extended into the setting of policy (Henkin 1996, 45–46). To some extent this distinction was academic, for the nature of war meant, as the Continental Congress recognized in its instructions to Washington, that since "all particulars cannot be foreseen, nor positive instructions for such emergencies so before hand given ... many things must be left to your prudent and discreet management" (Wormuth and Firmage 1986, 106). Since no attempt was made to specify where executive discretion left off and legislative oversight took over, nor even to say what the powers of commander in chief entailed, the framers left future presidents and congresses free to wrestle over the powers contained in the title of commander in chief.

The clauses pertaining to military and foreign policy that drew the delegates' greatest attention were those relating to the power to declare war and especially to treaty-making power. The Continental Congress had assumed both of these powers but since there was no chief executive there really was no other choice. Having committed to a separate executive branch, the delegates at the federal convention were faced with a momentous choice of what to do with these powers that had historically belonged to the king by virtue of his role as the representative of his people. Given the centuries of precedent they were overturning, it is striking how little dissent there was from the decision not to vest the power to declare war in the president. Only one delegate, Pierce Butler, expressed himself in favor of giving the president the power to declare war. All other delegates voicing an opinion agreed the legislature was the safest depository of such a power, though there was vigorous disagreement about whether that power was best vested in the Senate or in both houses and whether the words "declare war" were preferable to "make war." The treaty-making power was a more vexing question for the delegates. Not until two weeks before the end of the convention did the delegates decide against vesting the power in the Senate, opting instead to have the president and Senate share a role in the making of treaties. Thus control of foreign and military policy was, as Hamilton put it in *Federalist* 75, a "joint possession." One of the most fascinating stories in the development of the presidency is how this "joint possession" gradually became seen, even by Congress itself, as primarily a presidential dominion.[5]

---

5. That story would include a chapter on how presidents have sent American forces to fight in foreign countries several hundred times, although Congress has declared war on only five occasions: the War of 1812, the Mexican War of 1848, the Spanish-American War of 1898, World War I, and World War II. Another would explore the ways in which presidents since Theodore Roosevelt's time have increasingly used executive agreements as a way to avoid having to gain Senate approval of treaties. The most interesting chapter of all would be the way in which Congress itself has willingly acquiesced in and even required presidential dominance of foreign policy. Students interested in these developments should begin with Henkin (1996) but will also profit from Corwin (1957, chaps. 5–6), Schlesinger (1973), and Crabb and Holt (1992).

26. The Federal Convention of 1787

Prior to laying the Virginia Plan before the delegates on May 29, Edmund Randolph opened the convention's main business by enumerating the "defects of the confederation" that the plan was designed to remedy. The first defect he identified was that it "produced no security against foreign invasion; congress not being permitted to prevent a war nor to support it by their own authority." Elaborating on this defect, Randolph pointed out that although the Articles of Confederation gave Congress the exclusive power to negotiate treaties, Congress "could not cause infractions of treaties or of the law of nations, to be punished" (Farrand 1937, 1:19). This impacted the nation's security, since the failure of states to honor the nation's treaties gave foreign governments an excuse to renege on their own treaty commitments. For instance, Congress's inability to compel states to pay prewar debts to British merchants, as was required by the peace terms of 1783, allowed the British to renege on their own pledge to relinquish their strategically important northern forts (Marks 1973, 5–15). Nor had the national government been able to prevent states from entering into treaties or warring with Indians (4). Another related complaint was that although the Articles vested Congress with "the sole and exclusive right and power of determining on peace and war," the national government was dependent on the states to raise and maintain an army and navy. During the revolutionary war, self-preservation mixed with patriotic fervor generally induced the necessary cooperation from the states, but the onset of peace eroded the states' willingness to sacrifice for the whole. Lacking the ability to raise and maintain an effective army and navy, the national government was handicapped in its efforts to fight against the Indians, force the British from their northern posts, open up the Mississippi to American trade, combat the Barbary pirates, or even put down domestic rebellions such as Shays' Rebellion in Massachusetts (143). For the authors of the Virginia Plan, then, as for most of the rest of the delegates, the problems of war and peace were seen primarily through the prism of the relationship between the central government and the states rather than in terms of the proper relationship between the executive and the legislature. The priority placed on establishing national supremacy over the states may explain why there is no mention at all in the Virginia Plan of what roles the national legislature and the national executive would play in foreign affairs and national defense. Instead, the Virginia Plan said only that "the National Legislature ought to be impowered to enjoy the Legislative Rights vested in Congress by the Confed-

---

Gaillard Hunt and James Brown Scott, eds., *The Debates in the Federal Convention of 1787 Which Framed the Constitution of the United States of America Reported by James Madison* (New York: Oxford University Press, 1920), 37–39, 337, 340–43, 404–5, 418–19, 457–59, 506, 508, 528–34.

eration" and that "a National Executive ... ought to enjoy the Executive rights vested in Congress by the Confederation." Did this give the power of war and peace to the executive or to the legislature? When the convention began consideration of the National Executive on June 1, Charles Pinckney immediately leaped to his feet to express concern that this formulation would mean vesting the power of war and peace in the executive.

June 1

Mr. Pinckney was for a vigorous Executive but was afraid the Executive powers of the existing Congress might extend to peace and war ... which would render the Executive a monarchy, of the worst kind, to wit an elective one. ...

Mr. Rutledge ... said he was for vesting the Executive power in a single person, though he was not for giving him the power of war and peace. ...

Mr. Wilson ... did not consider the prerogatives of the British Monarch as a proper guide in defining the Executive powers. Some of these prerogatives were of a Legislative nature, among others that of war and peace. The only powers he conceived strictly Executive were those of executing the laws, and appointing officers not appertaining to and appointed by the Legislature. ...

Mr. Madison thought it would be proper, before a choice should be made between a unity and plurality in the Executive, to fix the extent of the Executive authority; that as certain powers were in their nature Executive, and must be given to that department whether administered by one or more persons, a definition of their extent would assist ... in determining how far they might be safely entrusted to a single officer. He accordingly moved that so much of the clause before the Committee as related to the powers of the Executive [that is, the part of the clause reading "and that besides a general authority to execute the National Laws, it ought to enjoy the Executive rights vested in Congress by the Confederation"] should be struck out and that after the words "that a national Executive ought to be instituted" there be inserted the words following ... "with power to carry into effect the national laws [and] to appoint to offices in cases not otherwise provided for ..."[6]

Mr. Wilson seconded the motion. ... The motion being ... agreed to: Connecticut divided, all the other States in the affirmative.

August 6

Mr. Rutledge delivered in the Report of the Committee of Detail as follows. ...

Article VII, Section 1. The Legislature of the United States shall have the power. ... To make war; To raise armies; To build and equip fleets; To call forth the aid of the militia, in order to execute the laws of the Union, enforce treaties, suppress insurrections, and repel invasions. ...

Article IX, Section 1. The Senate of the United States shall have the power to make treaties. ...

---

6. Rufus King's notes record Madison agreeing "with Wilson in his definition of executive powers—executive powers ... do not include the Rights of war and peace ... but the powers should be confined and defined" (Farrand 1937, 1:70).

Article X, Section 2. [The President] shall receive Ambassadors. ... He shall be commander in chief of the Army and Navy of the United States, and of the Militia of the Several States.

August 15

Mr. Mercer contended that the Senate ought not to have the power of treaties. This power belonged to the Executive department; adding that Treaties would not be final so as to alter the laws of the land till ratified by legislative authority. This was the case of Treaties in Great Britain. ...

Col. Mason did not say that a Treaty would repeal a law; but that the Senate by means of treaty might alienate territory ... without legislative sanction. The cessions of the British Islands in [the] West Indies by Treaty alone were an example. If Spain should possess herself of Georgia therefore the Senate might by treaty dismember the Union. ... The Senate [could] sell the whole Country by means of Treaties.

August 17

Mr. Pinckney opposed vesting [the power to make war] in the Legislature. Its proceedings were too slow. It would meet but once a year. The House of Representatives would be too numerous for such deliberations. The Senate would be the best depositary, being more acquainted with foreign affairs. ... If the States are equally represented in the Senate, so as to give no advantage to large States, the power will notwithstanding be safe, as the small have their all at stake in such cases as well as the large States. It would be singular for one authority to make war, and another peace.

Mr. Butler. The objections against the Legislature lie in great degree against the Senate. He was for vesting the power in the President, who will have all the requisite qualities and will not make war but when the Nation will support it.

Mr. Madison and Mr. Gerry moved to insert "declare," striking out "make" war; leaving to the Executive the power to repel sudden attacks.

Mr. Sherman thought it stood very well. The Executive should be able to repel and not to commence war. "Make" [is] better than "declare," the latter narrowing the power too much.

Mr. Gerry never expected to hear in a republic a motion to empower the Executive alone to declare war.

Mr. Ellsworth. There is a material difference between the cases of making war and making peace. It should be more easy to get out of war than into it. War also is a simple and overt declaration. Peace [is] attended with intricate and secret negotiations.

Mr. Mason was against giving the power of war to the Executive, because [the Executive is] not safely to be trusted with it; or to the Senate, because [the Senate is] not so constructed as to be entitled to it. He was for clogging rather than facilitating war; but for facilitating peace. He preferred "declare" to "make."

On the motion to insert declare in place of make, it was agreed to [7 yes; 2 no; 1 absent]. ... On the remark by Mr. King that "make" war might be understood to "conduct" it, which was an Executive function, Mr. Ellsworth gave up his objection and the vote of Connecticut was changed to ay [8 yes; 1 no; 1 absent].

Mr. Butler moved to give the Legislature power of peace, as they were to have that of war.

Mr. Gerry seconds him. Eight Senators may possibly exercise the power if vested in that body, and fourteen if all should be present; and may consequently give up part of the United States. The Senate are more liable to be corrupted by an Enemy than the whole Legislature.

On the motion for adding "and peace" after "war" [0 yes; 10 no].

August 23

Article IX, section 1 being resumed, to wit "The Senate of the U.S. shall have power to make treaties."

Mr. Madison observed that the Senate represented the States alone and that for this as well as other obvious reasons it was proper that the President should be an agent in Treaties.

Mr. Govr. Morris did not know that he should agree to refer the making of Treaties to the Senate at all, but for the present would move to add, as an amendment to the section after "Treaties"—"but no Treaty shall be binding on the U.S. which is not ratified by a law."—

Mr. Madison suggested the inconvenience of requiring a legal ratification of treaties of alliance. ...

Mr. Gorham. Many other disadvantages must be experienced if treaties of peace and all negotiations are to be previously ratified; and if not previously, the Ministers would be at a loss how to proceed. What would be the case in Great Britain if the King were to proceed in this manner? American Ministers must go abroad not instructed by the same Authority ... which is to ratify their proceedings.

Mr. Govr. Morris. As to treaties of alliance, they will oblige foreign powers to send their Ministers here, the very thing we should wish for. Such treaties could not be otherwise made, if his amendment should succeed. In general he was not solicitous to multiply and facilitate Treaties. He wished none to be made with Great Britain till she should be at war. Then a good bargain might be made with her. So with other foreign powers. The more difficulty in making treaties, the more value will be set on them.

Mr. Wilson. In the most important Treaties the King of Great Britain, being obliged to resort to Parliament for the execution of them, is under the same fetters as the amendment of Mr. Morris will impose on the Senate. ... Under the clause, without the amendment, the Senate alone can make a Treaty. ...

Mr. Dickinson concurred in the amendment, as most safe and proper, though he was sensible it was unfavorable to the little States, which would otherwise have an equal share in making Treaties.

Docr. Johnson thought there was something of solecism in saying that the acts of a Minister with plenipotentiary powers from one Body should depend for ratification on another Body. The example of the King of Great Britain was not parallel. Full and complete power was vested in him. If the Parliament should fail to provide the necessary means of execution, the Treaty would be violated.

Mr. Gorham, in answer to Mr. Govr. Morris, said that the negotiations on the spot were not to be desired by us, especially if the whole Legislature is to have anything to do with Treaties. It will be generally influenced by two or three men, who will be corrupted by the Ambassadors here. In such a Government as ours, it is necessary to guard against the Government itself being seduced.

Mr. Randolph, observing that almost every Speaker had made objections to the clause as it stood, moved, in order to a further consideration of the subject, that the Motion of Mr. Govr. Morris should be postponed, and on this question it was lost the States being equally divided.

On Mr. Govr. Morris's motion [1 yes; 8 no; 1 divided].

August 27

Mr. Sherman moved to amend the clause giving the Executive the command of the Militia, so as to read "and of the Militia of the several states, when called into the actual service of the U.S.," and on the Question [6 yes; 2 no; 3 absent].

September 4

Mr. Brearly from the Committee of Eleven made a further partial Report as follows. ... "The President by and with the advice and consent of the Senate, shall have power to make treaties ... But no Treaty shall be made without the consent of two thirds of the members present."

September 7

Mr. Wilson moved to add, after the word "Senate," the words "and House of Representatives." As treaties he said are to have the operation of laws, they ought to have the sanction of laws also. The circumstance of secrecy in the business of treaties formed the only objection, but this he thought, so far as it was inconsistent with obtaining the Legislative sanction, was outweighed by the necessity of the latter.

Mr. Sherman thought the only question that could be made was whether the power could be safely trusted to the Senate. He thought it could, and that the necessity of secrecy in the case of treaties forbade a reference of them to the whole Legislature.

Mr. Fitzsimmons seconded the motion of Mr. Wilson, and on the question [1 yes; 10 no].

The first sentence as to making treaties was then agreed to: nem. con.

Mr. Wilson thought it objectionable to require the concurrence of $^2/_3$ which puts it in the power of a minority to control the will of a majority.

Mr. King concurred in the objection, remarking that as the Executive was here joined in the business there was a check which did not exist in Congress where the concurrence of $^2/_3$ was required.

Mr. Madison moved to insert after the word "treaty" the words "except treaties of peace," allowing these to be made with less difficulty than other treaties—It was agreed to nem. con.

Mr. Madison then moved to authorize a concurrence of two thirds of the Senate to make treaties of peace, without the concurrence of the President. The President he said would necessarily derive so much power and importance from a state of war that he might be tempted, if authorized, to impede a treaty of peace. Mr. Butler seconded the motion.

Mr. Gorham thought the precaution unnecessary as the means of carrying on the war would not be in the hands of the President but of the Legislature.

Mr. Govr. Morris thought the power of the President in this case harmless, and that no peace ought to be made without the concurrence of the President, who was the general Guardian of the National interests.

Mr. Butler was strenuous for the motion, as a necessary security against ambitious and corrupt Presidents. ...

Mr. Gerry was of the opinion that in treaties of peace a greater rather than less proportion of votes was necessary than in other treaties. In treaties of peace the dearest interests will be at stake, as the fisheries, territory, etc. In treaties of peace also there is more danger to the extremities of the Continent, of being sacrificed, than on any other occasions.

Mr. Williamson thought that treaties of peace should be guarded at least by requiring the same concurrence as in other treaties.

On the motion of Mr. Madison and Mr. Butler [3 yes; 8 no].

On the part of the clause concerning treaties amended by the exception as to Treaties of peace [8 yes; 3 no].

September 8

Mr. King moved to strike out the "exception of Treaties of peace" from the general clause requiring two thirds of the Senate for making Treaties.

Mr. Wilson wished the requisition of two thirds to be struck out altogether. If the majority cannot be trusted, it was a proof, as observed by Mr. Gorham, that we were not fit for one society.

A reconsideration of the whole clause was agreed to.

Mr. Govr. Morris was against striking out the "exception of Treaties of peace." If two thirds of the Senate should be required for peace, the Legislature will be unwilling to make war. ... Besides, if a Majority of the Senate be for peace, and are not allowed to make it, they will be apt to effect their purpose in a more disagreeable mode of negativing the supplies for the war.

Mr. Williamson remarked that Treaties are to be made in the branch of the Government where there may be a majority of the States without a majority of the people. Eight men may be a majority of a quorum, and should not have the power to decide the conditions of peace. ...

Mr. Wilson. If two thirds are necessary to make peace, the minority may perpetuate war against the sense of the majority.

Mr. Gerry enlarged on the danger of putting the essential rights of the Union in the hands of so small a number as a majority of the Senate, representing perhaps, not one fifth of the people. The Senate will be corrupted by foreign influence. ...

On the question for striking "except Treaties of peace" [8 yes; 3 no].

Mr. Wilson and Mr. Dayton moved to strike out the clause requiring two thirds of the Senate for making Treaties [1 yes; 9 no; 1 divided].

On a question on the clause of the Report of the Committee of Eleven relating to Treaties by ⅔ of the Senate, all the States were ay, except Pennsylvania, New Jersey and Georgia.

27. George Mason, Henry Lee, and George Nicholas, Virginia Ratifying Convention, June 18, 1788

Although the commander in chief clause was not debated at all in the federal convention, it received considerable attention in several ratifying conventions, especially in Virginia and North Carolina. Of particular concern was the

Jonathan Elliot, ed., *The Debates in the Several State Constitutions on the Adoption of the Federal Constitution* (New York: Burt Franklin, 1888), 3:496–98.

prospect that the president might personally assume command of the army. Although virtually every state constitution entitled the chief executive "commander in chief," a number of states (including both Virginia and North Carolina) insisted, in the words of the Pennsylvania constitution, that he "shall not command in person, except advised thereto by the council" (Thorpe 1909, 4:3088). Fear of the executive assuming personal command of the army also surfaced briefly at the federal convention in the New Jersey Plan, which authorized the executive to "direct all military operations; provided that none of the persons composing the federal Executive shall on any occasion take command of any troops, so as personally to conduct any enterprise as General, or in [an]other capacity" (Farrand 1937, 1:244). The convention apparently never debated or voted on this part of the New Jersey Plan, but the fears it reflected were forcefully articulated at Virginia's ratifying convention by George Mason.

Mr. Mason, animadverting on the magnitude of the powers of the President, was alarmed at the additional power of commanding the army in person. He admitted the propriety of his being commander-in-chief, so far as to give orders and have a general superintendency, but he thought it would be dangerous to let him command in person, without any restraint, as he might make a bad use of it. He was, then, clearly of the opinion that the consent of a majority of both houses of Congress should be required before he could take the command in person. If at any time it should be necessary that he should take personal command, either on account of his superior abilities or other cause, then Congress would agree to it; and all dangers would be obviated by requiring their consent. He called to the gentlemen's recollection the extent of what the late commander-in-chief might have done, from his great abilities, and the strong attachment of both officers and soldiers towards him, if, instead of being disinterested, he had been an ambitious man. So disinterested and amiable a character as General Washington might never command again. The possibility of danger ought to be guarded against. ...

Mr. Lee reminded his honorable friend that it did not follow, of necessity, that the President should command in person; that he was to command as a civil officer, and might only take the command when he was a man of military talents, and the public safety required it. ...

Mr. Mason replied that he did not mean that the President was of necessity to command, but he might if he pleased; and if he was an ambitious man, he might make a dangerous use of it.

Mr. Nicholas. ... The army and navy were to be raised by Congress, and not by the President. It was on the same footing with our state government; for the governor, with the council, was to embody the militia, but, when actually embodied, they were under the sole command of the governor. The instance adduced was not similar. General Washington was not a President. As to possible danger, any commander might attempt to pervert what was intended for the common defence of the community to its destruction. The President, at the end of four years, was to relinquish all his offices. But if any other person was to have the command, the time would not be limited.

Mr. Mason answered that it did not resemble the state constitution, because the governor did not possess such extensive powers as the President, and had no influence over the navy. The liberty of the people had been destroyed by those who were military commanders only. The danger here was greater by the junction of great civil powers to the command of the army and fleet. Although Congress are to raise the army, said he, no security arises from that; for, in time of war, they must and ought to raise an army, which will be numerous, or otherwise, according to the nature of the war, and then the President is to command without any control.

28. North Carolina Ratifying Convention, July 24 and 28, 1788

The debate in the North Carolina convention picks up where the Virginia convention left off. In North Carolina, though, concerns about the commander in chief clause went beyond Mason's worry that a president might assume personal command of the army. Congress and not the president, some Anti-Federalists suggested, "ought to have power to direct the motions of the army." North Carolina Anti-Federalists also drew a bead on the treaty-making power, which they criticized for excluding the people's branch, the House of Representatives. They objected that the elected branches of government least accountable and most distant from the people were the ones entrusted with military and foreign policy. But their greatest fear was the central government itself, and their most profound worry was that they were about "to give a power to the general government to drag the inhabitants to any part of the world as long as they pleased." The Federalists were able to answer persuasively many of the Anti-Federalists' objections to specific clauses, but it is noteworthy that this more sweeping objection went unanswered.

Mr. [James] Iredell. ... In almost every country, the executive has the command of the military forces. From the nature of the thing, the command of armies ought to be delegated to one person only. The secrecy, despatch, and decision, which are necessary in military operations, can only be expected from one person. The President, therefore, is to command the military forces of the United States, and this power I think a proper one; at the same time it will be found to be sufficiently guarded. A very material difference may be observed between this power and the authority of the king of Great Britain under similar circumstances. The king of Great Britain is not only the commander-in-chief of the land and naval forces, but has power, in time of war, to raise fleets and armies. He has also authority to declare war. The President has not the power of declaring war by his own authority, nor that of raising fleets and armies. These powers are vested in other hands. The power of declaring war is expressly given to Congress, that is, to the two branches of the legislature. ... They have also expressly delegated to them the powers of raising and supporting armies, and of providing and maintaining a navy.[7]

Jonathan Elliot, ed., *The Debates in the Several State Constitutions on the Adoption of the Federal Constitution* (New York: Burt Franklin, 1888), 4:107–8, 114–16, 118–20.

7. Here Iredell follows Hamilton's line of argument in *Federalist 69*.

With regard to the militia, it must be observed that though he has the command of them when called into the actual service of the United States, yet he has not the power of calling them out. The power of calling them out is vested in Congress, for the purpose of executing the laws of the Union. When the militia are called out for any purpose, some person must command them; and who so proper as that person who has the best evidence of his possessing the general confidence of the people? I trust, therefore, that the power of commanding the militia, when called forth into the actual service of the United States, will not be objected to.

Mr. [William] Miller acknowledged that the explanation of this clause ... had obviated some objections which he had to it, but still he could not entirely approve of it. He could not see the necessity of vesting this power in the President. He thought that his influence would be too great in the country, and particularly over the military, by being the commander-in-chief of the army, navy, and militia. He thought he could too easily abuse such extensive powers, and was of the opinion that Congress ought to have power to direct the motions of the army. He considered it as a defect in the Constitution that it was not expressly provided that Congress should have the direction of the motions of the army.

Mr. [Richard Dobbs] Spaight answered that it was true that the command of the army and navy was given to the President, but that Congress, who had the power of raising armies, could certainly prevent any abuse of that authority in the President. [Congress] alone had the means of supporting armies, and ... the President was impeachable if he in any manner abused his trust. He was surprised that any objection should be made to giving the command of the army to one man; that it was well known that the direction of an army could not be properly exercised by a numerous body of men; that Congress had, in the last war, given the exclusive command of the army to the commander-in-chief, and that if they had not done so, perhaps the independence of America would not have been established.

Mr. [William] Porter. Mr. Chairman, there is a power vested in the Senate and President to make treaties, which shall be the supreme law of the land. Which among us can call them to account? I always thought that there could be no proper exercise of power without the suffrage of the people, yet the House of Representatives has no power to intermeddle with treaties. The President and seven senators, as nearly as I can remember, can make a treaty which will be of great advantage to the Northern States and equal injury to the Southern States. Yet, in the preamble of the Constitution, they say all the people have done it. I should be glad to know what power there is of calling the President and Senate to account. ...

Gov. [Samuel] Johnston. Mr. Chairman, in my opinion, if there be any difference between this Constitution and the Confederation with respect to treaties, the Constitution is more safe than the Confederation. We know that two members from each state have a right, by the Confederation, to give the vote of that state, and two thirds of the states have a right also to make treaties. By this Constitution two thirds of the senators cannot make treaties without the concurrence of the President. Here is, then, an additional guard. The calculation that seven or eight senators, with the President, can make treaties, is totally erroneous. Fourteen is a quorum; two thirds of which is ten. It is upon the improbable supposition that they will not attend that the objection is founded that ten men, with the President, can make treaties. Can it be reasonably supposed that they will not attend when the most important business is agitated, when the interests of their respective states are most immediately affected? ...

Mr. Porter recommended the most serious consideration when they were about to give away power; that they were not only about to give away power to legislate or make laws of a supreme nature, and to make treaties, which might sacrifice the most valuable interests of the community, but to give a power to the general government to drag the inhabitants to any part of the world as long as they pleased; that they ought not to put it in the power of any man, or any set of men, to do so. ... He observed that, as treaties were the supreme law of the land, the House of Representatives ought to have a vote in making them as well as in passing them.

Mr. J. [John] M'dowell. Mr. Chairman, permit me ... to make a few observations, to show how improper it is to place so much power in so few men, without any responsibility whatever. Let us consider what number of them is necessary to transact the most important business. Two thirds of the members present, with the President, can make a treaty. Fourteen of them are a quorum, two thirds of which are ten. These ten may make treaties and alliances. They may involve us in any difficulties, and dispose of us in any manner they please. Nay, eight is a majority of a quorum, and can do everything but make treaties. How unsafe are we when we have no power of bringing those to an account! ... Our lives and property are in the hands of eight or nine men. Will these gentlemen intrust their rights in this manner?

Mr. [William Richardson] Davie. Mr. Chairman, although treaties are mere conventional acts between the contracting parties, yet, by the law of nations, they are the supreme law of the land to their respective citizens or subjects. All civilized nations have concurred in considering them as paramount to an ordinary act of legislation. This concurrence is founded on the reciprocal convenience and solid advantages arising from it. A due observance of treaties makes nations more friendly to each other, and is the only means of rendering less frequent those mutual hostilities which tend to depopulate and ruin contending nations. It extends and facilitates that commercial intercourse, which, founded on the universal protection of private property, has, in a measure, made the world one nation.

The power of making treaties had, in all countries and governments, been placed in the executive departments. This has not only been grounded on the necessity and reason arising from that degree of secrecy, design, and despatch, which is always necessary in negotiations between nations, but to prevent their being impeded, or carried into effect, by the violence, animosity, and heat of parties, which too often infect numerous bodies. Both of these reasons preponderated in the foundation of this part of the system. ...

On the principle of the propriety of vesting this power in the executive department, it would seem that the whole power of making treaties ought to be left to the President, who, being elected by the people of the United States at large, will have their general interest at heart. But that jealousy of executive power which has shown itself so strongly in all the American governments would not admit this improvement. Interest, sir, has a most powerful influence over the human mind, and is the basis on which all the transactions of mankind are built. It was mentioned before that the extreme jealousy of the little states, and between the commercial states and the non-importing states, produced the necessity of giving an equality of suffrage to the Senate. The same causes made it indispensable to give to the senators, as representatives of states, the power of making, or rather ratifying treaties. Although it militates against every idea of just proportion that the little state of Rhode Island should have the same suffrage with Virginia, or the great commonwealth of Massachusetts, yet the small states would not consent to confederate without an equal voice in the formation of treaties. Without the equality, they apprehended that their interest would be neglected or sacrificed in negotiations. This difficulty could not be got over. It arose from the unalterable nature of things. Every man was convinced of the inflexibility of the little states in this point. It therefore became necessary to give them an absolute equality in making treaties.

29. Alexander Hamilton,
Federalist 74–75, March 25–26, 1788

For Alexander Hamilton the commander in chief clause hardly needed defending, since it was axiomatic for Hamilton (as it had been for Blackstone) that "the power of directing and employing the common strength forms an usual and essential part in the definition of the executive authority." A single paragraph in *Federalist* 74 sufficed to do the job. Treaty-making power was another matter, however; Hamilton devoted all of *Federalist* 75 to vindicating a clause he deemed to be one of "the best digested and most unexceptionable parts of the plan." Hamilton must have taken particular pride in this clause, since it closely resembled the plan of government he had presented to the convention on June 18. At a stage when most of the other delegates seemed inclined to regard treaty-making power as an exclusively legislative function, Hamilton presciently proposed to give the chief executive "with the advice and approbation of the Senate the power of making all treaties."

The President of the United States is to be "Commander in Chief of the army and navy of the United States, and of the militia of the several States when called into the actual service of the United States." The propriety of this provision is so evident in itself; and it is at the same time so consonant to the precedents of the State constitutions in general, that little need be said to explain or enforce it. Even those of them, which have in other respects coupled the Chief Magistrate with a Council, have for the most part concentrated the military authority in him alone. Of all the cares or concerns of government, the direction of war most peculiarly demands those qualities which distinguish the exercise of power by a single hand. The direction of war implies the direction of the common strength, and the power of directing and employing the common strength forms an usual and essential part in the definition of the executive authority. ...

The president is to have power "by and with the advice and consent of the senate, to make treaties, provided two-thirds of the senators present concur." Though this provision has been assailed on different grounds, with no small degree of vehemence, I scruple not to declare my firm persuasion, that it is one of the best digested and most unexceptionable parts of the plan. One ground of objection is the trite topic of the intermixture of powers; some contending that the president ought alone to possess the power of making treaties, and others that it ought to have been exclusively deposited in the senate. Another source of objection is derived from the small number of persons by whom a treaty may be made. Of those who espouse this objection, a part are of the opinion that the house of representatives ought to have been associated in the business, while another part seems to think that nothing more was necessary than to have substituted two-thirds of all the members of the senate to two-thirds of the members present. ...

New-York Packet, March 25, 1788. *New York Independent Journal*, March 26, 1788.

With regard to the intermixture of powers, I shall rely upon the explanations already given, in other places, of the true sense of the rule, upon which that objection is founded; and shall take it for granted, as an inference from them, that the union of the executive with the senate in the article of treaties is not an infringement of that rule. I venture to add that the particular nature of the power of making treaties indicates a peculiar propriety in that union. Though several writers on the subject of government place that power in the class of executive authorities, yet this is evidently an arbitrary disposition. For if we attend carefully to its operation, it will be found to partake more of the legislative than of the executive character, though it does not seem strictly to fall within the definition of either of them. The essence of the legislative authority is to enact laws, or in other words to prescribe rules for the regulation of the society. While the execution of the laws and the employment of the common strength, either for this purpose or for the common defense, seem to comprise all the functions of the executive magistrate. The power of making treaties is plainly neither the one nor the other. It relates neither to the execution of the subsisting laws, nor to the enaction of new ones, and still less to an exertion of the common strength. Its objects are contracts with foreign nations, which have the force of law, but derive it from the obligations of good faith. They are not rules prescribed by the sovereign to the subject, but agreements between sovereign and sovereign. The power in question seems therefore to form a distinct department, and to belong properly neither to the legislative nor to the executive. The qualities ... indispensable in the management of foreign negotiations point out the executive as the most fit agent in those transactions; while the vast importance of the trust, and the operation of treaties as laws, plead strongly for the participation of the whole or a part of the legislative body in the effect of making them.

However proper or safe it may be in governments where the executive magistrate is an hereditary monarch to commit to him the entire power of making treaties, it would be utterly unsafe and improper to entrust that power to an elective magistrate of four years duration. It has been remarked upon another occasion, and the remark is unquestionably just, that an hereditary monarch, though often the oppressor of his people, has personally too much at stake in the government to be in any material danger of being corrupted by foreign powers. But a man raised from the station of private citizen to the rank of chief magistrate, possessed of but a moderate or slender fortune, and looking forward to a period not very remote when he may probably be obliged to return to the station from which he was taken, might sometimes be under temptations to sacrifice his duty to his interest, which it would require superlative virtue to withstand. An avaricious man might be tempted to betray the interests of the state to the acquisition of wealth. An ambitious man might make his own aggrandizement, by the aid of a foreign power, the price of his treachery to his constituents. The history of human conduct does not warrant that exalted opinion of human virtue which would make it wise in a nation to commit interests of so delicate and momentous a kind as those which concern its intercourse with the rest of the world to the sole disposal of a magistrate, created and circumstanced as would be a president of the United States.

To have entrusted the power of making treaties to the senate alone would have been to relinquish the benefits of the constitutional agency of the president in the conduct of foreign negotiations. It is true that the senate would in that case have the option of employing him in this capacity, but they would also have the option of letting it alone, and pique or cabal might induce the latter rather than the former. Besides this, the ministerial servant of the senate could not be expected to enjoy the confidence and respect of foreign powers in the same degree with the constitutional representative of the nation, and of course would not be able to act with an equal degree of weight or efficacy. While the union would from this cause lose a considerable advantage in the management of its external concerns, the people would lose the additional security which would result from the cooperation of the executive. Though it would be imprudent to confide in him solely so important a trust; yet it cannot be doubted that his participation in it would materially add to the safety of the society. It must indeed be clear ... that the joint possession of the power in question by the president and senate would afford a greater prospect of security than the separate possession of it by either of them. And whoever has maturely weighed the circumstances, which must concur in the appointment of a president, will be satisfied that the office will always bid fair to be filled by men of such characters as to render their concurrence in the formation of treaties peculiarly desirable, as well on the score of wisdom as on that of integrity.

The remarks made in a former number ... will apply with conclusive force against the admission of the house of representatives to a share in the formation of treaties. The fluctuating and, taking its future increase into the account, the multitudinous composition of that body, forbid us to expect in it those qualities which are essential to the proper execution of such a trust. Accurate and comprehensive knowledge of foreign politics, a steady and systematic adherence to the same views, a nice and uniform sensibility to national character, decision, secrecy and dispatch, are incompatible with the genius of a body so valuable and so numerous. The very complication of the business, by introducing a necessity of the concurrence of so many different bodies, would of itself afford a solid objection. The greater frequency of the calls upon the house of representatives, and the greater length of time which it would often be necessary to keep them together when convened to obtain their sanction in the progressive states of a treaty, would be a source of so great inconvenience and expense as alone ought to condemn the project.

30. Pacificus
[Alexander Hamilton] I, June 29, 1793

In April 1793, with Congress out of session, George Washington unilaterally proclaimed America neutral in the war between France and Britain. Those Americans sympathetic to the French cause immediately objected that Washington had overstepped his constitutional bounds. The power to declare neutrality, they insisted, no less than the power to declare war, belonged to Congress. Hamilton, Washington's secretary of the Treasury, took it upon himself, under the pseudonym "Pacificus," to defend the president's policy and, more important, the president's constitutional right to issue a declaration of neutrality.

What department of our government is the proper one to make a declaration of neutrality, when the engagements of the nation permit, and its interests require that it should be done?

Letters of Pacificus and Helvidius on the Proclamation of Neutrality of 1793 (Washington: Gideon, 1845), 8–12, 14.

A correct mind will discern at once that it can belong neither to the legislative nor judicial department [and] of course must belong to the executive.

The legislative department is not the organ of intercourse between the United States and foreign nations. It is charged neither with making nor interpreting treaties. It is therefore not naturally that member of the government which is to pronounce the existing condition of the nation with regard to foreign powers, or to admonish the citizens of their obligations and duties in consequence; still less is it charged with enforcing the observance of those obligations and duties.

It is equally obvious that the act in question is foreign to the judiciary department. ... It is indeed charged with the interpretation of treaties, but it exercises this function only where contending parties bring before it a specific controversy. It has no concern with pronouncing upon the external political relations of treaties between government and government. This position is too plain to need being insisted upon.

It must then of necessity belong to the executive department to exercise the function in question. ... It appears to be connected with that department in various capacities: As the organ of intercourse between the nation and foreign nations; as the interpreter of the national treaties, in those cases in which the judiciary is not competent, that is, between government and government; as the power which is charged with execution of the laws, of which treaties form a part; as that which is charged with the command and disposition of the public force.

This view of the subject is so natural and obvious, so analogous to general theory and practice, that no doubt can be entertained of its justness, unless to be deduced from particular provisions of the constitution of the United States. Let us see, then, if cause for such doubt is to be found there.

The second article of the constitution of the United States ... establishes this general proposition, that "the EXECUTIVE POWER shall be vested in a President of the United States of America." The same article ... proceeds to designate particular cases of executive power. It declares, among other things, that the president shall be commander in chief of the army and navy of the United States, and of the militia of the several States, when called into the actual service of the United States; that he shall have power, by and with the advice of the senate, to make treaties; that it shall be his duty to receive ambassadors and other public ministers, and to take care that the laws be faithfully executed.

It would not be consistent with the rules of sound construction to consider this enumeration of particular authorities as derogating from the more comprehensive grant in the general clause, further than as it may be coupled with express restrictions or qualifications; as in regard to the cooperation of the senate in the appointment of officers and the making of treaties, which are plainly qualifications of the general executive powers of appointing officers and making treaties. The difficulty of a complete enumeration of all the cases of executive authority would naturally dictate the use of general terms, and would render it improbable that a specification of certain particulars was designed as a substitute for those terms, when antecedently used. The different mode of expression employed in the constitution in regard to the two powers, the legislative and the executive, serves to confirm this inference. In the article which gives the legislative powers of the government the expressions are, "All legislative powers herein granted shall be vested in a congress of the United States." In that which grants the executive power the expressions are, "The executive power shall be vested in a president of the United States."

The enumeration ought therefore to be considered as intended merely to specify the principal articles implied in the definition of executive power, leaving the rest to flow from the general grant of that power, interpreted in conformity with other parts of the constitution and with the principles of free government.

The general doctrine then of our constitution is that the executive power of the nation is vested in the president, subject only to the exceptions and qualifications which are expressed in the instrument. Two of these have been already noticed: the participation of the senate in the appointment of officers and in the making of treaties. A third remains to be mentioned: the right of the legislature "to declare war and grant letters of marque and reprisal."

With these exceptions the executive power of the United States is completely lodged in the president. ... It will follow, that if a proclamation of neutrality is merely an executive act, as, it is believed, has been shown, the step which has been taken by the president is liable to no just exception on the score of authority.

It may be said that this inference would be just if the power of declaring war had not been vested in the legislature, but that this power naturally includes the right of judging whether the nation is or is not under obligations to make war.

The answer is that however true this position may be, it will not follow that the executive is in any case excluded from a similar right of judgment in the execution of its own functions. If, on the one hand, the legislature have a right to declare war, it is, on the other, the duty of the executive to preserve peace till war is declared; and in fulfilling this duty, it must necessarily possess a right of judging what is the nature of the obligations which the treaties of the country impose on the government. And when it has concluded that there is nothing in them inconsistent with neutrality, it becomes both its province and its duty to enforce the laws incident to that state of the nation. The executive is charged with the execution of all laws, the laws of nations as well as the municipal law. ... It is consequently bound, by executing faithfully the laws of neutrality, when the country is in a neutral position, to avoid giving cause of war to foreign powers.

This is the direct end of the proclamation of neutrality. It declares to the United States their situation with regard to the contending parties, and makes known to the community that the laws incident to that state will be enforced. In doing this, it conforms to an established usage of nations, the operation of which ... is to obviate a responsibility on the part of the whole society for secret and unknown violations of the rights of any of the warring powers by its citizens. ...

It deserves to be remarked that as the participation of the senate in the making of treaties, and the power of the legislature to declare war, are exceptions out of the general "executive Power" vested in the President, they are to be construed strictly, and ought to be extended no further than is essential to their execution.

While, therefore, the legislature can alone declare war, can alone actually transfer the nation from a state of peace to a state of hostility, it belongs to the "executive power" to do whatever else the laws of nations, cooperating with the treaties of the country, enjoin in the intercourse of the United States with foreign powers.

In this distribution of authority, the wisdom of our constitution is manifested. It is the province and duty of the executive to preserve to the nation the blessings of peace. The legislature alone can interrupt them by placing the nation in a state of war.

31. Helvidius [James Madison] I, III, August 24, September 7, 1793

Thomas Jefferson, Washington's secretary of state, had acquiesced in Washington's decision to issue the neutrality proclamation, though not without strong misgivings. Upon reading Hamilton's expansive interpretation of "the executive Power," Jefferson's misgivings turned to alarm. To Madison he wrote, "For God's sake, my dear Sir, take up your pen, select the most striking heresies and cut him to pieces in face of the public" (Corwin 1957, 180). Madison took up the assignment and, under the pen name "Helvidius," assailed Hamilton's reading of the executive power, sometimes citing Hamilton (in the *Federalist*) to refute Hamilton. Interestingly, an 1802 edition of the *Federalist*, which was approved by Hamilton, included Hamilton's Pacificus letters. An 1818 edition of the *Federalist,* which continued to be reprinted well into the 1850s, also included Madison's Helvidius letters. Only with the arrival of the Civil War, in an 1863 edition by Henry Dawson, was the Pacificus-Helvidius exchange dropped from editions of the *Federalist* (Loss 1976, xiv).

Several pieces with the signature of PACIFICUS were lately published, which have been read with singular pleasure and applause by the foreigners and degenerate citizens among us who hate our republican government and the French revolution. ... Under colour of vindicating an important public act of a chief magistrate who enjoys the confidence and love of his country, principles are advanced which strike at the vitals of its constitution, as well as at its honour and true interest. ...

The substance of the first piece, sifted from its inconsistencies and its vague expressions, may be thrown into the following propositions: (1) That the powers of declaring war and making treaties are, in their nature, executive powers; (2) That being particularly vested by the constitution in other departments, they are to be considered as exceptions out of the general grant to the executive department; (3) That being, as exceptions, to be construed strictly, the powers not strictly within them remain with the executive. ...

If there be any countenance to these positions, it must be found either, first, in the writers of authority on public law; or, second, in the quality and operation of the powers to make war and treaties; or, third, in the constitution of the United States.

1. It would be of little use to enter far into the first source of information, not only because our own reason and our own constitution are the best guides; but because a just analysis and discrimination of the powers of government, according to their executive, legislative, and judiciary qualities, are not to be expected in the works of the most received jurists, who wrote before a critical attention was paid to those objects and with their eyes too much on monarchical governments, where all powers are confounded in

Letters of Pacificus and Helvidius on the Proclamation of Neutrality of 1793 (Washington: Gideon, 1845), 53–61, 75–76, 62.

the sovereignty of the prince. It will be found, however, I believe, that all of them ... speak of the powers to declare war, to conclude peace, and to form alliances, as among the highest acts of the sovereignty; of which the legislative power must at least be an integral and preeminent part.

Writers such as Locke and Montesquieu, who have discussed more the principles of liberty and the structure of government, lie under the same disadvantage of having written before these subjects were illuminated by the events and discussions which distinguish a very recent period. Both of them, too, are evidently warped by a regard to the particular government of England, to which one of them owed allegiance and the other professed an admiration bordering on idolatry. Montesquieu, however, has rather distinguished himself by enforcing the reasons and the importance of avoiding a confusion of the several powers of government than by enumerating and defining the powers which belong to each particular class. And Locke, notwithstanding the early date of his work on civil government, and the example of his own government before his eyes, admits that the particular powers in question, which, after some of the writers on public law, he calls federative, are really distinct from the executive, though almost always united with it and hardly to be separated into distinct hands. Had he not lived under a monarchy, in which these powers were united, or had he written by the lamp which truth now presents to lawgivers, the last observation would probably never have dropped from his pen. But let us quit a field of research which is more likely to perplex than to decide, and bring the question to other tests of which it will be more easy to judge.

2. If we consult ... the nature and operation of the two powers to declare war and to make treaties, it will be impossible not to see that they can never fall within a proper definition of executive powers. The natural province of the executive magistrate is to execute laws, as that of the legislature is to make laws. All his acts, therefore, properly executive, must presuppose the existence of the laws to be executed. A treaty is not an execution of laws; it does not presuppose the existence of laws. It is, on the contrary, to have itself the force of a law, and to be carried into execution, like all other laws, by the executive magistrate. To say then that the power of making treaties, which are confessedly laws, belongs naturally to the department which is to execute laws, is to say that the executive department naturally includes a legislative power. In theory this is an absurdity, in practice a tyranny.

The power to declare war is subject to similar reasoning. A declaration that there shall be war is not an execution of laws; it does not suppose pre-existing laws to be executed. It is not, in any respect, an act merely executive. It is, on the contrary, one of the most deliberate acts that can be performed; and when performed, has the effect of repealing all the laws operating in a state of peace, so far as they are inconsistent with a state of war; and of enacting, as a rule for the executive, a new code adapted to the relation between the society and its foreign enemy. In like manner, a conclusion of peace annuls all the laws peculiar to a state of war and revives the general laws incident to a state of peace.

These remarks will be strengthened by adding that treaties, particularly treaties of peace, have sometimes the effect of changing not only the external laws of the society, but operate also on the internal code, which is purely municipal, and to which the legislative authority of the country is of itself competent and complete.

From this view of the subject it must be evident that although the executive may be a convenient organ of preliminary communications with foreign governments on the subjects of treaty or war; and the proper agent for carrying into execution the final determinations of the competent authority; yet it can have no pretensions, from the nature of the powers in question compared with the nature of the executive trust, to that essential agency which gives validity to such determinations.

It must be further evident that if these powers be not in their nature purely legislative, they partake so much more of that than of any other quality that under a constitution leaving them to result to their most natural department, the legislature would be without a rival in its claim.

Another important inference to be noted is that the powers of making war and treaty being substantially of a legislative, not an executive nature, the rule of interpreting exceptions strictly must narrow, instead of enlarging, executive pretensions on those subjects.

3. It remains to be inquired whether there be anything in the constitution itself which shows that the powers of making war and peace are considered as of an executive nature, and as comprehended within a general grant of executive power.

It will not be pretended that this appears from any direct position to be found in the instrument. If it were deducible from any particular expressions it may be presumed that [Pacificus] would have saved us the trouble of the research. Does the doctrine, then, result from the actual distribution of powers among the several branches of the government? or from any fair analogy between the powers of war and treaty, and the enumerated powers vested in the executive alone?

Let us examine:

In the general distribution of powers, we find that of declaring war expressly vested in the congress, where every other legislative power is declared to be vested; and without any other qualification than what is common to every other legislative act. The constitutional idea of this power would seem then clearly to be that it is of a legislative and not an executive nature.

This conclusion becomes irresistible when it is recollected that the constitution cannot be supposed to have placed either any power legislative in its nature entirely among executive powers, or any power executive in its nature entirely among legislative powers, without charging the constitution with that kind of intermixture and consolidation of different powers which would violate a fundamental principle in the organization of free governments. If it were not unnecessary to enlarge on this topic here, it could be shown that the constitution was originally vindicated, and has been constantly expounded, with a disavowal of any such intermixture.

The power of treaties is vested jointly in the president and in the senate, which is a branch of the legislature. From this arrangement merely there can be no inference that would necessarily exclude the power from the executive class, since the senate is joined with the president in another power, that of appointing to offices, which, as far as relate to executive offices at least, is considered as of an executive nature. Yet on the other hand, there are sufficient indications that the power of treaties is regarded by the constitution as materially different from mere executive power, and as having more affinity to the legislative than to the executive character.

One circumstance indicating this is the constitutional regulation under which the senate give their consent in the case of treaties. In all other cases, the consent of the body is expressed by a majority of voices. In this particular case, a concurrence of two-thirds at least is made necessary, as a substitute or compensation for the other branch of the legislature, which, on certain occasions, could not be conveniently a party to the transaction.

But the conclusive circumstance is that treaties, when formed according to the constitutional mode, are confessedly to have force and operation of laws, and are to be a rule for the courts in controversies between man and man, as much as any other laws. They are even emphatically declared by the constitution to be "the supreme law of the land."

So far the argument from the constitution is precisely in opposition to the doctrine. As little will be gained in its favour from a comparison of the two powers with those particularly vested in the president alone. As there are but few, it will be most satisfactory to review them one by one.

"The president shall be commander in chief of the army and navy of the United States, and of the militia when called into the actual service of the United States."

There can be no relation worth examining between this power and the general power of making treaties. And instead of being analogous to the power of declaring war, it affords a striking illustration of the incompatibility of the two powers in the same hands. Those who are to conduct a war cannot in the nature of things, be proper or safe judges whether a war ought to be commenced, continued, or concluded. They are barred from the latter functions by a great principle in free government, analogous to that which separates the sword from the purse, or the power of executing from the power of enacting laws. ...

"He shall take care that the laws shall be faithfully executed. ..." To see the laws faithfully executed constitutes the essence of the executive authority. But what relation has it to the power of making treaties and war, that is, of determining what the laws shall be with regard to other nations? No other certainly than what subsists between the powers of executing and enacting laws; no other, consequently, than what forbids a coalition of the powers in the same department. ...

"He shall receive ambassadors, other public ministers, and consuls." ... Little, if anything, more was intended by the clause than to provide for a particular mode of communication, almost grown into a right among modern nations, by pointing out the department of the government most proper for the ceremony of admitting public ministers, of examining their credentials, and of authenticating their title to the privileges annexed to their character by the law of nations. This being the apparent design of the constitution, it would be highly improper to magnify the function into an important prerogative. ...

To show that the view here given of the clause is not a new construction, invented or strained for a particular occasion—I will take the liberty of recurring to [the *Federalist*], which contains the obvious and original gloss put on this part of the constitution by its friends and advocates.

"The president is also to be authorized to receive ambassadors and other public ministers. This, though it has been a rich theme of declamation, is more a matter of dignity than of authority. It is a circumstance which will be without consequence in the administration of the government; and it was far more convenient that it should be arranged in this manner than that there should be a necessity of convening the legislature, or one of its branches, upon every arrival of a foreign minister, though it were merely to take the place of a departed predecessor" [Hamilton, *Federalist* 69]. ...

Thus it appears that by whatever standard we try this doctrine, it must be condemned as no less vicious in theory than it would be dangerous in practice. It is countenanced neither by the writers on law, nor by the nature of the powers themselves, nor by any general arrangements ... particular expressions, or plausible analogies to be found in the constitution. Whence then can the writer have borrowed it? There is but one answer to this question: The power of making treaties and the power of declaring war are royal prerogatives in the British government, and are accordingly treated as executive prerogatives by British commentators.

Questions for Discussion

1. Whose interpretation of the scope of executive power do you find more persuasive, that of Pacificus (Hamilton) or Helvidius (Madison)?

2. Are Hamilton's arguments in *Federalist* 69, 74, and 75 consistent with the arguments he advances as Pacificus? Is Madison's position as Helvidius consistent with the views he expressed at the Constitutional Convention? If not, how do you explain the inconsistencies?

3. Today the president dominates military and foreign policy. Do you think this is contrary to what the framers intended when drafting the Constitution? Based on your readings of the convention and ratification debates, how would you characterize the original intent of the framers with regard to foreign affairs?

4. If a new constitutional convention were to be called today, would you alter any of the provisions relating to control over foreign and military policy in Article 1, section 8, or in Article 2, sections 2–3? How would you amend the commander in chief clause to make it clearer what this power entailed? Should the new constitution try to specify more precisely the scope of executive power as it relates to foreign relations and military policy?

8

The Power of Appointment

The President ... shall nominate, and by and with the Advice and Consent of the Senate, shall appoint Ambassadors, other public Ministers and Consuls, Judges of the supreme Court, and all other Officers of the United States, whose Appointments are not herein otherwise provided for, and which shall be established by Law: but the Congress may by Law vest the Appointment of such inferior Officers, as they think proper, in the President alone, in the Courts of Law, or in the Heads of Departments.

Article 2, section 2

No Senator or Representative shall, during the Time for which he was elected, be appointed to any civil Office under the Authority of the United States, which shall have been created, or the Emoluments whereof shall have been encreased during such time; and no Person holding any Office under the United States, shall be a member of either House during his Continuance in Office.

Article 1, section 6

No power loomed larger in the eighteenth-century Anglo-American imagination than the power of appointment to office. The Glorious Revolution of 1688, by reigning in the power of the monarch, was supposed to have made the British constitution the most perfect in the world, balanced as it now was between the king, House of Lords, and House of Commons. But this careful balancing of political and social forces, many feared, was being subverted by the control that the king (or the king's chief minister) exercised over the dispensing of offices and honors. Depriving the king of prerogative powers such as the veto meant little if the Crown could control Parliament by offering members lucrative offices, titles, and pensions. The Crown's power to create, vacate, and dispense offices held at the royal pleasure explained why despite having clipped "the wings of prerogative" at the end of the seventeenth century, Englishmen at the accession of George III could express with plausible alarm that because of the dramatic growth in government revenues "the in-

181

fluence of the crown is greater than ever it was in any period in our history" (Wood 1969, 143; also see Williams 1960, 141–43).

Most Americans of the revolutionary period blasted the Crown's appointment power as insidious "corruption," but others followed David Hume and William Blackstone in believing that such "influence" was a necessary instrument of effective governance. This position was articulated at the Constitutional Convention by Maryland's John Francis Mercer, who opposed making members of the legislature ineligible for executive offices on the grounds that "depriv[ing the Executive] of 'influence' " would make him "a mere phantom of authority" (August 14). This view was echoed by Alexander Hamilton, who lamented that Americans "have been taught to reprobate the danger of influence in the British government, without duly reflecting how it was necessary to support a good government" (June 18). A number of delegates rushed to disassociate themselves from these heretical views but such forthright defenses of executive influence hinted at the distance Americans had traversed since the early days of the Revolution, hints that would be confirmed in the final Constitution, which not only vested the power of appointment in the president but rejected the more sweeping prohibitions on legislative eligibility for public offices with which the convention began.

In the years leading up to the American Revolution, the Crown's power of appointment had been one of the primary targets of colonial resentment. Among the grievances against the king laid down in the Declaration of Independence was that "he has erected a multitude of new offices, and sent hither swarms of officers to harrass our people and eat out their substance." The country, it was widely believed, was being overrun with "fawning parasites and cringing courtiers" (Wood 1969, 78) who were being elevated to lucrative offices ahead of more qualified colonials. The corruption was not limited to the upper reaches of society but extended into local villages and towns. Through the conferring of offices and honors, complained one revolutionary petition in Massachusetts, "a secret poison has been spread thro'out all our Towns and great Multitudes have been secured for the corrupt Designs of an abandoned Administration" (146). It mattered not how menial the office for, as John Adams observed, "the Commission of a Subaltern, in the Militia, will tempt these little Minds, as much as Crowns, and Stars and Garters will greater ones" (147). The royal prerogative of "erecting and disposing of offices" (Blackstone [1783] 1978, 1:272) was sapping the virtue of America as it had already done in Britain. Or so it seemed to the colonists.

From the English perspective, such rhetoric must have seemed like paranoid delusions bred of fevered imaginations. Although the power of appointment in England remained securely in the hands of the king at the time of the American Revolution, in America many of the colonial assemblies had long since wrested large chunks of the appointment power away from the royal governors. Unlike in England, where treasury appointments were an unquestioned part of the Crown's prerogative, most colonial assemblies regarded it their "inherent right" to appoint the state's treasurer (Greene 1963, 221), and a number controlled the appointment of lesser revenue officers as well. In South Carolina, for instance, the lower house had secured almost complete control over the appointment of all officers who handled revenue, from the treasurer to tax collectors (224). Indeed a 1721 statute had asserted the "power, right and authority" of the South Carolina assembly (styled the House of Commons) to nominate and appoint all "civil officers which now do or hereafter may receive a settled salary out of the public treasury" (227). In addition, the assembly appointed unpaid commissioners to carry out a variety of state and local public works, from building forts and parish churches to maintaining local roads and bridges. South Carolina's royal governors periodically complained to the home government that "almost all the places of profit or of trust are disposed of by the General Assembly" (Greene [1888] 1966, 187), but there was little the governor or home government could do to reverse what had by mid-century become well-established precedents, precedents that had been built up earlier in the century when the Crown had paid scant attention to colonial affairs and the legislature had used its power of the purse to encroach upon the governor's prerogatives.

Although colonial assemblies typically exercised greater control over appointment to offices than did the House of Commons in England, colonial governors nonetheless often wielded substantial powers of appointment. Not all states had the strong tradition of legislative appointment of treasury officers and other civil officers that existed in South Carolina as well as in Massachusetts and Pennsylvania. In New Jersey, New Hampshire, and Georgia, the power of appointment remained largely in the hands of the governor (Greene [1888] 1966, 182). Moreover, in all the royal colonies the governor (with the advice and consent of the council) appointed judges as well as justices of the peace and sheriffs. In fact colonial governors at the time of the Revolution had greater control over the judiciary than did the Crown in England, since royal instructions issued to colonial governors mandated that judges serve during pleasure only. In England, in contrast, the Act of Settlement of 1701 required that judges be appointed during good behavior in order to ensure their independence from the crown. In colonial America, moreover, the executive could create courts, a power denied to the Crown in England (Greene 1963, 330–31; Bailyn 1970, 68). In addition, the power of colonial governors to appoint military officers—as in England—generally went unchallenged (South Carolina was a notable exception) and unchecked, since the governor acting as commander in chief was not required to seek the advice and consent of the council

(Greene [1888] 1966, 110–11). And, finally, only a few states had statutes that barred legislators from holding other public offices at the same time.[1]

Nor were governors shy about using the appointment powers they possessed to further their political or personal ends. Since political rule was maintained by building personal networks based on material interest and familial loyalty, in this era the personal really was political. In New Hampshire, for instance, Governor Benning Wentworth followed by his nephew, Governor John Wentworth, strategically dispensed offices and land to maintain tight control over the state's political system for thirty-five years. At the time of Benning Wentworth's retirement in 1767 the council that advised the governor included his brother, three brothers-in-law, and four nephews or cousins (Daniell 1981, 207); provincial offices were monopolized by Wentworth's friends and family, many of whom held multiple offices. One close ally of Wentworth on the council, for example, served simultaneously as chief justice of the Superior Court, provincial secretary, and a militia colonel. After taking over from his uncle in 1767, John Wentworth met increasing resistance to what critics derided as "family government" (207; Kruman 1997, 119), but he continued to use the patronage available to him to build political support, reward his friends, and punish his enemies. Upon assuming office, for instance, Wentworth successfully wooed an influential member of the assembly, Josiah Bartlett, first by appointing him justice of the peace and later lieutenant colonel in the militia (Wilderson 1994, 137). When a councilor turned on the governor, Wentworth retaliated by not renewing the councilor's judgeship (206). In the neighboring state of Massachusetts, Governors Francis Bernard and Thomas Hutchinson used the patronage available to them in the same way, cementing legislative support by offering loyal assemblymen such posts as militia officer or justice of the peace. Although justices of the peace were not paid, it was, as John Adams complained in 1774, "a great Acquisition in the Country, and such a Distinction to a Man among his Neighbors is enough to purchase and corrupt almost any Man" (Gross 1976, 37; Bailyn 1974, 177–78, 183–84).

When the American revolutionaries came to write their new state constitutions in 1776 and 1777, they moved to stamp out abuses of the appointment

---

1. South Carolina forbade salaried officers from serving in the legislature, and Virginia had laws disqualifying sheriffs from the legislature and requiring that a legislator appointed to other offices of profit must first resign his seat and then run for reelection, a law modeled on the English Place Act of 1707. New Jersey also had passed statutes modeled on the English Place Act. The most radical measure of all was passed by the Maryland assembly in 1757, which not only barred any officeholder from the assembly but also required that any person taking an office of trust or profit within six years of leaving the assembly must pay a fine of £1000. The upper house killed the measure. In 1770 the New York colonial assembly, after failing in earlier efforts to enact a law excluding all officers from the assembly, finally managed to pass an act disqualifying judicial officers from the legislature, only to have the act nullified by the Crown (Greene 1963, 227; Greene [1898] 1966, 158–59; Kruman 1997, 116–17).

power by further restricting the governors' power of appointment, beginning with the appointment of judges. Only Maryland drafted a constitution that retained the colonial pattern of giving the power of appointing judges to the governor with the advice and consent of an executive council. All the other constitutions drafted in 1776 and 1777 assigned the appointment of judges to the legislature or, in the case of Pennsylvania, to the twelve-member supreme executive council.[2] The power to choose justices of the peace, which in colonial times had been exercised by the governor, was now handed over to the legislature (as in Georgia, New Hampshire, New Jersey, North Carolina, and South Carolina) or to the people directly (as in Pennsylvania). In a few cases (Delaware and Virginia) the governor was denied the power of nomination but was allowed to select from a list presented to him by either the legislature (Delaware) or the county courts (Virginia). Again only in Maryland was the governor trusted with the power both to nominate and appoint justices of the peace. But since appointments had to be consented to by a five-person executive council selected annually by the legislature, even the power of Maryland's governor was circumscribed.

More remarkable still was the way in which governors were systematically stripped of their power to appoint military officers. The governor was excluded altogether from a role in military appointments in Delaware, New Hampshire, New Jersey, North Carolina, and South Carolina. In these states, "field and general officers" of the militia were typically appointed by the legislature, and "inferior officers" of the militia were generally chosen by the companies themselves (Thorpe 1909, 5:2596). Virginia retained some role for the governor in the appointment of military officers but the power was tightly constrained. The governor could appoint militia officers only "with the advice of the Privy Council" and "on recommendations from the respective County Courts." Moreover such officers served not at the pleasure of the governor but during good behavior (7:3817). Even Maryland would not allow the governor to appoint military officers without the advice and consent of the executive council.

The most innovative of the revolutionary state constitutions when it came to the appointment power was that of New York. Unable to agree whether the power of appointment should be lodged in the executive or the legislature, the convention's delegates finally settled their long and heated debate by creating a special Council of Appointment, composed of a popularly elected governor and four senators picked by the lower house. The council appointed most of the important state offices with the notable exception of the treas-

---

2. Delaware allowed the chief executive (styled the "president") to cast a vote together with the two houses of legislature but since there were thirty legislators, the president's impact on the appointment was minimal (Thorpe 1909, 1:564). The Georgia constitution did not specify legislative appointment of judges but it was the assembly that in fact appointed judges (Wood 1969, 148 n. 40; Kruman 1997, 122).

urer (5:2633), which remained, as it did in the other states, under the control of the assembly. New York was unique not only in crafting a council specially designed to handle appointments but also in the lack of attention it paid to excluding legislators from holding other public offices. The only public offices that a legislator could not hold were high-level judicial offices, sheriff, and treasurer. Adding to the potential influence of the council (and hence the governor) was that all commissioned military officers and many civil officers served "during pleasure," which meant the council could remove them whenever they pleased (5:2634).

The other revolutionary state constitutions generally betrayed far greater fear of the corrupting potential of the appointment power, even when it was largely or entirely exercised by the legislature. In New Jersey, for instance, the legislature appointed virtually every unelected public office but still barred all officers except justices of the peace (who were appointed by the legislature) from sitting in the assembly in order "that the legislative department of this government may, as much as possible, be preserved from all suspicion of corruption" (5:2598). In Pennsylvania, where the appointment power was lodged primarily in the hands of the twelve-member executive council, members of the assembly were barred from holding any other office, except in the militia (5:3084). The "usual effects" of "offices of profit," the Pennsylvania constitution explained, are "dependence and servility, unbecoming freemen, in the possessors and expectants" (5:3090). In Maryland, where the governor retained the lion's share of the appointment power, the constitution makers were even more vigilant in excluding legislators from public office. Maryland's legislators were flatly barred from holding "any office of profit, or receiv[ing] the profits of any office exercised by any other person, during the time for which he shall be elected" (3:1697). Maryland's prohibition was more sweeping than that in other states in that it required the legislator to wait for his term to expire before he could accept any position. Other state constitutions only required that the legislator resign his seat before accepting an office.

The only state constitution that neglected to make any provision restricting plural officeholding was that of New Hampshire, the first state to draw up a new, albeit temporary, constitution.[3] The omission probably has something to do with the fact that it was the briefest and least elaborated of all the rev-

---

3. Another exception to the general pattern of excluding legislators from holding offices was South Carolina's short-lived 1776 constitution. On the model of the English Place Act of 1707, it required that if a legislator "shall accept any place or emolument or any commission except in the militia" (Thorpe 1909, 6:3244), he had to vacate his seat but could then seek reelection. If elected, he could retain his legislative seat and the office to which he had been appointed. The state's revised constitution of 1778 kept this provision but amended it by offering a substantial list of offices that could not under any circumstances be held while serving in the legislature, including secretary of state, Treasury commissioner, customs officer, clerk of the court, legislature or privy council, sheriff, and commissary of military stores (6:3253).

olutionary state constitutions, but it may also have reflected the drafters' sense that such exclusionary rules had been rendered less important if not irrelevant by the constitution's abolition of the position of governor and its deliverance (in uncharacteristic detail) of the appointment power to the legislature. But if concentration of power in the hands of the governor and his council in colonial times was unacceptable, New Hampshire citizens quickly found that concentrated power in a few legislative hands was little better. If the Wentworths had used the power of appointment to control and corrupt the legislature and the judiciary, New Hampshire's new constitution allowed a similar concentration of authority. Meschech Weare, for instance, was president of the legislative council (the upper house), chief justice of the state supreme court, and chairman of the committee of safety, a protoexecutive body selected by and from the legislature. "During the first year of their tenure under the constitution," reports one historian, "the legislators took advantage of their unparalleled opportunities by appointing themselves and their friends to virtually every post of power and profit, military as well as civil, in the state" (Turner 1983, 15). This concentration of power in the hands of Weare and his council allies brought growing complaints from New Hampshire's citizenry. "The ambition of men is unbounded," one critic wrote, "and no man breathing should be intrusted with too much power nor with offices and places opposite in their institutions" (Kruman 1997, 118–19). Abolishing or even just emasculating the governor, citizens learned, did not serve to check power but only to concentrate it. Power, many came to believe, was to be tamed instead through separation of powers, which meant both barring plural officeholding and ensuring that each branch of government, including the executive, was sufficiently independent and resourceful to resist the encroachments of the other (Turner 1983, 23).

This emerging perspective reached fruition in the Massachusetts constitution of 1780, drafted by John Adams. The Massachusetts constitution minced no words in affirming a commitment to strict separation of powers: "the legislative department shall never exercise the executive and judicial powers, or either of them: the executive shall never exercise the legislative and judicial powers, or either of them: the judicial shall never exercise the legislative and executive powers, or either of them" (Thorpe 1909, 3:1893). For Adams, the key was to ensure that each branch had an independent base of power so that no branch would be "under the undue influence" of another branch (3:1903). For the executive this meant that he should be elected by the people rather than by the legislature, for judges it meant that they should hold their offices during good behavior, and for legislators it meant that they were barred from holding a long list of public offices, including treasurer, commissary-general, judges or clerks of the supreme court, attorney general, solicitor general, sheriffs, registers of probate or deeds, customs officers, and naval officers (3:1909). Legislators were even barred from serving as "president, professor or instructor of Harvard College" (3:1909).[4] A legislator who accepted any of these offices would automatically have his seat vacated and then filled. Having safeguarded the legislature from executive influence, the governor was then granted the power to appoint, with the advice and consent of a ten-member executive council,[5] "all judicial officers, the attorney-general, the solicitor-general, all sheriffs, coroners, and registers of probate" (3:1902). The governor (with the advice but not the consent of council) was also given the power to appoint all officers of the Continental Army and all officers of forts and garrisons.[6] At the time the Massachusetts constitution was enacted, only Maryland vested comparable appointment powers in the governor.

New Hampshire followed the lead of its larger neighbor to the south. The contrast between the state's 1784 constitution, which was closely modeled, often verbatim, on the Massachusetts constitution, and its 1776 constitution, which had no executive at all apart from an interim committee of safety, indicates the degree to which attitudes toward executive power had shifted in the first decade of the new republic. Whereas the 1776 constitution had placed the power of appointment entirely in the hands of the legislature, the new constitution dramatically scaled back the legislature's role in appointments, allowing it to choose only the treasurer, secretary, and commissary general (and in so doing went even further than the Massachusetts constitution, which permitted the legislature also to appoint naval officers, notaries public, the receiver-general, and major-generals). Apart from the offices of treasurer, secretary, and commissary general, all executive officers as well as all judicial officers and top military officers in New Hampshire were to be appointed by a popularly elected president together with a five-person council chosen by both houses of the legislature.[7]

---

4. Massachusetts did not remove this particular prohibition until it passed a constitutional amendment in 1877.

5. Nine members of the council were selected annually from among the senators by a joint ballot of the two houses of the legislature. Upon their selection to the executive council, the senators had to give up their seats in the Senate and the remaining senators constituted the Senate for that year, thus preserving the separation of powers that Adams desired. The tenth member of the council was a popularly elected lieutenant governor (Thorpe 1909, 3:1903-4).

6. The governor, though, had no power over appointments to the militia because militia officers, from captains to field officers to brigadier generals, were democratically elected by their immediate subordinates. Only if the militia refused or failed to make a selection did the governor, with the advice of council, have the power to fill militia offices (Thorpe 1909, 3:1902).

7. A closer investigation of New Hampshire's revised constitution, however, reveals a more complex story that portrays the continuing vitality of Americans' fears of executive power. The original constitution (drafted in 1781), which was virtually identical to the Massachusetts constitution in most respects, was rejected three times in three years by New Hampshire voters. To gain approval for the new plan of government, New Hampshire's constitution makers were forced to change a number of key items, including weakening the chief executive. It did this, most importantly, by depriving him of the qualified veto Adams had given the Massachusetts governor and, most symbolically, by changing his title from governor to president (Turner 1983, 26-29). New Hampshire also weakened the chief executive's power of appointment by giving the power of appointment jointly to the president and council, whereas in Massachusetts the governor was

As the federal convention delegates assembled in Philadelphia in May 1787 and surveyed their state constitutions, they would have seen a growing consensus on the principle (though not the details) of excluding legislators from executive or judicial offices[8] but a bewildering variety of appointment schemes. Maryland, Massachusetts, and New Hampshire vested the lion's share of the appointment power in a chief executive with the advice and consent of a council. The legislature also had a minimal role in the appointment process in Pennsylvania and New York, in the former case because the power was vested in an executive council, and in the latter case because the power was vested in a specially constituted five-person council of appointment that included the governor. In four states, Georgia, New Jersey, North Carolina, and South Carolina, the legislature was given almost total control over appointments. The two remaining states, Delaware and Virginia, represented more mixed cases. In Virginia the legislature controlled the appointment of judges and legal officers, but a number of posts, including militia officers, justices of the peace, and sheriffs, were appointed by the governor with the advice of an executive council (styled a privy council) and upon the recommendation of county courts. In Delaware the role of the legislature and the executive in the appointment of officers was about evenly balanced. The president and privy council were given exclusive power to appoint a wide variety of judicial officers from the attorney general to clerks of the court, whereas the legislature had the dominant or exclusive role in the selection of judges and military officers. The attempt to balance executive and legislative powers was particularly striking in the innovative scheme used to appoint justices of the peace, by which the president and privy council chose twelve justices of the peace from each county from a list of twenty-four nominees provided by the assembly. Delaware's 1776 constitution also included a clause that shows that Americans, even at the height of their revolutionary antiexecutive fervor, were a long way from thinking of the power of appointment (apart from the power to appoint the treasurer, which all states seemed to accept as a legisla-

---

only required to seek the advice of council in appointing military officers. Moreover, whereas Massachusetts required members of the governor's council to quit their seats in the legislature, New Hampshire's council members retained their seats in the legislature, though they were barred from "intermeddl[ing]" with impeachment proceedings (Thorpe 1909, 4:2465–66). Compromising separation of powers still further, the president was made the presiding officer in the Senate as well as a voting member of that body (4:2463). Although New Hampshire's constitution is a reliable measure of how far Americans had traveled since 1776, it also dramatizes the great distance they still needed to go before they arrived at the Constitution.

8. The point should not be overdrawn. There was still plenty of plural officeholding in a number of the states, though nothing like what had been customary in the colonial era. When John Sullivan was defeated for the New Hampshire presidency in 1785, he remained speaker of the house, a member of the council, and a major general of the militia (Turner 1983, 64), though the new 1784 constitution meant he could not also retain his former post as attorney general. To take another example, in South Carolina, as Charles Pinckney pointed out in the federal convention (August 14), state judges commonly served in the legislature.

tive function) as a legislative responsibility: "the president," read article 16 of the Delaware constitution, "may appoint, during pleasure, until otherwise directed by the legislature, all necessary civil officers not hereinbefore mentioned" (Thorpe 1909, 1:565). The constitutions drafted by Massachusetts and New Hampshire in the 1780s reveal that an understanding of the appointment power as properly an executive function was steadily but slowly gaining adherents in the years leading up to the federal convention.

32. The Federal Convention of 1787

The debate over the appointment power was among the most contentious the delegates faced. The delegates agreed that it was the legislature and not the executive that should have the power to create offices, but there the agreement ended. Among the questions they faced were: who would appoint government officials and military officers? who would appoint the national judiciary? and, finally, what sort of restrictions or prohibitions, if any, should be placed on legislators accepting appointments to public office? The convention's starting point, the Virginia Plan, proposed answers to the last two of these questions but gave little guidance on the first. In the Virginia Plan the judiciary, as was the case in most of the state constitutions, was to be selected by the legislature and to hold office during good behavior. And members of the House and Senate were "to be ineligible to any [state or national] office ... during term of service and for [the] space of ___ after [the] expiration thereof," an exclusionary rule that went well beyond what existed in any of the state constitutions, none of which barred legislators from assuming office after their term had expired or made legislators ineligible for an appointment even if they resigned their seat (Farrand 1937, 1:20–21). As to the rest of the appointment power, the Virginia Plan made no specific provision, though the last sentence of the seventh resolution did say that the "National Executive ... ought to enjoy the Executive rights vested in Congress by the Confederation." Since the Continental Congress exercised all legislative and executive powers, this sentence did nothing to clarify what counted as "executive rights." When the convention began consideration of the seventh resolution on June 1, the delegates quickly embraced Madison's proposal to strike this sentence and substitute one that specifically granted the executive the power "to appoint to offices

---

Gaillard Hunt and James Brown Scott, eds., *The Debates in the Federal Convention of 1787 Which Framed the Constitution of the United States of America Reported by James Madison* (New York: Oxford University Press, 1920), 56–57, 97, 274–77, 300–3, 337, 341–43, 415, 455, 464–65, 506, 508, 528–29, 562–63, 572; 24, 93–94, 150–55, 173–74, 203, 337, 340, 395–96, 398–99, 401, 502, 504–6. Madison's and Mason's comments on June 22 are from the notes of Abraham Yates in Jonathan Elliot, ed., *The Debates in the Several State Constitutions on the Adoption of the Federal Constitution* (New York: Burt Franklin, 1888), 1:437–38.

in cases not otherwise provided for." That was the easy part. Everything after that pertaining to the appointment power came much harder.

Appointing Judges, Ambassadors, and Other Officers

June 5

The clause, "that the National Judiciary be chosen by the National Legislature," being under consideration.

Mr. Wilson opposed the appointment of judges by the National Legislature. Experience showed the impropriety of such appointments by numerous bodies. Intrigue, partiality, and concealment were the necessary consequences. A principal reason for unity in the Executive was that officers might be appointed by a single, responsible person.

Mr. Rutledge was by no means disposed to grant so great a power to any single person. The people will think we are leaning too much towards Monarchy. ...

Docr. Franklin observed that two modes of choosing the judges had been mentioned, to wit, by the Legislature and by the Executive. He wished such other modes to be suggested as might occur to other gentlemen; it being a point of great moment. ...

Mr. Madison disliked the election of the Judges by the Legislature or any numerous body. Besides the danger of intrigue and partiality, many of the members were not judges of the requisite qualifications. The Legislative talents, which were very different from those of a Judge, commonly recommended men to the favor of Legislative Assemblies. It was known too that the accidental circumstances of presence and absence, of being a member or not a member, had a very undue influence on the appointment. On the other hand he was not satisfied with referring the appointment to the Executive. He rather inclined to give it to the Senatorial branch ... as being sufficiently stable and independent to follow their deliberate judgments. He hinted this only and moved that the appointment by the Legislature might be struck out and a blank left to be hereafter filled on maturer reflection. Mr. Wilson seconds it. On the question for striking out [9 yes; 2 no].

June 13

Mr. Pinckney and Mr. Sherman moved ... [that] the Judges of [the supreme tribunal should] be appointed by the national Legislature.

Mr. Madison objected to an appointment by the whole Legislature. ... He proposed that the appointment should be made by the Senate, which as a less numerous and more select body would be more competent judges, and which was sufficiently numerous to justify such a confidence in them.

Mr. Sherman and Mr. Pinckney withdrew their motion, and the appointment by the Senate was agreed to.

July 18

"The Judges ... to be appointed by the second branch of the National Legislature."

Mr. Gorham would prefer an appointment by the second branch to an appointment by the whole Legislature, but he thought even that branch too numerous and too little personally responsible to ensure a good choice. He suggested that the Judges be appointed by the Executive with the advice and consent of the second branch, in the mode prescribed by the constitution of Massachusetts. This mode had been long practiced in that country, and was found to answer perfectly well.

Mr. Wilson still would prefer an appointment by the Executive but, if that could not be attained, would prefer ... the mode suggested by Mr. Gorham. He thought it his duty however to move in the first instance "that the Judges be appointed by the Executive." Mr. Govr. Morris seconded the motion.

Mr. L. Martin was strenuous for an appointment by the second branch. Being taken from all the States it would be best informed of characters and most capable of making a fit choice.

Mr. Sherman concurred in the observations of Mr. Martin, adding that the Judges ought to be diffused, which would be more likely to be attended to by the second branch than by the Executive.

Mr. Mason. The mode of appointing the Judges may depend in some degree on the mode of trying impeachments of the Executive. If the Judges were to form a tribunal for that purpose, they surely ought not to be appointed by the Executive. There were insuperable objections besides against referring the appointment to the Executive. He mentioned as one, that as the seat of Government must be in some one State, and the Executive would remain in office for a considerable time, for 4, 5 or 6 years at least, he would insensibly form local and personal attachments within the particular State that would deprive equal merit elsewhere of an equal chance of promotion.

Mr. Gorham. As the Executive will be responsible ... for a judicious and faithful discharge of his trust, he will be careful to look through all the States for proper characters. The Senators will be as likely [as the Executive] to form their attachments at the seat of Government where they reside. If they can not get the man of the particular State to which they may respectively belong, they will be indifferent to the rest. Public bodies feel no personal responsibility, and give full play to intrigue and cabal. Rhode Island is a full illustration of the insensibility to character, produced by a participation of numbers ... and of the length to which a public body may carry wickedness and cabal. ...

Mr. Madison suggested that the Judges might be appointed by the Executive with the concurrence of $\frac{1}{3}$ at least of the second branch. This would unite the advantage of responsibility in the Executive with the security afforded in the second branch against any incautious or corrupt nomination by the Executive.

Mr. Sherman was clearly for an election by the Senate. It would be composed of men nearly equal to the Executive, and would of course have on the whole more wisdom. They would bring into their deliberations a more diffusive knowledge of characters. It would be less easy for candidates to intrigue with them than with the Executive Magistrate. For these reasons he thought there would be a better security for a proper choice in the Senate than in the Executive.

Mr. Randolph. It is true that when the appointment of the Judges was vested in the second branch an equality of votes had not been given to it. Yet he had rather leave the appointment there than give it to the Executive. He thought the advantage of personal responsibility might be gained in the Senate by requiring the respective votes of the members to be entered on the Journal. He thought too that the hope of receiving appointments would be more diffusive if they depended on the Senate, the members of which would be diffusively known, than if they depended on a single man who could not be personally known to a very great extent. ...

Mr. Bedford thought there were solid reasons against leaving the appointment to the Executive. He must trust more to information than the Senate. It would put it in his power to gain over the larger States by gratifying them with a preference of their citizens. The responsibility of the Executive so much talked of was chimerical. He could not be punished for mistakes.

Mr. Gorham remarked that the Senate could have no better information than the Executive. They must, like him, trust to information from the members belonging to the particular State where the Candidates resided. The Executive would certainly be more answerable for a good appointment, as the whole blame of a bad one would fall on him alone. He did not mean that he would be answerable under any other penalty than that of public censure, which with honorable minds was a sufficient one.

On the question for referring the appointment of the Judges to the Executive, instead of the second branch [2 yes; 6 no; 1 absent].

Mr. Gorham moved "that the Judges be nominated and appointed by the Executive, by and with the advice and consent of the second branch, and every such nomination shall be made at least ____ days prior to such appointment." This mode he said had been ratified by the experience of 140 years in Massachusetts. If the appointment should be left to either branch of the Legislature, it will be a mere piece of jobbing.

Mr. Govr. Morris seconded and supported the motion.

Mr. Sherman thought it less objectionable than an absolute appointment by the Executive, but disliked it as too much fettering the Senate.

Question on Mr. Gorham's motion [4 yes; 4 no; 1 absent].

July 21

Mr. Madison [moved] "that the Judges should be nominated by the Executive and such nomination become appointments unless disagreed to by ⅔ of the second branch of the Legislature." ...

Mr. Madison stated as his reasons for the motion. 1. that it secured the responsibility of the Executive who would in general be more capable and likely to select fit characters than the Legislature, or even the second branch of it, who might hide their selfish motive under the number concerned in the appointment. 2. that in case of any flagrant partiality or error in the nomination it might be fairly presumed that ⅔ of the second branch would join in putting a negative on it. 3. that as the second branch was very differently constituted when the appointment of the Judges was formerly referred to it, and was now to be composed of equal votes from all the States, the principle of compromise which had prevailed in other instances required in this that their should be a concurrence of two authorities, in one of which the people, in the other the States, should be represented. The Executive Magistrate would be considered as a national officer, acting for and equally sympathising with every part of the United States. If the second branch alone should have this power, the Judges might be appointed by a minority of the people, though by a majority of the States, which could not be justified on any principle, as their proceedings were to relate to the people rather than to the States. And as it would moreover throw the appointments entirely into the hands of the Northern States, a perpetual ground of jealousy and discontent would be furnished to the Southern States.

Mr. Pinckney was for placing the appointment in the second branch exclusively. The Executive will possess neither the requisite knowledge of characters nor confidence of the people for so high a trust.

Mr. Randolph would have preferred the mode of appointment proposed formerly by Mr. Gorham, as adopted in the Constitution of Massachusetts, but thought the motion pending so great an improvement of the clause as it stands that he anxiously wished it success. He laid great stress on the responsibility of the Executive as a security for fit appointments. Appointments by the Legislatures have generally resulted from cabal, from personal regard, or some other consideration than a title derived from the proper qualifications. The same inconveniences will proportionally prevail if the appointments be referred to either branch of the Legislature or to any other authority administered by a number of individuals.

Mr. Ellsworth would prefer a negative in the Executive on a nomination by the second branch, the negative to be overruled by a concurrence of ⅔ of the second branch, to the mode proposed by the motion but preferred an absolute appointment by the second branch to either. The Executive will be regarded by the people with a jealous eye. Every power for augmenting unnecessarily his influence will be disliked. As he will be stationary it was not to be supposed he could have a better knowledge of characters. He will be more open to caresses and intrigues than the Senate. The right to supersede his nomination will be ideal only. A nomination under such circumstances will be equivalent to an appointment.

Mr. Govr. Morris supported the motion. 1. The States in their corporate capacity will frequently have an interest staked on the determination of the Judges. [Because] in the Senate the States are to vote, the Judges ought not to be appointed by the Senate. Next to the impropriety of being Judge in one's own cause, is the appointment of the Judge. 2. It had been said the Executive would be uninformed of characters. The reverse was the truth. The Senate will be so. They must take the character of candidates from the flattering pictures drawn by their friends. The Executive in the necessary intercourse with every part of the U.S., required by the nature of his administration, will or may have the best possible information. 3. It had been said that a jealousy would be entertained of the Executive. If the Executive can be safely trusted with the command of the army, there cannot surely be any reasonable ground of jealousy in the present case. He added that if the objections against an appointment of the Executive by the Legislature had the weight that had been allowed there must be some weight in the objection to an appointment of the Judges by the Legislature or by any part of it.

Mr. Gerry. The appointment of the Judges like every other part of the Constitution should be so modelled as to give satisfaction both to the people and to the States. The mode under consideration will give satisfaction to neither. He could not conceive that the Executive could be as well informed of characters throughout the Union. It appeared to him also a strong objection that ⅔ of the Senate were required to reject a nomination of the Executive. The Senate would be constituted in the same manner as [the Continental] Congress. And the appointments of Congress have been generally good.

Mr. Madison observed that he was not anxious that ⅔ should be necessary to disagree to a nomination. He had given this form to his motion chiefly to vary it the more clearly from one which had just been rejected. He was content to obviate the objection last made, and accordingly so varied the motion as to let a majority reject.

Col. Mason found it his duty to differ from his colleagues in their opinions and reasonings on this subject. Notwithstanding the form of the proposition by which the appointment seemed to be divided between the Executive and Senate, the appointment was substantially vested in the former alone. The false complaisance which usually prevails in such cases will prevent a disagreement to the first nominations. He considered the appointment by the Executive as a dangerous prerogative. It might even give him an influence over the Judiciary department itself. He did not think the difference of interest between the Northern and Southern States could be properly brought into this argument. It would operate and require some precautions in the case of regulating navigation, commerce and imposts, but he could not see that it had any connection with the Judiciary department.

On the question, the motion now being that the executive should nominate, and such nominations should become appointments unless disagreed to by the Senate [3 yes; 6 no].

On the question for agreeing to the clause as it stands by which the Judges are to be appointed by the second branch [6 yes; 3 no].

August 6

Mr. Rutledge delivered in the Report of the Committee of Detail as follows. ...

Article VII, Sect. 1. The Legislature of the United States shall have the power ... to appoint a Treasurer by ballot. ...

Article IX, Section 1. "The Senate of the United States shall have power ... to appoint Ambassadors, and Judges of the supreme Court. ..."

Article X, Section 2. [The President] shall take care that the laws of the United States be duly and faithfully executed ... and shall appoint officers in all cases not otherwise provided for by this Constitution.

August 17

Article VII, section 1 resumed. On the clause "to appoint Treasurer by ballot." ...

Mr. Gorham moved to insert "joint" before ballot, as more convenient as well as reasonable, than to require the separate concurrence of the Senate.

Mr. Pinckney seconds the motion. Mr. Sherman opposed it as favoring the larger States.

Mr. Read moved to strike out the clause, leaving the appointment of the Treasurer as of other officers to the Executive. The Legislature was an improper body for appointments. Those of the State legislatures were a proof of it. The Executive being responsible would make a good choice.

Mr. Mercer seconds the motion of Mr. Read.

On the motion for inserting the word "joint" before ballot [7 yes; 3 no].

Col. Mason, in opposition to Mr. Read's motion, desired it might be considered to whom the money would belong; if to the people, the legislature representing the people ought to appoint the keepers of it.

On striking out the clause [4 yes; 6 no].

August 23

Article IX being next for consideration,

Mr. Govr. Morris argued against the appointment of officers by the Senate. He considered the body as too numerous for the purpose, as subject to cabal, and as devoid of responsibility. If Judges were to be tried by the Senate according to a late report of a Committee it was particularly wrong to let the Senate have the filling of vacancies which its own decrees were to create.

Mr. Wilson was of the same opinion and for like reasons. ...

The several clauses of Article IX, Section 1 were then ... postponed after inserting "and other public Ministers" next after "Ambassadors."

August 24

Article X, Section 2, being taken up. ...

Mr. Sherman objected to the sentence, "and shall appoint officers in all cases not otherwise provided for by this Constitution." He admitted it to be proper that many officers in the Executive Department should be so appointed, but contended that many ought not, as general officers in the army in time of peace. Herein lay the corruption in Great Britain. If the Executive can model the army, he may set up an absolute Government, taking advantage of the close of a war and an army commanded by his creatures. James II was not obeyed by his officers because they had been appointed by his predecessors not by himself. He moved to insert "or by law" after the word "Constitution."

On motion of Mr. Madison "officers" was struck out and "to offices" inserted, in order to obviate doubts that he might appoint officers without a previous creation of the offices by the Legislature.

On the question for inserting "or by law" as moved by Mr. Sherman [1 yes; 9 no; 1 absent].

Mr. Dickinson moved to strike out the words "and shall appoint to offices in all cases not otherwise provided for by this Constitution" and insert—"and shall appoint to all offices established by this Constitution, except in cases herein otherwise provided for, and to all offices which may hereafter be created by law." ...

On Mr. Dickinson's motion, it passed in the affirmative [6 yes; 4 no; 1 absent].

September 4

Mr. Brearly from the Committee of Eleven made a further partial Report as follows. ... "The President ... shall nominate and by and with the advice and consent of the Senate shall appoint ambassadors, and other public Ministers, Judges of the Supreme Court, and all other Officers of the U.S., whose appointments are not otherwise herein provided for."

September 7

Mr. Wilson objected to the mode of appointing as blending a branch of the Legislature with the Executive. Good laws are of no effect without a good Executive, and there can be no good Executive without a responsible appointment of officers to execute. Responsibility is in a manner destroyed by such an agency of the Senate. ...

Mr. Pinckney was against joining the Senate in these appointments, except in the instance of Ambassadors whom he thought ought not to be appointed by the President.

Mr. Govr. Morris said that as the President was to nominate, there would be responsibility, and as the Senate was to concur, there would be security. As Congress now make appointments there is no responsibility.

Mr. Gerry. The idea of responsibility in the nomination to offices is chimerical. The President can not know all characters, and can therefore always plead ignorance.

Mr. King ... differed from those who thought the Senate would sit constantly. He did not suppose it was meant that all the minute officers were to be appointed by the Senate, or any other original source, but [rather] by the higher officers of the departments to which they belong. ...

On the question on these words in the clause viz—"He shall nominate and by and with the advice and consent of the Senate, shall appoint ambassadors, and other public ministers (and Consuls), Judges of the Supreme Court." Agreed to nem. con., the insertion of "and consuls" having first taken place.

On the question on the following words "And all other officers of the U.S." [9 yes; 2 no].

On the motion of Mr. Spaight—"that the President shall have power to fill up all vacancies that may happen during recess of the Senate by granting Commissions which shall expire at the end of the next Session of the Senate" it was agreed to nem. con.

September 14

Article 1, section 8. The Congress "may by joint ballot appoint a Treasurer."

Mr. Rutledge moved to strike out this power, and let the Treasurer be appointed in the same manner with other officers.

Mr. Gorham and Mr. King said that the motion, if agreed to, would have a mischievous tendency. The people are accustomed and attached to that mode of appointing Treasurers, and the innovation will multiply objections to the System.

Mr. Govr. Morris remarked that if the Treasurer be not appointed by the Legislature, he will be more narrowly watched, and more readily impeached.

Mr. Sherman. As the Houses appropriate money, it is best for them to appoint the officer who is to keep it; and to appoint him as they make the appropriation, not by joint, but several votes.

General Pinckney. The Treasurer is appointed by joint ballot in South Carolina. The consequence is that bad appointments are made, and the Legislature will not listen to the faults of their own officer.

On the motion to strike out [8 yes; 3 no].[9]

September 15

Mr. Govr. Morris moved to annex "but the Congress may by law vest the appointment of such inferior officers as they think proper, in the President alone, in the Courts of law, or in the heads of Departments." Mr. Sherman seconded the motion.

Mr. Madison. It does not go far enough if it be necessary at all. Superior officers below heads of Departments ought in some cases to have the appointment of the lesser offices. ...

On the motion [5 yes; 5 no; 1 divided].

The motion being lost by an equal division of votes, it was urged that it be put a second time, some such provision being too necessary to be omitted, and on a second question it was agreed to nem. con. ...

---

9. The states opposed were Virginia, Massachusetts, Pennsylvania, the three largest states, which strongly suggests that it was less political philosophy than state interests that determined this late decision to take the power of selecting the treasurer away from the legislature, where it was vested in every state constitution.

After "Officers of the U.S. whose appointments are not otherwise provided for," were added the words "and which shall be established by law."

Legislative Indigibility to Office

May 29

Resolutions proposed by Mr. Randolph in Convention. ...

4. Resolved that the members of the first branch of the National Legislature ought to be ... ineligible to any office established by a particular State, or under the authority of the United States, except those peculiarly belonging to the functions of the first branch, during the term of service, and for the space of ___ after its expiration.

5. Resolved that the members of the second branch of the National Legislature ought to be ... ineligible to any office established by a particular State, or under the authority of the United States, except those peculiarly belonging to the functions of the second branch, during the term of service, and for the space of ___ after the expiration thereof.

June 12

On a question for making Members of the National legislature ineligible to any Office under the National Government for the term of 3 years after ceasing to be members [1 yes; 10 no].

On the question for such ineligibility for one year [8 yes; 2 no; 1 divided].

June 22

Mr. Gorham moved to strike out the ... ineligibility of members of the 1st branch to offices during the term of their membership and for one year after. He considered it as unnecessary and injurious. It was true abuses had been displayed in Great Britain but no one could say how far they might have contributed to preserve the due influence of the Government nor what might have ensued in case the contrary theory had been tried.

Mr. Butler opposed it. This precaution against intrigue was necessary. He appealed to the example of Great Britain where men got into Parliament that they might get offices for themselves or their friends. This w..s the source of the corruption that ruined their Government.

Mr. King thought we were refining too much. Such a restriction on the members would discourage merit. It would also give a pretext to the Executive for bad appointments, as he might always plead this as a bar to the choice he wished to have made.

Mr. Wilson ... suggested also the fatal consequences in time of war of rendering perhaps the best Commanders ineligible: appealing to our situation during the late war, and indirectly leading to a recollection of the appointment of the Commander in Chief out of Congress. ...

Mr. Madison. Some gentlemen give too much weight and others too little to this subject. If you have no exclusive clause, there may be danger of creating offices or augmenting the stipends of those already created in order to gratify some members. ... Such an instance has fallen within my own observation. I am therefore of the opinion that no office ought to be open to a member which may be created or augmented while he is in the legislature.

Mr. Mason. It seems as if it were taken for granted that all offices will be filled by the executive, while I think many will remain in the gift of the legislature. In either case, it is necessary to shut the door against corruption. If otherwise, they make or multiply offices in order to fill them. ... If not checked we shall have ambassadors to every petty state in Europe, the little republic of St. Marino not excepted. We must in the present system remove the temptation. I admire many parts of the British constitution and government, but I detest their corruption. Why has the power of the crown so ... remarkably increased the last century? A stranger, by reading their laws, would suppose it considerably diminished; and yet, by the sole power of appointing the increased officers of the government, corruption pervades every town and village in the kingdom. If such a restriction should abridge the right of election, it is still necessary, as it will prevent the people from ruining themselves. And will not the same causes here produce the same effects? I consider this clause as the corner-stone on which our liberties depend; and if we strike it out we are erecting a fabric for our destruction. ...

Col. Hamilton. There are inconveniences on both sides. We must take man as we find him and, if we expect him to serve the public, must interest his passions in doing so. A reliance on pure patriotism had been the source of many of our errors. He thought the remark of Mr. Gorham a just one. It was impossible to say what would be the effect in Great Britain of such a reform as had been urged. It was known that one of the ablest politicians [Mr. Hume] had pronounced all that influence on the side of the crown, which went under the name of corruption, an essential part of the weight which maintained the equilibrium of the Constitution.[10]

On Mr. Gorham's motion for striking out "ineligibility" [4 yes; 4 no; 3 divided].

June 23

General Pinckney moves to strike out the ineligibility of members of the 1st branch to offices established "by a particular State." He argued from the inconvenience to which such a restriction would expose both the members of the 1st branch and the States wishing for their services; [and] from the smallness of the object to be attained by the restriction. ...

Mr. Sherman seconds the motion [8 yes; 3 no].

Mr. Madison renewed his motion ... to render the members of the first branch "ineligible during their term of service, and for one year after, to such offices only as should be established, or the emoluments thereof, augmented by the Legislature of the United States during the time of their being members." He supposed that the unnecessary creation of offices, and increase of salaries, were the evils most experienced, and that if the door was shut against them, it might properly be left open for the appointment of members to other offices as an encouragement to legislative service. ...

Mr. Rutledge was for preserving the Legislature as pure as possible, by shutting the door against appointments of its own members to offices, which was one source of its corruption.

Mr. Mason. The motion of my colleague is but a partial remedy for the evil. He appealed to him as a witness of the shameful partiality of the Legislature of Virginia to its own members. He enlarged on abuses and corruption in the British Parliament, connected with the appointment of its members. ...

---

10. In "Of the Independency of Parliament," Hume had written, "We may ... give to this influence what name we please; we may call it by the invidious appellations of corruption and dependence; but some degree and some kind of it are inseparable from the very nature of the constitution, and necessary to the preservation of our mixed government" (1777, 44).

Mr. King remarked that ... the idea of preventing intrigue and solicitation of offices was chimerical. You say that no member shall himself be eligible to any office. Will this restrain him from availing himself of the same means which would gain appointments for himself, to gain them for his son, his brother, or any other object of his partiality. We were losing therefore the advantages on one side, without avoiding the evils on the other.

Mr. Wilson supported the motion. The proper cure he said for corruption in the Legislature was to take from it the power of appointing to offices. One branch of corruption would indeed remain, that of creating unnecessary offices, or granting unnecessary salaries, and for that the amendment would be a proper remedy. ...

Mr. Sherman observed that the motion did not go far enough. It might be evaded by the creation of a new office, the translation to it of a person from another office, and the appointment of a member of the Legislature to the latter. A new Embassy might be established to a new court and an ambassador taken from another, in order to create a vacancy for a favorite member. ...

Mr. Gerry thought there was great weight in the objection of Mr. Sherman. He added as another objection against admitting the eligibility of members in any case that it would produce intrigues of ambitious men for displacing proper officers, in order to create vacancies for themselves. In answer to Mr. King he observed that although members if disqualified themselves might still intrigue and cabal for their sons, brothers, etc., yet as their own interest would be dearer to them than those of their nearest connections it might be expected they would go to greater lengths to promote it.

Mr. Madison had been led to this motion as a middle ground between an eligibility in all cases and an absolute disqualification. He admitted the probable abuses of an eligibility of the members to offices, particularly within the gift of the Legislature. He had witnessed the partiality of such bodies to their own members, as had been remarked of the Virginia assembly by his colleague (Col. Mason). He appealed however to him in turn to vouch another fact not less notorious in Virginia, that the backwardness of the best citizens to engage in the legislative service gave but too great success to unfit characters. The question was not to be viewed on one side only. The advantages and disadvantages on both ought to be fairly compared. The objects to be aimed at were to fill all offices with the fittest characters, and to draw the wisest and most worthy citizens into the Legislative service. ...

On the question for agreeing to the motion of Mr. Madison [2 yes; 8 no; 1 divided].

On the ineligibility of the members during the term for which they were elected [8 yes; 2 no; 1 divided].

On ... extending ineligibility of members to one year after the term for which they were elected Col. Mason thought this essential to guard against evasions by resignations, and stipulations for office to be fulfilled at the expiration of the legislative term. Mr. Gerry had known such a case. Mr. Hamilton [said that] evasions could not be prevented: as by proxies, by friends holding for a year and them opening the way, etc. Mr. Rutledge admitted the possibility of evasions but was for controlling them as possible [4 yes; 6 no; 1 divided].

June 26

Mr. Williamson moved a resolution so penned as to admit of the two following questions: 1. whether the members of the Senate should be ineligible to and incapable of holding offices under the United States; 2. whether ... under the particular States. ...

Mr. Gerry and Mr. Madison moved to add to Mr. Williamson's first question: "and for 1 year thereafter." On this amendment [7 yes; 4 no].

On Mr. Williamson's first question as amended, namely, ineligible and incapable [to federal offices] for 1 year [it was] agreed unanimously.

On the second question as to ineligibility ... to State offices [8 yes; 4 no].

July 2

Mr. Govr. Morris ... disliked the exclusion of the second branch from holding offices. It is dangerous. ... It deprives the Executive of the principal source of influence. ... Besides shall the best, the most able, the most virtuous citizens not be permitted to hold offices? Who then are to hold them?

August 6

Mr. Rutledge delivered in the Report of the Committee of Detail as follows. ...

Article VI, Section 9. The members of each House shall be ineligible to, and incapable of holding any office under the authority of the United States, during the time for which they shall respectively be elected: and the members of the Senate shall be ineligible to, and incapable of holding any such office for one year afterwards. ...

August 14

Article VI, section 9 taken up.[11]

Mr. Pinckney argued that making the members ineligible to offices was degrading to them, and the more improper as their election into the Legislature implied that they had the confidence of the people. ... He moved to ... take up the following proposition: "the members of each House shall be incapable of holding any office under the U.S. for which they or any of others for their benefit receive any salary, fees, or emoluments of any kind—and the acceptance of such office shall vacate their seats respectively." ...

Mr. Mercer. ... Governments can only be maintained by force or influence. The Executive has not force, deprive him of influence by rendering the members of the Legislature ineligible to Executive offices and he becomes a mere phantom of authority. The Aristocratic part will not even let him in for a share of the plunder. The Legislature must and will be composed of wealth and abilities, and the people will be governed by a Junto. ... Without such an influence, the war will be between the aristocracy and the people. He wished it to be between the Aristocracy and the Executive. ...

Mr. Govr. Morris. ... He was against rendering the members of the Legislature ineligible to offices. He was for rendering them eligible again after having vacated their Seats by accepting office. Why should we not avail ourselves of their services if the people choose to

---

11. The debate over this section absorbed the better part of the day. Those speaking in favor of Pinckney's resolution were Mercer, Morris, and Wilson, all of whom delivered lengthy speeches and spoke more than once. Those speaking in opposition were Gerry, Mason, and Ellsworth as well as Sherman, Williamson, and Randolph.

give them their confidence? There can be little danger of corruption either among the people or the [state] Legislatures who are to be the Electors. If they say, we see their merits, we honor the men, we choose to renew our confidence in them, have they not a right to give them a preference, and can they be properly abridged of it?

Mr. Williamson ... did not wish to ... expunge the present Section. He had scarcely seen a single corrupt measure in the Legislature of North Carolina which could not be traced up to office hunting.

Mr Sherman. The Constitution should lay as few temptations as possible in the way of those in power. ...

Mr. Pinckney. No State has rendered the members of the Legislature ineligible to offices. In South Carolina the Judges are eligible into the Legislature. It cannot be supposed then that the motion will be offensive to the people. If the State Constitutions should be revised he believed restrictions of this sort would be rather diminished than multiplied. ...

Mr. Randolph had been and should continue uniformly opposed to the striking out of the [ineligibility] clause; as opening a door for influence and corruption. ...

A general postponement was agreed to.

September 1

Mr. Brearly from the Committee of Eleven ... made the following partial report.

That in lieu of the 9th section of article 6 the words following be inserted: "The members of each House shall be ineligible to any civil office under the authority of the U.S. during the time for which they shall respectively be elected, and no person holding an office under the U.S. shall be a member of either House during his continuance in office."

September 3

Mr King moved to insert the word "created" before the [first] "during" in the Report of the Committee. ...

Mr. Williamson seconded the motion. He did not see why members of the Legislature should be ineligible to vacancies happening during the term of their election.

Mr Sherman was for entirely incapacitating members of the Legislature. He thought their eligibility to offices would give too much influence to the Executive. He said the incapacity ought at least to be extended to cases where salaries should be increased, as well as created, during the term of the member. He mentioned also the expedient by which the restriction could be evaded to wit: an existing officer might be translated to an office created and a member of the Legislature be then put into the office vacated.

Mr Govr. Morris contended that the eligibility of members to office would lessen the influence of the Executive. If they cannot be appointed themselves, the Executive will appoint their relations and friends, retaining the service and votes of the members for his purposes in the Legislature. Whereas the appointment of the members deprives him of such an advantage. ...

Mr. Gorham was in favor of the amendment. Without it we go further than has been done in any of the States, or indeed any other Country. The experience of the State Governments, where there was no such ineligibility, proved that it was not necessary; on the contrary that the eligibility was among the inducements for fit men to enter into the Legislative service.

Mr. Randolph was inflexibly fixed against inviting men into the Legislature by the prospect of being appointed to offices.

Mr. Baldwin remarked that the example of the States was not applicable. The Legislatures there are so numerous that an exclusion of their members would not leave proper men for offices. The case would be otherwise in the General Government.

Col. Mason. Instead of excluding merit, the ineligibility will keep out corruption by excluding office-hunters.

Mr. Wilson considered the exclusion of members of the Legislature as increasing the influence of the Executive, as observed by Mr. Govr. Morris, at the same time that it would diminish the general energy of the Government. He said that the legal disqualification for office would be odious to those who did not wish for office but did not wish either to be marked by so degrading a distinction. ...

On the question of Mr. King's motion [5 yes; 5 no].

The amendment being thus lost by the equal division of the States, Mr. Williamson moved to insert the words "created or the emoluments whereof shall have been increased" before the word "during" in the Report of the committee.

Mr. King seconded the motion, and on the question [5 yes; 4 no; 1 divided].

The last clause rendering a seat in the Legislature and an office incompatible was agreed to.

The Report as amended and agreed to is as follows: "The members of each House shall be ineligible to any Civil office under the authority of the United States, created, or the emoluments whereof shall have been increased during the time for which they shall respectively be elected. And no person holding any office under the U. S. shall be a member of either House during his continuance in office."

33. Luther Martin,
"The Genuine Information," 1788

Comparing the form that legislative exclusion took in the final Constitution with the formulation in the original Virginia Plan, or even with the Committee of Detail's August 6 report, shows, as Luther Martin points out, how much the clause had been watered down. This watering down occurred in three distinct ways. The first occurred on June 23 and June 26, when the convention agreed, by healthy majorities, that Representatives and then Senators should not be barred from holding state offices, a weakening of the original Virginia Plan that Martin endorsed. The second part of the original Virginia Plan's exclusionary clause to be eliminated was the prohibition on legislators after their term of service had finished. The Virginia Plan had left the precise number of years blank and on June 12 the convention filled in the blank with one

---

"The Genuine Information, Delivered to the Legislature of the State of Maryland, Relative to the Proceedings of the General Convention, Held at Philadelphia, in 1787, By Luther Martin," in Jonathan Elliot, ed., *The Debates in the Several State Constitutions on the Adoption of the Federal Constitution* (New York: Burt Franklin, 1888), 1:365–66.

year. Ten days later, on June 23, the one-year prohibition was removed in a close vote, only to be resurrected three days later, though now the one-year ban applied only to senators. This one-year prohibition against senators was written into the Committee of Detail's report of August 6 but then, without any floor debate, was dropped in the September 1 report of the Committee on Postponed Matters. The third part of the Virginia Plan's original exclusionary clause to be weakened was the bar on legislators being eligible for offices during their elected term. The Brearly Committee had preserved this aspect of the Virginia Plan, but on September 3 the delegates decided, by the narrowest of margins, to modify the clause so that legislators would be ineligible only for those federal offices that had been "created or the emoluments whereof shall have been increased during the time for which they shall respectively be elected," a proposal that was essentially the same as the one that Madison had proposed and the convention had decisively rejected on June 23. It was the convention's late change of heart on September 3 that was particularly disheartening to Martin, who argues that the Constitution thus opened the gates to corruption of the legislature by the executive. Yet despite Martin's alarm the final form of the Constitution's exclusionary clause, which requires legislators to vacate their seats if they are appointed to fill any federal office, was far closer to the spirit and letter of the state constitutions than was the more draconian prohibition in the Virginian Plan with which the convention began.

In the sixth section of the first article, it is provided that senators and representatives may be appointed to any civil office under the authority of the United States, except such as shall have been created, or the emoluments of which have been increased, during the time for which they were elected. Upon this subject, sir, there was a great diversity of sentiment among the members of the Convention. As the propositions were reported by the committee of the whole house, a senator or representative could not be appointed to any office under a particular state, or under the United States, during the time for which they were chosen, nor to any office under the United States until one year after the expiration of that time. It was said—and in my opinion justly—that no good reason could be assigned why a senator or representative should be incapacitated to hold an office in his own government, since it can only bind h..n more closely to his state and attach him the more to its interests, which, as its representative, he is bound to consult and sacredly guard as far as is consistent with the welfare of the Union; and, according to this idea, the clause which prevented senators or delegates from holding offices in their own states was rejected by a considerable majority. But, sir, we sacredly endeavored to preserve all that part of the resolution which prevented them from being eligible to offices under the United States, as we considered it essentially necessary to preserve the integrity, independence, and dignity of the legislature, and to secure its members from corruption.

I was in the number of those who were extremely solicitous to preserve this part of the report, but there was a powerful opposition made by such who wished the members of the legislature to be eligible to offices under the United States. Three different times did they attempt to procure an alteration, and as often failed—a majority firmly adhering to the resolution as reported by the committee; however, an alteration was at length, by dint of perseverance, obtained even within the last twelve days of the Convention—for it happened after I left Philadelphia. As to the exception that they cannot be appointed to offices created by themselves, or the emoluments of which are by themselves increased, it is certainly of little consequence, since they may easily evade it by creating new offices to which may be appointed the persons who fill the offices before created, and thereby vacancies will be made which may be filled by the members who for that purpose have created the new offices.

It is true the acceptance of an office vacates their seat, nor can they be reelected during their continuance in office; but it was said that the evil would first take place; that the price for the office would be paid before it was obtained; that vacating the seat of the person who was appointed to office made way for the admission of a new member who would come there as desirous to obtain an office as he whom he succeeded and as ready to pay the price necessary to obtain it; in fine, that it would be only driving away the flies that were filled to make room for those that were hungry. And as the system is now reported, the President having the power to nominate to all offices, it must be evident that there is no possible security for the integrity and independence of the legislature, but that they are most unduly placed under the influence of the President, and exposed to bribery and corruption.

34. John Adams to Roger Sherman, July 1789

Luther Martin's concern about the corrupting potential of the president's appointment power was echoed by several other Anti-Federalists. "An Old Whig," for instance, worried that the president had been made "the fountain of all honors in the United States" (Storing 1981, 3:37). Similarly, the Impartial Examiner fretted that by "dispensing honor and profit throughout America ... copious streams of influence must flow from [the president]" (5:196). At least as common, however, were Anti-Federalist objections to the appointment clause that singled out the Senate's role in the appointment process. The Federal Farmer, for instance, feared that the Senate would use its power over appointments not "to advise, but to order and dictate in fact" and would reduce the president to "a mere primus inter pares." "With these efficient means of influence," the Federal Farmer continued, the Senate "will not only dictate, probably, to the president, but manage the house ... and under appearances of a balanced system, in reality, govern alone" (2:304; also see 4:26; 5:113; 6:119).

Anti-Federalists, though, were far from the only ones with strong misgivings about the founders' design of the appointment power. In this letter to convention delegate Roger Sherman, John Adams, the draftsman of the 1780 Massachusetts constitution, explains his objections to the Senate's role in the appointment process. The decision in Philadelphia not to have an executive

Charles Francis Adams, ed., *The Works of John Adams* (Boston: Charles C. Little and James Brown, 1851), 6:432–36.

council left people like Adams, who believed in a strict separation of powers, in something of a dilemma. To include the Senate in the appointment process not only violated the separation of powers but would, as Adams predicted, result in making "the whole business of this government ... infinitely delayed." But if the Senate were excluded from the appointment process, as Adams believed it should be, then the president would exercise the power alone, a concentration of power in the chief executive that few Americans of the founding period were ready to contemplate. Certainly no state constitution allowed the governor to make important civil appointments without the advice and consent of a council.

There is another sense and another degree in which the executive is blended with the legislature, which is liable to great and just objection; which excites alarms, jealousies and apprehensions, in a very great degree. I mean ... the negative of the senate upon appointments to office, [which] is liable to the following objections:

1. It takes away, or, at least ... it lessens the responsibility of the president. The blame of an injudicious, weak, or wicked appointment, is shared so much between him and the senate, that his part of it will be too small. Who can censure him, without censuring the senate, and the legislatures who appoint them? All their friends will be interested to vindicate the president in order to screen them from censure. ...

2. It turns the minds and attention of the people to the senate, a branch of the legislature, in executive matters. It interests another branch of the legislature in the management of the executive. It divides the people between the executive and the senate; whereas all the people ought to be united to watch the executive, to oppose its encroachments, and resist its ambition. Senators and representatives, and their constituents, in short, the aristocratical and democratical divisions of society, ought to be united on all occasions to oppose the executive or the monarchical branch, when it attempts to overleap its limits. But how can this union be effected when the aristocratical branch has pledged its reputation to the executive, by consenting to an appointment?

3. It has a natural tendency to excite ambition in the senate. An active, ardent spirit who is rich and able, and has a great reputation and influence, will be solicited by candidates for office. Not to introduce the idea of bribery, because, though it certainly would force itself in other countries and will probably here when we grow populous and rich, it is not yet to be dreaded, I hope, [but] ambition must come in already. A senator of great influence will be naturally ambitious and desirous of increasing his influence. Will he not be under a temptation to use his influence with the president as well as his brother senators to appoint persons to office in the several states who will exert themselves in elections to get out his enemies or opposers, both in the senate and house of representatives, and to get in his friends, perhaps his instruments? Suppose a senator to aim at the treasury office for himself, his brother, father, or son. Suppose him to aim at the president's chair, or vice-president's, at the next election, or at the office of war, foreign, or domestic affairs. Will he not naturally be tempted to make use of his whole patronage, his whole influence, in advising to appointments, both with president and senators, to get such persons nominated as will exert themselves in elections of president, vice-president, senators, and house of representatives, to increase his interest and promote his views? In this point of view, I am very apprehensive that this defect in our constitution will have an unhappy tendency to introduce corruption of the grossest

kinds, both of ambition and avarice, into all our elections, and this will be the worst of poisons to our constitution. It will not only destroy the present form of government, but render it almost impossible to substitute in its place any free government, even a better limited-monarchy, or any other than a despotism or a simple monarchy.

4. To avoid the evil under the last head, it will be in danger of dividing the continent into two or three nations, a case that presents no prospect but of perpetual war.

5. This negative on appointments is in danger of involving the senate in reproach, censure, obloquy, and suspicion without doing any good. Will the senate use their negative or not? If not, why should they have it? Many will censure them for not using it; many will ridicule them and call them servile. If they do use it, the very first instance of it will expose the senators to the resentment of not only the disappointed candidate and all his friends, but of the president and all his friends, and these will be most of the officers of government through the nation.

6. We shall very soon have parties formed, a court and country party, and these parties will have names given them. One party in the house of representatives will support the president and his measures and ministers, the other will oppose them. A similar party will be in the senate; these parties will study with all their arts, perhaps with intrigue, perhaps with corruption, at every election to increase their own friends and diminish their opposers. Suppose such parties formed in the senate, and then consider what factious divisions we shall have there upon every nomination.

7. The senate have not time. ...

You are of [the] opinion "that the concurrence of the senate in the appointments to office, will strengthen the hands of the executive, and secure the confidence of the people, much better than a select council, and will be less expensive."

But in every one of these ideas, I have the misfortune to differ from you.

It will weaken the hands of the executive by lessening the obligation, gratitude, and attachment of the candidate to the president, by dividing his attachment between the executive and legislative, which are natural enemies. Officers of government, instead of having a single eye and undivided attachment to the executive branch, as they ought to have, consistent with law and the constitution, will be constantly tempted to be factious with their factious patrons in the senate. The president's own officers, in a thousand instances, will oppose his just and constitutional exertions, and screen themselves under the wings of their patrons and party in the legislature. Nor will it secure the confidence of the people. The people will have more confidence in the executive, in executive matters, than in the senate. The people will be constantly jealous of factious schemes in the senators to unduly influence the executive, to serve each other's private views. The people will also be jealous that the influence of the senate will be employed to conceal, connive at, and defend guilt in executive officers, instead of being a guard and watch upon them, and a terror to them. A council, selected by the president himself, at his pleasure, from among the senators, representatives, and a nation at large, would be purely responsible. In that case, the senate would be a terror to privy counsellors; its honor would never be pledged to support any measure or instrument of the executive beyond justice, law, and the constitution. Nor would a privy council be more expensive. The whole senate must now deliberate on every appointment, and if they ever find time for it you will find that a great deal of time will be required and consumed in this service. Then, the president might have a constant executive council; now, he has none.

I said, under the seventh head, that the senate would not have time. You will find that the whole business of this government will be infinitely delayed by this negative of the senate on treaties and appointments. Indian treaties and consular conventions have been already waiting for months, and the senate have not been able to find a moment of time to attend to them; and this evil must constantly increase. So that the senate must be constantly sitting, and must be paid as long as they sit. ...

But I have tired your patience. Is there any truth in these broken hints and crude surmises, or not? To me they appear well founded and very important.

35. Alexander Hamilton, *Federalist* 76–77, April 1–2, 1788

In Hamilton's marathon speech to the convention on June 18, he dwelled on the importance of executive influence. By influence, Hamilton explained, "he did not mean corruption, but a dispensation of those regular honors and emoluments, which produce an attachment to the Govt." Hamilton's vision was, as historian Forrest McDonald observes, of a government "approximating the British system of government by cabinet ministers" (1994, 207). That is why in the plan of government he presented to the delegates at the close of his long oration there was no mention of excluding legislators from holding offices. Consistent with this ministerial vision was Hamilton's plan to give the chief executive "sole appointment" of the heads of the executive departments, not only of War and Foreign Affairs but, more radically, of Treasury as well. To be sure, much of Hamilton's plan of appointment—specifically his plan to vest the chief executive, subject to the approval of the Senate, with the power to choose all federal officers, including ambassadors and judges—was remarkably prescient. Not until the Brearly Committee report of September 4 was the power to appoint "ambassadors, and other public Ministers, [and] Judges of the Supreme Court" wrested away from the Senate and given to the president, in exactly the manner that Hamilton had suggested more than two months earlier. But the convergence in plans disguises a divergence in visions. Most of the framers were focused on separation of powers; their interest, as historian J. R. Pole has observed, was "to withdraw the executive as far as possible from the legislative process while investing it with genuine executive powers" (1971, 369). Hamilton, in contrast, envisioned the appointment power as a means by which the executive could gain support in the legislature, though in *Federalist* 76–77 he is at pains to emphasize the politically correct themes of independence and checks and balances and to deny that the power of appointments would give the executive influence over the Senate, pointing in support of his position to the exclusionary clause that he

New-York Packet, April 1, 1788. New York *Independent Journal*, April 2, 1788. The first ten paragraphs are from *Federalist* 76; the last eight from *Federalist* 77.

had opposed at the convention. Not until the Constitution had finally been adopted and Hamilton was safely ensconced as President Washington's first secretary of the Treasury would Hamilton be able to resume his quest for some form of ministerial government.

It has been observed in a former paper "that the true test of a good government is its aptitude and tendency to produce a good administration." If the justness of this observation be admitted, the mode of appointing the officers of the United States ... must when examined be allowed to be entitled to particular commendation. It is not easy to conceive a plan better calculated than this to produce a judicious choice of men for filling the offices of the Union; and it will not need proof that on this point must essentially depend the character of its administration.

It will be agreed on all hands that the power of appointment in ordinary cases ought to be modified in one of three ways. It ought either to be vested in a single man, or in a select assembly of a moderate number, or in a single man with the concurrence of such an assembly. The exercise of it by the people at large will be readily admitted to be impracticable, as, waving every other consideration, it would leave them little time to do anything else. ...

Those who have themselves reflected upon the subject, or who have attended to the observations made in other parts of these papers in relation to the appointment of the President, will I presume agree to the position that there would always be great probability of having the place supplied by a man of abilities, at least respectable. Premising this, I proceed to lay it down as a rule, that one man of discernment is better fitted to analyze and estimate the peculiar qualities adapted to particular offices than a body of men of equal, or perhaps even of superior discernment.

The sole and undivided responsibility of one man will naturally beget a livelier sense of duty and a more exact regard to reputation. He will on this account feel himself under stronger obligations, and more interested to investigate with care the qualities requisite to the station to be filled, and to prefer with impartiality the persons who may have the fairest pretensions to them. He will have fewer personal attachments to gratify than a body of men, who may each be supposed to have an equal number, and will be so much the less liable to be misled by the sentiments of friendship and of affection. A single well directed man, by a single understanding, cannot be distracted and warped by that diversity of views, feelings and interests which frequently distract and warp the resolutions of a collective body. There is nothing so apt to agitate the passions of mankind as personal considerations, whether they relate to ourselves or to others, who are to be the objects of our choice or preference. Hence, in every exercise of the power of appointing to officers by an assembly of men, we must expect to see a full display of all the private and party likings and dislikes, partialities and antipathies, attachments and animosities, which are felt by those who compose the assembly. The choice which may at any time happen to be made under such circumstances will of course be the result either of a victory gained by one party over the other, or of a compromise between the parties. In either case, the intrinsic merit of the candidate will be too often out of sight. In the first, the qualifications best adapted to uniting the suffrages of the party will be more considered than those which fit the person for the station. In the last the coalition will commonly turn upon some interested equivalent—"Give us the man we wish for this office, and you shall have the one you wish for that." This will be the usual condition of the bargain. And it will rarely happen that the advancement of the public service will be the primary object either of party victories or of party negotiations.

The truth of the principles here advanced seems to have been felt by the most intelligent of those who have found fault with the provision made in this respect by the Convention. They contend that the President ought solely to have been authorized to make the appointments under the Federal Government. But it is easy to show that every advantage to be expected from such an arrangement would in substance by derived from the power of nomination, which is proposed to be conferred upon him, while several disadvantages which might attend the absolute power of appointment in the hands of that officer would be avoided. In the act of nomination his judgment alone would be exercised; and as it would be his sole duty to point out the man, who with the approbation of the Senate should fill an office, his responsibility would be as complete as if he were to make the final appointment. There can in this view be no difference between nomination and appointing. The same motives which would influence a proper discharge of his duty in one case would exist in the other. And as no man could be appointed, but upon his previous nomination, every man who might be appointed would be in fact his choice.

But might not his nomination be overruled? I grant it might, yet this could only be to make place for another nomination by himself. The person ultimately appointed must be the object of his preference, though perhaps not in the first degree. It is also not very probable that his nomination would often be overruled. The Senate could not be tempted by the preference they might feel to another to reject the one proposed, because they could not assure themselves that the person they might wish would be brought forward by a second or by any subsequent nomination. They could not even be certain that a future nomination would present a candidate in any degree more acceptable to them. And as their dissent might cast a kind of stigma upon the individual rejected, and might have the appearance of a reflection upon the judgment of the chief magistrate, it is not likely that their sanction would often be refused where there were not special and strong reasons for the refusal.

To what purpose then require the co-operation of the Senate? I answer that the necessity of their concurrence would have a powerful, though in general a silent operation. It would be an excellent check upon a spirit of favoritism in the President, and would tend greatly to preventing the appointment of unfit characters from State prejudice, from family connection, from personal attachment, or from a view to popularity. And, in addition to this, it would be an efficacious source of stability in the administration.

It will readily be comprehended that a man who had himself the sole disposition of offices would be governed much more by his private inclinations and interests than when he was bound to submit the propriety of his choice to the discussion and determination of a different and independent body, and that body an entire branch of the Legislature. The possibility of rejection would be a strong motive to [take] care in proposing. The danger to his own reputation and ... to his political existence from betraying a spirit of favoritism or an unbecoming pursuit of popularity to the observation of a body, whose opinion would have great weight in forming that of the public, could not fail to operate as a barrier. ... He would be both ashamed and afraid to bring forward for the most distinguished or lucrative stations, candidates who had no other merit than that of coming from the same State to which he particularly belonged, or of being in some way or other personally allied to him, or of possessing the necessary insignificance and pliancy to render them the obsequious instruments of his pleasure.

To this reasoning it has been objected that the President, by the influence of the power of nomination, may secure the compliance of the Senate to his views. The supposition of universal venality in human nature is little less an error in political reasoning than the supposition of universal rectitude. The institution of delegated power implies that there is a portion of virtue and honor among mankind, which may be a reasonable foundation of confidence. And experience justifies the theory. It has been found to exist in the most corrupt periods of the most corrupt governments. The venality of the British House of Commons has been long a topic of accusation against that body ... and it cannot be doubted that the charge is to a considerable extent well founded. But it is as little to be doubted that there is always a large proportion of the body which consists of independent and public spirited men, who have an influential weight in the councils of the nation. Hence it is (the present reign not excepted) that the sense of that body is often seen to control the inclinations of the monarch, both with regard to men and to measures. Though it might therefore be allowable to suppose that the executive might occasionally influence some individuals in the Senate, yet the supposition that he could in general purchase the integrity of the whole body would be forced and improbable. A man disposed to view human nature as it is, without either flattering its virtues or exaggerating its vices, will see sufficient ground of confidence in the probity of the Senate to rest satisfied not only that it will be impracticable to the Executive to corrupt or seduce a majority of its members, but that the necessity of its co-operation in the business of appointments will be a considerable and salutary restraint upon the conduct of that magistrate. Nor is the integrity of the Senate the only reliance. The constitution has provided some important guards against the danger of executive influence upon the legislative body: It declares that "No Senator, or representative shall, during the time for which he was elected, be appointed to any civil office under the United States, which shall have been created, or the emoluments whereof shall have been increased during such time; and no person holding any office under the United States shall be a member of either house during his continuance in office." ...

It has been mentioned as one of the advantages to be expected from the co-operation of the Senate in the business of appointments, that it would contribute to the stability of the administration. The consent of that body would be necessary to displace as well as to appoint. A change of the chief magistrate therefore would not occasion so violent or so general a revolution in the officers of the government as might be expected if he were the sole disposer of offices. Where a man in any station had given satisfactory evidence of his fitness for it, a new president would be restrained from attempting a change in favor of a person more agreeable to him by the apprehension that the discountenance of the Senate might frustrate the attempt and bring some degree of discredit upon himself. Those who can best estimate the value of a steady administration will be most disposed to prize a provision which connects the official existence of public men with the approbation or disapprobation of that body, which from the greater permanency of its own composition, will in all probability be less subject to inconstancy than any other member of the government.

To this union of the Senate with the president in the article of appointments, it has in some cases been objected that it would serve to give the president an undue influence over the Senate; and in others, that it would have an opposite tendency; a strong proof that neither suggestion is true.

To state the first in its proper form is to refute it. It amounts to this—The president would have an improper influence over the Senate because the Senate would have the power of restraining him. This is an absurdity in terms. It cannot admit of a doubt that the entire power of appointment would enable him much more effectually to establish a dangerous empire over that body than a mere power of nomination subject to their control.

Let us take a view of the converse of the proposition—"The Senate would influence the executive." ... In what manner is this influence to be exerted? In relation to what objects? The power of influencing a person, in the sense in which it is here used, must imply a power of conferring a benefit upon him. How could the Senate confer a benefit upon the president by the manner of employing their right of negative upon his nominations? If it be said they might sometimes gratify him by an acquiescence in a favorite choice when public motives might dictate a different conduct, I answer that the instances in which the president could be personally interested in the result would be too few to admit of his being materially affected by the compliances of the Senate. The power which can originate the disposition of honors and emoluments is more likely to attract than to be attracted by the power which can merely obstruct their course. If by influencing the president be meant restraining him, this is precisely what must have been intended. And it has been shown that the restraint would be salutary, at the same time that it would not be such as to destroy a single advantage to be looked for from the uncontrolled agency of that magistrate. The right of nomination would produce all the good of that of appointment and would in a great measure avoid its ills.

Upon a comparison of the plan for the appointment of the officers of the proposed government with that which is established by the constitution of [New York] a decided preference must be given to the former. In that plan the power of nomination is unequivocally vested in the executive. And as there would be a necessity for submitting each nomination to the judgment of an entire branch of the legislature, the circumstances attending an appointment ... would naturally become matters of notoriety, and the public would be at no loss to determine what part had been performed by the different actors. The blame of a bad nomination would fall upon the president singly and absolutely. The censure of rejecting a good one would lie entirely at the door of the Senate. ... If an ill appointment should be made, the executive for nominating and the Senate for approving would participate, though in different degrees, in the opprobrium and disgrace.

The reverse of all this characterizes the manner of appointment in this state. The council of appointment consists of from three to five persons, of whom the governor is always one. This small body, shut up in a private apartment, impenetrable to the public eye, proceed to the execution of the trust committed to them. It is known that the governor claims the right of nomination, upon the strength of some ambiguous expressions in the constitution; but it is not known to what extent or in what manner he exercises it, nor upon what occasions he is contradicted or opposed. The censure of a bad appointment, on account of the uncertainty of its author and for want of a determinate object, has neither poignancy nor duration. And while an unbounded field for cabal and intrigue lies open, all idea of responsibility is lost. The most that the public can know is that the governor claims the right of nomination; that two out of the considerable number of four men can too often be managed without much difficulty; that if some of the members of a particular council should happen to be of an uncomplying character, it is frequently not impossible to get rid of their opposition by regulating the times of meeting in such a manner as to render their attendance inconvenient; and that, from whatever cause it may proceed, a great number of very improper appointments are from time to time made. Whether a governor of this state avails himself of the ascendant [power] he must necessarily have ... to prefer to offices men who are best qualified for them, or whether he prostitutes that advantage to the advancement of persons whose chief merit is their implicit devotion to his will, and to the support of a despicable and dangerous system of personal influence, are questions which unfortunately for the community can only be the subjects of speculation and conjecture.

Every mere council of appointment, however constituted, will be a conclave, in which cabal and intrigue will have their full scope. Their number, without an unwarrantable increase of expense, cannot be large enough to preclude a facility of combination. And as each member will have his friends and connections to provide for, the desire of mutual gratification will beget a scandalous bartering of votes and bargaining for places. The private attachments of one man might easily be satisfied, but to satisfy the private attachments of a dozen, or of twenty men, would occasion a monopoly of all the principal employments of the government in a few families, and would lead more directly to an aristocracy or an oligarchy than any measure that could be contrived. If to avoid an accumulation of offices there was to be a frequent change in the persons who were to compose the council, this would involve the mischiefs of a mutable administration in their full extent. Such a council would also be more liable to executive influence than the Senate, because they would be fewer in number and would act less immediately under the public inspection. Such a council in fine as a substitute for the plan of the convention would be productive of an increase of expenses, a multiplication of the evils which spring from favoritism and intrigue in the distribution of the public honors, a decrease of stability in the administration of the government, and a diminution of the security against an undue influence of the executive. ...

I could not with the propriety conclude my observations on the subject of appointments without taking notice of a scheme for which there has appeared some, though but a few advocates; I mean that of uniting the house of representatives in the power of making [appointments]. I shall however do little more than mention it, as I cannot imagine that it is likely to gain the countenance of any considerable part of the community. A body so fluctuating, and at the same time so numerous, can never be deemed proper for the exercise of that power. Its unfitness will appear manifest to all when it is recollected that in half a century it may consist of three or four hundred persons. All the advantages of the stability, both of the executive and of the Senate, would be defeated by this union, and infinite delays and embarrassments would be occasioned. The example of most of the states in their local constitutions encourages us to reprobate the idea.

36. House of Representatives, May 19, June 16–18, 1789

The delegates at the federal convention debated and settled many weighty and divisive questions, but they also managed to ignore a few key questions. One such issue immediately confronted the first Congress as it set about establishing the executive departments of Foreign Affairs, War, and Treasury. How the department heads would be appointed was crystal clear, but the Constitution was silent as to how these department heads should be removed. They could be impeached, of course, but was that the only grounds for removal? Did they serve during good behavior, like judges? Tench Coxe suggested this in his early defense of the Constitution in which he tried to allay

The Debates and Proceedings in the Congress of the United States (Washington, D.C.: Gales and Seaton, 1834), 1st Congress, 1st session, 1:397 (May 19), 1:504 (June 17), 1:480–82 (June 16), 1:506–7, 1:517–19 (June 17), 1:533–35 (June 18).

Anti-Federalist alarm by downplaying the president's powers (Jensen, Kaminski, and Saladino 1976–, 13:251). Few members of Congress, however, found this theory either plausible or desirable. But if department heads did not serve during good behavior, then at whose pleasure did they serve? One group in the House, including former constitutional delegates Elbridge Gerry and Roger Sherman, argued that just as the department heads could be appointed only with the consent of the Senate so department heads could only be removed with Senate approval. In support of their position they could point to the arguments Federalists themselves had used when presenting the Constitution for ratification. Hamilton, for instance, in *Federalist* 77 had confidently assured the citizens of New York that "the consent of [the Senate] would be necessary to displace as well as to appoint." This argument was met on the House floor by an opposing theory, advanced most powerfully by Madison, that removal of officers was an executive function and that the Constitution clearly vested the executive power in the president. The president only shared his executive powers when the Constitution specified an exception, as it did in the case of appointments. Madison's argument rested not only on constitutional grounds but on policy grounds as well: allowing the Senate to block the removal of officers would erode executive responsibility and debilitate the presidency. Others agreed with Madison that it was wise to vest the power of removal in the president but did not accept Madison's constitutional theory. They argued instead that Congress, which the Constitution vested with the power to "make all laws which shall be necessary and proper for carrying into execution ... all ... powers vested by this constitution in any department or officers" (Thach 1923, 150), was free to vest the power of removal wherever it chose. Without necessarily reaching agreement on the constitutional questions the House agreed, by a vote of 29 to 22, to exclude the Senate from the removal process. The following month, the Senate concurred.[12]

Mr. Theoderick Bland: The constitution declares that the President and the Senate shall appoint, and it naturally follows that the power which appoints shall remove also. ... A new President might, by turning out the great officers, bring about a change of the ministry and

---

12. This is far from the end of the story, however. The president's right to dismiss officers continued to be challenged periodically throughout the nineteenth century. President Andrew Jackson's dismissal of Treasury secretary William Duane in 1834 led the Senate formally to censure the president. In 1867 Congress passed the Tenure of Office Act, which required the president to obtain the consent of the Senate before removing any officers that had been appointed with the advice and consent of the Senate. The following year President Andrew Johnson fired his secretary of war, Edwin Stanton, without consulting the Senate, and the House then impeached Johnson. A decade later Congress passed a law mandating that "postmasters of the first, second and third classes shall be appointed and may be removed by the President with the advice and consent of the Senate" (Corwin 1957, 86). The matter was not definitively settled as a constitutional matter until the 1926 Supreme Court ruling in *Myers v. U.S.*, in which the Court held that Article 2 of the Constitution gave the power of removal to the president. For an introduction to these developments, see Corwin 1957, 81–95.

throw the affairs of the Union into disorder. Would not this in fact make the President a monarch, and give him absolute power over all the great departments of Government?

Mr. Thomas Lawrence: It has been said by some gentlemen that if [the power of removal] is lodged in [the president], it will be subject to abuse; that there may be a change of officers and a complete revolution throughout the whole executive department upon the election of every new President. I admit this may be the case, and contend that it should be the case, if the President thinks it necessary. I contend that every President ought to have those men about him in whom he can place the most confidence, provided the Senate approve his choice. ...

Mr. James Madison: It is evidently the intention of the constitution that the first Magistrate should be responsible for the executive department. So far therefore as we do not make the officers who are to aid him in the duties of that department responsible to him, he is not responsible to his country. Is there no danger that an officer, when he is appointed by the concurrence of the Senate, and has friends in that body, may choose rather to risk his establishment on the favor of that branch than rest it upon the discharge of his duties to the satisfaction of the executive branch, which is constitutionally authorized to inspect and control his conduct? And if it should happen that the officers connect themselves with the Senate, they may mutually support each other, and for want of efficacy reduce the power of the President to a mere vapor, in which case his responsibility would be annihilated and the expectation of it unjust. The high executive officers, joined in cabal with the Senate, would lay the foundation of discord and end in an assumption of the executive power, only to be removed by a revolution in the Government. I believe no principle is more clearly laid down in the Constitution than that of responsibility. ...

I conceive that if any power whatsoever is in its nature executive, it is the power of appointing, overseeing, and controlling those who execute the laws. If the constitution had not qualified the power of the President in appointing to office, by associating the Senate with him in that business, would it not be clear that he would have the right, by virtue of his executive power, to make such appointment? Should we be authorized, in defiance of that clause in the Constitution—"The executive power shall be vested in a President"—to unite the Senate with the President in the appointment to office? I conceive not. If it is admitted that we should not be authorized to do this, I think it may be disputed whether we have a right to associate them in removing persons from office, the one power being as much of an executive nature as the other; and the first only is authorized by being excepted out of the general rule established by the constitution in these words, "the Executive power shall be vested in the President." ...

Mr. James Jackson: It has been mentioned that in all Governments the Executive Magistrate has the power of dismissing officers under him. This may hold good in Europe, where monarchs claim their powers jure divino, but it never can be admitted in America, under a constitution delegating only enumerated powers. It requires more than a mere ipse dixit [an arbitrary or dogmatic statement] to demonstrate that any power is in its nature executive, and consequently given to the President of the United States by the present constitution; but [even] if this power is incident to the executive branch of Government, it does not follow that it vests in the President alone, because he alone does not possess all executive powers [under this constitution]. ...

It has been observed that the President ought to have this power to remove a man when he becomes obnoxious to the people or disagreeable to himself. Are we, then, to have all the officers the mere creatures of the President? This thirst of power will introduce a treasury bench into the House, and we shall have ministers obtrude upon us to govern and direct the measures of the Legislature, and to support the influence of their master. ... I suppose these circumstances must take place, because they have taken place in other countries. The executive power falls to the ground in England if it cannot be supported by the Parliament; therefore a high game of corruption is played and a majority secured to the ministry by the introduction of placemen and pensioners. ...

Mr. Madison: Everything relative to the merits of the question, as distinguished from a constitutional question, seems to turn on the danger of such a power vested in the President alone. But when I consider the checks under which he lies in the exercise of this power, I own to you I feel no apprehensions but what arise from the dangers incidental to the power itself; for dangers will be incidental to it, vest it where you please. I will not reiterate what was said before with respect to the mode of election, and the extreme improbability that any citizen will be selected from the mass of citizens who is not highly distinguished by his abilities and worth; in this alone we have no small security for faithful exercise of this power. But, throwing that out of the question, let us consider the restraints he will feel after he is placed in that elevated station. ...

In the first place, he will be impeachable by this House, before the Senate, for such an act of mal-administration; for I contend that the wanton removal of meritorious officers would subject him to impeachment and removal from his own high trust. But what can be his motives for displacing a worthy man? It must be that he may fill the place with an unworthy creature of his own. Can he accomplish this end? No; he can place no man in the vacancy whom the Senate shall not approve; and if he could fill the vacancy with the man he might choose, I am sure he would have little inducement to make an improper removal. Let us consider the consequences. The injured man will be supported by the popular opinion; the community will take side with him against the President; it will facilitate those combinations and give success to those exertions which will be pursued to prevent his reelection. To displace a man of high merit, and who from his station may be supposed a man of extensive influence, are considerations which will excite serious reflections beforehand in the mind of any man who may fill the Presidential chair. The friends of those individuals and the public sympathy will be against him. If this should not produce his impeachment before the Senate, it will amount to an impeachment before the community, who will have the power of punishment by refusing to reelect him.

But suppose this persecuted individual cannot obtain revenge in this mode. There are other modes in which he could make the situation of the President very inconvenient. ... If he had not influence enough to direct the vengeance of the whole community, he may probably be able to obtain an appointment in one or the other branch of the Legislature, and being a man of weight, talents, and influence ... he may prove to the President troublesome indeed. We have seen examples in the history of other nations which justify the remark I now have made. Though the prerogatives of the British King are great as his rank, and it is unquestionably known that he has a positive influence over both branches of the legislative body, yet there have been examples in which the appointment and removal of ministers have been found to be dictated by one or other of those branches. Now if this be the case with an hereditary Monarch, possessed of those high prerogatives and furnished with so many means of influence, can we suppose a President, elected for four years only, dependent upon the popular voice, impeachable by the Legislature, little if at all distinguished for wealth, personal talents, or influence from the head of the department himself—I say, will he bid defiance to all these considerations, and wantonly dismiss a meritorious and virtuous officer?

Such abuse of power exceeds my conception. If anything takes place in the ordinary course of business of this kind, my imagination cannot extend to it on any rational principle.

But let us not consider the question on one side only; there are dangers to be contemplated on the other. Vest this power in the Senate jointly with the President and you abolish at once that great principle of unity and responsibility in the executive department which was intended for the security of liberty and the public good. If the President should possess alone the power of removal from office, those who are employed in the execution of the law will be in their proper situation and the chain of dependence be preserved. The lowest officers, the middle grade, and the highest will depend, as they ought, on the President, and the President on the community. The chain of dependence therefore terminates in the supreme body, namely, in the people, who will possess besides, in aid of their original power, the decisive engine of impeachment.

Take the other supposition: that the power should be vested in the Senate on the principle that the power to displace is necessarily connected with the power to appoint. It is declared by the constitution that we may by law vest the appointment of inferior officers in the heads of departments, the power of removal being incidental, as stated by some gentlemen. Where does this terminate? If you begin with the subordinate officers, they are dependent on their superior, he on the next superior, and he on—whom? On the Senate ... a body possessing that proportion of aristocratic power which the constitution no doubt thought wise to be established in the system, but which some have strongly excepted against. And let me ask gentlemen, is there equal security in this case as in the other? Shall we trust the Senate, responsible to individual Legislatures, rather than the person who is responsible to the whole community? It is true, the Senate do not hold their offices for life, like aristocracies recorded in the historic page. Yet the fact is they will not possess that responsibility for the exercise of Executive powers which would render it safe for us to vest such powers in them.

But what an aspect will this give to the Executive? Instead of keeping the departments of Government distinct, you make an Executive out of one branch of the Legislature; you make the Executive a two-headed monster. ... [Y]ou destroy the great principle of responsibility and perhaps have the creature divided in its will, defeating the very purposes for which a unity in the Executive was instituted. ... You link together two branches of the Government which the preservation of liberty requires to be constantly separated. ...

Mr. Alexander White: It is not contended that the power which this bill proposes to vest is given to the President in express terms by the constitution, or that it can be inferred from any particular clause in that instrument. It is sought for from another source, the general nature of executive power. It is on this principle the clause is advocated. ... It was said by [Mr. Madison] that the constitution having invested the President with a general executive power, thereby all those powers were vested which were not expressly excepted, and therefore he possessed the power of removal. This is a doctrine not to be learned in American Governments [and] is no part of the constitution of the Union. Each State has an Executive Magistrate, but look at his powers and I believe it will not be found that he has in any one ... the right of appointing or removing officers. In Virginia ... all the great officers are appointed by the General Assembly. Few, if any, of a subordinate nature are appointed by the Governor without some modification. The case is generally the same in the other States. If the doctrine of the gentleman is to be supported by examples, it must be by those brought from beyond the Atlantic. We must also look there for rules to circumscribe the latitude of this principle, if indeed it can be limited.

Upon the principle by which the executive powers are expounded must the legislative be determined. Hence we are to infer that Congress have all legislative powers not expressly excepted in the constitution. If this is the case and the President is invested with all executive powers not excepted, I do not know that there can be a more arbitrary Government. The President will have the powers of the most absolute Monarch and the Legislature all the powers of the most sovereign Legislature, except in those particular instances in which the constitution has defined their limits. This I take to be a clear and necessary deduction from the principle on which the clause in the bill is founded.

I will mention the exceptions, and then let gentlemen form their opinion of the Government, if it is thus constituted. The President is limited in the appointment of ambassadors, consuls, judges, and all other officers, and in making treaties, but no further. Take from him these and give him all other powers exercised by Monarchs, and see what they will be. There are also exceptions to the legislative power, such as: they shall not for a certain period prohibit the importation of slaves; that direct taxes shall be apportioned in a particular manner; that duties, imposts, and excises shall be uniform; that they shall grant no titles of nobility, no bill of attainder; no ex post facto law shall be passed; no preference in commerce to be given; no money to be drawn but by law. These are the exceptions to the legislative powers. Now give them all the powers which the Parliament of Great Britain have, and what kind of Government is yours? I cannot describe it. It appears to me as absolute and extensive as any despotism. Then we must adhere to the limits described in the constitution. If we advance one step beyond its boundaries, where are we to draw the line to circumscribe our powers or secure the liberties of our fellow-citizens?

Questions for Discussion

1. Imagine a dialogue over the appointment power among Alexander Hamilton, John Adams, and George Mason. On what would their disagreements center? Their agreements?

2. How would American politics be different today if the delegates had stuck with the appointment and exclusion provisions in the original Virginia Plan?

3. Had the delegates at the Constitutional Convention taken up the question of the power of removal, how do you think it would have been settled? Which delegates would have insisted on involving the Senate in the removal process? Which delegates would have preferred to vest the power of removal exclusively in the president? Where do you think the power of removal should be vested?

4. How would the relationship between the executive and legislative branches have been altered if Congress in 1789 had decided that the Constitution required that department heads could not be removed without the consent of the Senate?

9

Pardon Power

> The President ... shall have Power to grant Reprieves and Pardons for Offences against the United States, except in Cases of Impeachment.
>
> Article 2, section 2

The pardon power received little scrutiny at the convention. It was not until the end of August that the delegates even took up the subject, and then only briefly. The only serious debate over the power to grant pardons came two days before the convention's close, when the delegates entertained a last-minute amendment from Edmund Randolph that would have prohibited the president from pardoning in cases of treason. The relative lack of debate is particularly striking, since the president's pardon power went well beyond the pardon power in the states.

Georgia's constitution carved out a single exception to its grant of executive power to the governor: he was forbidden to grant pardons or remit fines. The governor could reprieve a criminal or suspend a fine but only until the next meeting of the assembly, which was given the broad power to "determine therein as they shall judge fit" (Thorpe 1909, 2:781). In New Jersey the power to pardon was exercised jointly by the governor and the legislative council sitting as a "Court of Appeals" (5:2596). The governors of Massachusetts and New Hampshire could only grant pardons "by and with the advice of council" and even then they were forbidden to pardon before conviction (3:1901, 4:2464), as was the New Jersey Court of Appeals. New York did not permit the governor to pardon for treason or murder, though he could grant a reprieve until the legislature's next meeting (5:2633). The same limitation in cases of treason and murder applied in Pennsylvania, where the pardon power was lodged in the twelve-person executive council. Moreover, even state constitutions enacted immediately after the adoption of the new federal Constitution often opted for these stricter limitations on the pardon power. Georgia's revised constitution of 1789 granted the governor the power to pardon but withheld it in cases of treason and murder; it also insisted that pardons could only occur after conviction. South Carolina's new constitution of 1790 (its previous two constitutions of 1776 and 1778 had made no provision at all for pardons) also refused to allow pardons prior to conviction, as did New Hampshire's constitution of 1792.[1] Even the colonial governors were not permitted to grant pardons in cases of treason or murder, though they could issue a reprieve until the Crown determined the offender's fate (Greene [1888] 1966, 125–26).

If it counts as something of a surprise that the framers chose neither to exempt treason (as Randolph proposed) nor to limit pardons to after conviction (as Luther Martin proposed), it comes as no surprise at all that the framers exempted impeachment. No state that permitted impeachment procedures allowed the governor to pardon impeachments. For the framers it was a settled maxim that the executive should not be able to pardon an impeached officer. This maxim had been steeled in England's constitutional crisis of a century earlier, a crisis that had been precipitated in part by King Charles II's effort to use the pardon power to preempt the House of Commons's impeachment of the Earl of Danby, the king's leading minister in Parliament. The Commons refused to accept Danby's pardon, and the king responded by dissolving Parliament. The Act of Settlement of 1701 included a declaration "that no pardon under the great seal of England [shall] be pleadable to an impeachment by the Commons in Parliament" (Adler 1989a, 214). In other words, the monarch was forbidden to employ the pardon power to prevent the Commons from prosecuting impeachment and holding accountable the king's ministers. In one respect, then—and one respect only—the president's pardon power was made more limited than the king's. Unlike the president, the king could offer a pardon after impeachment had been determined, whereas in the United States no impeached official can ever be pardoned (though if the official resigns before he is impeached, as Richard Nixon did, then the president can still pardon him).

Why did the framers not place greater restrictions on the president's pardon power? Here, after all, was a royal prerogative that had been subject to great abuse in the past. Kings had sold pardons for a fee, and Edward I (1272–1307) even used pardons to raise armies: a year's service in the king's armies could bring a pardon for murder or robbery. Use of the pardon to advance political objectives or protect political allies was commonplace. Among Parliament's many complaints against the Catholic King James II (before he

---

1. The other two constitutions (Pennsylvania in 1790 and Delaware in 1792) written in this post-ratification period exactly followed the pardon clause of the new federal constitution. Vermont, which had been admitted as a state in 1791, drew up a new constitution in 1793, but the plan of government was identical to that of its 1786 constitution. The pardon provision in Vermont's 1786 and 1793 constitutions, as well as its original constitution of 1777, was modeled on Pennsylvania's 1776 constitution: the pardon was vested in a "Supreme executive council" and did not extend to treason, murder, or impeachment.

fled to France in a bloodless "Glorious Revolution") was that he had pardoned scores of Catholics before they had been brought to trial (McDonald 1994, 34). Given a history replete with abuse of this power, why did the framers retain this most ancient of royal prerogatives in a virtually unrestricted manner?

In England, according to William Blackstone, the king possessed the power to pardon on the theory that all criminal offenses were against the Crown. "It is reasonable," Blackstone surmises, "that only he who is injured should have the power of forgiving" (Adler 1989a, 213). The pardon, in this formulation, is bestowed as an act of mercy, a gift of grace.[2] But if this theory justifies the royal prerogative, it hardly seems a persuasive grounds on which to rest the pardon power in a republican executive. Indeed Blackstone himself thought that the pardon power was incompatible with a democratic form of government; only a monarchy was suited to the pardon power because only a monarchical regime acknowledged a person who acts "in a superior sphere" and could thus act above or outside the law ([1783] 1978, 4:397). For the framers, though, the English conception of pardons as "an act of grace" (Adler 1989a, 211) was subordinate to more pragmatic concerns. When Martin suggested that pardons prior to convictions be outlawed, he quickly withdrew the motion after being met with James Wilson's objection that a pardon before conviction might be needed "in order to obtain the testimony of accomplices." The "principal argument" for vesting the pardon power in the executive, Hamilton maintained in *Federalist* 74, was that "in seasons of insurrection or rebellion, there are often critical moments, when a well timed offer of pardon to the insurgents or rebels may restore the tranquility of the commonwealth." The legislature, because it was not always in session, would often not be able to capitalize on these "critical moments." The presidential pardon, in short, was seen primarily as "an instrument of law enforcement" and not, as in England, an act of clemency "opposed to the law" (Corwin 1957, 159).

Anti-Federalists were not persuaded that the pardon power needed to be unlimited to be effective, though few if any deemed the issue vital enough to warrant a sustained critique. Virtually all Anti-Federalists (and more than a few Federalists) would have shared the Federal Farmer's desire to see "the power to reprieve and pardon ... more cautiously lodged, and under some limitations" (Storing 1981, 2:348). Anti-Federalists were particularly frightened by the prospect, first broached by Randolph at the federal convention, that a president might use the pardon power to cover up his own misdeeds. As "Centinel" expressed the fear, the president may "shelter the traitors whom he himself ... [has] excited to plot against the liberties of the nation" (2:151; also

---

2. Blackstone also emphasizes the pardon's role in securing popular support for the monarch, an argument that none of the framers made for the presidential pardon. "These repeated acts of goodness," Blackstone explained, "coming immediately from his own hand, endear the sovereign to his subjects, and contribute more than anything to root in their hearts that filial affection, and personal loyalty, which are the sure establishment of a prince" ([1783] 1978, 4:398).

see 2:142, 2:67). The Anti-Federalists' alarm that a president might use the pardon to conceal his own crimes still rings relevant today. In the 1980s there were fears that Ronald Reagan might pardon Oliver North, John Poindexter, and other subordinates as a way of concealing his own actions in the Iran-Contra affair. When President George Bush pardoned Reagan's defense secretary, Caspar Weinberger, independent counsel Lawrence Walsh accused the president of trying to avoid facing "searching questions" about his own role in the affair (Pious 1996, 303). And more recently, concerns have been expressed that Bill Clinton might use the pardon to cover up possible wrongdoing by the president.

It is the pardon of specific individuals that usually draws the most attention—none more so than Gerald Ford's pardon of Richard Nixon, which precipitated a twenty-point drop in Ford's popular approval rating. But presidents have also used the pardon power to grant general or blanket amnesties to entire categories of people, particularly during or immediately after major wars or domestic uprisings. Having crushed the Whiskey Rebellion in western Pennsylvania in 1794, President Washington promptly issued an amnesty to all who had participated in the rebellion. During the Civil War period, Presidents Abraham Lincoln and Andrew Johnson issued amnesties that covered approximately 200,000 people. In more recent times, Presidents Gerald Ford and Jimmy Carter granted amnesties to more than 10,000 people who had evaded the draft during the Vietnam War. If Anti-Federalists were right to worry about possible abuses of the presidential pardon, defenders of the president's pardon power were right that it would often serve society's need to forgive rather than to punish.

37. The Federal Convention of 1787

On July 27 the five-member Committee of Detail began its deliberations; its task, as the title of the committee suggests, was to prepare a constitution that fleshed out the details and filled in the gaps in a manner "conformable" to the resolutions the convention had adopted. Also referred to the committee were the proposals contained in the New Jersey and Pinckney Plans. None of the resolutions or plans referred to the Committee of Detail made any mention of the pardon power. Edmund Randolph, who had presented the original Virginia Plan to the convention, was assigned the task of drawing up the committee's first draft. That draft, which closely followed the adopted resolutions, included no mention of the pardoning power. The power to pardon was

Gaillard Hunt and James Brown Scott, eds., *The Debates in the Federal Convention of 1787 Which Framed the Constitution of the United States of America Reported by James Madison* (New York: Oxford University Press, 1920), 337, 343, 471–72, 571–72.

introduced into the committee's report by chair John Rutledge, who, in the margins of Randolph's draft, added, "The power of pardoning vested in the Executive ... [H]is pardon shall not however, be pleadable to an Impeachmt." (Farrand 1937, 2:146). Although the impeachment exemption was common in the states, Rutledge's language suggests that he was influenced more by the English example ("no pardon [shall] be pleadable to an impeachment" is the language of the 1701 Settlement) than he was by the example of the states, none of which used anything resembling Rutledge's language or the phrasing in the committee's final report, which was the handiwork of James Wilson.

August 6

Mr. Rutledge delivered in the Report of the Committee of Detail as follows. ...
    Article X, section 2. ... "The President ... shall have power to grant reprieves and pardons; but his pardon shall not be pleadable in bar of an impeachment."

August 25

Mr. Sherman moved to amend the "power to grant reprieves & pardons" so as to read "to grant reprieves until the ensuing session of the Senate, and pardons with consent of the Senate."
    On the question [1 yes; 8 no].
    "Except in cases of impeachment" inserted nem. con. after "pardons."
    On the question to agree to—"but his pardon shall not be pleadable in bar" [4 yes; 6 no].

August 27

Mr. L. Martin moved to insert the words "after conviction" after the words "reprieves and pardons."
    Mr. Wilson objected that pardon before conviction might be necessary in order to obtain the testimony of accomplices. He stated the case of forgeries which this might particularly happen. Mr. Martin withdrew his motion.

September 15

Article II, section 2. "he shall have power to grant reprieves and pardons for offences against the U.S., except in cases of impeachment."
    Mr. Randolph moved to [add] "except cases of treason." The prerogative of pardon in these cases was too great a trust. The President may himself be guilty. The traitors may be his own instruments.
    Col. Mason supported the motion.
    Mr. Govr. Morris had rather there should be no pardon for treason than let the power devolve on the Legislature.
    Mr. Wilson. Pardon is necessary for cases of treason, and is best placed in the hands of the Executive. If he be himself a party to the guilt he can be impeached and prosecuted.

Mr. King thought it would be inconsistent with the Constitutional separation of the Executive & Legislative powers to let the prerogative be exercised by the latter. A Legislative body is utterly unfit for the purpose. They are governed too much by the passions of the moment. In Massachusetts, one assembly would have hung all the insurgents in that State, the next was equally disposed to pardon them all. He suggested the expedient of requiring the concurrence of the Senate in acts of pardon.

Mr. Madison admitted the force of objections to the Legislature, but the pardon of treasons was so peculiarly improper for the President that he should acquiesce in the transfer of it to the former rather than leave it altogether in the hands of the latter. He would prefer ... an association of the Senate as a Council of advice with the President.

Mr. Randolph could not admit the Senate into a share of the Power. The great danger to liberty lay in a combination between the President and that body. ...

On the motion of Mr. Randolph [2 yes; 8 no; 1 divided].

38. James Madison and George Mason, Virginia Ratifying Convention, June 18, 1788

The convention's rejection of Randolph's treason exemption did not set well with either Randolph or Mason. In a public letter explaining why he had not signed the Constitution, Randolph identified the convention's decision to grant the president the power to pardon treason, even prior to conviction, as one of its major failings (Storing 1981, 2:97). Mason's published objections highlighted the same issue. The president, he complained, had been given "the unrestrained power of granting pardons for treason, which may be sometimes exercised to screen from punishment those whom he had secretly instigated to commit the crime, and thereby prevent a discovery of his own guilt" (Farrand 1937, 2:638). At the Virginia ratifying convention, Randolph (who had by then decided to support the Constitution) was awkwardly silent, but Mason pushed his case against the president's unrestrained pardon power. It is instructive to contrast Madison's uncompromising defense of the unlimited presidential pardon at the Virginia ratifying convention with the strong doubts he expressed on this issue at the Constitutional Convention. Had Madison changed his mind? Or had his views at the federal convention been crafted to conciliate and perhaps gain the support of his Virginia colleagues? Alternatively, were the views Madison expressed in the secrecy of the Philadelphia Convention closer to his real views, but now he was willing to use any arguments to defend the Constitution and see it ratified?

Mr. Mason. ... I conceive that the President ought not to have the power of pardoning, because he may frequently pardon crimes which were advised by himself. It may happen, at

---

Jonathan Elliot, ed., *The Debates in the Several State Constitutions on the Adoption of the Federal Constitution* (New York: Burt Franklin, 1888), 3:497–98.

some future day, that he will establish a monarchy and destroy the republic. If he has the power of granting pardons before indictment or conviction, may he not stop inquiry and prevent detection? The case of treason ought at least to be excepted. ...

Mr. Madison, adverting to Mr. Mason's objection to the President's power of pardoning, said it would be extremely improper to vest it in the House of Representatives, and not much less so to place it in the Senate; because numerous bodies were actuated more or less by passion, and might, in the moment of vengeance, forget humanity. It was an established practice in Massachusetts for the legislature to determine in such cases. It was found ... that two different sessions, before each of which the question came with respect to pardoning the delinquents of [Shays'] rebellion, were governed precisely by different sentiments: the one would execute with universal vengeance, and the other would extend general mercy.

There is one security in this case to which gentleman may not have adverted: if the President be connected in any suspicious manner with any person, and there be grounds to believe he will shelter him, the House of Representatives can impeach him; they can remove him if found guilty; they can suspend him when suspected, and the power will devolve on the Vice-President. Should he be suspected, also he may likewise be suspended till he be impeached and removed, and the legislature may make a temporary appointment. This is a great security.

Mr. Mason vindicated the conduct of the assemblies mentioned by the gentleman last up. He insisted they were both right; for, in the first instance, when such ideas of severity prevailed, a rebellion was in existence. In such circumstance, it was right to be rigid. But after it was over, it would be wrong to exercise unnecessary severity.

Mr. Madison replied that the honorable member had misunderstood the fact, for the first assembly was after the rebellion was over. The decision must have been improper in one or the other case. It marks this important truth ... that numerous bodies of men are improper to exercise this power. The universal experience of mankind proves it.

39. Alexander Hamilton, *Federalist* 74, March 25, 1788

The issue of the pardoning power was first broached at the federal convention by Alexander Hamilton in his long speech of June 18. Hamilton's plan for a new government gave the chief executive the power to pardon all offenses except treason, a crime that the executive could not pardon without the approval of the Senate. This is the only instance in which the chief executive envisioned by Hamilton was actually more limited in his power than the president that emerged from the federal convention. In *Federalist* 74 Hamilton thus found himself defending a presidential power (that is, to pardon treason without legislative assent) that he himself had not been ready to grant in his own plan. Hamilton's admission in this essay that there were "strong reasons" against allowing the executive alone to pardon treason was certainly

New-York Packet, March 25, 1788.

genuine, but one suspects that Hamilton, given his strong proexecutive bias, had little difficulty persuading himself that the Constitution's unlimited pardon power was superior, especially since the Senate he had proposed to implicate in the pardon power was to serve during good behavior and would, unlike the Senate under the Constitution, thereby be removed from the "taint" of popular passions.

The President ... is also to be authorized "to grant reprieves and pardons for offences against the United States except in cases of impeachment." Humanity and good policy conspired to dictate that the benign prerogative of pardoning should be as little as possible fettered or embarrassed. The criminal code of every country partakes so much of necessary severity that without an easy access to exceptions in favor of unfortunate guilt, justice would wear a countenance too sanguinary and cruel. As the sense of responsibility is always strongest in proportion as it is undivided, it may be inferred that a single man would be most ready to attend to the force of those motives which might plead for a mitigation of the rigor of the law, and least apt to yield to considerations which were calculated to shelter a fit object of its vengeance. The reflection that the fate of a fellow creature depended on his sole fiat would naturally inspire scrupulousness and caution. The dread of being accused of weakness or connivance would beget equal circumspection, though of a different kind. On the other hand, as men generally derive confidence from their numbers, they might often encourage each other in an act of obduracy, and might be less sensible to the apprehension of suspicion or censure for an injudicious or affected clemency. On these accounts, one man appears to be a more eligible dispenser of the mercy of the government than a body of men.

The expediency of vesting the power of pardoning in the President has, if I mistake not, been only contested in relation to the crime of treason. This, it has been urged, ought to have depended upon the assent of one or both of the branches of the legislative body. I shall not deny that there are strong reasons to be assigned for requiring in this particular the concurrence of that body or of a part of it. As treason is a crime levelled at the immediate being of the society. When the laws have once ascertained the guilt of the offender, there seems a fitness in referring the expediency of an act of mercy towards him to the judgment of the Legislature. And this ought the rather to be the case, as the supposition of the connivance of the Chief Magistrate ought not to be entirely excluded. But there are also strong objections to such a plan. It is not to be doubted that a single man of prudence and good sense is better fitted, in delicate conjunctures, to balance the motives which may plead for and against the remission of the punishment, than any numerous body whatever. It deserves particular attention that treason will often be connected with seditions, which embrace a large proportion of the community, as lately happened in Massachusetts. In every such case, we might expect to see the representation of the people tainted with the same spirit, which had given birth to the offence. And when parties were pretty equally matched, the secret sympathy of the friends and favorers of the condemned person, availing itself of the good nature and weakness of others, might frequently bestow impunity where the terror of an example was necessary. On the other hand, when the sedition had proceeded from causes which had inflamed the resentments of the major party, they might often be found obstinate and inexorable when policy demanded a conduct of forbearance and clemency. But the principal argument for reposing the power of pardoning in this case in the Chief Magistrate is this: In seasons of insurrection or rebellion there are often critical moments when a well timed offer of pardon to the insurgents or rebels may restore the tranquility of the commonwealth, and which, if suffered to pass unimproved, it may never be possible afterwards to recall. The dilatory process of convening the Legislature, or one of its branches, for the purpose of obtaining its sanction to the measure would frequently be the occasion of letting slip the golden opportunity. The loss of a week, a day, an hour, may sometimes be fatal. If it should be observed that a discretionary power with a view to such contingencies might be occasionally conferred upon the President, it may be answered in the first place that it is questionable whether, in a limited constitution, that power could be delegated by law; and in the second place, that it would generally be impolitic beforehand to take any step which might hold out the prospect of impunity. A proceeding of this kind, out of the usual course, would be likely to be construed into an argument of timidity or of weakness, and would have a tendency to embolden guilt.

40. James Iredell, North Carolina Ratifying Convention, July 28, 1788

The first sustained defense of the pardon power came not from Hamilton but from North Carolina lawyer James Iredell. Writing as "Marcus," he penned an answer to George Mason's objection to the pardon power. The essay, written in January, was published on March 5, three weeks before the publication of *Federalist* 74. Iredell at first attempted to answer Mason by pointing to state practices, arguing that to exempt treason would "abridge this power of pardoning in a manner altogether unexampled" (Jensen, Kaminski, and Saladino 1976–, 16:323). The truth, though, as we have seen, was that Mason's proposal to exempt treason from the executive's pardon power was anything but novel, a fact that Iredell was forced to acknowledge in a footnote he added to the text. At the North Carolina ratifying convention in July, Iredell seized the opportunity to mount a more persuasive defense of the pardon power (though during the debate no North Carolina Anti-Federalist seems to have criticized the pardon provision) that elaborated in greater detail on the positive benefits to be gained from granting the president a relatively free hand to pardon.

Another power that he has is to grant pardons, except in cases of impeachment. I believe it is the sense of a great part of America that this power should be exercised by their governors. It is in several states on the same footing that it is here. It is the genius of a republican government that the laws should be rigidly executed, without the influence of favor or ill-will. ... When a man commits a crime, however powerful he or his friends may be, ... he should be punished for it, and, on the other hand, though he should be universally hated by his country, his real guilt alone, as to the particular charge, is to operate against him. This

---

Jonathan Elliot, ed., *The Debates in the Several State Constitutions on the Adoption of the Federal Constitution* (New York: Burt Franklin, 1888), 4:110–14.

strict and scrupulous observance of justice is proper in all governments, but it is particularly indispensable in a republican one because, in such a government, the law is superior to every man, and no man is superior to another. But, though this general principle be unquestionable, surely there is no gentleman ... who is not aware that there ought to be exceptions to it, because there may be many instances where, though a man offends against the letter of the law, yet peculiar circumstances in his case may entitle him to mercy. It is impossible for any general law to foresee and provide for all possible cases that may arise, and therefore an inflexible adherence to it in every instance might frequently be the cause of very great injustice. For this reason, such a power ought to exist somewhere, and where could it be more properly vested than in a man who had received such strong proofs of his possessing the highest confidence of the people? ...

Another reason for the President possessing this authority is [that] it is often necessary to convict a man by means of his accomplices. We have sufficient experience of that in this country. A criminal would often go unpunished were not this method to be pursued against him. In my opinion, till an accomplice's own danger is removed, his evidence ought to be regarded with great diffidence. If, in civil causes of property, a witness must be entirely disinterested, how much more proper is it he should be so in cases of life and death! This power is naturally vested in the President because it is his duty to watch over the public safety, and as that may frequently require the evidence of accomplices to bring great offenders to justice he ought to be intrusted with the most effectual means of procuring it.

I beg leave further to observe that, for another reason, I think there is a propriety in leaving this power to the general discretion of the executive magistrate, rather than to fetter it in any manner which has been proposed. It may happen that many men, upon plausible pretences, may be seduced into very dangerous measures against their country. They may aim, by an insurrection, to redress imaginary grievances, at the same time believing, upon false suggestion, that their exertions are necessary to save their country from destruction. Upon cool reflection, however, they possibly are convinced of their error, and clearly see through the treachery and villainy of their leaders. In this situation, if the President possessed the power of pardoning, they probably would throw themselves on the equity of the government, and the whole body be peaceably broken up. Thus, at a critical moment, the President might, perhaps, prevent a civil war. But if there was no authority to pardon, in that delicate exigency, what would be the consequence? The principle of self-preservation would prevent their parting. Would it not be natural for them to say, "We shall be punished if we disband. Were we sure of mercy, we would peaceably part. But we know not that there is any chance of this. We may as well meet one kind of death as another. We may as well die in the field as at the gallows." I therefore submit to the committee if this power be not highly necessary for such a purpose.

We have seen a happy instance of the good effect of such an exercise of mercy in the state of Massachusetts, where, very lately, there was so formidable an insurrection. I believe a great majority of the insurgents were drawn into it by false artifices. They at length saw their error, and were willing to disband. Government, by a wise exercise of lenity, after having shown its power, generally granted a pardon, and the whole party were dispersed. There is now as much peace in that country as in any state in the Union.

A particular instance which occurs to me shows the utility of this power very strongly. Suppose we were involved in war. It would be then necessary to know the designs of the enemy. This kind of knowledge cannot always be procured but by means of spies—a set of wretches whom all nations despise but whom all employ; and, as they would assuredly be used against us, a principle of self-defence would urge and justify the use of them on our part. Suppose, therefore, the President could prevail upon a man of some importance to go over to the enemy in order to give him secret information of his measures. He goes off privately to the enemy. He feigns resentment against his country from some ill usage, either real or pretended, and is received, possibly, into favor and confidence. The people would not know the purpose for which he was employed. In the meantime, he secretly informs the President of the enemy's designs and by this means, perhaps, those designs are counteracted, and the country saved from destruction. After his business is executed he returns into his own country, where the people, not knowing he had rendered them any service, are naturally exasperated against him for his supposed treason. I would ask any gentleman whether the President ought not to have the power of pardoning this man. Suppose the concurrence of the Senate, or any other body, was necessary; would this obnoxious person be properly safe? We know in every country there is a strong prejudice against the executive authority. If a prejudice of this kind, on such an occasion, prevailed against the President, the President might be suspected of being influenced by corrupt motives and the application in favor of this man be rejected. Such a thing might very possibly happen when the prejudices of party were strong; ... no man, so clearly entitled as in the case I have supposed, ought to have his life exposed to so hazardous a contingency.

The power of impeachment is given by this Constitution to bring great offenders to punishment. It is calculated to bring them to punishment for a crime which it is not easy to describe, but which everyone must be convinced is a high crime and misdemeanor against the government. This power is lodged in those who represent the great body of the people, because the occasion for its exercise will arise from acts of great injury to the community, and the objects of it may be such as cannot be easily reached by an ordinary tribunal. The trial belongs to the Senate, lest an inferior tribunal should be too much awed by so powerful an accuser. After trials thus solemnly conducted, it is not probable that it would happen once in a thousand times that a man actually convicted would be entitled to mercy; and if the President had the power of pardoning in such a case, this great check upon high officers of state would lose much of its influence. It seems, therefore, proper that the general power of pardoning should be abridged in this particular instance. ...

The regulations altogether, in my opinion, are as wisely contrived as they could be. It is impossible for imperfect beings to form a perfect system. If the present one may be productive of possible inconveniences, we are not to reject it for that reason, but to inquire whether any other system could be devised which would be attended with fewer inconveniences in proportion to the advantages resulting.

Questions for Discussion

1. If you were designing a new federal constitution today, would you include the power to pardon? If so, where do you think this power would be most safely lodged? In the presidency, as it is now? Or would you rather see it lodged in one or both houses of Congress, in the Supreme Court, or perhaps in some specially constituted board or committee established specifically to hear pardon appeals?

2. What would you think of requiring the president to seek the "advice and consent" of the Senate on pardons, as he currently must do with appointments and treaties? What restrictions, if any, would you want to see placed on the pardon power?

3. Should a president or any other public official or set of officials have the power to pardon individuals before they have been convicted or even tried? Should pardons extend to serious offenses like treason or murder?

IV

Removing
the President

10

Impeachment

The President, Vice President and all civil Officers of the United States, shall be removed from Office on Impeachment for, and Conviction of, Treason, Bribery, or other high Crimes and Misdemeanors.

Article 2, section 4

The House of Representatives ... shall have the sole Power of Impeachment.

Article 1, section 2

The Senate shall have the sole Power to try all Impeachments. When sitting for that Purpose, they shall be on Oath or Affirmation. When the President of the United States is tried, the Chief Justice shall preside. And no person shall be convicted without the Concurrence of two thirds of the Members present.

Judgment in cases of Impeachment shall not extend further than to removal from Office, and disqualification to hold and enjoy any Office of honor, trust or Profit under the United States: but the Party convicted shall nevertheless be liable and subject to Indictment, trial, Judgment and Punishment, according to Law.

Article 1, section 3

The idea of impeachment has deep roots in English history, reaching as far back as the fourteenth century. Impeachment by the House of Commons was originally a means to reach those whose "exalted station" put them beyond the reach of "the usual course of justice" (Berger 1973, 60–61). In the seventeenth century impeachment became a vital tool in Parliament's struggle to rein in the power of the monarchy and to make ministers of the Crown accountable to Parliament. The king himself was not impeachable but his most powerful ministers and councillors were. Throughout the seventeenth and early eighteenth centuries impeachment was often used as a political instrument to protest or block unpopular royal policies. The House of Commons recognized few limits on its right to impeach: it claimed the right to impeach a peer or a commoner, in or out of political office, for "treason or any other crime or misdemeanor" (Hoffer and Hull 1984, 5). Checking the House's proclivity to criminalize political dif-

233

ferences was the requirement that all impeachments be tried in the House of Lords, which included the royal judges. The House of Lords, the realm's highest appeals court, "granted the accused counsel in matters of law, allowed a full hearing of his defense, and permitted him to summon his own witnesses" (5). The proceedings, in the judgment of Peter Hoffer and N.E.H. Hull, "were more often than not fair, dignified and learned" (4). Between 1626 and 1715, fifty-seven men were impeached for "high crimes and misdemeanors," but only five of these were actually convicted in the House of Lords (6). The Commons, though, usually did not need a conviction to secure its political objectives. Indeed, in many instances "the Commons did not even prosecute—the impeachment itself was sufficient warning or inconvenience to the accused" (4).

As an instrument for constraining the king's ministers, impeachment had been effective but crude. Criminalizing political differences made politics an extremely dangerous game for those who played it at the highest level. Having beaten back royal absolutism and having established the principle of ministerial accountability to Parliament, the Commons found its aims could be served more quickly, quietly, and safely by other means, such as a vote of no confidence in a minister (Berger 1973, 2, 97). By 1718 "the century of impeachment" in England had come to a close, and over the next seventy years impeachment would, with a few notable exceptions, play little role in English politics (Hoffer and Hull 1984, 8–9, 267).

If impeachment was largely absent in the seven decades of parliamentary history prior to the Constitutional Convention, how did impeachment end up assuming so prominent a part in the Constitution? More puzzling still, why would the framers imagine that impeachment, steeped in the bloody battles between king and Parliament, was relevant to republican America, in which there was no monarch, no Parliament, and no House of Lords? No known republic, ancient or modern, had ever employed impeachment (Hoffer and Hull 1984, 268). Why, moreover, would a nation so fearful of "the omnipotent power of the British Parliament" (James Iredell, quoted in Berger 1973, 53) resurrect one of Parliament's most unlimited powers? Part of the answer is that impeachment was readily assimilated to the republican dread of power and corruption. Impeachment could serve as yet one more check on the appetites of avaricious politicians (Hull and Hoffer 1984, 61). Also important was the American colonial experience with imperial authorities who repeatedly denied that colonial assemblies had the right to impeach anyone. Only Parliament, they insisted, had the power to impeach; if the colonies had a grievance with a colonial official it must be handled through an appeal or petition to the royal governor or the Crown. Faced with this challenge to their self-governance, colonial Americans, most importantly John Adams, responded by arguing that impeachment, though nowhere explicitly granted to the colonial assemblies, was among the fundamental "Rights and Privileges of Englishmen." Just as "the House of Commons in England is the grand Inquest of the Nation," Adams insisted, so the Massachusetts "House of Representatives is the Grand Inquest of this Province" (12). Impeachment, then, far from being a symbol of Parliamentary despotism, was an integral part of the effort to reclaim, through revolution, the colonists' inherent "Rights and Privileges."

Yet the American revolutionaries were uncertain how to adapt this English institution to American soil. Neither of the first two state constitutions, those drafted by New Hampshire and South Carolina, made any mention of impeachment. Two of the other ten state constitutions drafted in 1776 and 1777, those of Maryland and Georgia, also made no provision for impeachment. New Jersey gave the assembly the power to impeach for "misbehavior" but that power did not extend to impeaching the governor (Thorpe 1909, 5:2596). Among the other five state constitutions adopted during these first two years there was substantial variation in the impeachment process, particularly relating to the impeachment trial. The power to bring articles of impeachment was lodged either in the lower house (Delaware, Virginia, and New York), in both houses (North Carolina), or in a unicameral legislature (Pennsylvania). Each state seemed to have its own ideas about where impeachments should be tried. In Delaware the power to try impeachments was lodged in the upper house, in Pennsylvania the members of the supreme executive council including the president were the judges in impeachment cases, and in Virginia impeachments were tried in the supreme court (called the General Court), except for supreme court justices, who would be tried in the court of appeals. Particularly innovative was New York, which set up a special court for the trial of impeachments that was to consist of "the president of the senate ... and the senators, chancellor, and judges of the supreme court, or the major part of them" (5:2635). Each of the three state constitutions drafted in the decade after 1777 vested impeachment in the lower house, but the states continued to try out different schemes for the trial of impeachment. The South Carolina constitution of 1778 vested the power to try impeachments in "the senators and such of the judges of this State as are not members of the house of representatives." The 1778 Massachusetts constitution, which was rejected by the voters, proposed an impeachment trial court consisting of the governor and the Senate. The redrafted constitution, adopted in 1780, made the Senate alone the impeachment court, as did the 1784 New Hampshire constitution, which copied the Massachusetts impeachment provisions verbatim. The most complex scheme was offered by Thomas Jefferson, who in 1783 proposed amending the Virginia constitution. Under Jefferson's elaborate scheme "a court of Impeachments" was "to consist of three members of the Council of state, one of each of the Superior courts of Chancery, Common law, and Admiralty, two members of the House of Delegates and one of the Senate" (Boyd 1950–, 6:301).[1] It was with good reason that Madison would later remark that establishing a court in which to try impeachments was

---

1. Jefferson, perhaps because he had come close to being impeached as a wartime governor in Virginia, was never particularly enamored with the impeachment power.

"among the most puzzling articles of a republican Constitution" (6:313). The diversity of plans provided poignant testimony to the difficulty Americans had in coming up with a functional equivalent of the House of Lords.

Uncertainty about where to lodge the power to try impeachments persisted through the Constitutional Convention. The Virginia Plan, following the provision in Virginia's constitution, empowered the national judiciary to "hear and determine ... impeachments of any National officers" (Farrand 1937, 1:22). The New Jersey Plan, though different from the Virginia Plan in many other respects, also proposed giving the national judiciary the "authority to hear and determine ... all impeachments of federal officers" (1:244). Hamilton's long speech of June 18 recommended a special court that would consist of the chief justice of each state's highest court. Yet another solution, modeled on the revised South Carolina constitution of 1778, was offered in the Pinckney Plan: impeachments would be tried "before the Senate and the judges of the federal judicial Court" (2:136, 159, 3:608).[2] The Committee of Detail, which had before it each of these plans (except Hamilton's), as well as various state constitutions, followed the Virginia and New Jersey Plans in giving the Supreme Court the power to try impeachments in the draft constitution it reported to the convention on August 6. The Committee of Detail's report, like the Virginia and New Jersey Plans, reflected the framers' sense that impeachment trials should be impartial and follow legal rules and procedures. Since the Senate (unlike the House of Lords) was not a judicial body, there existed a compelling case to give this essentially judicial function to the courts. On top of this, delegates who worried about executive dependence on the legislature (and at this point the plan was still for the president to be selected by Congress) did not want to give the legislative branch the power both to impeach the president and to sit as judges on his impeachment.

Yet doubts persisted about this solution. If judges were to try impeachment, who would try the judges? Impeachment, as Rufus King argued, was particularly important for judges, since unlike a governor or president, who could be removed through the electoral process, a judge served during good behavior. And state experience during the revolutionary period had shown that it was the more politically insulated judicial officials who were most likely to attract impeachment charges. The Committee of Detail tried to meet this concern by making the Senate the court for impeachment trials involving Supreme Court justices. Yet toward the end of August, Morris introduced an additional difficulty: the proposal then before the convention to make the chief justice of the supreme court a member of the president's privy council would make the supreme court unsuitable to try even the impeachment of the executive. Without any debate the convention unanimously agreed to postpone this vexing question. The issue was then taken up by the Brearly Committee on Postponed

---

2. Later in the convention (July 20), though, Pinckney was a leading advocate of eliminating impeachment altogether.

Matters, an eleven-member committee composed of one delegate from each state. Changes the Brearly Committee made in the appointment power (now the president rather than the Senate would appoint federal judges) and in the mode of presidential selection (substituting the electoral college for legislative election) made it more attractive to lodge the power to try impeachments in the Senate (because neither the judiciary nor the executive now owed their appointment to the Senate) and correspondingly less desirable to give it to the Supreme Court (because the president would then be tried by a court he had chosen). The Brearly Committee's recommendation that the power to try impeachments be shifted from the Supreme Court to the Senate brought sharp objections from Madison and Pinckney, who worried that this would make the president "improperly dependent" on the legislature. The convention disagreed, however, and decisively approved the committee's proposal, with only the two largest states, Pennsylvania and Virginia, voting against granting the Senate the power to try impeachments.

Helping to allay concerns about impeachment becoming a partisan tool was the committee's stipulation that two-thirds of all members present vote for conviction. The two-thirds provision was an American invention. The House of Lords, like the House of Commons (and colonial legislatures), used a simple majority on all votes, including conviction upon impeachment, but it was not invented in Philadelphia. Instead the framers borrowed the idea directly from the state constitutions, specifically those of New York (1777) and South Carolina (1778), both of which required two-thirds of the members present for an individual to be convicted in an impeachment trial.[3] A two-thirds vote was designed to help the Senate rise above partisanship and deliberate in a relatively dispassionate way, much as the House of Lords did in England. The two-thirds provision thus made impeachment safe for a republic.

Also helping to tame impeachment was the requirement, introduced by Gouverneur Morris on September 8, that all senators be placed under oath before the trial. Here again the framers took their cue from the later state constitutions. South Carolina's revised 1778 constitution had been the first American constitution to require that "previous to the trial of every impeachment, the members of the said court shall respectively be sworn truly and impartially to try and determine the charge in question according to evidence" (Thorpe 1909, 6:3254). This provision proved so popular that it was copied virtually verbatim in the Massachusetts (1780) and New Hampshire (1784) constitutions. The wording adopted in the federal Constitution is more spare and economical—"they shall be on Oath or Affirmation"—but the idea was the same: to ensure that impeachment trials would be guided by an impartial weighing of the evidence rather than by political partisanship.

---

3. New York and South Carolina also required that two-thirds of the representatives present in the lower house vote for an impeachment in order for it to proceed to trial, a provision that was evidently never even considered in the Constitutional Convention.

The framers borrowed even more directly from the state constitutions in crafting the seventh paragraph of Article 1, section 3: "Judgment in Cases of Impeachment shall not extend further than to removal from Office, and disqualification to hold and enjoy any Office of honor, Trust or Profit under the United States: but that Party convicted shall nevertheless be liable and subject to Indictment, Trial, Judgment and Punishment, according to Law." This provision, which emerged out of the work of the Committee of Detail, was taken directly from the New York constitution of 1777 (the same wording also appears in the constitutions of Massachusetts and New Hampshire). That the delegates adopted this provision unanimously and without debate is yet another indication of how far Americans had come in republicanizing impeachment. In England the House of Lords could not only remove impeached officials from office but could also mete out legal punishment for the crime. A number of the early state constitutions, like those in Virginia and Delaware, followed the English precedent in giving the impeachment court the power to subject the guilty party "to such pains and penalties as the laws shall direct" (1:566; 7:3818). In adopting New York's innovation of separating removal or disbarment from office (which an impeachment court could impose on the guilty) from criminal punishment (which only the regular courts could impose), the framers again indicated a desire to limit the scope of the impeachment power.

Yet for all the framers' intention to limit the impeachment power they were in the end maddeningly imprecise about what constituted an impeachable offense. It was clear that (unlike in England) only public officials could be impeached,[4] and treason and bribery were relatively well-defined terms, but it was not at all clear what constituted "other high Crimes and Misdemeanors." No state constitution used this phrase. The most influential state constitutions spoke instead of "misconduct and mal-administration in their offices" (Massachusetts) or "mal and corrupt conduct in their respective officers" (New York and South Carolina). The Committee of Detail's initial report in early August

---

4. There is a little more room for debate as to whether the framers intended "civil officers" to include senators and representatives. The preponderance of the evidence, though, suggests that most of those who framed and debated the Constitution shared Archibald Maclaine's view that "members of the legislative body are never, as such, liable to impeachment" (Elliot 1888, 4:35). Legislators were representatives of the people rather than "civil officers," and their punishment was to come from the voters. In addition, as James Monroe pointed out, since legislators already had the power to expel their own members, impeachment of legislators would be redundant (Kurland and Lerner 1987, 2:160). Only one person at the federal convention proposed making senators impeachable—Alexander Hamilton—but Hamilton's Senate was to serve "during good behavior" and so lacked the check of elections. Moreover, not only did Hamilton exempt representatives from impeachment but his language, which specified that "Governors Senators and all officers of the United States" be liable for impeachment, clearly suggests that he did not consider senators to be "officers of the United States" (cf. Berger 1973, 218). Some legal scholars may wish it were otherwise, but the acquittal of North Carolina senator William Blount in 1799 on the ground that senators were not "civil officers" settled this question to all intents and purposes (Wood 1969, 523).

had made "treason, bribery, or corruption" impeachable offenses but the Committee on Postponed Matters had removed "corruption" from the list out of a concern over the vagueness of the term, a justifiable concern since Americans often used the term "corruption" to describe patronage appointments made by the executive.[5] When the convention began debate on this clause, George Mason immediately objected that it dangerously narrowed the scope of impeachment. In his home state of Virginia, the constitution (which he had drafted) provided for impeachment in cases of "maladministration, corruption, or other means, by which the safety of the Commonwealth may be endangered." Drawing upon the state model, Mason proposed to add to the list of impeachable offenses, "maladministration," a term which was an impeachable offense not only in Virginia but also in Delaware, North Carolina, Pennsylvania, Massachusetts, and New Hampshire. Fellow Virginian James Madison opposed Mason's motion, arguing that the term was too vague and that it would put the president at the mercy of the Senate. Mason countered by proposing "high crimes and misdemeanors against the State," and the motion was quickly carried.

The question of what the framers meant by "high crimes and misdemeanors" remains something of a puzzle. The phrase was first used in impeachment proceedings in England in 1386 at a time when there was actually no such crime as a misdemeanor. What we today think of misdemeanors—lesser crimes—were then known as "trespasses." By the middle of the sixteenth century misdemeanor had become a common designation for ordinary crimes, but the criminal category of "misdemeanor" bore no relation to the notion of a "high misdemeanor." "High crimes and misdemeanors," as legal historian Raoul Berger has shown, retained a specific meaning in English law denoting "a category of political crimes against the state." So, for instance, William Blackstone, writing in 1757, could write that "the first and principal [high misdemeanor] is the mal-administration of such high officers, as are in the public trust and employment. This is usually punished by the method of parliamentary impeachment." Berger argues that the framers retained this traditional understanding of "high crimes and misdemeanors," and that the "high" adopted by the convention was intended to modify not only crimes but misdemeanors (1973, 61–62). That this distinction between "high misdemeanors" and "misdemeanors" may not have been as clear in the framers' mind as it was in English law is suggested by Madison's concern, voiced immediately after the convention had approved the phrase "high crimes and misdemeanors," that allowing the Senate to try the president would be especially dangerous now that "he was to be impeached ... for any act which might be

---

5. At the beginning of the convention, on June 2, the delegates had agreed without debate to make "mal-practice or neglect of duty" the grounds for impeachment, but the Committee of Detail opted to strike this provision and replace it with "treason, bribery or corruption" (Farrand 1937, 2:145).

called a misdemeanor." Still Berger seems essentially correct that Mason and probably most of the framers thought of "high crimes and misdemeanors" in terms of "great offenses," particularly when they had the president in mind. When proposing to add "maladministration" to the list of impeachable offenses, Mason reasoned that treason (which had been given a precise definition in the Constitution[6]) "will not reach many great and dangerous offenses," including "attempts to subvert the Constitution." In offering to substitute "high crimes and misdemeanors," Mason seems to have been seeking a more precise and yet still familiar way of designating the "great and dangerous offenses" he believed should be grounds for impeachment.

Ultimately though the difficulty of deciding what constitutes an impeachable offense is an inherent problem in what after all is a political and not a legal process. Limiting impeachment to criminal offenses would simplify matters but that does not appear to be a limitation intended by the framers (Labovitz 1978, 27). Instead, the framers wanted impeachment to be able to reach offenses that might not be violations of criminal law yet nonetheless constituted serious abuse of power that threatened the constitutional structure of government. Substituting "serious wrongdoing" or "great and dangerous offenses" for "high crimes and misdemeanors" might be an improvement but would not remove the problems of political judgment that lie at the core of the impeachment process (Labovitz 1978, 255–56). The legislature would still need to evaluate whether a president's behavior was a "great and dangerous" offense or just an ordinary offense, whether the wrongdoing was serious or just naughty.

Madison's worry that an impeachment clause that went beyond well-defined criminal acts such as treason or bribery would make the president unduly dependent on the legislature was put to the test in the impeachment trial of Andrew Johnson. Republicans in Congress were increasingly frustrated that Johnson (who became president after Lincoln was assassinated) refused to go along with the party's policy for dealing with the defeated southern states; after initially rejecting impeachment, the House reversed itself a few months later after Johnson fired secretary of war Edwin Stanton and appointed an interim secretary, in apparent violation of the recently passed Tenure of Office Act.[7] Because southern states were not represented in Congress in the immediate aftermath of the Civil War, the normal political checks on the impeachment power were absent. The two-thirds clause normally ensures that a sizable number of the president's own party must defect in order

---

6. Article 3, section 3 of the Constitution specifies that "Treason against the United States, shall consist only in levying War against them, or in adhering to their Enemies, giving them Aid and Comfort."

7. The Tenure of Office Act had been passed (over Johnson's veto) in the spring of 1867 largely to prevent Johnson from removing Republicans. The act mandated that any presidential appointee requiring the consent of the Senate would continue to hold office until the Senate had confirmed his successor. Johnson refused to abide by the statute because in his view it invaded the president's constitutional prerogatives. The Tenure of Office Act was repealed by Congress in 1887.

to get a conviction; in Johnson's case over three-quarters of the Senate were Republicans, so a single party could push through a conviction without any support from the other party. Yet even with this huge numerical advantage the Republicans fell one vote short of the necessary two-thirds. Johnson's trial showed that Madison's concerns were not misplaced, but the president's acquittal also showcased the effectiveness of the constitutional safeguards the framers had erected to prevent a president from being removed for merely partisan policy disagreements. Bill Clinton's recent brush with impeachment arguably teaches a similar lesson.

41. The Federal Convention of 1787

Throughout American history the impeachment power has been used largely to oust corrupt or derelict judges, yet ironically the removal of judges did not figure prominently in the framers' debate over impeachment, which was couched almost entirely in terms of removing the president. Removal of judges was peripheral largely because the framers viewed the judiciary (in Hamilton's famous phrase) as "the least dangerous branch." The executive magistrate, in contrast, despite the limited power of most state executives, still had the capacity to stir deep and profound fears of monarchy, corrupting influence, and devious ministers. Even Madison, a steadfast proponent of a strong, independent president, believed that impeachment was vital because the chief executive, unlike the legislature, was a single person. And one man, either through "loss of capacity or corruption," could easily act in ways that would be "fatal to the Republic."

May 29

Resolutions proposed by Mr. Randolph in Convention. ...
9. Resolved that a National Judiciary be established [and] that the jurisdiction ... of the supreme tribunal shall be to hear and determine ... impeachments of any National officers.

June 2

Mr. Dickinson moved "that the Executive be made removeable by the National Legislature on the request of a majority of the Legislatures of individual States." It was necessary he said to place the power of removing somewhere. He did not like the plan of impeaching the great

---

Gaillard Hunt and James Brown Scott, eds., *The Debates in the Federal Convention of 1787 Which Framed the Constitution of the United States of America Reported by James Madison* (New York: Oxford University Press, 1920), 23, 25, 46–48, 283, 289–93, 337–38, 343–44, 428–29, 472, 506–8, 535–37, 561.

officers of State. He did not know how provision could be made for removal of them in a better mode than that which he had proposed. He had no idea of abolishing the State Governments as some gentlemen seemed inclined to do. The happiness of this Country in his opinion required considerable powers to be left in the hands of the States.

Mr. Bedford seconded the motion.

Mr. Sherman contended that the National Legislature should have power to remove the Executive at pleasure.

Mr. Mason. Some mode of displacing an unfit magistrate is rendered indispensable by the fallibility of those who choose, as well as by the corruptibility of the man chosen. He opposed decidedly ... making the Executive the mere creature of the Legislature as a violation of the fundamental principle of good Government.

Mr. Madison and Mr. Wilson observed that it would leave an equality of agency in the small with the great States; that it would enable a minority of the people to prevent the removal of an officer who had rendered himself justly criminal in the eyes of a majority; that it would open a door for intrigues against him in States where his administration though just might be unpopular, and might tempt him to pay court to particular States whose leading partisans he might fear, or wish to engage as his partisans. They both thought it bad policy to introduce such a mixture of the State authorities, where their agency could be otherwise supplied.

Mr. Dickinson considered the business as so important that no man ought to be silent or reserved. He went into a discourse of some length, the sum of which was that the Legislative, Executive, and Judiciary departments ought to be made as independent as possible, but that such an Executive as some seemed to have in contemplation was not consistent with a republic; that a firm Executive could only exist in a limited monarchy. In the British Government itself the weight of the Executive arises from the attachments which the Crown draws to itself, and not merely from the force of its prerogatives. In place of these attachments we must look out for something else. One source of stability is the double branch of the Legislature. The division of the Country into distinct States formed the other principle source of stability. This division ought therefore to be maintained, and considerable powers to be left with the States. ... Without this, and in case of a consolidation of the States into one great Republic, we might read its fate in the history of smaller ones. ...

On Mr. Dickinson's motion for making the Executive removeable by the National Legislature at the request of a majority of State Legislatures ... all the States [were] in the negative except Delaware. ...

Mr. Williamson seconded by Mr. Davie moved to [make the executive] "removeable on impeachment and conviction of mal-practice or neglect of duty"—which was agreed to.

July 19

Govr. Morris. The Executive is ... to be impeachable. This is a dangerous part of the plan. It will hold him in such dependence that he will be no check on the Legislature, will not be a firm guardian of the people and of the public interest. He will be the tool of a faction, of some leading demagogue in the Legislature. ... As to the danger from an unimpeachable magistrate he could not regard it as formidable. There must be certain great officers of State—a minister of finance, of war, of foreign affairs etc.—[and] these he presumes will exercise their functions in subordination to the Executive and will be amenable by impeachment to the public Justice. Without these ministers the Executive can do nothing of consequence.

July 20

"To be removeable on impeachment and conviction for malpractice or neglect of duty."

Mr. Pinckney and Mr. Govr. Morris moved to strike out this part of the Resolution. Mr. Pinckney observed he ought not to be impeachable while in office.[8]

Mr. Davie. If he be not impeachable while in office, he will spare no efforts or means whatever to get himself reelected. He considered this as an essential security for the good behavior of the Executive.

Mr. Wilson concurred in the necessity of making the Executive impeachable while in office.

Mr. Govr. Morris. He can do no criminal act without coadjutors who may be punished. In case he should be reelected, that will be sufficient proof of his innocence. Besides who is to impeach? Is the impeachment to suspend his functions? If it is not the mischief will go on. If it is the impeachment will be nearly equivalent to a displacement, and will render the Executive dependent on those who are to impeach.

Col. Mason. No point is of more importance than that the right of impeachment should be continued. Shall any man be above justice? Above all, shall that man be above it who can commit the most extensive injustice? When great crimes were committed he was for punishing the principal as well as a the coadjutors. ...

Docr. Franklin was for retaining the clause as favorable to the Executive. History furnishes one example only of a first Magistrate being formally brought to public Justice. Everybody cried out against this as unconstitutional. What was the practice before this in cases where the chief Magistrate rendered himself obnoxious? Why recourse was had to assassination in which he was not only deprived of his life but of the opportunity of vindicating his character. It would be ... best ... therefore to provide in the Constitution for the regular punishment of the Executive where his misconduct should deserve it, and for his honorable acquittal when he should be unjustly accused.

Mr. Govr. Morris admits corruption and some few other offenses ... ought to be impeachable, but thought the cases ought to be enumerated and defined.

Mr. Madison thought it indispensable that some provision should be made for defending the Community against the incapacity, negligence or perfidy of the chief Magistrate. The limitation of the period of his service was not a sufficient security. He might lose his capacity after his appointment.[9] He might pervert his administration into a scheme of speculation

---

8. Two states—Delaware and Virginia—specified that impeachment articles could only be brought against the chief executive "when he is out of office" (Thorpe 1909, 1:566; 7:3818).

9. The framers gave surprisingly little attention to the problem of presidential incapacity (they might have paid closer attention to this problem had King George III had his first bout of insanity in 1786 rather than in 1788). The August 6 report of the Committee of Detail included a provision that "in the case of his ... disability to discharge the powers and duties of his office, the President of the Senate shall exercise those powers and duties, until another President of the United States be chosen, or until the disability of the President be removed." On August 27 there was a brief discussion of the difficulties of having the president of the Senate as the temporary successor, and John Dickinson, in seconding the postponement of the matter, remarked that the provision was "too vague." He wanted to know "the extent of the term 'disability' and who is to be the judge of it" (Farrand 1937, 2:427). The delegates never returned to the subject and so never answered Dickinson's charge. Article 2, section 1 of the Constitution speaks of both "inability" and "disability," but the terms are not defined and no process is specified by which a president would be determined disabled. The omission of such a process was finally remedied by the Twenty-fifth Amendment (see appendix 5), which was ratified in 1967.

or oppression. He might betray his trust to foreign powers. The case of the Executive magistracy was very distinguishable from that of the Legislature or of any other public body holding offices of limited duration. It could not be presumed that all or even a majority of the members of an Assembly would either lose their capacity for discharging, or be bribed to betray, their trust. Besides the restraints of their personal integrity and honor, the difficulty of acting in concert for purposes of corruption was security to the public. And if one or a few members only should be seduced, the soundness of the remaining members would maintain the integrity and fidelity of the body. In the case of the Executive Magistracy, which was to be administered by a single man, loss of capacity or corruption was more within the compass of probable events, and either of them might be fatal to the Republic.

Mr. Pinckney did not see the necessity of impeachments. He was sure they ought not to issue from the Legislature who would in that case hold them as a rod over the Executive, and by that means effectually destroy his independence. His revisionary power in particular would be rendered altogether insignificant.

Mr. Gerry urged the necessity of impeachments. A good magistrate will not fear them. A bad one ought to be kept in fear of them. He hoped the maxim would never be adopted here that the chief magistrate could do no wrong.

Mr. King expressed his apprehensions that an extreme caution in favor of liberty might enervate the Government we were forming. He wished the House to recur to the primitive axiom that the three great departments of Governments should be separate and independent: that the Executive and Judiciary should be so as well as the Legislative. ... Would this be the case if the Executive should be impeachable? It had been said that the Judiciary would be impeachable. But it should have been remembered at the same time that the Judiciary hold their places not for a limited time, but during good behavior. It is necessary therefore that a forum should be established for trying misbehavior. Was the Executive to hold his place during good behavior? The Executive was to hold his place for a limited term, like the members of the Legislature. Like them ... he would periodically be tried for his behavior by his electors, who would continue or discontinue him in trust according to the manner in which he had discharged it. Like them, therefore, he ought to be subject to no ... impeachment. He ought not to be impeachable unless he held his office during good behavior, a tenure which would be most agreeable to him, provided an independent and effectual forum could be devised. But under no circumstances ought he to be impeachable by the Legislature. This would be destructive of his independence and of the principles of the Constitution. He relied on the vigor of the Executive as a great security for the public liberties.

Mr. Randolph. The propriety of impeachments was a favorite principle with him. Guilt wherever found ought to be punished. The Executive will have great opportunities of abusing his power, particularly in time of war when the military force, and in some respects the public money, will be in his hands. Should no regular punishment be provided, it will be irregularly inflicted by tumults and insurrections. He is aware of the necessity of proceeding with a cautious hand and of excluding as much as possible the influence of the Legislature from the business. He suggested for consideration an idea which had fallen [from Col. Hamilton] of composing a forum out of the Judges belonging to the States, and even of requiring some preliminary inquest whether just grounds of impeachment existed.

Docr. Franklin mentioned the case of the Prince of Orange during the late war. An agreement was made between France and Holland, by which their two fleets were to unite at a certain time and place. The Dutch fleet did not appear. Everybody began to wonder at it. At length it was suspected that the Statholder was at the bottom of the matter. This suspicion prevailed more and more. Yet as he could not be impeached and no regular examination took place he remained in his office, and strengthening his own party as the party opposed to him became formidable, he gave birth to the most violent animosities and contentions. Had he been impeachable a regular and peaceable inquiry would have taken place and he would if guilty have been duly punished, [and] if innocent restored to the confidence of the public.

Mr. King remarked that the case of the Statholder was not applicable. He held his place for life and was not periodically elected. In the former case impeachments are proper to secure good behaviour. In the latter they are unnecessary; the periodical responsibility to the electors being an equivalent security.

Mr. Wilson observed that if the idea were to be pursued, the Senators who are to hold their places during the same term with the Executive ought to be subject to impeachment and removal.

Mr. Pinckney apprehended that some gentleman reasoned on a supposition that the Executive was to have powers which would not be committed to him. He presumed that his powers would be so circumscribed as to render impeachments unnecessary.

Mr. Govr. Morris's opinion had been changed by the arguments used in the discussion.[10] He was now sensible of the necessity of impeachments if the Executive was to continue for any time in office. Our Executive was not like a Magistrate having a life interest, much less like one having a hereditary interest in his office. He may be bribed by a greater interest to betray his trust, and no one would say that we ought to expose ourselves to the danger of seeing the first Magistrate in foreign pay without being able to guard against it by displacing him. One would think the King of England well secured against bribery. He has as it were a fee simple in the whole Kingdom. Yet Charles II was bribed by Louis XIV. The Executive ought therefore to be impeachable for treachery. Corrupting his electors and incapacity were other causes of impeachment. For the latter he should be punished not as a man but as an officer and punished only by degradation from his office. This Magistrate is not the King but the prime-Minister. The people are the King. When we make him amenable to Justice however we should take care to provide some mode that will not make him dependent on the Legislature. ...

On the question, shall the Executive be removeable on impeachments [8 yes; 2 no].

August 6

Mr. Rutledge delivered in the Report of the Committee of detail as follows. ...

Article IV, section 6. The House of Representatives shall have the sole power of impeachment.[11]

Article X, section 2. [The President] shall be removed from his office on impeachment by the House of Representatives, and conviction in the supreme Court, of treason, bribery, or corruption.

Article XI, section 3. The Jurisdiction of the Supreme Court shall extend ... to the trial of impeachment of Officers of the United States.

---

10. This episode illustrates Madison's recollection that Morris "added, what is too rare, a candid surrender of his opinions, when the lights of discussion satisfied him, that they had been too hastily formed, and a readiness to aid in making the best of measures in which he had been overruled" (Rutland 1994, 311).

11. This section was unanimously agreed to without debate on August 9.

Article XI, section 5. Judgment, in cases of Impeachment, shall not extend further than to removal from Office, and disqualification to hold and enjoy any office of honor, trust or profit, under the United States. But that party convicted shall, nevertheless be liable and subject to indictment, trial, judgment and punishment according to law.

August 20

Mr. Govr. Morris, seconded by Mr. Pinckney, submitted the following propositions which were ... referred to the Committee of Detail. ...

"Each of the officers [making up the president's Council of State] shall be liable to impeachment and removal from office for neglect of duty, malversation,[12] or corruption."

August 27

The clause for removing the President on impeachment by the House of Representatives and conviction in the supreme Court, of Treason, Bribery or corruption, was postponed ... at the instance of Mr. Govr. Morris, who thought the tribunal an improper one, particularly if the first judge was to be of the privy Council [as the Committee of Detail had recommended in its report of August 22].

September 4

The Committee of Eleven ... report that in their opinion the following additions and alterations should be made to the Report before the Convention. ...

"The Senate of the U.S. shall have power to try all impeachments; but no person shall be convicted without the concurrence of two thirds of the members present. ...

The vice-president shall be ex officio President of the Senate, except when they sit to try the impeachment of the President, in which case the Chief Justice shall preside. ...

[The President] shall be removed from office on impeachment by the House of Representatives, and conviction by the Senate, for Treason, or bribery." ...

Govr. Morris [explained that] a conclusive reason for making the Senate instead of the Supreme Court the Judge of impeachments was that the latter was to try the President after the trial of the impeachment.

September 8

The clause referring to the Senate the trial of impeachments against the President for Treason and bribery was taken up.

Col. Mason. Why is the provision restrained to Treason and bribery only? Treason as defined in the Constitution will not reach many great and dangerous offenses. Hastings is not

---

12. The *Oxford English Dictionary* defines "malversation" as "corrupt behavior in an office."

guilty of Treason.[13] Attempts to subvert the Constitution may not be Treason as above defined. ... He moved to add after "bribery" "or maladministration." Mr. Gerry seconded him.

Mr. Madison. So vague a term will be equivalent to a tenure during pleasure of the Senate.

Mr. Govr. Morris. It will not be put in force and can do no harm. An election of every four years will prevent maladministration.

Col. Mason withdrew "maladministration" and substitutes "other high crimes and misdemeanors against the State."

On the question thus altered [8 yes; 3 no].

Mr. Madison objected to a trial of the President by the Senate, especially as he was to be impeached by the other branch of the Legislature, and for any act which might be called a misdemeanor. The President under these circumstances was made improperly dependent. He would prefer the Supreme Court for the trial of impeachments, or rather a tribunal of which that should form a part.

Mr. Govr. Morris thought no other tribunal than the Senate could be trusted. The supreme Court were too few in number and might be warped or corrupted. He was against a dependence of the Executive on the Legislature, considering the Legislative tyranny the great danger to be apprehended; but there could be no danger that the Senate would say untruly on their oaths that the President was guilty of crimes or facts, especially as in four years he can be turned out.

Mr. Pinckney disapproved of making the Senate the Court of Impeachments, as rendering the President too dependent on the Legislature. If he opposes a favorite law, the two Houses will combine against him, and under the influence of heat and faction throw him out of office.

Mr. Williamson thought there was more danger of too much lenity than too much rigor towards the President, considering the number of cases in which the Senate was associated with the President.

Mr. Sherman regarded the Supreme Court as improper to try the President because the Judges would be appointed by him.

On motion by Mr. Madison to strike out the words—"by the Senate" after the word "conviction" [2 yes; 9 no].

In the amendment of Col. Mason just agreed to, the word "State" after the words "misdemeanors against" was struck out and the words "United States" inserted unanimously, in order to remove ambiguity.

On the question to agree to clause as amended [10 yes; 1 no].

On motion "The vice-President and other Civil officers of the U.S. shall be removed from office on impeachment and conviction as aforesaid" was added to the clause on the subject of impeachments. ...

Mr. Govr. Morris moved to add ... the words "and every member shall be on oath" which being agreed to, and a question taken on the clause so amended, namely "The Senate of the U.S. shall

---

13. Just prior to the opening of the convention, the House of Commons had charged Warren Hastings with "high crimes and misdemeanors" for his conduct during his tenure as governor-general of India. As Mason's comment indicates, the case (which the Commons had been pursuing ever since Hastings resigned his post at the beginning of 1785) attracted wide interest in the Anglo-American world. The prosecution of Hastings's impeachment was led by Edmund Burke who, in his opening argument before the House of Lords, declared, "It is by this tribunal that statesmen, who abuse their powers, are accused by statesmen, and tried by statesmen, not upon the niceties of a narrow jurisprudence, but upon the enlarged and solid principles of state morality" (Labovitz 1978, 251). The case dragged on for seven years before the Lords finally acquitted Hastings in 1795.

have power to try all impeachments but no person shall be convicted without the concurrence of two thirds of the members present; and every member shall be on oath" [9 yes; 2 no].

September 14

Mr. Rutledge and Mr. Govr. Morris moved "that persons impeached be suspended from their office until they be tried and acquitted."

Mr. Madison. The President is made too dependent already on the Legislature by the power of one branch to try him in consequence of an impeachment by the other. The intermediate suspension will put him in the power of one branch only. They can at any moment, in order to make way for the functions of another who will be more favorable to their views, vote a temporary removal of the existing magistrate.

Mr. King concurred in the opposition to the amendment.

On the question to agree to it [3 yes; 8 no].

42. Luther Martin, "The Genuine Information," 1788

At the federal convention, critics of the impeachment clause, like Pinckney and Gouverneur Morris, worried about impeachment's deleterious effect on executive independence. After the close of the convention, though, Anti-Federalists expressed the opposite concern—that the check would be totally ineffective—because, as Luther Martin suggests here, the Senate would be unlikely to convict a president, since its advice and consent function meant that it might very well be complicit in the offending measures. Martin goes still further in contending that even the House of Representatives would be unlikely to bring articles of impeachment against the president, though this was not a widely shared fear. Ironically, Martin would later be a central player in the most important impeachment proceeding in the early republic, an impeachment that involved not the president but a supreme court justice, Samuel Chase. The same Martin who in 1788 had dismissed impeachment as largely ineffective labored strenuously in Chase's defense in 1805 to curtail the power of impeachment. Impeachment, Martin told the Senate in the Chase trial, "cannot change the law, and make that punishable which was not before criminal." If the legislature could remove "for acts which are not contrary to law ... you leave your judges, and all your other officers at the mercy of the prevailing party" (Labovitz 1978, 41). Chase was acquitted but the debate about what constituted an impeachable offense had only just begun.

"The Genuine Information, Delivered to the Legislature of the State of Maryland, Relative to the Proceedings of the General Convention, Held at Philadelphia, in 1787, By Luther Martin," in Jonathan Elliot, ed., *The Debates in the Several State Constitutions on the Adoption of the Federal Constitution* (New York: Burt Franklin, 1888), 1:379–80.

The only appearance of responsibility in the President which the system holds up to our view is the provision for impeachment. But ... when we reflect that he cannot be impeached but by the House ... and that the members of this house are rendered dependent upon and unduly under the influence of the President, by being appointable to offices of which he has the sole nomination ... there is little reason to believe that a majority will ever concur in impeaching the President, let his conduct be ever so reprehensible; especially ... as the final event of that impeachment will depend upon a different body, and the members of the House of Delegates will be certain, should the decision be ultimately in favor of the President, to become thereby the objects of his displeasure, and to bar to themselves every avenue to the emoluments of government.

Should [the President], contrary to probability, be impeached, he is afterwards to be tried and adjudged by the Senate, and without the concurrence of two-thirds of the members who shall be present, he cannot be convicted. This Senate being constituted a privy council to the President, it is probable many of its leading and influential members may have advised or concurred in the very measures for which he may be impeached. The members of the Senate also are ... placed as unduly under the influence of ... the President as the members of the other branch, since they also are appointable to offices and cannot obtain them but through the favor of the President.

There will be great, important, and valuable offices under this government, should it take place, more than sufficient to enable him to hold out the expectation of one of them to each of the senators. Under these circumstances, will any person conceive it to be difficult for the President always to secure to himself more than one third of that body? Or can it reasonably be believed that a criminal will be convicted who is constitutionally empowered to bribe his judges, at the head of whom is to preside ... the chief justice, [an] officer [who], in his original appointment, must be nominated by the President and will, therefore, probably, be appointed not so much for his eminence in legal knowledge, and for his integrity, as from favoritism and influence. ... The President, knowing that in case of impeachment the chief justice is to preside at his trial, will naturally wish to fill that office with a person of whose voice and influence he shall consider himself secure. These are reasons to induce a belief that there will be but little probability of the President ever being either impeached or convicted. [Moreover,] vested with the powers which the system gives him, and with the influence attendant upon those powers, to him it would be of little consequence whether he was impeached or convicted, since he will be able to set both at defiance. These considerations occasioned a part of the Convention to give a negative to this part of the system establishing the executive as it is now offered for our acceptance.

43. James Iredell, North Carolina Ratifying Convention, July 28, 1788

For many of the framers the most troubling aspect of the impeachment clause related to the Senate's involvement in the treaty-making process.

Jonathan Elliot, ed., *The Debates in the Several State Constitutions on the Adoption of the Federal Constitution* (New York: Burt Franklin, 1888), 4:125–27.

Those who knew their English history were aware, as Edmund Randolph pointed out in the Virginia ratifying convention, that treaties had been the most common occasions for impeachment proceedings (Elliot 1888, 3:401). James Monroe clearly grasped the danger: Could the Senate, "the very persons who advised [the president] to perpetrate the act," be expected to then convict the president for making the treaty. "Is this any security?" he asked (4:489). The most direct and compelling answer to Monroe's question came not at the Virginia ratifying convention but a month later from North Carolinian James Iredell, who distinguished between disagreements of policy (an error of the head) and villainous conduct (an error of the heart). Monroe's objection would be valid if impeachment was used, as it had been in England, to punish errors of the head, but in the United States there was no need to fear the Senate's role because impeachments were to be limited to errors of the heart.

[The treaty-making clause] is objected to as improper because if the President or Senate should abuse their trust there is not sufficient responsibility, since he can only be tried by the Senate by whose advice he acted; and the Senate cannot be tried at all. I beg leave to observe that when any man is impeached, it must be for an error of the heart, and not of the head. God forbid that a man, in any country in the world, should be liable to be punished for want of judgment. This is not the case here. As to errors of the heart, there is sufficient responsibility. Should these be committed, there is a ready way to bring him to punishment. This is a responsibility which answers every purpose that could be desired by a people jealous of their liberty. I presume that if the President with the advice of the Senate should make a treaty with a foreign power, and that treaty should be deemed unwise or against the interest of the country, yet if nothing could be objected against it but the difference of opinion between them and their constituents they could not justly be [punished]. If they were punishable for exercising their own judgment and not that of their constituents, no man who regarded his reputation would accept the office either of a senator or President. Whatever mistake a man may make, he ought not to be punished for it, nor his posterity rendered infamous. But if a man be a villain, and willfully abuse his trust, he is to be held up as a public offender and ignominiously punished. A public officer ought not to act from a principle of fear. Were he punishable for want of judgment he would be continually in dread, but when he knows that nothing but real guilt can disgrace him he may do his duty firmly, if he be an honest man; and if he be not, a just fear of disgrace may, perhaps, as to the public, have nearly the effect of an intrinsic principle of virtue. According to these principles, I suppose the only instances in which the President would be liable to impeachment would be where he had received a bribe or had acted from some corrupt motive or other. If the President had received a bribe [from a foreign power], without the privity or knowledge of the Senate ... and, under the influence of that bribe, had address enough with the Senate, by artifices and misrepresentations, to seduce their consent to a pernicious treaty ... would not that Senate be as competent to try him as any other persons whatsoever? Would they not exclaim against his villainy? Would they not feel a particular resentment against him for being made the instrument of his treacherous purposes? In this situation, if any objection could be made against the Senate as a proper tribunal it might more properly be made by the President himself, lest their resentment should operate too strongly. ...

The President must certainly be punishable for giving false information to the Senate. He is to regulate all intercourse with foreign powers, and it is his duty to impart to the Senate every material intelligence he receives. If it should appear that he has not given them full information but has concealed important intelligence which he ought to have communicated, and by that means induced them to enter into measures injurious to their country, and which they would not have consented to had the true state of things been disclosed to them,—in this case, I ask whether upon an impeachment for a misdemeanor upon such an account the Senate would probably favor him.

44. Alexander Hamilton,
Federalist 65, March 7, 1788

Hamilton did not participate in the debate over impeachment at the federal convention, but the plan of government he presented to the convention on June 18 included a provision to vest the trial of impeachments in a specially constituted court made up of the chief justice of each state supreme court. Given Hamilton's admiration for the British system, in which impeachments were tried in the House of Lords, it might seem surprising that he chose not to have impeachments tried in the Senate, whose members, in Hamilton's plan, were to serve life terms. Most likely, Hamilton worried that to have impeachments tried in the Senate would make the president and his subordinates dangerously dependent upon the legislature. And judging by the lukewarm endorsement of the impeachment provision at the close of *Federalist* 65, it is clear that Hamilton continued to harbor reservations about the wisdom of giving the Senate the power to try impeachments. Yet here, as so often in the *Federalist*, Hamilton bravely set out to defend what he himself mistrusted.

A well constituted court for the trial of impeachments is an object not more to be desired than difficult to be obtained in a government wholly elective. The subjects of its jurisdiction are those offenses which proceed from the misconduct of public men, or in other words from the abuse or violation of some public trust. They are of a nature which may with peculiar propriety be denominated political, as they relate chiefly to injuries done immediately to the society itself. The prosecution of them, for this reason, will seldom fail to agitate the passions of the whole community, and to divide it into parties, more or less friendly or inimical, to the accused. In many cases, it will connect itself with the pre-existing factions, and will enlist all their animosities, partialities, influence, and interest on one side, or the other; and in such cases there will always be the greatest danger that the decision will be regulated more by the comparative strength of parties than by the real demonstration of innocence or guilt.

The delicacy and magnitude of a trust which so deeply concerns the political reputation and existence of every man engaged in the administration of public affairs, speak for them-

---

New-York Packet, March 7, 1788.

selves. The difficulty of placing it rightly in a government resting entirely on the basis of periodical elections will as readily be perceived when it is considered that the most conspicuous characters in it will ... be too often the leaders or the tools of the most cunning or the most numerous faction, and on this account can hardly be expected to possess the requisite neutrality toward those whose conduct may be the subject of scrutiny.

The Convention, it appears, thought the Senate the most fit depositary of this important trust. Those who can best discern the intrinsic difficulty of the thing will be the least hasty in condemning that opinion; and will be most inclined to allow due weight to the arguments which may be supposed to have produced it.

What it may be asked is the true spirit of the institution itself? Is it not designed as a method of national inquest into the conduct of public men? If this be the design of it, who can so properly be the inquisitors for the nation as the representatives of the nation themselves? It is not disputed that the power of originating the inquiry ... ought to be lodged in the hands of one branch of the legislative body; will not the reasons which indicate the propriety of this arrangement strongly plead for an admission of the other branch of that body to a share in the inquiry? The model from which the idea of this institution has been borrowed pointed out that course to the Convention: In Great Britain it is the province of the House of Commons to [originate] the impeachment, and of the House of Lords to decide upon it. Several of the State constitutions have followed the example. ... The latter as [well as] the former seem to have regarded the practice of impeachments as a bridle in the hands of the legislative body upon the executive servants of the government. Is not this the true light in which it ought to be regarded?

Where else than in the Senate could have been found a tribunal sufficiently independent? What other body would be likely to feel confidence enough in its own situation to preserve unawed and uninfluenced the necessary impartiality between an individual accused and the representatives of the people, his accusers?

Could the Supreme Court have been relied upon as answering this description? It is much to be doubted whether the members of this tribunal would, at all times, be endowed with so eminent a portion of fortitude as would be called for in the execution of so difficult task; and it is still more to be doubted whether they would possess the degree of credit and authority, which might, on certain occasions, be indispensable towards reconciling the people to a decision that should happen to clash with an accusation brought by their immediate representatives. A deficiency in the first would be fatal to the accused; in the last, dangerous to the public tranquility. The hazard in both these respects could only be avoided, if at all, by rendering that tribunal more numerous than would [be] consist[ent] with a reasonable attention to economy. ... The awful discretion which a court of impeachments must necessarily have to doom to 'honor or to infamy the most ... distinguished characters of the community forbids the commitment of the trust to a small number of persons.

These considerations alone seem sufficient to authorize a conclusion that the Supreme Court would have been an improper substitute for the Senate as a court of impeachments. There remains a further consideration which will not a little strengthen this conclusion. ... The punishment, which may be the consequence of conviction upon impeachment, is not to terminate the chastisement of the offender. After having been sentenced to a perpetual ostracism from the esteem and confidence, and honors and emoluments of his country, he will still be liable to prosecution and punishment in the ordinary course of law. Would it be proper that the persons who had disposed of his fame and his most valuable rights as a citizen in one trial, should in another trial, for the same offense, be also the disposers of his life and his fortune? Would there not be the greatest reason to apprehend that error in the first sentence would be the parent of error in the second sentence? That the strong bias of one decision would be apt to overrule the influence of any new lights which might be brought to vary the complexion of another decision? Those who know human nature will not hesitate to answer these questions in the affirmative. ...

Would it have been desirable to have composed the court for the trial of impeachments of persons wholly distinct from the other departments of the government? There are weighty arguments ... against as [well as] in favor of such a plan. To some minds it will not appear a trivial objection that it would tend to increase the complexity of the political machine, and to add a new spring to the government, the utility of which would at best be questionable. But an objection which will not be thought by any unworthy of attention is [that] a court formed upon such a plan would be attended either with heavy expense, or might in practice be subject to a variety of casualties and inconveniences. It must either consist of permanent officers stationary at the seat of government, and of course entitled to fixed and regular stipends, or of certain officers of the State governments, to be called upon whenever an impeachment was actually pending. It will not be easy to imagine any third mode materially different which could rationally be proposed. As the court ... ought to be numerous, the first scheme will be reprobated by every man who can compare the extent of the public wants with the means of supplying them. The second will be espoused with caution by those who will seriously consider the difficulty of collecting men dispersed over the whole union, the injury to the innocent from the procrastinated determination of the charges which might be brought against them, the advantage to the guilty from the opportunities which delay would afford to intrigue and corruption, and in some cases the detriment to the State from the prolonged inaction of men whose firm and faithful execution of their duty might have exposed them to the persecution of an intemperate or designing majority in the House of Representatives. Though this latter supposition may seem harsh, and might not be likely often to be verified, yet it ought not to be forgotten that the demon of faction will at certain seasons extend his sceptre over all numerous bodies of men.

But though one or the other of the substitutes which have been examined, or some other that might be devised, should be thought preferable to the plan in this respect reported by the Convention, it will not follow that the Constitution ought for this reason to be rejected. If mankind were to resolve to agree in no institution until every part of it had been adjusted to the most exact standard of perfection, society would soon become a general scene of anarchy and the world a desert. Where is the standard of perfection to be found? Who will undertake to unite the discordant opinions of a whole community in the same judgment of it, and prevail upon one conceited projector to renounce his infallible criterion for the fallible criterion of his more conceited neighbor? To answer the purpose of the adversaries of the Constitution, they ought to prove not merely that particular provisions in it are not the best which might have been imagined, but that the plan upon the whole is bad and pernicious.

Questions for Discussion

1. What difference would it have made to American history if Mason's original formulation of "maladministration" had been adopted rather than his substitute phrase, "high crimes and misdemeanors"?

2. Would the impeachment process be improved if impeachment trials had been lodged in the Supreme Court, as the original Virginia Plan posited? What are the advantages to having impeachment tried in the Senate?

3. Would the United States be better off if the president had not been made impeachable, as Charles Pinckney, Rufus King, and Gouverneur Morris urged?

V

Debating Presidential Power

11

Goldilocks and the Three Branches: A President Too Strong, Too Weak, or Just Right?

Throughout this nation's history, Americans have disagreed sharply about presidential power. Prior to the Civil War, the Whig party coalition was built upon a shared opposition to a strong presidency, while Democrats championed the presidency as the voice of the people. In the decades between World War II and the Vietnam War, liberal Democrats tended to look to the presidency as the truest representative of the public interest while denigrating Congress as the bastion of parochial special interests and unaccountable (southern) committee chairmen. Conservative southern Democrats and Republicans could be counted on to sound alarms about presidential power and to defend the deliberative process of the people's branch. In recent decades attitudes toward the presidency have generally not split neatly along party lines, but attitudes remain sharply divided. In the wake of Vietnam and Watergate, there was a strong feeling, including or perhaps especially among disillusioned liberals, that the president had grown out of control, that it had become, in Arthur Schlesinger's famous phrase "the imperial presidency" (1973).

No sooner had the "imperial presidency" battle cry been taken up than experience intervened. The troubled presidencies of Gerald Ford and Jimmy Carter brought a new round of hand-wringing, only this time the theme was of an "imperiled presidency" (Ford 1980; Cronin 1980), an "impotent" presidency (Hodgson 1980, 13), a "tethered presidency" (Franck 1981). The presidencies of Ronald Reagan, George Bush, and Bill Clinton have done nothing to resolve this disagreement. Some continue to see presidential weakness, lamenting "the beleaguered presidency" (Wildavsky 1991), the "impeded presidency" (Hoxie 1998), or the "shrinking presidency"; others still see the president as too powerful and unaccountable, an "out-of-control presidency" in the words of Michael Lind (1995). The labels proliferate, the words change, but the song remains the same. The debate is as old as the United States itself.

257

"How do you like our new constitution?" Thomas Jefferson inquired of John Adams in November 1787. The Virginian confessed that he found "things in it which stagger all my dispositions to subscribe to what such an assembly has proposed." No part of the new government disturbed Jefferson more than the presidency, which seemed "a bad edition of a Polish king."

> He may be reelected from 4 years to 4 years for life. Reason and experience prove to us that a chief magistrate, so continuable, is an officer for life. When one or two generations shall have proved that this is an officer for life, it becomes on every succession worthy of intrigue, of bribery, of force, and even of foreign interference. It will be of great consequence to France and England to have America governed by a Galloman or Angloman. Once in office, and possessing the military force of the union, without either the aid or check of a council, he would not be easily dethroned, even if the people could be induced to withdraw their votes from him. I wish that at the end of the 4 years they had made him forever ineligible a second time. (Boyd 1950–, 12:350–51)

Where Jefferson saw too much presidential power, his friend Adams saw too little. "You are afraid of the one—I, of the few," Adams wrote back to Jefferson. "You are apprehensive of Monarchy; I, of Aristocracy." Adams volunteered that he would have preferred to "have given more Power to the President and less to the Senate." Taking note of Jefferson's apprehension that the president will be reelected as long as he lives, Adams was blunt: "So much the better as it appears to me" (12:396).[1]

This exchange of letters between Jefferson and Adams, both of whom supported the Constitution, indicates that the debate over presidential power was not reducible to the dispute between Federalists and Anti-Federalists. Supporters of the Constitution disagreed about whether the presidency was, as Jefferson believed, too strong or, as Adams believed, too weak. A similar division existed among Anti-Federalists who opposed the Constitution, some of whom believed the basic problem with the presidency was its weakness relative to the Senate while others ominously predicted the president "will be a king to all intents and purposes, and one of the most dangerous kind too: a king elected to command a standing army" (Storing 1981, 3:128).

So who is right? Is the president too strong or too weak? The question is inherently contestable, since the answer depends not only on one's empirical

---

1. Adams explained that he, too, was "apprehensive of foreign Interference" but noted that "as often as Elections happen, the danger of foreign influence recurs. The less frequently they happen the less danger.—And if the Same Man may be chosen again, [and] it is probable he will be, [then] the danger of foreign Influence will be less. Foreigners, seeing little Prospect will have less Courage for Enterprize." Adams confessed that he looked upon "Elections to offices which are great objects of Ambition" with nothing short of "terror." "Experiments of this kind," he reminded Jefferson, "have been so often tryed, and so universally found productive of Horrors, that there is great Reason to dread them" (Boyd 1950–, 12:396).

judgment about the existing state of presidential power (about which we might, in theory at least, come to agree) but also on one's normative vision for what the presidency should be (a question on which there will inevitably be sharp differences). Although this centuries-long dispute will never be settled, and concerns about presidential weakness will continue to find expression, it is likely that it is the fear of presidential power that will continue to touch the deepest nerve in American political culture. The founding generation's fears of a president becoming a king may seem remote and exaggerated to people today (although see Reedy 1970), but if Americans have ceased to worry about a president donning a crown they remain hypersensitive to the uses and abuses of executive power. Today, as during the founding period, it is the prospect of the imperial presidency rather than the imperiled presidency that is most likely to haunt American dreams.

Too Strong

45. Patrick Henry, Virginia Ratifying Convention, June 5, 1788

Patrick Henry, Jefferson said, was "the greatest orator that ever lived" (Rutland 1994, 188). Hailed as "the trumpet of the revolution," Henry dominated Virginia's politics for most of its first fifteen years. In 1776 he was elected the state's first governor, a position he was elected to on five occasions. When not in the governor's chair, he was the commanding figure in the state's legislature. According to George Washington, Henry had "only to say, let this be law, and it is law." Henry's political stature and oratorical skills made him not only the most well-known but also the most dangerous opponent of the proposed Constitution. At the Virginia ratifying convention, Henry dominated the debate; his speeches, by one count, "amounted to one-fourth of all those presented." For hours on end Henry assailed the proposed government as a threat to the people's liberties. So vivid were his speeches that one observer "involuntarily felt his wrists to assure himself that the fetters were not already pressing his flesh" (190). Where Madison's speeches defending the Constitution were coldly precise and logical, Henry's were impassioned and sweeping. Madison's comments were tightly focused on specific sections and clauses of the Constitution, whereas Henry preferred to direct attention to the big picture, which he painted in broad strokes and bright, dramatic colors.

Jonathan Elliot, ed., *The Debates in the Several State Constitutions on the Adoption of the Federal Constitution* (New York: Burt Franklin, 1888), 3:58–60.

This Constitution is said to have beautiful features, but when I come to examine these features, sir, they appear to me horribly frightful. Among other deformities, it has an awful squinting; it squints towards monarchy; and does not this raise indignation in the breast of every true American?

Your President may easily become king. ... If your American chief be a man of ambition and abilities, how easy is it for him to render himself absolute! The army is in his hands, and if he be a man of address, it will be attached to him, and it will be the subject of long meditation with him to seize the first auspicious moment to accomplish his design; and, sir, will the American spirit solely relieve you when this happens? I would rather infinitely—and I am sure most of this Convention are of the same opinion—have a king, lords, and commons, than a government so replete with such insupportable evils. If we make a king, we may prescribe the rules by which he shall rule his people, and interpose such checks as shall prevent him from infringing them; but the President, in the field, at the head of his army, can prescribe the terms on which he shall reign master, so far that it will puzzle any American ever to get his neck from under the galling yoke. I cannot with patience think of this idea. If ever he violates the laws, one of two things will happen: he will come at the head of his army to carry everything before him; or he will give bail, or do what Mr. Chief Justice will order him. If he be guilty, will not the recollection of his crimes teach him to make one bold push for the American throne? Will not the immense difference between being master of everything, and being ignominiously tried and punished, powerfully excite him to make this bold push? But, sir, where is the existing force to punish him? Can he not, at the head of his army, beat down every opposition? Away with your President, we shall have a king. The army will salute him [as] monarch. Your militia will leave you and assist in making him king, and fight against you. And what have you to oppose this force? What will then become of you and your rights? Will not absolute despotism ensue?

46. An Old Whig, November 1, 1787

We do not know who wrote under the pseudonym "An Old Whig" (see Storing 1981, 3:17; Jensen, Kaminski, and Saladino 1976–, 13:376), but his fears of "an elective King" were echoed by many Anti-Federalist writers and orators. The concern is less with this or that specific power that had been vested in the president than with the overall package of powers that had been bestowed upon the president. To concentrate power in a single person and then to make this person elected was the worst of all possible worlds. With the stakes so high, such elections would result in "a scene of horror and confusion." And what will stop a president who does not wish to relinquish this exalted station from using his power as commander in chief to establish a military government. Far better, if so much power is to be given to a single person, to make the office hereditary, as in Britain. Or, better yet, draft a new Constitution that does not trust so much power to the hands of any one man.

Philadelphia *Independent Gazetteer*, November 1, 1787.

The office of President of the United States appears to me to be clothed with such powers as are dangerous. To be the fountain of all honors in the United States, commander in chief of the army, navy and militia, with the power of making treaties and of granting pardons, and to be vested with an authority to put a negative upon all laws unless two thirds of both houses shall persist in enacting it ... is in reality to be a King, as much a King as the King of Great Britain, and a King too of the worst kind: an elective King. If such powers as these are to be trusted in the hands of any man, they ought for the sake of preserving the peace of the community at once to be made hereditary. Much as I abhor kingly government, yet I venture to pronounce where kings are admitted to rule they should most certainly be vested with hereditary power. The election of a King, whether it be in America or Poland, will be a scene of horror and confusion, and I am perfectly serious when I declare that, as a friend to my country, I shall despair of any happiness in the United States until his office is either reduced to a lower pitch of power or made perpetual and hereditary.

When I say that our future President will be as much a king as the king of Great Britain, I only ask of my readers to look into the constitution of that country, and then tell me what important prerogative the King of Great Britain is entitled to which does not also belong to the President. ... The King of Great Britain it is true can create nobility which our President cannot, but our President will have the power of making all the great men, which comes to the same thing. All the difference is that we shall be embroiled in contention about the choice of the man, whilst they are at peace under the security of an hereditary succession. To be tumbled headlong from the pinnacle of greatness and be reduced to a shadow of departed royalty is a shock almost too great for human nature to endure. It will cost a man many struggles to resign such eminent powers, and ere long we shall find someone who will be very unwilling to part with them. Let us suppose this man to be a favorite with his army, and that they are unwilling to part with their beloved commander in chief. Or to make the thing familiar, let us suppose a future President and commander in chief adored by his army and the militia to as great a degree as our late illustrious commander in chief; and we have only to suppose one thing more, that this man is without the virtue, the moderation and love of liberty which possessed the mind of our late general, and this country will be involved at once in war and tyranny. So far is it from ... being improbable that the man who shall hereafter be in a situation to make the attempt to perpetuate his own power should want the virtues of General Washington, that it is perhaps a chance of one hundred millions to one that the next age will not furnish an example of so disinterested a use of great power. We may also suppose, without trespassing upon the bounds of probability, that this man may not have the means of supporting in private life the dignity of his former station; that, like Caesar, he may be at once ambitious and poor, and deeply involved in debt. Such a man would die a thousand deaths rather than sink from the heights of splendor and power into obscurity and wretchedness. We are certainly ... giving our president too much or too little, and in the course of less than twenty years we shall find that we have given him enough to enable him to take all.

It would be infinitely more prudent to give him at once as much as would content him so that we might be able to retain the rest in peace, for ... once power is seized by violence not the least fragment of liberty will survive the shock. I would therefore advise my countrymen seriously to ask themselves this question: Whether they are prepared to receive a king? If they are, to say [so] at once, and make the kingly office hereditary, [and] frame a constitution that should set bounds to his power, and, as far as possible, secure the liberty of the subject. If we are not prepared to receive a king, let us call another convention to revise the proposed constitution, and form it anew on the principles of confederacy of free republics; but by no means, under pretence of a republic, ... lay the foundation for a military government, which is the worst of all tyrannies.

47. Cato IV and V, November 8 and 22, 1787

Cato's criticisms of Article 2 are perhaps the best-known Anti-Federalist writings on the presidency. Those few scholarly collections on the presidency that include something from the founding period other than Hamilton's *Federalist* essays almost always select Cato (see, e.g., Pfiffner and Davidson 1997, 18–22; Bailey and Shafritz 1988, 15–19), and for sound reasons. Of all the Anti-Federalist writings on the presidency, Cato is one of the few to glimpse that the president's power might come not only from the specific powers he was granted but also from the "vague and inexplicit" nature of Article 2. At the time of the ratification debate, it was generally assumed that the New York governor, George Clinton, had penned the Cato essays (Kaminski 1993, 131), an attribution that remained largely unchallenged until the 1960s. Linda De Pauw (1966, 283–92) suggested that the author was more likely Abraham Yates, a close political associate of Governor Clinton. More recently, Herbert Storing concludes that "the weight of evidence still inclines toward Clinton as Cato; but the question is surely open. For most purposes it is better to regard him simply as–Cato" (1981, 2:103).

I shall begin with observations on the executive branch of this new system; and though it is not the first in order, as arranged therein, yet being the *chief,* is perhaps entitled by the rules of rank to the first consideration. ...

   It is remarked by Montesquieu, in treating of republics, that "in all magistracies, the greatness of the power must be compensated by the brevity of the duration; and that a longer time than a year would be dangerous." It is therefore obvious to the least intelligent mind ... why great power in the hands of a magistrate, and that power connected with a considerable duration, may be dangerous to the liberties of a republic. The deposit of vast trusts in the hands of a single magistrate, enables him ... to create a numerous train of dependents, [which] tempts his ambition [and] gives him the means and time to perfect and execute his designs–"he therefore fancies that he may be great and glorious by oppressing his fellow citizens, and raising himself to permanent grandeur on the ruins of his country." And here it may be necessary to compare the vast and important powers of the president, together with his continuance in office with the foregoing doctrine: his eminent magisterial situation will attach many adherents to him, and he will be surrounded by expectants and courtiers; his power of nomination and influence on all appointments; the strong posts in each state comprised within his superintendence, and garrisoned by troops under his direction; his control over the army, militia, and navy; the unrestrained power of granting pardons for treason, which may be used to screen from punishment those whom he had secretly instigated to commit the crime, and thereby prevent a discovery of his own guilt; [and] his duration in office for four years. These and various other principles evidently prove the truth of the position that if the president is possessed of ambition, he has power and time sufficient to ruin his country.

Though the president, during the sitting of the legislature, is assisted by the senate, yet he is without a constitutional council in their recess. He will therefore be unsupported by proper information and advice, and will generally be directed by minions and favorites, or a council of state will grow out of the principal officers of the great departments, the most dangerous council in a free country.

The ten miles square, which is to become the seat of government, will of course be the place of residence for the president and the great officers of state. The same observations of a great man [Montesquieu] will apply to the court of a president possessing the powers of a monarch that is observed of that of a monarch—"ambition with idleness, baseness with pride, the thirst of riches without labour, aversion to truth, flattery, treason, perfidy, violation of engagements, contempt of civil duties, hope from the magistrate's weakness; but above all, the perpetual ridicule of virtue"; these, [Montesquieu] remarks, are the characteristics by which the courts in all ages have been distinguished. ...

The establishment of a vice-president is as unnecessary as it is dangerous. This officer, for want of other employment, is made president of the senate, thereby blending the executive and legislative powers, besides always giving to some one state, from which he is to come, an unjust preeminence.

It is a maxim in republics that the representative of the people should be of their immediate choice, but by the manner in which the president is chosen he arrives to this office at the fourth or fifth hand. Nor does the highest vote ... determine the choice, for it is only necessary that he should be taken from the highest of five. ...

Compare your past opinions and sentiments with the present proposed establishment, and you will find ... that it will lead you into a system which you heretofore reprobated as odious. Every American whig, not long since, bore his emphatic testimony against a monarchical government, though limited, because of the dangerous inequality that it created among citizens as relative to their rights and property. And wherein does this president, invested with his powers and prerogatives, essentially differ from the king of Great Britain, save as to name, the creation of nobility and some immaterial incidents, the offspring of absurdity and locality. The direct prerogatives of the president ... are among the following: It is necessary, in order to distinguish him from the rest of the community and enable him to keep and maintain his court, that the compensation for his services, or in other words, his revenue, should be such as to enable him to appear with the splendor of a prince; he has the power of receiving ambassadors from, and a great influence on their appointments to foreign courts, [and] also [the power] to make treaties, leagues, and alliances with foreign states, assisted by the senate, which when made, become the supreme law of the land; he is a constituent part of the legislative power, for every bill which shall pass the house of representatives and senate is to be presented to him for approbation—if he approves of it, he is to sign it, if he disapproves, he is to return it with objections, which in many cases will amount to a complete negative; [though] the king of Great Britain has the express power of making peace or war, yet he never thinks it prudent so to do without the advice of his parliament from whom he is to derive his support, and therefore these powers, in both president and king, are substantially the same; he is the generalissimo of the nation, and of course, has the command

and control of the army, navy and militia; he is the general conservator of the peace of the union [and] may pardon all offences, except in cases of impeachment; and [he is] the principal fountain of all offices and employments. Will not the exercise of these powers therefore tend either to the establishment of a vile and arbitrary aristocracy, or monarchy? ...

You must, however, my countrymen, beware that the advocates of this new system do not deceive you by a fallacious resemblance between it and your own state government, which you so much prize. ... If you examine you will perceive that the chief magistrate of this state is your immediate choice, controlled and checked by a just and full representation of the people, divested of the prerogative of influencing war and peace, making treaties, receiving and sending embassies, and commanding standing armies and navies, which belong to the power of the confederation, and will be convinced that this government is not more like a true picture of your own than an Angel of darkness resembles an Angel of light. ...

In my last number I endeavored to prove that the language of the article relative to the establishment of the executive of this new government was vague and inexplicit, that the great powers of the President, connected with his duration in office, would lead to oppression and ruin. That he would be governed by favorites and flatterers, or that a dangerous council would be collected from the great officers of state; that the ten miles square ... would be the asylum of the base, idle, avaricious and ambitious, and that the court would possess a language and manners different from yours; that a vice-president is as unnecessary as he is dangerous in his influence; that the president cannot represent you because he is not of your own immediate choice; that if you adopt this government you will incline to an arbitrary and odious aristocracy or monarchy; that the president possessed of the power given him by this frame of government differs but very immaterially from the establishment of monarchy in Great Britain. And I warned you to beware of the fallacious resemblance that is held out to you by the advocates of this new system between it and your own state governments.

And here I cannot help remarking that inexplicitness seems to pervade this whole political fabric. Certainty in political compacts, which Mr. [Edward] Coke calls "the mother and nurse of repose and quietness," the want of which induced men to engage in political society, has ever been held by a wise and free people as essential to their security. ... On the one hand it fixes barriers which the ambitious and tyrannically disposed magistrate dare not overleap, and on the other, becomes a wall of safety to the community. Otherwise stipulations between the governors and governed are nugatory, and you might as well deposit the important powers of legislation and execution in one or a few and permit them to govern according to their disposition and will. But the world is too full of examples which prove that "to live by one man's will became the cause of all men's misery." Before the existence of express political compacts it was reasonably implied that the magistrate should govern with wisdom and justice, but mere implication was too feeble to restrain the unbridled ambition of a bad man, or afford security against negligence, cruelty, or any other defect of mind. It is alleged that the opinions and manners of the people of America are capable to resist and prevent an extension of prerogative or oppression, but you must recollect that opinion and manners are mutable, and may not always be a permanent obstruction against the encroachments of government; that the progress of a commercial society begets luxury, the parent of inequality, the foe to virtue, and the enemy to restraint; and that ambition and voluptuousness aided by flattery will teach magistrates, where limits are not explicitly fixed, to have separate and distinct interests from the people. Besides it will not be denied that government assimilates the manners and opinions of the community to it. Therefore, a general presumption that rulers will govern well is not a sufficient security. You are then under a sacred obligation to provide for the safety of your posterity, and would you now basely desert their interests when by a small share of prudence you may transmit to them a beautiful political patrimony, which will prevent the necessity of their travelling through seas of blood to obtain that which your wisdom might have secured. It is a duty you owe likewise to your own reputation, for you have a great name to lose. You are characterized as cautious, prudent and jealous in politics. Whence is it, therefore, that you are about to precipitate yourselves into a sea of uncertainty, and adopt a system so vague and which has discarded so many of your valuable rights. Is it because you do not believe that an American can be a tyrant? If this be the case you rest on a weak basis. Americans are like other men in similar situations. When the manners and opinions of the community are changed by the causes I mentioned before, and your political compact inexplicit, your posterity will find that great power connected with ambition, luxury, and flattery will as readily produce a Caesar, Caligula, Nero, and Domitian in America, as the same causes did in the Roman empire.

Too Weak

48. Alexander Hamilton's Speech to the Federal Convention, June 18, 1787

On September 17, the last day of the Constitutional Convention, with the delegates preparing to sign the historic document, Hamilton rose to address the convention one last time. He urged his fellow delegates to affix their signatures to the document. "No man's ideas," he reminded the delegates, "were more remote from the plan than his were known to be." Though the Constitution was far from the plan of government Hamilton would have preferred, it offered "the chance of good," whereas rejection of the document meant almost certain "anarchy and Convulsion" (Farrand 1937, 2:645–46). The delegates knew just how far Hamilton's own ideas were from the final Constitution because Hamilton had presented his own vision to the convention three months earlier in a five-hour speech on June 18. In this speech we encounter a far different Hamilton from the one we are familiar with from the *Federalist*.

Mr. Hamilton had been hitherto silent on the business before the convention, partly from respect to others whose superior abilities, age and experience rendered him unwilling to bring forward ideas dissimilar to theirs, and partly from his delicate situation with respect to his own state, to whose sentiments as expressed by his colleagues he could by no means accede. The crisis however which now marked our affairs was too serious to permit any scruples whatever to prevail over the duty imposed on every man to contribute his efforts for the public safety and happiness. ...

Gaillard Hunt and James Brown Scott, eds., *The Debates in the Federal Convention of 1787 Which Framed the Constitution of the United States of America Reported by James Madison* (New York: Oxford University Press, 1920), 111–13, 115–19.

What then is to be done? The extent of the country to be governed discouraged him. ... [He was] almost led to despair that a republican government could be established over so great an extent. He was sensible at the same time that it would be unwise to propose one of any other form. In his private opinion he had no scruple in declaring, supported as he was by the opinions of so many of the wise and good, that the British government was the best in the world, and that he doubted much whether anything short of it would do in America. He hoped gentlemen of different opinions would bear with him in this, and begged them to recollect the change of opinion on this subject which had taken place and was still going on. It was once thought that the power of Congress was amply sufficient to secure the end of their institution. The error was now seen by everyone. The members most tenacious of republicanism, he observed, were as loud as any in declaiming against the vices of democracy. This progress of the public mind led him to anticipate the time when others as well as himself would join in the praise bestowed by Mr. Necker on the British constitution, namely, that it is the only government in the world "which unites public strength with individual security." In every community where industry is encouraged, there will be a division of it into the few and the many. Hence separate interests will arise. There will be debtors and creditors, etc. Give all power to the few, they will oppress the many. Both therefore ought to have power, that each may defend itself against the other. To the want of this check we owe our paper money, instalment laws, etc. To the proper adjustment of it the British owe the excellence of their constitution.

Their House of Lords is a most noble institution. Having nothing to hope for by a change, and a sufficient interest by means of their property in being faithful to the national interest, they form a permanent barrier against every pernicious innovation, whether attempted on the part of the Crown or of the Commons. No temporary Senate will have firmness enough to answer the purpose. ... Gentlemen differ in their opinions concerning the necessary checks, from the different estimates they form of the human passions. They suppose seven years a sufficient period to give the Senate an adequate firmness [without] duly considering the amazing violence and turbulence of the democratic spirit. When a great object of government is pursued, which seizes the popular passions, they spread like wild fire and become irresistible. He appealed to the gentlemen from the New England states whether experience had not there verified the remark.

As to the executive, it seemed to be admitted that no good one could be established on republican principles. Was not this giving up the merits of the question: for can there be a good government without a good executive? The English model was the only good one on this subject. The hereditary interest of the king was so interwoven with that of the Nation, and his personal emoluments so great, that he was placed above the danger of being corrupted from abroad—and at the same time was both sufficiently independent and sufficiently controlled to answer the purpose of the institution at home. One of the weak sides of republics was their being liable to foreign influence and corruption. Men of little character, acquiring great power, become easily the tools of intermeddling neighbors. Sweden was a striking instance. ...

What is the inference from all these observations? That we ought to go as far in order to attain stability and permanency, as republican principles will admit. Let one branch of the legislature hold their places for life or at least during good behavior. Let the executive also be for life. He appealed to the feelings of the members present whether a term of seven years would induce the sacrifices of private affairs which an acceptance of public trust would require, so as to ensure the services of the best citizens. On this plan we should have in the

Senate a permanent will, a weighty interest, which would answer essential purposes. But is this a republican government, it will be asked? Yes if all the magistrates are appointed, and vacancies are filled, by the people, or a process of election originating with the people. He was sensible that an executive constituted as he proposed would have in fact but little of the power and independence that might be necessary. On the ... plan of appointing him for 7 years, he thought the executive ought to have but little power. He would be ambitious, with the means of making creatures; and as the object of his ambition would be to prolong his power, it is probable that in case of war he would avail himself of the emergency to evade or refuse a degradation from his place. An executive for life has not this motive for forgetting his fidelity, and will therefore be a safer depository of power.

It will be objected probably that such an executive will be an elective monarch, and will give birth to the tumults which characterize that form of government. He would reply that *monarch* is an indefinite term. It marks not either the degree or duration of power. If this executive magistrate would be a monarch for life, the other proposed by the report from the Committee of the Whole would be a monarch for seven years. The circumstance of being elective was also applicable to both. It had been observed by judicious writers that elective monarchies would be the best if they could be guarded against the tumults excited by the ambition and intrigues of competitors. He was not sure that tumults were an inseparable evil. He rather thought this character of elective monarchies had been taken rather from particular cases than from general principles. The election of Roman emperors was made by the army. In Poland the election is made by great rival princes with independent power and ample means of raising commotions. In the German empire, the appointment is made by the electors and princes, who have equal motives and means for exciting cabals and parties. Might not such a mode of election be devised among ourselves as will defend the community against these effects in any dangerous degree?

Having made these observations he would read ... a sketch of a plan which he should prefer to either of those under consideration. He was aware that it went beyond the ideas of most members. But will such a plan be adopted out of doors? In return he would ask will the people adopt the [Virginia] plan? At present they will adopt neither. But he sees the Union dissolving or already dissolved; he sees evils operating in the states which must soon cure the people of their fondness for democracies; he sees that a great progress has been already made and is still going on in the public mind. He thinks therefore that the people will in time be unshackled from their prejudices; and whenever that happens they will themselves not be satisfied at stopping where the plan of Mr. Randolph would place them, but be ready to go as far at least as he proposes. He did not mean to offer the paper he had sketched as a proposition to the Committee. It was meant only to give a more correct view of his ideas, and to suggest the amendments which he should probably propose to the plan of Mr. Randolph in the proper stages of its future discussion. He read his sketch in the words following:

I. "The Supreme Legislative power of the United States of America to be vested in two different bodies of men; the one to be called the Assembly, the other the Senate. ...

II. The Assembly to consist of persons elected by the people to serve for three years.

III. The Senate to consist of persons elected to serve during good behavior; their election to be made by electors chosen for that purpose by the people. ...

IV. The supreme Executive authority of the United States to be vested in a Governour to be elected to serve during good behavior—the election to be made by Electors chosen by the people in ... Election Districts. The authorities and functions of the Executive to be as follows: to have a negative on all laws about to be passed, and the execution of all laws passed;

to have the direction of war when authorized or begun; to have with the advice and approbation of the Senate the power of making all treaties; to have the sole appointment of the heads or chief officers of the departments of Finance, War and Foreign Affairs; to have the nomination of all other officers (Ambassadors to foreign Nations included) subject to the approbation or rejection of the Senate; to have the power of pardoning all offences except Treason, which he shall not pardon without the approbation of the Senate. ...

VI. The Senate to have the sole power of declaring war, the power of advising and approving all Treaties, the power of approving or rejecting all appointments of officers except the heads or chiefs of the departments of Finance, War, and Foreign Affairs. ...

IX. The Governour, Senators and all officers of the United States to be liable to impeachment for mal- and corrupt conduct, and upon conviction to be removed from office and disqualified for holding any place of trust or profit. All impeachments to be tried by a Court to consist of the Chief or Judge of the superior Court of Law of each State. ...

X. All laws of the particular States contrary to the Constitution or laws of the United States to be utterly void; and the better to prevent such laws being passed, the Governour or president of each State shall be appointed by the general Government and shall have a negative upon the laws about to be passed in the State of which he is Governour or President."

49. Samuel Spencer, North Carolina Ratifying Convention, July 28, 1788

No Anti-Federalists shared Hamilton's expansive vision of the presidency, but a sizable number agreed that the president was too weak, specifically vis-à-vis the Senate. They worried, as Pennsylvania's Samuel Bryan did, that "the President ... would be a mere pageant of state, unless he coincides with the views of the Senate." He would become either "the head of the aristocratic junto in [the Senate], or its minion" (Storing 1981, 2:142). The problem, as many Anti-Federalists saw it, was that the Senate, through its advice and consent function, had assumed the role of an executive council. The Senate was thus a dangerous and potentially tyrannical mixture of executive powers (especially respecting appointments), judicial powers (particularly the trying of impeachments), and legislative powers. The president would be both safer and stronger, these Anti-Federalists maintained, if a president was constrained and assisted by a purely executive council. The following speech by Judge Samuel Spencer, a North Carolina Anti-Federalist, exemplifies this strain in Anti-Federalist thinking.

It is an essential article in our Constitution that the legislative, the executive, and the supreme judicial powers of government ought to be forever separate and distinct from each

Jonathan Elliot, ed., *The Debates in the Several State Constitutions on the Adoption of the Federal Constitution* (New York: Burt Franklin, 1888), 4:116–18.

other. The Senate, in the proposed government of the United States, are possessed of the legislative authority in conjunction with the House of Representatives. They are likewise possessed of the sole power of trying all impeachments, which, not being restrained to the officers of the United States, may be intended to include all the officers of the several states in the Union. And by this clause they possess the chief of the executive power; they are, in effect, to form treaties, which are to be the law of the land; and they have obviously, in effect, the appointment of all the officers of the United States. The President may nominate, but they have a negative upon his nomination, till he has exhausted the number of those he wishes to be appointed. He will be obliged, finally, to acquiesce in the appointment of those whom the Senate shall nominate, or else no appointment will take place. Hence it is easy to perceive that the President, in order to do any business or to answer any purpose in this department of his office, and to keep himself out of perpetual hot water, will be under a necessity to form a connection with that powerful body, and be contented to put himself at the head of the leading members who compose it. I do not expect, at this day, that the outline and organization of this proposed government will be materially altered. But I cannot but be of the opinion that the government would have been infinitely better and more secure if the President had been provided with a standing council, composed of one member from each of the states, the duration of whose office might have been the same as that of the President's office, or for any other period that might have been thought more proper; for it can hardly be supposed, if two senators can be sent from each state who are fit to give counsel to the President, that one such cannot be found in each state qualified for that purpose. Upon this plan, one half the expense of the Senate, as a standing council to the President in the recess of Congress, would evidently be saved; each state would have equal weight in this council, as it has now in the Senate. And what renders this plan the more eligible is that two very important consequences would result from it. ... The first is that the whole executive department, being separate and distinct from that of the legislative and judicial, would be amenable to the justice of the land: the President and his council, or either or any of them, might be impeached, tried, and condemned, for any misdemeanor in office. Whereas, on the present plan proposed, the Senate, who are to advise the President, and who, in effect, are possessed of the chief executive powers, let their conduct be what it will, are not amenable to the public justice of their country: if they may be impeached, there is no tribunal invested with jurisdiction to try them. It is true that the proposed Constitution provides that when the President is tried, the chief justice shall preside. But I take this to be little more than a farce. What can the Senate try him for? For doing that which they have advised him to do, and which, without their advice, he would not have done. Except what he may do in a military capacity—when, I presume, he will be entitled to be tried by a court martial of general officers—he can do nothing in the executive department without the advice of the Senate, unless it be to grant pardons, and adjourn the two Houses of Congress to some day to which they cannot agree to adjourn themselves, probably to some term that may be convenient to the leading members of the Senate.

I cannot conceive, therefore, that the President can ever be tried by the Senate with any effect, or to any purpose for any misdemeanor in his office, unless it should extend to high treason, or unless they should wish to fix the odium of any measure on him in order to exculpate themselves, ... which I cannot suppose will ever happen.

Another important consequence of the plan I wish had taken place is that the office of the President being thereby unconnected with that of the legislative, as well as the judicial, he would have that independence which is necessary to form the intended check upon the acts passed by the legislature before they obtain the sanction of laws. But, on the present plan, from the necessary connection of the President's office with that of the Senate, I have little ground to hope that his firmness will long prevail against the overbearing power and influence of the Senate ... for he will soon find that, unless he inclines to compound with them, they can easily hinder and control him in the principal articles of his office. But if nothing else could be said in favor of the plan of a standing council to the President, independent of the Senate, the dividing the power of the latter would be sufficient to recommend it; it being of the utmost importance towards the security of the government and the liberties of the citizens under it. For I think it must be obvious to every unprejudiced mind that ... combining in the Senate the power of legislation with a controlling share in the appointment of all the officers of the United States (except those chosen by the people) and the power of trying all impeachments that may be found against such officers, invests the Senate at once with such an enormity of power and with such an overbearing and uncontrollable influence, as is incompatible with every idea of safety to the liberties of a free country and is calculated to swallow up all other powers and to render that body a despotic aristocracy.

Just Right

50. James Wilson, Pennsylvania Ratifying Convention, December 11, 1787

Fears that the president would be reduced to an instrument of an all-powerful, aristocratic Senate were widespread among Pennsylvania Anti-Federalists. On December 6, at the Pennsylvania ratifying convention, John Smilie, a leader of the Anti-Federalist opposition, delivered a long speech detailing his side's objections to the proposed constitution. "The balance of power," he complained, "is in the Senate. Their share in the executive department will corrupt the legislature, and detracts from the proper power of the President, and will make the President merely a tool to the Senate" (Jensen, Kaminiski, and Saladino 1976–, 2:508). Smilie's objections to the Senate's power closely echoed concerns that James Wilson himself had voiced in the closing days of the Constitutional Convention, when he had characterized the convention's plan as "having a dangerous tendency to aristocracy; as throwing a dangerous power into the hands of the Senate." The president, Wilson had fretted, "will not be the man of the people as he ought to be, but the Minion of the Senate" (September 6). Even after the federal convention had removed the Senate entirely from the process of presidential selection, Wilson continued to object that the Senate's role in the appointment of officers was "blending a branch of the Legislature with the Executive" in a manner that undermined

---

Jonathan Elliot, ed., *The Debates in the Several State Constitutions on the Adoption of the Federal Constitution* (New York: Burt Franklin, 1888), 2:510–14.

executive independence and responsibility (September 7). But at the ratifying convention Wilson buried his own reservations and vigorously refuted Smilie's charge that the executive would be a tool of the Senate. A majority of the convention evidently agreed with Wilson—the convention approved the Constitution by a 2 to 1 margin—but a minority remained unconvinced and filed a dissenting report that echoed Smilie's concerns. "The president general," the minority report reiterated, "is dangerously connected with the senate; his coincidence with the views of the ruling junto in that body is made essential to his weight and importance in the government, which will destroy all independency and purity in the executive department" (2:635).

The objection against the powers of the President is not that they are too many or too great; but, to state it in the gentleman's [John Smilie] own language, they are so trifling that the President is no more than the *tool* of the Senate.

Now, sir, I do not apprehend this to be the case, because I see that he may do a great many things independent of the Senate; and, with respect to the executive powers of government in which the Senate participates, they can do nothing without him. Now, I would ask, which is most likely to be the tool of the other? Clearly, sir, [the president] holds the helm, and the vessel can proceed neither in one direction nor another without his concurrence. It was expected by many that the cry would have been against the powers of the President as a monarchical power; indeed the echo of such sound was heard some time before the rise of the late Convention. There were men, at that time, determined to make an attack upon whatever system should be proposed, but they mistook the point of direction. Had the President possessed those powers, which the opposition on this floor are willing to consign him, of making treaties and appointing officers, with the advice of a council of state, the clamor would have been that the House of Representatives and the Senate were the tools of the monarch. This, sir, is but conjecture, but I leave it to those who are acquainted with the current of the politics pursued by the enemies to this system to determine whether it is a reasonable conjecture or not. ...

If gentlemen will look into this article, and read for themselves, they will find that there is no well-grounded reason to suspect the President will be the tool of the Senate. "The President shall be commander in chief of the army and navy of the United States, and of the militia of the several states, when called into the actual service of the United States. He may require the opinion, in writing, of the principal officers in each of the executive departments, upon any subject relative to the duties of their respective offices; and he shall have power to grant reprieves and pardons, for offences against the United States." Must the President, after all, be called the tool of the Senate? I do not mean to insinuate that he has more powers than he ought to have, but merely to declare that they are of such a nature as to place him above expressions of contempt.

There is another power of no small magnitude entrusted to this officer. "He shall take care that the laws be faithfully executed."

I apprehend that in the administration of this government it will not be found necessary for the Senate always to sit. I know some gentlemen have insinuated and conjectured that this will be the case, but I am inclined to a contrary opinion. ... From the nature of their business, I do not think it will be necessary for them to attend longer than the House of Representatives. Besides their legislative powers, they possess three others: trying impeachments, concurring in making treaties, and in appointing officers. With regard to their power in mak-

ing treaties, it is of importance that it should be very seldom exercised. We are happily removed from the vortex of European politics, and the fewer and the more simple our negotiations with European powers, the better they will be. If such be the case, it will be but once
in a number of years that a single treaty will come before the Senate.[2] I think, therefore, that
on this account it will be unnecessary to sit constantly. With regard to the trial of impeachments, I hope it is what will seldom happen. In this observation, the experience of the ten
last years support me. Now, there is only left the power of concurring in the appointment of
officers; but care is taken in this Constitution that this branch of business may be done without their presence. The President is authorized to fill up all vacancies that may happen during the recess of the Senate, by granting commissions which shall expire at the end of their
next session; so that, on the whole, the Senate need not sit longer than the House of Representatives ... and no doubt if apprehensions are entertained of the Senate, the House of
Representatives will not provide pay for them one day longer than is necessary. But what (it
will be asked) is this great power of the President? He can fill the offices only by temporary
appointments. True, but every person knows the advantage of being once introduced into an
office; it is often of more importance than the highest recommendation.

Having now done with the legislative and executive branches of this government, I shall
just remark that, upon the whole of the executive, it appears that the gentlemen in opposition state nothing as exceptionable but the deficiency of powers in the President; but rather
seem to allow some degree of political merit in this department of government.

51. An American Citizen [Tench Coxe], "On the Federal Government," No. 1, September 26, 1787

This widely circulated essay by "An American Citizen" was the first published
defense of the presidency. Whereas James Wilson at the Pennsylvania ratifying convention found himself having to defend the presidency against
charges that it was too weak, Tench Coxe anticipated (correctly) that the
major criticism of Article 2 would be that the president was too strong and
too closely resembled a king. Coxe emphasizes how far short of a king the
American president would be. America, he assures the country, had nothing
to fear from a creature whose powers were so "limited and transitory."

Philadelphia *Independent Gazetteer*, September 26, 1787.

2. Wilson's forecast was reasonably accurate in the short term. At the time of the Constitution treaties tended to be far less important that the conventions of international law. In the nation's first quarter century only thirteen treaties were sent to the Senate, an average of one every
two years. Between December 1805 and February 1816 not a single treaty was sent to the Senate. Our policy, Jefferson explained at the midpoint of his two terms as president, "is to have [no
treaties] with any nation, as far as can be avoided" (McDonald 1994, 385). After the conclusion
of the War of 1812, however, treaties became a much more significant instrument of foreign relations. Between 1815 and 1869, the Senate considered 220 treaties, or four treaties a year, eight
times the number of treaties that had been submitted in the opening quarter century (388).

Let us consider awhile that which is now proposed to us. Let us compare it with the so much boasted British form of government, and see how much more it favors the people and how completely it secures their rights, remembering at the same time that we did not dissolve our connection with that country so much on account of its constitution as the perversion and mal-administration of it.

In the first place let us look at the nature and powers of the head of that country, and those of the ostensible head of ours.

The British king is the great bishop or supreme head of an established church, with an immense patronage annexed. In this capacity he commands a number of votes in the House of Lords, by creating bishops, who, besides their great incomes, have votes in that assembly and are judges in the last resort. They have also many honorable and lucrative places to bestow, and thus from their wealth, learning, dignities, powers and patronage give a great luster and an enormous influence to the Crown.

In America our president will not only be without these influencing advantages, but they will be in the possession of the people at large, to strengthen their hands in the event of a contest with him. All religious funds, honors and powers are in the gift of numberless, unconnected, disunited, and contending corporations, wherein the principle of perfect equality universally prevails. In short, danger from ecclesiastical tyranny, that longstanding and still remaining curse of the people, that sacrilegious engine of royal power in some countries, can be feared by no man in the United States. In Britain their king is for life; in America our president will always be one of the people at the end of four years. In that country the king is hereditary and may be an idiot, a knave, or a tyrant by nature, or ignorant from neglect of his education, yet cannot be removed, for "he can do no wrong." In America, as the president is to be one of the people at the end of his short term, so will he and his fellow citizens remember that he was originally one of the people, and that he is created by their breath. Further, he cannot be an idiot, probably not a knave or a tyrant, for those whom nature makes so discover it before the age of thirty-five, until which period he cannot be elected. It appears we have not admitted that he can do no wrong, but have rather presupposed he may and will sometimes do wrong, by providing for his impeachment, his trial, and his peaceable and complete removal.

In England the king has a power to create members of the upper house who are judges in the highest court, as well as legislators. Our president not only cannot make members of the upper house, but their creation, like his own, is by the people through their representatives, and a member of assembly may and will be as certainly dismissed at the end of his year for electing a weak or wicked Senator, as for any other blunder or misconduct.

The king of England has legislative power, while our president can only use it when the other servants of the people are divided. But in all great cases affecting the national interests or safety, his modified and restrained power must give way to the sense of two-thirds of the legislature. In fact it amounts to no more than a serious duty imposed upon him to request both houses to reconsider any matter on which he entertains doubts or feels apprehensions, and here the people have a strong hold upon him from his sole and personal responsibility.

The president of the upper house (or the chancellor) in England is appointed by the king, while our vice-president, who is chosen by the people through the electors and the senate, is not at all dependent on the president, but may exercise equal powers on some occasions. In all royal governments an helpless infant or an inexperienced youth may wear the crown. Our president must be matured by the experience of years, and being born among us, his character at thirty-five must be fully understood. Wisdom, virtue, and active qualities of mind and body can alone make him the first servant of a free and enlightened people.

Our president will fall very far short indeed of any prince in his annual income, which will not be hereditary, but the absolute allowance of the people passing through the hands of their other servants from year to year as it becomes necessary. There will be no burdens on the nation to provide for his heir or other branches of his family. It is probable, from the state of property in America and other circumstances, that many citizens will exceed him in show and expense, those dazzling trappings of kingly rank and power. He will have no authority to make a treaty without two-thirds of the Senate, nor can he appoint ambassadors or other great officers without their approbation, which will remove the idea of patronage and influence, and of personal obligation and dependence. The appointment of even the inferior officers may be taken out of his hands by an act of Congress at any time; he can create no nobility or title of honor, nor take away offices during good behavior. His person is not so much protected as that of a member of the House of Representatives, for he may be proceeded against like any other man in the ordinary course of law. He appoints no officer of the separate states. He will have no influence from placemen in the legislature, nor can he prorogue or dissolve it. He will have no power over the treasures of the state, and lastly, as he is created through the electors by the people at large, he must ever look up to the support of his creators. From such a servant with powers so limited and transitory, there can be no danger, especially when we consider the solid foundations on which our national liberties are immovably fixed by the other provisions of this excellent constitution. Whatever of dignity or authority he possesses is a delegated part of their majesty and their political omnipotence, transiently vested in him by the people themselves for their own happiness.

52. Alexander Hamilton, *Federalist* 69, March 14, 1788

In this justly famous essay, Hamilton takes up the line of defense pursued by Coxe. Hamilton, though, compares the presidency not only with the British monarchy but also, more tellingly, with the New York governorship. In a direct response to Cato, Hamilton maintains that the president's powers are roughly comparable and often decidedly less than the powers possessed by the New York governor. Hamilton also finds the powers of the president to be radically unlike the powers possessed by a king.

The first thing which strikes our attention is that the executive authority, with few exceptions, is to be vested in a single magistrate. This will scarcely, however, be considered as a point upon which any comparison can be grounded; for if, in this particular, there be a resemblance to the King of Great Britain, there is not less a resemblance to the Grand Seignior, to the khan of Tartary, to the Man of the Seven Mountains, or to the governor of New York.

New-York Packet, March 14, 1788.

That magistrate is to be elected for four years, and is to be reeligible as often as the people of the United States shall think him worthy of their confidence. In these circumstances there is a total dissimilitude between him and a king of Great Britain, who is an hereditary monarch, possessing the crown as a patrimony descendible to his heirs forever; but there is a close analogy between him and a governor of New York, who is elected for three years and is reeligible without limitation or intermission. If we consider how much less time would be requisite for establishing a dangerous influence in a single state than for establishing a like influence throughout the United States, we must conclude that a duration of four years for the chief magistrate of the Union is a degree of permanency far less to be dreaded in that office than a duration of three years for a corresponding office in a single state.

The president of the United States would be liable to be impeached, tried, and, upon conviction of treason, bribery, or other high crimes or misdemeanors, removed from office; and would afterwards be liable to prosecution and punishment in the ordinary course of law. The person of the king of Great Britain is sacred and inviolable; there is no constitutional tribunal to which he is amenable, no punishment to which he can be subjected without involving the crisis of a national revolution. In this delicate and important circumstance of personal responsibility, the president of confederated America would stand upon no better ground than a governor of New York, and upon worse ground than the governors of Maryland and Delaware.

The president of the United States is to have power to return a bill, which shall have passed the two branches of the legislature, for reconsideration; but the bill so returned is to become a law, if, upon that reconsideration, it be approved by two thirds of both houses. The king of Great Britain, on his part, has an absolute negative upon the acts of the two houses of Parliament. The disuse of that power for a considerable time past does not affect the reality of its existence, and is to be ascribed wholly to the crown's having found the means of substituting influence for authority, or the art of gaining a majority in one or the other of the two houses. ... The qualified negative of the president differs widely from this absolute negative of the British sovereign, and tallies exactly with the revisionary authority of the council of revision of this state, of which the governor is a constituent part. In this respect the power of the president would exceed that of the governor of New York, because the former would possess, singly, what the latter shares with the chancellor and judges; but it would be precisely the same with that of the governor of Massachusetts, whose constitution, as to this article, seems to have been the original from which the convention have copied.

The president is to be the "commander-in-chief of the army and navy of the United States, and of the militia of the several States, when called into the actual service of the United States. He is to have power to grant reprieves and pardons for offences against the United States, except in cases of impeachment; to recommend to the consideration of Congress such measures as he shall judge necessary and expedient; to convene, on extraordinary occasions, both houses of the legislature, or either of them, and, in case of disagreement between them with respect to the time of adjournment, to adjourn them to such time as he shall think proper; to take care that the laws be faithfully executed; and to commission all officers of the United States." In most of the particulars, the power of the president will resemble equally that of the king of Great Britain and of the governor of New York. The most material point of difference are these:

First, the president will have only the occasional command of such part of the militia of the nation as by legislative provision may be called into the actual service of the Union. The king of Great Britain and the governor of New York have at all times the entire command of all the militia within their several jurisdictions. In this article, therefore, the power of the president would be inferior to that of either the monarch or the governor.

Secondly, the president is to be commander-in-chief of the army and navy of the United States. In this respect his authority would be nominally the same with that of the King of Great Britain, but in substance much inferior to it. It would amount to nothing more than the supreme command and direction of the military and naval forces, and first general and admiral of the Confederacy; while that of the British king extends to the declaring of war and to the raising and regulating of fleets and armies, all of which, by the Constitution under consideration, would appertain to the legislature. The governor of New York, on the other hand, is by the constitution of the state vested only with the command of its militia and navy. But the constitutions of several of the states expressly declare their governors to be commanders-in-chief as well of the army as navy; and it may well be a question whether those of New Hampshire and Massachusetts, in particular, do not in this instance confer larger powers upon their respective governors than could be claimed by a president of the United States.

Thirdly, the power of the president in respect to pardons would extend to all cases except those of impeachment. The governor of New York may pardon in all cases, even in those of impeachment, except of treason and murder. Is not the power of the governor, in this article, on a calculation of political consequences, greater than that of the president? All conspiracies and plots against the government which have not been matured into actual treason may be screened from punishment of every kind by the interposition of the prerogative of pardoning. If a governor of New York, therefore, should be at the head of any such conspiracy, until the design had been ripened into actual hostility, he could insure his accomplices and adherents an entire impunity. A president of the Union, on the other hand, though he may even pardon treason, when prosecuted in the ordinary course of law, could shelter no offender, in any degree, from the effects of impeachment and conviction. Would not the prospect of a total indemnity for all the preliminary steps be a greater temptation to undertake and persevere in an enterprise against the public liberty than the mere prospect of an exemption from death and confiscation, if the final execution of the design, upon an actual appeal to arms, should miscarry? Would this last expectation have any influence at all when the probability was computed that the person who was to afford that exemption might himself be involved in the consequences of the measure, and might be incapacitated by his agency in it from affording the desired impunity? The better to judge of this matter, it will be necessary to recollect that, by the proposed Constitution, the offence of treason is limited "to levying war upon the United States, and adhering to their enemies, giving them aid and comfort"; and that by the laws of New York it is confined within similar bounds.

Fourthly, the president can only adjourn the national legislature in the single case of disagreement about the time of adjournment. The British monarch may prorogue or even dissolve the Parliament. The governor of New York may also prorogue the legislature of this state for a limited time, a power which, in certain situations, may be employed to very important purposes.

The president is to have power, with the advice and consent of the Senate, to make treaties, provided two-thirds of the senators present concur. The king of Great Britain is the sole and absolute representative of the nation in all foreign transactions. He can of his own accord make treaties of peace, commerce, alliance, and of every other description. It has been insinuated that his authority in this respect is not conclusive, and that his conventions with foreign powers are subject to the revision, and stand in need of the ratification, of Parliament. But I believe this doctrine was never heard of until it was broached upon the present occasion. Every jurist of that kingdom, and every other man acquainted with its Constitution, knows ... that the prerogative of making treaties exists in the crown in its utmost plentitude, and that the compacts entered into by the royal authority have the most complete legal validity and perfection, independent of any other sanction. The Parliament, it is true, is sometimes seen employing itself in altering the existing laws to conform them to the stipulation in a new treaty, and this may have possibly given birth to the imagination that its cooperation was necessary to the obligatory efficacy of the treaty. But this parliamentary interposition proceeds from a different cause: from the necessity of adjusting a most artificial and intricate system of revenue and commercial laws to the changes made in them by the operation of the treaty, and of adapting new provisions and precautions to the new state of things to keep the machine from running into disorder. In this respect, therefore, there is no comparison between the intended power of the president and the actual power of the British sovereign. The one can perform alone what the other can do only with the concurrence of a branch of the legislature. It must be admitted that, in this instance, the power of the federal executive would exceed that of any state executive. But this arises naturally from the sovereign power which relates to treaties. If the Confederacy were to be dissolved, it would become a question whether the executives of the several states were not solely invested with that delicate and important prerogative.

The president is also to be authorized to receive ambassadors and other public ministers. This, though it has been a rich theme of declamation, is more a matter of dignity than of authority. It is a circumstance which will be without consequence in the administration of the government, and it was far more convenient that it should be arranged in this manner than that there should be a necessity of convening the legislature, or one of its branches, upon every arrival of a foreign minister, though it were merely to take the place of a departed predecessor.

The president is to nominate, and, with the advice and consent of the Senate, to appoint ambassadors and other public ministers, judges of the Supreme Court, and in general all officers of the United States established by law, and whose appointments are not otherwise provided for by the Constitution. The king of Great Britain is emphatically and truly styled the fountain of honor. He not only appoints to all offices, but can create offices. He can confer titles of nobility at pleasure, and has the disposal of an immense number of church preferments. There is evidently a great inferiority in the power of the president, in this particular, to that of the British king, nor is it equal to that of the governor of New York, if we are to interpret the meaning of the constitution of the state by the practice which has obtained under it. The power of appointment is with us lodged in a council, composed of the governor and four members of the Senate, chosen by the Assembly. The governor claims, and has frequently exercised, the right of nomination, and is entitled to a casting vote in the appointment. If he really has the right of nominating, his authority is in this respect equal to that of the president, and exceeds it in the article of the casting vote. In the national government, if the Senate should be divided, no appointment could be made; in the government of New York if the council shall be divided, the governor can turn the scale and confirm his own nomination. If we compare the publicity which must necessarily attend the mode of appointment by the president and an entire branch of the national legislature with the privacy in the mode of appointment by the governor of New York, closeted in a secret apartment with at most four and frequently with only two persons; and if we at the same time consider how much more easy it must be to influence the small number of which a council of appointment consists than the considerable number of which the national Senate would consist, we cannot hesitate to pronounce that the power of the chief magistrate of this state, in the disposition of offices, must, in practice, be greatly superior to that of the chief magistrate of the Union.

Hence it appears that, except as to the concurrent authority of the president in the article of treaties, it would be difficult to determine whether that magistrate would, in the aggregate, possess more or less power than the governor of New York. And it appears yet more unequivocally that there is no pretence for the parallel which has been attempted between him and the king of Great Britain. But to render the contrast in this respect still more striking, it may be of use to throw the principal circumstances of dissimilitude into a closer group.

The president of the United States would be an officer elected by the people for four years; the King of Great Britain is a perpetual and hereditary prince. The one would be amenable to personal punishment and disgrace; the person of the other is sacred and inviolable. The one would have a qualified negative upon the acts of the legislative body; the other has an absolute negative. The one would have a right to command the military and naval forces of the nation; the other, in addition to this right, possesses that of declaring war, and of raising and regulating fleets and armies by his own authority. The one would have a concurrent power with a branch of the legislature in the formation of treaties; the other is the sole possessor of the power of making treaties. The one would have a like concurrent authority in appointing to offices; the other is the sole author of all appointments. The one can confer no privileges whatever; the other can make denizens of aliens, noblemen of commoners, [and] can erect corporations with all the rights incident to corporate bodies. The one can prescribe no rules concerning the commerce or currency of the nation; the other is in several respects the arbiter of commerce, and in this capacity can establish markets and fairs, can regulate weights and measures, can lay embargoes for a limited time, can coin money, can authorize or prohibit the circulation of foreign coin. The one has no particle of spiritual jurisdiction; the other is the supreme head and governor of the national church! What answer shall we give to those who would persuade us that things so unlike resemble each other? The same that ought to be given to those who tell us that a government, the whole power of which would be in the hands of the elective and periodical servants of the people, is an aristocracy, a monarchy, and a despotism.

Questions for Discussion

1. Imagine Alexander Hamilton, having finished writing his *Federalist* essays defending the presidency, now picks up his pen to write a personal letter to a trusted family member or friend, a letter that he knows will never be read by any person in public life. What would he say in that letter, and how would it compare to what he wrote in the *Federalist*?

2. In what ways, if any, is the president like the British monarch?

3. Is the president created by the Constitution too strong or too weak? In your judgment, are the strengths or weaknesses of the contemporary presidency a product of the Constitution or have they developed in spite of the Constitution?

4. The date is June 25, 1788. Virginia has just voted to ratify the Constitution, becoming the tenth state to do so. A group of disgusted Anti-Federalists decide that their only chance to reverse the tide is to meet in secret and draw up an alternative constitution that they can then present to the states for approval. Only in this way, they decide, will they be able to offer the nation a positive alternative to the Constitution drafted the previous summer in Philadelphia. Eight men meet in George Mason's spacious kitchen. In addition to Mason, they are fellow Virginian Patrick Henry, Samuel Spencer of North Carolina, Luther Martin of Maryland, Elbridge Gerry of Massachusetts, Cato, An Old Whig, and the Federal Farmer (all three of whom show up in disguise so we still don't know who they are). For their first meeting they decide to focus only on the presidency and executive power. Your assignment is to draft the constitutional executive that you think these eight men would come up with.

5. Which of the Federalists and Anti-Federalists do you think were most prescient about the future shape of the presidency? Consider, for example, the debate about the veto power. Morris and Hamilton both believed a two-thirds override would not be sufficient to protect presidential power and to protect the community from bad laws. Were they right? You might also consider the debate over impeachment, tenure in office, or the electoral college.

6. What is the single biggest mistake the framers made in creating the presidency?

7. Would you say that the advocates of a strong presidency at the federal convention and the ratifying conventions are more democratic or less democratic than those who favored a weaker presidency? Name names, and find specific passages that support your interpretation.

8. Surveying the essays and speeches made in favor of and opposed to the presidency created at the Constitutional Convention, what do you think is the most telling argument advanced by each side? Why do you find this argument particularly effective? On balance, which side do you find marshals the more persuasive arguments about the presidency?

Appendixes

Appendix 1: Chronology

Federal Convention in Philadelphia, 1787

Monday, May 14: Convention scheduled to begin

Friday, May 25: Convention opens with necessary quorum of seven states (N.Y., N.J., Pa., Va., S.C., N.C., Del.); Washington selected president of convention

Tuesday, May 29: Virginia Plan presented to convention by Edmund Randolph

Friday, June 15: New Jersey Plan presented to convention by William Paterson

Tuesday, June 19: New Jersey Plan voted down by convention

Tuesday, July 10: New York delegation leaves

Sunday, July 22: New Hampshire delegation arrives

Tuesday, July 24: Five-member Committee of Detail (John Rutledge, chair; Oliver Ellsworth, Nathaniel Gorham, Edmund Randolph, James Wilson) elected to draw up a constitution "conformable to the Resolutions passed by the Convention"

Thursday, July 26: Convention approves ten-day recess to give Committee of Detail time to draft a constitution

Monday, August 6: Convention reconvenes: draft of constitution prepared by Committee of Detail read to convention

Friday, August 31: Convention votes to have new constitution ratified by conventions elected by people rather than ratified by state legislatures; requires nine states to ratify

Friday, August 31: Committee on Postponed Matters (David Brearly, chair; Abraham Baldwin, Pierce Butler, Daniel Carroll, John Dickinson, Nicholas Gilman, Rufus King, James Madison, Gouverneur Morris, Roger Sherman, Hugh Williamson), composed of one delegate from each state, appointed to deal with all postponed matters, including question of presidential selection

Tuesday, September 4: Committee on Postponed Matters submits its compromise plan on presidential selection, including proposal for electoral college

Saturday, September 8: Convention elects five-member Committee of Style (William Samuel Johnson, chair; Alexander Hamilton, Rufus King,

James Madison, Gouverneur Morris) to finalize the language of the Constitution

Wednesday, September 12: Committee of Style lays Constitution before the convention

Monday, September 17: Delegates sign Constitution and vote to dissolve convention; three (Elbridge Gerry, George Mason, and Edmund Randolph) refuse to sign

Ratification

October 27, 1787: First of the *Federalist* essays by "Publius" published

December 7, 1787: Delaware unanimously ratifies Constitution

December 12, 1787: Pennsylvania ratifies Constitution, 46 to 23

December 18, 1787: New Jersey unanimously ratifies Constitution

December 31, 1787: Georgia unanimously ratifies Constitution

January 9, 1788: Connecticut ratifies Constitution, 128 to 40

February 6, 1788: Massachusetts ratifies Constitution, 187 to 168

February 22, 1788: New Hampshire refuses to ratify but adjourns until June rather than reject Constitution

March 11–April 2, 1788: Hamilton's *Federalist* essays on the executive (67–77) are published

March 24, 1788: Rhode Island referendum on Constitution boycotted; rejects Constitution, 2,711 to 239

April 26, 1788: Maryland ratifies Constitution, 63 to 11

May 23, 1788: South Carolina ratifies Constitution, 149 to 73

June 21, 1788: New Hamphsire ratifies Constitution, 57 to 40; is ninth state to ratify, thus satisfying Convention requirements

June 25, 1788: Virginia ratifies Constitution, 89 to 79

July 26, 1788: New York ratifies Constitution, 30 to 27

August 2, 1788: North Carolina declines to ratify Constitution, 180 to 80

November 21, 1789: North Carolina ratifies Constitution, 194 to 77

May 29, 1790: Rhode Island ratifies Constitution, 34 to 32

Appendix 2: Delegates to the Constitutional Convention

Connecticut
  Oliver Ellsworth
  William Samuel Johnson
  Roger Sherman
  John Dickinson
  George Read

Delaware
  Richard Bassett
  Gunning Bedford
  Jacob Broom

Georgia
  Abraham Baldwin
  William Few
  William Houston
  William Pierce
Maryland
  Daniel Carroll
  Daniel of St. Thomas Jenifer
  Luther Martin
  James McHenry
  John Francis Mercer
Massachusetts
  Elbridge Gerry
  Nathaniel Gorham
  Rufus King
  Caleb Strong
New Hampshire
  Nicholas Gilman
  John Langdon
New Jersey
  David Brearly
  Jonathan Dayton
  William Churchill Houston
  William Livingston
  William Paterson
New York
  Alexander Hamilton
  John Lansing
  Robert Yates

North Carolina
  William Blount
  William Richardson Davie
  Alexander Martin
  Richard Dobbs Spaight
  Hugh Williamson
Pennsylvania
  George Clymer
  Thomas Fitzsimmons
  Benhamin Franklin
  Jared Ingersoll
  Thomas Mifflin
  Gouverneur Morris
  Robert Morris
  James Wilson
South Carolina
  Pierce Butler
  Charles Pinckney
  Charles Cotesworth Pinckney
  John Rutledge
Virginia
  John Blair
  James Madison
  George Mason
  James McClurg
  Edmund Randolph
  George Washington
  George Wythe

Appendix 3: Convention Reports and Resolutions

A. The Virginia Plan, May 29, 1787

7. Resolved that a National Executive be instituted; to be chosen by the National Legislature for the term of ___ years, to receive punctually at stated times, a fixed compensation for the services rendered, in which no increase or diminution shall be made so as affect the Magistracy, existing at the time of increase or diminution, and to be ineligible a second time; and that besides

a general authority to execute the National laws, it ought to enjoy the Executive rights vested in Congress by the Confederation.

8. Resolved that the Executive and a convenient number of the National Judiciary, ought to compose a Council of revision with authority to examine every act of the National Legislature before it shall operate, & every act of a particular Legislature before a Negative thereon shall be final; and that the dissent of the said Council shall amount to a rejection, unless the Act of the National Legislature be again passed, or that of a particular Legislature be again negatived by ___ of the members of each branch.

9. Resolved that a National Judiciary be established to consist of one or more supreme tribunals, and of inferior tribunals to be chosen by the National Legislature. ...

B. The Report of the Committee of the Whole on Mr. Randolph's Propositions, June 13, 1787

9. Resolved that a national Executive be instituted to consist of a single person, to be chosen by the National Legislature for the term of seven years, with power to carry into execution the national laws, to appoint to offices in cases not otherwise provided for—to be ineligible a second time, & to be removeable on impeachment and conviction of malpractices, or neglect of duty—to receive a fixed stipend by which he may be compensated for the devotion of his time to public service to be paid out of the national Treasury.

10. Resolved that the National Executive shall have a right to negative any Legislative Act, which shall not be afterwards passed unless by two thirds of each branch of the National Legislature.

11. Resolved that a National Judiciary be established to consist of one supreme tribunal; the Judges of which to be appointed by the second Branch of the National Legislature. ...

C. New Jersey Plan, June 15, 1787

4. Resolved that the United States in Congress be authorized to elect a federal Executive to consist of ___ persons, to continue in office for the term of ___ years, to receive punctually at stated times a fixed compensation for their services, in which no increase or diminution shall be made so as to affect the persons composing the Executive at the time of such increase or diminution, to be paid out of the federal treasury; to be incapable of holding any other office or appointment during their term of service, and for ___ years thereafter; to be ineligible a second time, & removeable by Congress on application by a majority of the Executives of the several States; that the Executives

besides their general authority to execute the federal acts ought to appoint all federal officers not otherwise provided for, & to direct all military operations; provided, that none of the persons composing the federal Executive shall on any occasion take command of any troops, so as personally to conduct any military enterprise as General, or in other capacity.

5. Resolved that a federal Judiciary be established, to consist of a supreme Tribunal the Judges of which to be appointed by the Executive, & to hold their offices during good behaviour. ...

D. Resolutions Referred to the Committee of Detail, July 26, 1787

That a national Executive be instituted to consist of a single Person—to be chosen for the Term of six Years—with Power to carry into Execution the national Laws—to appoint to Offices in Cases not otherwise provided for—to be removeable on Impeachment and Conviction of mal Practice or Neglect of Duty—to receive a fixed Compensation for the Devotion of his Time to public Service—to be paid out of the public Treasury.

That the national Executive shall have a Right to negative any legislative Act, which shall not be afterwards passed, unless by two third Parts of each Branch of the national Legislative.

That a national Judiciary be established to consist of one Supreme Tribunal—the Judges of which shall be appointed by the second Branch of the national Legislature.

E. Report of Committee of Detail, August 6, 1787

Article VI
Sect. 13. Every bill, which shall have passed the House of Representatives and the Senate, shall, before it becomes a law, be presented to the President of the United States for his revision: if, upon such revision, he approve of it, he shall signify his approbation by signing it: But if, upon such revision, it shall appear to him improper for being passed into a law, he shall return it, together with his objections against it, to that House in which it shall have originated, who shall enter the objections at large on their journal, and proceed to reconsider the bill. But if after such reconsideration, two thirds of that House shall, notwithstanding the objections of the President, agree to pass it, it shall together with his objections, be sent to the other House, by which it shall likewise be reconsidered, and if approved by two thirds of the other House also, it shall become a law. But in all such cases, the votes of both Houses shall be determined by yeas and nays; and the names of the persons voting for or against the bill shall be entered in the journal of each House respectively. If any bill shall not be returned by the President within seven days after it shall

have been presented to him, it shall be a law, unless the legislature, by their adjournment, prevent its return; in which case, it shall not be a law. ...

Article IX
Sect. 1. The Senate of the United States shall have power to make treaties, and to appoint Ambassadors, and Judges of the Supreme Court. ...

Article X
Sect. 1. The Executive Power of the United States shall be vested in a single person. His stile shall be, "The President of the United States of America"; and his title shall be, "His Excellency." He shall be elected by ballot by the Legislature. He shall hold his office during the term of seven years; but shall not be elected a second time.

Sect. 2. He shall, from time to time, give information to the Legislature, of the state of the Union: he may recommend to their consideration such measures as he shall judge necessary and expedient: he may convene them on extraordinary occasions. In case of disagreement between the two Houses, with regard to the time of adjournment, he may adjourn them to such time as he thinks proper: he shall take care that the laws of the United States be duly and faithfully executed: he shall commission all the officers of the United States; and shall appoint officers in all cases not otherwise provided for by this Constitution. He shall receive Ambassadors, and may correspond with the supreme Executives of the several States. He shall have power to grant reprieves and pardons; but his pardon shall not be pleadable in bar of an impeachment. He shall be commander in chief of the Army and navy of the United States, and of the Militia of the several States. He shall, at stated times, receive for his services a compensation, which shall neither be increased nor diminished during his continuance in office. Before he shall enter on the duties of his department, he shall take the following oath or affirmation: "I –– solemnly swear (or affirm), that I will faithfully execute the office of President of the United States of America." He shall be removed from his office on impeachment by the House of Representatives, and conviction in the Supreme Court, of treason, bribery, or corruption. In case of his removal as aforesaid, death, resignation, or disability to discharge the powers and duties of his office, the President of the Senate shall exercise those powers and duties until another President of the United States be chosen, or until the disability of the President be removed.

Appendix 4: The Constitution of 1787

Article I
Section 2. ... The House of Representatives ... shall have the sole Power of Impeachment.

Section 3. ... The Senate shall have the sole Power to try all Impeachments. When sitting for that Purpose, they shall be on Oath or Affirmation. When the President of the United States is tried, the Chief Justice shall preside. And no Person shall be convicted without the Concurrence of two thirds of the Members present.

Judgment in Cases of Impeachment shall not extend further than to removal from Office, and disqualification to hold and enjoy any Office of honor, Trust or Profit under the United States: but the Party convicted shall nevertheless be liable and subject to Indictment, Trial, Judgment and Punishment, according to Law. ...

Section 7. ... Every Bill which shall have passed the House of Representatives and the Senate, shall, before it become a Law, be presented to the President of the United States; If he approve he shall sign it, but if not he shall return it, with his Objections to that House in which it shall have originated, who shall enter the Objections at large on their Journal, and proceed to reconsider it. If after such Reconsideration two thirds of that House shall agree to pass the Bill, it shall be sent, together with the Objections, to the other House, by which it shall likewise be reconsidered, and if approved by two thirds of that House, it shall become a Law. But in all such Cases the Votes of both Houses shall be determined by yeas and Nays, and the Names of the Persons voting for and against the Bill shall be entered on the Journal of each House respectively. If any Bill shall not be returned by the President within ten Days (Sundays excepted) after it shall have been presented to him, the Same shall be a Law, in like Manner as if he had signed it, unless the Congress by their Adjournment prevent its Return, in which Case it shall not be a Law.

Every Order, Resolution, or Vote to which the Concurrence of the Senate and House of Representatives may be necessary (except on a question of Adjournment) shall be presented to the President of the United States; and before the Same shall take Effect, shall be approved by him, or being disapproved by him, shall be repassed by two thirds of the Senate and House of Representatives, according to the Rules and Limitations prescribed in the Case of a Bill. ...

Article 2

Section 1. The executive Power shall be vested in a President of the United States of America. He shall hold his Office during the Term of four Years, and, together with the Vice President, chosen for the same Term, be elected, as follows

Each State shall appoint, in such Manner as the Legislature thereof may direct, a Number of Electors, equal to the whole Number of Senators and Representatives to which the State may be entitled in the Congress: but no Senator or Representative, or Person holding an Office of Trust or Profit under the United States, shall be appointed an Elector.

The Electors shall meet in their respective States, and vote by Ballot for two Persons, of whom one at least shall not be an Inhabitant of the same State with themselves. And they shall make a List of all the Persons voted for, and of the Number of Votes for each; which List they shall sign and certify, and transmit sealed to the Seat of the Government of the United States, directed to the President of the Senate. The President of the Senate shall, in the Presence of the Senate and House of Representatives, open all the Certificates, and the Votes shall then be counted. The Person having the greatest Number of Votes shall be the President, if such Number be a Majority of the whole Number of Electors appointed; and if there be more than one who have such Majority, and have an equal Number of Votes, then the House of Representatives shall immediately chuse by Ballot one of them for President; and if no Person have a Majority, then from the five highest on the List the said House shall in like Manner chuse the President. But in chusing the President, the Votes shall be taken by States, the Representation from each State having one Vote; A quorum for this Purpose shall consist of a Member or Members from two thirds of the States, and a Majority of all the States shall be necessary to a Choice. In every Case, after the Choice of the President, the Person having the greatest Number of Votes of the Electors shall be the Vice President. But if there should remain two or more who have equal Votes, the Senate shall chuse from them by Ballot the Vice President.

The Congress may determine the Time of chusing the Electors, and the Day on which they shall give their Votes; which Day shall be the same throughout the United States.

No Person except a natural born Citizen, or a Citizen of the United States, at the time of the Adoption of this Constitution, shall be eligible to the Office of President; neither shall any Person be eligible to that Office who shall not have attained to the Age of thirty five Years, and been fourteen Years a Resident within the United States.

In Case of the Removal of the President from Office, or of his Death, Resignation, or Inability to discharge the Powers and Duties of the said Office, the Same shall devolve on the Vice President, and the Congress may by Law provide for the Case of Removal, Death, Resignation or Inability, both of the President and Vice President, declaring what Officer shall then act as President, and such Officer shall act accordingly, until the Disability be removed, or a President shall be elected.

The President shall, at stated Times, receive for his Service, a Compensation, which shall neither be encreased nor diminished during the Period for which he shall have been elected, and he shall not receive within that Period any other Emolument from the United States, or any of them.

Before he enter on the Execution of his office, he shall take the following Oath or Affirmation:—"I do solemnly swear (or affirm) that I will faithfully execute the Office of President of the United States, and will to the best of my Ability, preserve, protect and defend the Constitution of the Untied States."

Section 2. The President shall be Commander in Chief of the Army and Navy of the United States, and of the Militia of the several States, when called into the actual Service of the United States; he may require the Opinion, in writing, of the principal Officer in each of the executive Departments, upon any Subject relating to the Duties of their respective Offices, and he shall have Power to grant Reprieves and Pardons for Offences against the United States, except in Cases of Impeachment.

He shall have Power, by and with the Advice and Consent of the Senate, to make Treaties, provided two thirds of the Senators present concur; and he shall nominate; and by and with the Advice and Consent of the Senate, shall appoint Ambassadors, other public Ministers and Consuls, Judges of the Supreme Court, and all other Officers of the United States, whose Appointments are not herein otherwise provided for, and which shall be established by Law: but the Congress may by Law vest the Appointment of such inferior Officers, as they think proper, in the President alone, in the Courts of Law, or in the Heads of Departments.

The President shall have Power to fill up all Vacancies that may happen during the Recess of the Senate, by granting Commissions which shall expire at the End of their next Session.

Section 3. He shall from time to time give to the Congress Information of the State of the Union, and recommend to their Consideration such Measures as he shall judge necessary and expedient; he may, on extraordinary Occasions, convene both Houses, or either of them, and in Case of Disagreement between them, with Respect to the Time of Adjournment, he may adjourn them to such Time as he shall think proper; he shall receive Ambassadors and other public Ministers; he shall take Care that the Laws be faithfully executed, and shall Commission all the Officers of the United States.

Section 4. The President, Vice President and all civil Officers of the United States, shall be removed from Office on Impeachment for, and Conviction of, Treason, Bribery, or other high Crimes and Misdemeanors.

Appendix 5: Amendments to the Constitution

Twelfth Amendment (1804)

The Electors shall meet in their respective states, and vote by ballot for President and Vice-President, one of whom, at least, shall not be an inhabitant of the same state with themselves; they shall name in their ballots the person voted for as President, and in distinct ballots the person voted for as Vice-President, and they shall make distinct lists of all persons voted for as President, and of all persons voted for as Vice-President, and of the number of votes for each, which lists they shall sign and certify, and transmit sealed to the seat of the government of the United States, directed to the President of the Senate;— The President of the Senate shall, in the presence of the Senate and House of Representatives, open all the certificates and the votes shall then be counted;— The person having the greatest number of votes for President, shall be the President, if such number be a majority of the whole number of Electors appointed; and if no person have such majority, then from the persons having the highest numbers not exceeding three on the list of those voted for as President, the House of Representatives shall choose immediately, by ballot, the President. But in choosing the President, the votes shall be taken by states, the representation from each state having one vote; a quorum for this purpose shall consist of a member or members from two-thirds of the states, and a majority of all the states shall be necessary to a choice. And if the House of Representatives shall not choose a President whenever the right of choice shall devolve upon them, before the fourth day of March next following, then the Vice-President shall act as President, as in the case of the death or other constitutional disability of the President. —The person having the greatest number of votes as Vice-President, shall be the Vice-President, if such number be a majority of the whole number of Electors appointed, and if no person have a majority, then from the two highest numbers on the list, the Senate shall choose the Vice-President; a quorum for the purpose shall consist of two-thirds of the whole number of Senators, and a majority of the whole number shall be necessary to a choice. But no person constitutionally ineligible to the office of President shall be eligible to that of Vice-President of the United States.

Twentieth Amendment (1933)

Section 1. The terms of the President and Vice President shall end at noon on the 20th day of January, and the terms of Senators and Representatives at noon on the 3d day of January, of the years in which such terms would have ended if this article had not been ratified; and the terms of their successors shall then begin. ...

Section 3. If, at the time fixed for the beginning of the term of the President, the President elect shall have died, the Vice President elect shall become President. If a President shall not have been chosen before the time fixed for the beginning of his term, or if the President elect shall have failed to qualify, then the Vice President elect shall act as President until a President shall have qualified; and the Congress may by law provide for the case wherein neither a President elect nor a Vice President elect shall have qualified, declaring who shall then act as President, or the manner in which one who is to act shall be selected, and such person shall act accordingly until a President or Vice President shall have qualified.

Section 4. The Congress may by law provide for the case of the death of any of the persons from whom the House of Representatives may choose a President whenever the right of choice shall have devolved upon them, and for the case of the death of any of the persons from whom the Senate may choose a Vice President whenever the right of choice shall have devolved upon them. ...

Twenty-second Amendment (1951)

Section 1. No person shall be elected to the office of the President more than twice, and no person who has held the office of President, or acted as President, for more than two years of a term to which some other person was elected President shall be elected to the office of President more than once. But this Article shall not apply to any person holding the office of President when this Article was proposed by the Congress, and shall not prevent any person who may be holding the office of President, or acting as President, during the term within which this Article becomes operative from holding the office of President or acting as President during the remainder of such term. ...

Twenty-fifth Amendment (1967)

Section 1. In case of the removal of the President from office or of his death or resignation, the Vice President shall become President.

Section 2. Whenever there is a vacancy in the office of the Vice President, the President shall nominate a Vice President who shall take the office upon confirmation by a majority vote of both houses of Congress.

Section 3. Whenever the President transmits to the President pro tempore of the Senate and the Speaker of the House of Representatives his written declaration that he is unable to discharge the powers and duties of his office, and until he transmits to them a written declaration to the contrary, such powers and duties shall be discharged by the Vice President as Acting President.

Section 4. Whenever the Vice President and a majority of either the principal officers of the executive departments or of such other body as Congress may by law provide, transmit to the President pro tempore of the Senate and the Speaker of the House of Representatives their written declaration that the President is unable to discharge the powers and duties of his office, the Vice President shall immediately assume the powers and duties of the office as Acting President.

Thereafter, when the President transmits to the President pro tempore of the Senate and the Speaker of the House of Representatives his written declaration that no inability exists, he shall resume the powers and duties of his office unless the Vice President and a majority of either the principal officers of the executive department or of such other body as Congress may by law provide, transmit within four days to the President pro tempore of the Senate and the Speaker of the House of Representatives their written declaration that the President is unable to discharge the powers and duties of his office. Thereupon Congress shall decide the issue, assembling within forty-eight hours for that purpose if not in session. If the Congress, within twenty-one days after receipt of the latter written declaration, or, if Congress is not in session, within twenty-one days after Congress is required to assemble, determines by two-thirds vote of both Houses that the President is unable to discharge the powers and duties of his office, the Vice President shall continue to discharge the same as Acting President; otherwise, the President shall resume the powers and duties of his office.

References

Adler, David Gray. 1989a. "The President's Pardon Power." In *Inventing the American Presidency,* edited by Thomas E. Cronin. Lawrence: University Press of Kansas.

Adler, David Gray. 1989b. "The President's War-Making Power." In *Inventing the American Presidency,* edited by Thomas E. Cronin. Lawrence: University Press of Kansas.

Allan, Herbert S. 1948. *John Hancock: Patriot in Purple.* New York: Macmillan.

Bailey, Harry A., Jr., and Jay M. Shafritz, eds. 1988. *The American Presidency: Historical and Contemporary Perspectives.* Pacific Grove, Calif.: Brooks/Cole Publishing.

Bailyn, Bernard. 1970. *The Origins of American Politics.* New York: Vintage.

Bailyn, Bernard. 1974. *The Ordeal of Thomas Hutchinson: Loyalism and the Destruction of the First British Empire.* Cambridge, Mass.: Belknap.

Berger, Raoul. 1973. *Impeachment: The Constitutional Problems.* Cambridge: Harvard University Press.

Berns, Walter, ed. 1992. *After the People Vote: A Guide to the Electoral College.* Rev. and enl. ed. Washington, D.C.: AEI Press.

Blackstone, William. [1783] 1978. *Commentaries on the Laws of England.* Reprint of 9th ed. New York: Garland.

Borden, Morten, ed. 1965. *The Antifederalist Papers.* East Lansing: Michigan State University Press.

Boyd, Julian P. 1950–. *The Papers of Thomas Jefferson.* Princeton: Princeton University Press.

Bradford, M. E. 1984. *Founding Fathers: Brief Lives of the Framers of the United States Constitution.* 2d ed. Lawrence: University Press of Kansas.

Casper, Gerhard. 1997. *Separating Power: Essays on the Founding Period.* Cambridge: Harvard University Press.

Charleton, James H., Robert G. Ferris, and Mary C. Ryan, eds. 1986. *Framers of the Constitution.* Washington, D.C.: National Archives and Records Administration.

Collier, Christopher. 1971. *Roger Sherman's Connecticut: Yankee Politics and the American Revolution.* Middletown, Conn.: Wesleyan University Press.

Collier, Christopher, and James Lincoln Collier. 1986. *Decision in Philadelphia: The Constitutional Convention of 1787.* New York: Random House.

Cooke, Jacob E., ed. 1961. *The Federalist.* Cleveland: Meridian.

Corwin, Edward S. 1957. *The President: Office and Powers, 1787–1957.* 4th rev. ed. New York University Press.

Crabb, Cecil V., Jr., and Pat M. Holt. 1992. *Invitation to Struggle: Congress, the President and Foreign Policy.* 4th ed. Washington, D.C.: Congressional Quarterly.

Cronin, Thomas E. 1980. "An Imperiled Presidency." In *The Post-Imperial Presidency,* edited by Vincent Davis. New Brunswick, N.J.: Transaction.

Cronin, Thomas E., ed. 1989. *Inventing the American Presidency.* Lawrence: University Press of Kansas.

Daniell, Jere R. 1981. *Colonial New Hampshire: A History.* Millwood, N.Y.: KTO Press.

De Pauw, Linda Grant. 1966. *The Eleventh Pillar: New York State and the Federal Constitution.* Ithaca, N.Y.: Cornell University Press.

DiClerico, Robert E. 1987. "James Wilson's Presidency." *Presidential Studies Quarterly* 17 (Spring): 301-18.

Elliot, Jonathan, ed. 1888. *The Debates in the Several State Constitutions on the Adoption of the Federal Constitution.* 5 vols. New York: Burt Franklin.

Farrand, Max. 1913. *The Framing of the Constitution of the United States.* New Haven: Yale University Press.

Farrand, Max, ed. 1937. *The Records of the Federal Convention.* 4 vols. New Haven: Yale University Press.

Fischer, David Hackett. 1965. *The Revolution of American Conservatism: The Federalist Party in the Era of Jeffersonian Democracy.* New York: Harper and Row.

Flexner, James Thomas. 1969. *George Washington and the New Nation, 1783-1793.* Boston: Little, Brown.

Flower, Milton E. 1983. *John Dickinson: Conservative Revolutionary.* Charlottesville: University Press of Virginia.

Ford, Gerald. 1980. "Imperiled, Not Imperial." *Time,* November 10, 30-31.

Ford, Paul Leicester, ed. [1888] 1968. *Pamphlets of the Constitution of the United States.* New York: Da Capo.

Franck, Thomas, M., ed. 1981. *The Tethered Presidency: Congressional Restraints on Executive Power.* New York University Press.

Glennon, Michael J. 1992. *When No Majority Rules: The Electoral College and Presidential Succession.* Washington, D.C.: Congressional Quarterly.

Greene, Evarts Boutell. [1898] 1966. *The Provincial Governor in the English Colonies of North America.* New York: Russell and Russell.

Greene, Jack P. 1963. *The Quest for Power: The Lower Houses of Assembly in the Southern Royal Colonies, 1689-1776.* Chapel Hill: University of North Carolina Press.

Greene, Jack P. 1979. "Character, Persona, and Authority: A Study of Alternative Styles of Political Leadership in Revolutionary Virginia." In *The Revolutionary War in the South: Power, Conflict, and Leadership,* edited by Robert W. Higgins. Durham, N.C.: Duke University Press.

Gross, Robert A. 1976. *The Minutemen and Their World.* New York: Hill and Wang.

Handlin, Oscar, and Mary Handlin, eds. 1966. *Popular Sources of Political Authority: Documents on the Massachusetts Constitution of 1780.* Cambridge: Harvard University Press.

Haw, James. 1997. *John and Edward Rutledge of South Carolina.* Athens: University of Georgia Press.

Henkin, Louis. 1996. *Foreign Affairs and the United States Constitution.* 2d ed. Oxford: Clarendon.

Hobson, Charles F. 1979. "The Negative on State Laws: James Madison, the Constitution, and the Crisis of Republican Government." *William and Mary Quarterly* 36 (April): 215-35.

Hodgson, Godfrey. 1980. *All Things to All Men: The False Promise of the American Presidency*. New York: Simon and Schuster.

Hoffer, Peter Charles, and N. E. H. Hull. 1984. *Impeachment in America, 1635–1805*. New Haven: Yale University Press.

Holcombe, Arthur N. 1956. "The Role of Washington in the Framing of the Constitution." *Huntington Library Quarterly*, August, 317–34.

Hoxie, R. Gordon. 1998. "The Not–So–Imperial Presidency." In *Points of View: Readings in American Government and Politics*, edited by Robert E. DiClerico and Allan S. Hammock. 7th ed. Boston: McGraw-Hill.

Hume, David. 1777. "Of the Independency of Parliament." In *Essays and Treatises on Several Subjects*. 2 vols. London: T. Cadell.

Hutchinson, William T., et al., eds. 1962–. *The Papers of James Madison*. Chicago: University of Chicago Press.

Hutson, James H., ed. 1987. *Supplement to Max Farrand's The Records of the Federal Convention of 1787*. New Haven: Yale University Press.

Jefferson, Thomas. 1954. *Notes on the State of Virginia*, edited by William Peden. Chapel Hill: University of North Carolina Press.

Jensen, Merrill, John P. Kaminski, and Gaspare Saladino. 1976–. *The Documentary History of the Ratification of the Constitution*. Madison: State Historical Society of Wisconsin.

Jillson, Calvin C., and Rick K. Wilson. 1990. "Leadership and Coordination in Legislatures: The 'President' of the First American Congresses: 1774–1789." *Congress and the Presidency* 17 (Autumn):85–107.

Kaminski, John P. 1993. *George Clinton: Yeoman Politician of the New Republic*. Madison, Wis.: Madison House Publishers.

Ketcham, Ralph. 1984. *Presidents above Party: The First American Presidency*. Chapel Hill: University of North Carolina Press.

Kruman, Marc W. 1997. *Between Authority and Liberty: State Constitution Making in Revolutionary America*. Chapel Hill: University of North Carolina Press.

Kurland, Philip B., and Ralph Lerner, ed. 1987. *The Founders' Constitution*. 5 vols. Chicago: University of Chicago Press.

Labaree, Leonard W., et al., eds. 1959–. *The Papers of Benjamin Franklin*. New Haven: Yale University Press.

Labovitz, John R. 1978. *Presidential Impeachment*. New Haven: Yale University Press.

Lienesch, Michael. 1989. "North Carolina: Preserving Rights." In *Ratifying the Constitution*, edited by Michael Allen Gillespie and Michael Lienesch. Lawrence: University Press of Kansas.

Lind, Michael. 1995. "The Out–of–Control Presidency." *New Republic*, August 14, 18–23.

Locke, John. 1965. *Two Treatises of Government*, edited by Peter Laslett. New York: Mentor.

Longley, Lawrence D. 1994. "Yes—The Electoral College Should Be Abolished." In *Controversial Issues in Presidential Selection*, edited by Gary L. Rose. 2d ed. Albany: State University of New York Press.

Longley, Lawrence D. 1998. "The Electoral College Should Be Abolished." In *Points of View: Readings in American Government and Politics*, edited by Robert E. DiClerico and Allan S. Hammock. 7th ed. Boston: McGraw-Hill.

Loss, Richard. 1976. Introduction to *The Letters of Pacificus and Helvidius (1845) with the Letters of Americanus*. Delmar, N.Y.: Scholars' Facsimiles & Reprints.

Lutz, Donald S. 1984. "The Relative Influence of European Writers on late Eighteenth-Century American Political Thought." *American Political Science Review* 78 (March): 189-97.

McCloskey, Robert Green, ed. 1967. *The Works of James Wilson*. 2 vols. Cambridge: Harvard University Press.

McCormick, Richard P. 1982. *The Presidential Game: The Origins of American Presidential Politics*. New York: Oxford University Press.

McDonald, Forrest. 1982. *Alexander Hamilton: A Biography*. New York: Norton.

McDonald, Forrest. 1994. *The American Presidency: An Intellectual History*. Lawrence: University Press of Kansas.

McDonald, Forrest, and Ellen Shapiro McDonald. 1988. *Requiem: Variations on Eighteenth-Century Themes*. Lawrence: University Press of Kansas.

Main, Jackson Turner. 1967. *The Upper House in Revolutionary America, 1763-1788*. Madison: University of Wisconsin Press.

Marks, Frederick W. 1973. *Independence on Trial: Foreign Affairs and the Making of the Constitution*. Baton Rouge: Louisiana State University Press.

Marston, Jerrilyn Greene. 1987. *King and Congress: The Transfer of Political Legitimacy, 1774-1776*. Princeton: Princeton University Press.

Milkis, Sidney M., and Michael Nelson. 1994. *The American Presidency: Origins and Development, 1776-1993*. 2d ed. Washington, D.C.: Congressional Quarterly.

Miller, William Lee. 1992. *The Business of May Next: James Madison and the Founding*. Charlottesville: University Press of Virginia.

Moe, Ronald C. 1987. "The Founders and Their Experience with the Executive Veto." *Presidential Studies Quarterly* 17 (Spring): 413-32.

Montesquieu. 1977. *The Spirit of Laws*, edited by David Wallace Carrithers. Berkeley: University of California Press.

Nelson, Michael. 1989. "Qualifications for President." In *Inventing the American Presidency*, edited by Thomas E. Cronin. Lawrence: University Press of Kansas.

Peirce, Neal R., and Lawrence D. Longley. 1981. *The People's President: The Electoral College in American History and the Direct Vote Alternative*. Rev. ed. New Haven: Yale University Press.

Pfiffner, James P., and Roger H. Davidson, eds. 1997. *Understanding the Presidency*. New York: Longman.

Phelps, Glenn A. 1993. *George Washington and American Constitutionalism*. Lawrence: University Press of Kansas.

Pious, Richard M. 1996. *The Presidency*. Boston: Allyn and Bacon.

Pole, J. R. 1971. *Political Representation in England and the Origins of the American Republic*. Berkeley: University of California Press.

Purcell, Richard J. 1918. *Connecticut in Transition, 1775-1818*. Washington: American Historical Association.

Rakove, Jack N. 1994. *Original Meanings: Politics and Ideas in the Making of the Constitution*. New York: Knopf.

Reedy, George. 1970. *The Twilight of the Presidency*. New York: New American Library.

Roche, John P. 1961. "The Founding Fathers: A Reform Caucus in Action." *American Political Science Review* 55 (December): 799-816.

Rossiter, Clinton. 1987. *1787: The Grand Convention*. New York: Norton.

Rutland, Robert A. 1961. *George Mason: Reluctant Statesman*. Williamsburg, Va.: Colonial Williamsburg.

Rutland, Robert A., ed. 1970. *The Papers of George Mason, 1725–1792*. 3 vols. Chapel Hill: University of North Carolina Press.

Rutland, Robert A., ed. 1994. *James Madison and the American Nation, 1751–1836: An Encyclopedia*. New York: Simon and Schuster.

Schlesinger, Arthur M., Jr. 1973. *The Imperial Presidency*. Boston: Houghton Mifflin.

Schwartz, Barry. 1987. *George Washington: The Making of an American Symbol*. New York: Free Press.

Slonin, Shlomo. 1986. "The Electoral College at Philadelphia: The Evolution of an Ad Hoc Congress for the Selection of a President." *Journal of American History* 73 (June): 35–58.

Smith, Page. 1962. *John Adams*. 2 vols. Garden City, N.Y.: Doubleday.

Spitzer, Robert J. 1988. *The Presidential Veto: Touchstone of the American Presidency*. Albany: State University of New York Press.

Spitzer, Robert J. 1997. "The Constitutionality of the Presidential Line–Item Veto." *Political Science Quarterly* 112 (November): 261–83.

St. John, Jeffrey. 1987. *Constitutional Journal: A Correspondent's Report from the Convention of 1787*. Ottawa, Ill.: Jameson.

Stein, Charles W. 1943. *The Third–Term Tradition: Its Rise and Collapse in American Politics*. New York: Columbia University Press.

Storing, Herbert J., ed. 1981. *The Complete Anti–Federalist*. 7 vols. Chicago: University of Chicago Press.

Stourzh, Gerald. 1970. *Alexander Hamilton and the Idea of Republican Government*. Stanford: Stanford University Press.

Syrett, Harold C., ed. 1961–1987. *The Papers of Alexander Hamilton*. New York: Columbia University Press.

Thach, Charles C., Jr. 1923. *The Creation of the Presidency, 1775–1789*. Baltimore: Johns Hopkins University Press.

Thorpe, Francis Newton, ed. 1909. *The Federal and State Constitutions, Colonial Charters, and Other Organic Laws of the States, Territories, and Colonies Now or Heretofore Forming the United States of America*. 7 vols. Washington, D.C.: Government Printing Office.

Turner, Lynn Warren. 1983. *The Ninth State: New Hampshire's Formative Years*. Chapel Hill: University of North Carolina Press.

Warren, Charles. 1929. *The Making of the Constitution*. Boston: Little, Brown.

Webking, Robert H. 1987. "Melancton Smith and the Letters from the Federal Farmer." *William and Mary Quarterly* 44 (July): 510–28.

Wildavsky, Aaron. 1991. *The Beleaguered Presidency*. New Brunswick, N.J.: Transaction.

Wilderson, Paul W. 1994. *Governor John Wentworth and the American Revolution: The English Connection*. Hanover: University Press of New England.

Williams, E. Neville, ed. 1960. *The Eighteenth–Century Constitution, 1688–1815: Documents and Commentary*. Cambridge: Cambridge University Press.

Wood, Gordon S. 1969. *The Creation of the American Republic, 1776–1787*. Chapel Hill: University of North Carolina Press.

Wood, Gordon S. 1974. "The Authorship of the Letters from the Federal Farmer." *William and Mary Quarterly* 31 (April): 299–308.

Wormuth, Francis D., and Edwin B. Firmage. 1986. *To Chain the Dog of War: The War Power of Congress in History and Law.* Dallas: Southern Methodist University Press.

Wright, Esmond. 1986. *Franklin of Philadelphia.* Cambridge, Mass.: Belknap.

Young, Alfred F. 1980. "Conservatives, the Constitution, and the 'Spirit of Accommodation.'" In *How Democratic Is the Constitution?* Edited by Robert A. Goldwin and William A. Schambra. Washington, D.C.: AEI Press.

Index

About the Editor

Richard J. Ellis is Mark O. Hatfield Professor of Politics at Willamette University. Among his many books are *Speaking to the People: The Rhetorical Presidency in Historical Perspective* (1998), *The Dark Side of the Left: Illiberal Egalitarianism in America* (1998), and *Presidential Lightning Rods: The Politics of Blame Avoidance* (1994).